THIN LIZZY
A PEOPLE'S HISTORY

Richard Houghton

Spenwood Books
Manchester, UK

First published in Great Britain 2022
by Spenwood Books Ltd
2 College Street, Higham Ferrers, NN10 8DZ.

A CIP record for this book is available from the British Library.

ISBN 978-1-9168896-3-7

Printed and bound by Sound Performance Ltd,
3 Greenwich Quay, Clarence Road, Greenwich,
London, SE8 3EY.

Design by Bruce Graham, The Night Owl.

BY THE SAME AUTHOR

You Had to Be There: The Rolling Stones 1962 - 69

The Beatles - I Was There

The Who - I Was There

Pink Floyd - I Was There

The Rolling Stones - I Was There

Jimi Hendrix - The Day I Was There

Led Zeppelin - The Day I Was There

The Smiths - The Day I Was There

The Jam - The Day I Was There (with Neil Cossar)

Black Sabbath - The Day I Was There

Rush - The Day I Was There

The Wedding Present - Sometimes These Words Just Don't Have To Be Said (with David Gedge)

Orchestral Manoeuvres in the Dark - Pretending To See The Future

Simple Minds - Heart of the Crowd

Shaun Ryder's Book of Mumbo Jumbo

Cream - A People's History

Queen – A People's History

Jethro Tull – Lend Me Your Ears

Tell me the legends of long ago

ACKNOWLEDGEMENTS

I am indebted to my many hundreds of contributors who, after realising that I wasn't trying to sell them life insurance or double glazing, responded positively to my unsolicited approaches via Facebook about sharing their Thin Lizzy memories with me. An invaluable resource for cross checking gig dates was the excellent thinlizzyguide.com but there were still some dates (notably the appearance at the Nag's Head in Wollaston) where I wasn't able to pin down the date of the gig that Thin Lizzy played.

I'd particularly like to thank: John Truman; Roddie Cleere; Robin George; Steve Newton, whose website earofnewt.com and Patreon page patreon.com/earofnewt are worth checking out; Marc Whybrow-Price; Cris Martin, whose website is www.rockdawn.co.uk; Joe Elliott; Simon Matthews; Steve Caudle; Kjell Görlitz; Kevin Julie; Bruce Graham for his design expertise; Dave Evely at Sound Performance; Andy Small; Bruce Koziarski (web wizard); Deaglàn Penston; Ken Sweeney; Thomas Stevenson; Jon Valentine; Hugh Jones; Malcolm Wyatt, proof-reader extraordinaire; and Mark Stanway, for permission to an extract from *Close to the Mark*.

And I'd like to thank Kate Sullivan once again for her continued love and support.

CONTENTS

Introduction ... 9

Crumlin ... 11

In Britain ... 15

1972 ... 21

Whiskey ... 25

1974 ... 40

1975 ... 48

1976 ... 59

1977 ... 91

1978 ... 133

1979 ... 170

1980 ... 212

1981 ... 242

1982 ... 269

1983 ... 280

1984 ... 340

1985 ... 350

Post Lizzy ... 361

Encores ... 367

Postscript ... 383

Warriors ... 384

INTRODUCTION

The tale of Thin Lizzy has often been often told, and always ends the same, with the sad and untimely death of Phil Lynott at the age of just 36. But there is another Thin Lizzy story. A story of great songs, great performances, rock and roll magic and outstanding gigs by one of the most fondly remembered bands in music history.

Thin Lizzy first began performing over 50 years ago and it is only when researching this book that the penny dropped that it is now more than 50 years since Phil, Brian and Eric first performed as a three piece under the name Thin Lizzy.

This is the Thin Lizzy story told in the words of over 400 fans, or 'supporters' as Phil preferred to call them. It is not an attempt to chronicle every Thin Lizzy show, or every appearance by Phil Lynott, who could often to be found getting up on stage and jamming with other artists when Lizzy weren't on the road, or after hours at a club when they were. I do not apologise for the gaps in the story. I have not, for example, endeavoured to cover in great detail the origins of the band in their years in Ireland before Thin Lizzy came together, even though Phil, Eric, Gary and Brian Downey all played in a number of bands before Thin Lizzy. Other books have done this already.

Not many bands granted fans ready access backstage so that they coulds just hang out with the boys. Not many bands were so generous with their time and made themselves so available to people who wanted to meet them. Thin Lizzy were one of those bands.

Thin Lizzy have continued to perform with different line ups since Phil Lynott died. Whilst it is fantastic that the songs the band wrote and performed in Phil's lifetime continue to be played, and many tribute bands also celebrate their music by playing shows around the world, for many fans Thin Lizzy died when Phil died.

I was lucky enough to see Thin Lizzy five times, beginning with an under amplified appearance at the Reading Festival in 1977, when the bootleg tape my friend Roger was trying to record on his cassette player captured more of my running commentary than it did the band's performance, and ending with the *Thunder and Lightning* tour in April 1983 at the Queens Hall in Leeds. I remember the timpani wheeled on from the sides of the stage for 'Do Anything You Want To' on the Black Rose tour and Scott and Gary hammering away at the kettle drums. But most of all I remember the sheer stage presence and the show Thin Lizzy put on every time I saw them. The police lights. The sirens. The flash bombs. The dry ice.

And, most of all, Phil going through his whole catalogue of stage moves - the clenched fist, legs apart, pointing his guitar machine gun-like into the audience, encouraging the audience to sing along. And yet it didn't feel cliched because he had a huge grin on his face. It was Phil, loving life and the adulation of the audience - feeding off their energy and giving it back to them.

Sometimes when you see rock stars in tight leather trousers throwing shapes on stage, it frankly looks a bit crap. Phil rose above all that and demonstrated what you could do if you were good at your craft, but also what you could do if you were passionate about your music. There was no 'us and them' with Lizzy. Phil made you feel that the band and the audience were one.

What I remember most about Thin Lizzy is coming out of a show, being completely exhilarated by what I'd just seen and straight away thinking, 'When can I go see them again?'

Are you ready?

CRUMLIN

1964, DUBLIN, IRELAND

I WAS THERE: KEVIN BERGIN

In the mid to late Sixties I used to go from England to my grandmother's in Dublin for the two weeks of the old factory fortnight. She lived in Crumlin, on the Clonmacnoise Road. I'd play in her back garden. I was five or six years old.

My grandmother said, 'There's a boy comes to the fence. If you see him, you can talk to him. He's got relatives in England.' The fence was iron railings and beyond it was a bit of waste ground. I was out there in the garden when this lad came to the back fence. I think he was just curious that there was somebody in the back garden and I got talking to him. He said, 'My mother came over from Manchester and I'm here now, living in Dublin. My name's Phil.'

He'd come over most days and we'd go off and play. I knew that he was a bit older than me and I was a bit in awe of him because he said, 'Come on, I'll show you round.' Crumlin is quite a big estate, laid out on these weird grid patterns and circles. When you go up one section of the Clonmacnoise Road it goes into another one of these circles where there's a big piece of grass. I remember there was a kiosk there and Phil said, 'Be careful of this guy. He's the ice cream man. But he's blind. You have to be telling him what you want. He knows where everything is.'

After the two weeks were up, I said, 'I'm going back home now,' and Phil said, 'Next time you're over, come and meet up and we'll have a talk.' Every time I went back on the factory fortnight after that, if he was there, I'd talk to him.

He seemed to be a loner. I don't think the other kids were that bothered about playing with him. I was too young to appreciate the fact that he was black and Irish. To meet him was just something different. He was a bit disappointed when I told him I was a Leicester City fan because he was a big Man United fan even then, and a bit obsessed with Georgie Best.

When I'm in Ireland I say I'm from Dublin. When I'm in Dublin I say I'm from Crumlin. When I'm in Crumlin I say I'm from Lakeland Road, and when I'm on Lakeland Road I say I'm a Lynott. **Phil Lynott**

He moved away from Dublin with Thin Lizzy in 1970 and we lost contact. But one day my grandmother said, 'I've got a message from this Phil. He'd like to meet you in town.' I went up into Dublin and we met in a pub and it went on from there. Every time I went over, if he was in town or wasn't on tour, Phil would meet up with me. He'd always say, 'Oh Kev, I'm in town.' We used to meet up in the Baggot Inn. All the rock bands used to go in there. And one particular time we went in, around 1971, Phil said, 'My friend Gary's playing here tonight. He's only a young lad but he's a terrific guitarist and he's got a band called Skid Row.' And that was Gary Moore. I met Gary through Phil that night and I got to know all that early Dublin scene.

DUBLIN

1964/65, DUBLIN, IRELAND

I WAS THERE: JIM KEOGH

The first time I met Phil he arrived at my door with the two brothers who were in the Black Eagles with him, Danny and Frankie Smith. I was the drummer in a band called the Mustangs and we were actually rehearsing in our parlour. I don't know what they were looking for. We were all only 15 or 16. They arrived at the hall door and we just had a general chit chat for 20 minutes or half an hour about music and about getting going and things like that.

I met him a few times briefly in and out of gigs around the town after that. He was a nice lad. We always got on very well. The next time we met up was when both bands were booked for a band session at a function room run by the local priests. Two bands showed up for the one gig. There was a bit of animosity between my father and Joe Smith, the father of the two lads from the Black Eagles, over this, but it was the priest's fault. And it ended amicably and didn't come to fisticuffs in the end.

COUNTDOWN CLUB

DECEMBER 1969, DUBLIN, IRELAND

PHILIP AND BRIAN MEET ERIC BELL AND ERIC WRIXON.

THIN LIZZY FORMED

JANUARY 1970, DUBLIN, IRELAND

Having most recently performed under the name Orphanage, Philip Lynott, Brian Downey join forces with Eric Bell and Eric Wrixon and name themselves Thin Lizzy. The band's formation is reported in the Irish press in February 1970.

The band took their name from a Dandy cartoon character, Tin Lizzie

CLOGHRAN NATIONAL SCHOOL

13 FEBRUARY 1970, DUBLIN, IRELAND

The first appearance by Thin Lizzy.

1 MARCH 1970

TOWN HALL, NEWBRIDGE, IRELAND

Lizzy appear billed as 'Ireland's newest super group'.

ZIG ZAG DISCOTHEQUE, THE CAROUSEL
24 APRIL 1970, BELFAST, UK

After a series of dates south of the border, the band appears in Belfast billed as 'Tin Lizzie'. Incorrect billings of the band as 'Tin Lizzie', 'Thin Lizzie' and 'Tin Lizzy' persist over the coming months.

JULY 1970, DUBLIN, IRELAND

Eric Wrixon quits.

'THE FARMER' RELEASED
31 JULY 1970

'The Farmer', Thin Lizzy's first single, is released.

SISTERS CLUB, LONDON, UK
19 MARCH 1971

Thin Lizzy's UK mainland and London debut.

Photo - Andy Small

CLOUDS

8 APRIL 1971, DERBY, UK

I WAS THERE: SID LLOYD

They were billed as Tin Lizzy on the poster and were on the side stage, supporting Status Quo, the main act.

I WAS THERE: PAUL SEVERN

Phil Lynott broke a string and had to borrow a bass from Quo's bass player, Alan Lancaster. I had gone to see Quo. I worked at the printers that printed the flyers and I remember the typo getting through that called them Tin Lizzy.

Photo Sid Lloyd

'Tin Lizzy' were billed to appear at Clouds in Derby

MY BROTHER WAS THERE: PETER SCHOFIELD

My brother was there. Phil Lynott had a piss next to him and said 'hi'. Phil was wearing a long black leather coat which set my bro off wanting one. We called him Shaft after he did!

I WAS THERE: CHAD FOSTER

I saw Thin Lizzy at a club called Cleopatra's in my home city of Derby with the line-up of Phil Lynott, Eric Bell and Brian Downey. When I saw them, Lizzy were a trio of young Irish guys who were hungry for success and they played their hearts out. It was early in their career and they played stuff like 'Whiskey' and 'Black Boys', which is still my favourite Lizzy song of all time.

I heard that Thin Lizzy came about when Phil wanted to be front man for the legendary Skid Row, formed by drummer Noel Bridgeman, bassist Brendan 'Brush' Shields and the dear departed Gary Moore, who was only 17 years old at the time and already a brilliantly talented guitarist. Phil was rejected but as a consolation, Brush taught him to play bass and the rest is history.

Phil named the band after a cartoon character in *The Dandy* comic called 'Tin Lizzie', but Phil replaced 'Tin' with 'Thin' knowing that the Irish would pronounce it 'Tin' anyway.

BASTON PLAYING FIELDS
10 APRIL 1971, PETERBOROUGH, UK

I WAS THERE: DEBORAH KNOWLES

We used to dance to live groups in those days. When I saw them at Baston, there was hardly anyone there, so although there wasn't much of a vibe it meant my friend and I had the floor to ourselves and got an up close and personal view. I was a bit of a groupie in those days. I went backstage and found out they were playing in a pub somewhere in Peterborough the next day. As it was a bank holiday we decided to hitch there. It was up close and personal again but this time with an atmosphere. I was chatting to Phil and he was so lovely. They gave us a lift to the main road so it was easier for us to get a lift home. They mentioned that the album was out and apologised that they couldn't take us all the way home as they were going in the other direction. I expect they had to be careful with petrol and I had no idea where there was a garage that might have been open in those days. I didn't want to be the reason they ran out!

Photo Deborah Knowles

Deborah Knowles saw Lizzy in a playing field marquee

I got their debut album that week and played it to death. I still have it. The only other time I saw them was at the Reading Festival. I lived rural and didn't drive. Otherwise, I'd have seen them much more often.

RISLEY REMAND CENTRE

29 APRIL 1971, RISLEY, UK

I WAS THERE: ADRIAN FELTON

I saw Thin Lizzy a number of times as they regularly played at our college - Padgate College in Warrington. As a result of the contact and friendship between Phil and students and staff in the Sociology Department at the college, they played a gig at Risley Remand Centre. At the time, Risley had a high number of suicides which earned it the name 'Grisley Risley'.

THIN LIZZY RELEASED

30 APRIL 1971

Recorded at Decca Studios in January 1971, Lizzy were very much finding their feet with their first album. One critic was later to describe the album as 'surprisingly mellow'.

BURLESQUE ROSE & CROWN

23 MAY 1971, WISBECH, UK

I WAS THERE: STEVE ALLEN

I ran a club in Peterborough between 1969 and 1971 called Cloud Nine. On Saturday nights it was disco and soul bands, including all the well-known acts of that era such as Jimmy Ruffin and Lee Dorsey. On Sunday nights I organised an event called *The Night of Good Sounds*, which was effectively progressive rock and folk rock, which was happening everywhere at that time, primarily at London venues, but which was spreading out across the country to places like Friars in Aylesbury and Cloud Nine.

I'd booked a band called Skid Row, which featured Gary Moore, and whose manager was Ted Carroll. I became quite friendly with Ted. We ran quite a relaxed, fan-based operation and after the club closed, we used to go for a Chinese meal with the musicians. On the second of the two occasions that I booked Skid Row, in January 1971, Ted came to the Chinese restaurant along with the boys from Skid Row and said, 'I've got a band you really must use. They're called Thin Lizzy.' I said, 'By all means. You brought me Skid Row and they always bring the crowd in and fill the hall so I'd be very happy to use them.'

Unfortunately, at that point the venue had to close because the landlord wanted to sell it for redevelopment - he got an offer he couldn't refuse! – and so I lost my premises. But I had a club in Wisbech called the Burlesque Club and so Thin Lizzy played there. They were on a guarantee of £10 against 50 per cent at the door and ended up getting paid £15 for a 75 minute spot.

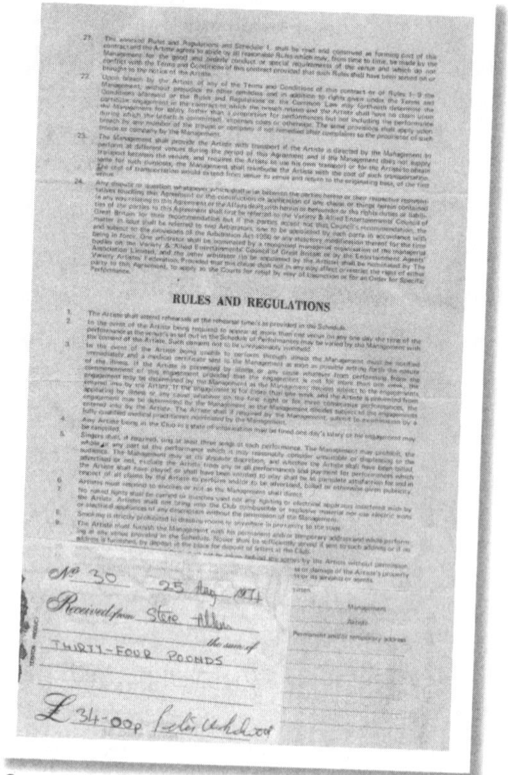

RULES AND REGULATIONS

No 30 25 May 1971
Received from Steve Allen
the sum of THIRTY-FOUR POUNDS
£34-00p

Steve Allen booked Lizzy in the early days

GRANARY CLUB

17 MAY 1971, BRISTOL, UK

I WAS THERE: PINS CUMBERLIDGE

They played a lot in Bristol over the years and always included the Colston Hall on their tours, but I do remember they played at the old Granary Club in the early years when Eric Bell was with them. I used to queue up outside the box office of the Colston Hall early in the morning on the first day of ticket sales to get seats as close to the stage as I could. The thing I loved about Lizzy was that they always wanted to take the audience on a journey when they played live. Crowd participation was important to them. They whipped the crowd up and in return the applause was always raucous and loud. Phil was always the ultimate smooth showman, talking to the audience between songs, and the rest of the band were slick tight and edgy. I always loved the drum solos Brian Downey performed. I loved the rock bands of the day back then and saw Deep Purple, Black Sabbath, Uriah Heep, Jethro Tull, Hawkwind and many others. Thin Lizzy were right up there among the best. A fantastic live act.

CLOUD NINE AT THE HALCYON

23 MAY 1971, PETERBOROUGH, UK

I WAS THERE: STEVE ALLEN

After the Wisbech gig, I put them on in a little pub in Peterborough called the Halcyon with a music back room which is where we moved to after we lost our Peterborough premises. We nearly broke the glass in the pub windows because they were so bloody noisy. But they were fantastic. The fee was £20 against 50 per cent of the door and we paid them £34, an improvement on the £15 they earned from the Wisbech gig.

NEW DAY EP RELEASED

20 AUGUST 1971

The four track 'maxi-single' – comprising 'Dublin', 'Remembering Part 2', 'Old Moon Madness' and 'Things Ain't Working Out Down at the Farm' - was released on Phil's 22nd birthday.

BOROUGH HALL

4 OCTOBER 1971, STAFFORD, UK

I WAS THERE: ALLAN ATKINS

I remember opening for Thin Lizzy when I fronted a young Judas Priest back in October 1971 at Stafford Borough Hall, which was the first time that the venue had opened for rock bands. It was a great gig and we kicked off first playing to a full crowd for around 40 minutes. Then came on Strife, who were a three piece band from Liverpool, and finally Thin Lizzy, who featured Brian Downey on drums, Eric Bell on guitar and the great Phil Lynott on bass and vocals. They played a storming set and went down really well. I didn't know much about them at the time and had never seen them play live before, but they made a big impression on me and I followed their every move after the gig watching them grow into the mighty band they became.

Allan Atkins shared a bill with Thin Lizzy

We all sat and talked in the dressing room after the show and I shared a spliff with Phil and found out we had a lot in common. We were both born in West Bromwich, although I was a couple of years older. There must have been something in the water there because Robert Plant was also born there.

DUBLIN, IRELAND

I WAS THERE: ALAN MADIGAN

My older sister was a 'very dear friend' of Philip's in the early Seventies. She was one of the few popular models at the time. Philip used to phone regularly and once I opened the door to him enquiring 'is Madedeine there?' in his unmistakeable accent. He seemed impossibly tall and exotic – I'd never seen a black man. We lived in a large house in D12, not far from his family home. I remember a typewritten lyric sheet for 'Whiskey' being dropped in plus most of the early albums. I became a huge Lizzy fan in my teens and witnessed the *Thunder and Lightning* show at the RDS, sitting on top of the fire exit door.

TOTTON COLLEGE
17 FEBRUARY 1972, SOUTHAMPTON, UK

I WAS THERE: DAVID GOODHAND, AGE 17

David Goodhand saw Lizzy with Eric Bell

My friend Geoff and I used to go into Southampton and listen to tracks or a whole album in the listening booths in the record shops, which ended up being a right pain for the people behind the counter because you were in there for hours listening to different stuff and then you walked out without buying anything! But it was a great way of finding out about music apart from what you heard if you listened to the pirate stations. The BBC was useless.

Geoff bought the Thin Lizzy *New Day* EP that came out just after their first album. It had four tracks on it. 'Dublin' was just gorgeous and it was all about Phil leaving Dublin and all his friends. It was poetry. 'Remembering Part 2' was mainly Eric Bell on guitar. Eric was very underrated as a guitarist. And then there was 'Old Moon Madness' and 'Things Ain't Working Out Down at the Farm'. Geoff played the EP to me and I said, 'Oh, that sounds pretty good.' In those days we couldn't really afford an LP. You had your summer jobs and your paper rounds and that was it. We were saving up for various LPs and Thin Lizzy wasn't top of the list.

And then Geoff said to me, 'Oh, they are coming to Totton College,' so we trekked across Southampton to Totton College on the west of town, which was a few bus rides, to see a gig with Arrival, Barabbas and Thin Lizzy. I wore my jeans with red cord flares that my mum had sewed into them along with my tie-dye shirt, orange hat and furry coat. When I was dressed like this my dad always used to say, 'Where's the circus?'

We got there at about 6.30pm so that we could be down at the front. It was just a school hall in a sixth form college. There weren't many people there. Lizzy were on first and as soon as they came on you thought, 'Wow, these guys really know their stuff. They've got a great stage presence.' Phil wasn't as upfront as he became later on but this tall black bass-playing singer with an Irish accent was a real presence. From memory Eric introduced quite a few of the songs whilst Phil did most of the vocals. And at 16, 17 you were taken by the guitarist because he is normally the leader of the band so we were watching Eric.

Phil was very nervous at the start but you could see his confidence grow during the gig. They played 'Things Ain't Working Out Down at the Farm' and I'm pretty sure they played 'Remembering' and then a number of tracks off *Shades of a Blue Orphanage* because they were promoting that album which came out later in '72. Jeff and I both went out and bought it.

They played for about an hour. We were calling out for an encore but they didn't come back out because of the time restriction with there being two other bands on the bill. I remember trying to talk to Eric and Phil afterwards. Eric was more forthcoming. Other than tell them they were great, we didn't get to say much.

We didn't stay until the end. We'd seen what we'd come to see.

I WAS THERE: STUART DEBELL, AGE 16

Our entertainment committee had paid £50 to secure Lizzy's appearance and when the three of them came on stage, we thought this was a Jimi Hendrix tribute band. What a surprise when they started playing - it was raw, unique and exciting. They only played about three numbers but the response was rapturous and we wanted more. That never happened because the headliners Arrival would have had to cut down their set. At the end of the concert, a few of us congregated up in the lighting and sound booth - somebody had a bottle of secret vodka because most of us were underage, and teachers were present and prowling about looking for miscreants. We became aware that someone was stood in the doorway and panic gripped us, but on turning round and expecting the worst, there was Mr Phil Lynott himself. In his soft spoken Irish way, he said he'd heard we had some alcohol. There were immediate denials but he gave a very knowing look and promised he would say nothing, so we found him a tea cup and for about ten minutes he chatted with us. Did we enjoy Lizzy's set? Unanimous agreement from us that Thin Lizzy had been the highlight and would be very successful.

SHADES OF A BLUE ORPHANAGE
RELEASED 10 MARCH 1972

Lizzy's second album was recorded in late 1971 at De Lane Lea Studios in Wembley, London. Like its predecessor it failed to make any inroads into the charts.

TECHNICAL COLLEGE
10 MARCH 1972, GLOUCESTER, UK

I WAS THERE: DAWN GILLIAMS

I saw Lizzy when I lived in Gloucester. I think I was 17. I know I was a starstruck teenager. We sneaked in the back and ended up getting a ride home with them. I left but my friend stayed. I think Phil fancied my friend. They were nice lads.

DRILL HALL
3 JUNE 1972, PETERBOROUGH, UK

I WAS THERE: KEITH LUCKEY

My band Butch supported Thin Lizzy twice. The first time was at the Drill Hall in Peterborough. Earlier the same day, Thin Lizzy had appeared at an event in Liverpool and then driven about 150 miles to get to Peterborough. My major memory of the gig was that, after we had played our set, my wife Chris and I were sitting on a bench in the changing room. Phil was sitting next to Chris, smoking an enormous hand-rolled cigarette and chatting away to us. Suddenly somebody

Photo Steve Allen

Thin Lizzy were supported by Butch

called, 'Come on Phil, we are on.' Phil smiled, handed the cigarette to Chris and off he went. Chris took a puff of the cigarette and nearly coughed her heart up, at which point she handed it to me. I had a great evening watching Thin Lizzy live, smoking a funny cigarette and getting paid for it!

The second gig was supporting Thin Lizzy at RAF Coningsby in Lincolnshire. Try as I might I cannot find a record of this gig anywhere on any of the various listing sites. It must either have been in late 1972 or in 1973. I don't remember too much about the gig except to say that before the gig Phil spent some time sitting in our dressing room 'socialising' and telling tales. I also remember that when Lizzy played they were incredibly loud.

Keith Luckey and wife Chris enjoyed one of Phil's 'funny' cigarettes

I WAS THERE: STEVE ALLEN

Having booked them twice we obviously became chums with Phil and the other members of the band. And I then booked them for a larger venue in Peterborough called the Drill Hall in London Road, which again we filled out. This was the big one. They got paid a straight £80 fee. Subsequently, the band Butch that I managed played support to them at one of the local RAF bases.

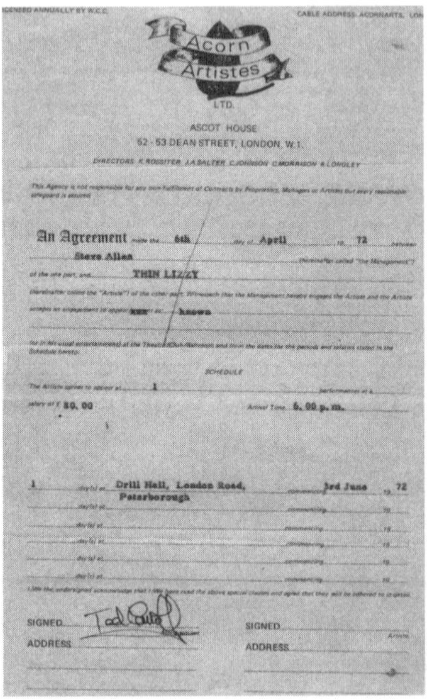

Acorn Artistes LTD.

ASCOT HOUSE
52 - 53 DEAN STREET, LONDON, W.1.

An Agreement ... 6th ... April ... 72 ...
Steve Allen
THIN LIZZY
known

SCHEDULE

1
£ 80. 00 ... 6. 00 p. m.

1 ... Drill Hall, London Road, Peterborough ... 3rd June ... 72

SIGNED
ADDRESS

SIGNED
ADDRESS

Steve Allen booked Thin Lizzy three times in total including Peterborough's Drill Hall

In July 1972, Lizzy returned to Ireland for a short tour, taking in the South and the North of the country. Return trips to Ireland were a frequent feature of Lizzy's touring schedule.

RED ISLAND

4 AUGUST 1972, SKERRIES, IRELAND

I WAS THERE: FRANK LOUGHREY, AGE 17

I saw Thin Lizzy play in my hometown of Skerries away back in 1972, in a venue called Red Island. I'll always remember Phil Lynott had a glass guitar on stage. The band hung around the town during the day, out on the beach, etc. My brother was also a big fan and had seen them before they hit the big time as Skid Row. They also played in small clubs and venues around Ireland, including in Skerries Rugby Club and a pub called The Milestone in Balbriggan, just four miles down the road.

'WHISKEY IN THE JAR' RELEASED 3 NOVEMBER 1972

'Whiskey in the Jar' was released against the band's wishes. It was to reach number 6 in the UK charts and top the Irish charts.

In July 1972, Thin Lizzy supported Slade at Starkers Royal Ballroom in Bournemouth, UK. In August, they shared a bill with David Bowie. And in November they went out on their first major tour, again supporting Slade, appearing above the unknown Suzi Quatro (Suzi's name was misspelt as Susi in music press ads for the tour).

CITY HALL

3 NOVEMBER 1972, NEWCASTLE-UPON-TYNE, UK

I WAS THERE: COLIN PETERSEN

I saw Thin Lizzy twice, in 1972 and 1976, both times at the Newcastle City Hall. The first time was as a support band, the second as headliners when in their pomp. In November 1972, they were supporting Slade. I hadn't heard much of them but a mate at school persuaded me to go as he really liked them. I remember being very disappointed by them, and thinking that they were very average and the material uninspiring.

Colin Petersen (right) saw Lizzy twice

By contrast the surprise additional support band that night was excellent; the Suzi Quatro Band. I think it might have been their first UK gig, or first significant gig. It was before her chart stuff and they played a short but rocking set including an excellent version of 'Free Electric Band'. I wasn't particularly a Slade fan - they were at that time very much a chart band - but they were very good, a tight band and very entertaining. I did own *Slade Alive* but that was a different set list from what we saw that night, which incorporated a lot of their hits up to then.

CIVIC HALL

6 NOVEMBER 1972, WOLVERHAMPTON, UK

I WAS THERE: STEVE MURTAGH

I was asked to go to a concert with a mate, It was Slade, so I jumped at the chance, but I had no idea who was supporting them. I was new to concerts, so no arriving after the warm ups or going straight to the bar. It was directly to our seats, and sit down waiting for the fun to begin.

We were looking forward to a good show!

First of all, this little woman came on with her band. She had a massive bass guitar that seemed bigger than her. It was Suzi Quatro! They only had a short slot, but they were very good. I think they did 'Can the Can', but my memory may be playing tricks about that.

Steve Murtagh first saw Thin Lizzy supporting Slade

She then introduced another band, at which point lots of obvious regulars came in from the bar, as this band was obviously popular. It was Thin Lizzy. They were a three piece group, and from the start had something about them. Their single 'Whiskey in the Jar' had just been released and the place erupted when they started that. I was well impressed!

They rattled off a couple of real rockers, and I was hooked immediately. The Irish drawl of Phil was mesmerising, and he knew how to get the audience going. It really was a great set. They did well and left to rapturous applause, which was rare for a Slade support band! Slade then came on and did an amazing show. What a night. I was hooked on Lizzy from then on.

TOWN HALL

19 NOVEMBER 1972, BIRMINGHAM, UK

I WAS THERE: JEFF COLLINS

I first came aware of Lizzy when 'Whiskey' was released, around the time I went to see Slade at Birmingham Town Hall. Lizzy were the support band. The thing I remember most is Phil's long legs. His bass looked like a little banjo!

GUILDHALL

2 DECEMBER 1972, PLYMOUTH, UK

I WAS THERE: PAUL GREGORY

Tickets were £1. The Guildhall was packed to capacity. Slade were headlining, and Thin Lizzy and Suzi Quatro were support. Suzi came on first and then Lizzy as a three piece, with Lynott, Bell and Downey. 'Whiskey in the Jar' had just been released. I certainly remember them doing it although apart from that I have no memory of the evening, apart from Slade being brilliant, with Noddy wearing his mirror hat and Dave Hill with his Superyob guitar.

NATIONAL STADIUM

10 JANUARY 1973, DUBLIN, IRELAND

I WAS THERE: ALAN KEOGH, AGE 17

I saw them in a place called the Stadium on the South Circular Road. It's five to ten minutes from where Phil used to live. It was a lovely venue, but it's not used for rock music any more. It looked like the Hollywood Bowl. It was intimate and a great place to see them. No matter where you sat, you could get up close and personal.

We all felt so proud of Phil when he went forward with his music, whether it was in the UK or in the States or wherever. We were real proud that we had the first rocker from Ireland, and still to this day THE rocker from Ireland. It was great to see that he did so well. I was devastated when Phil died. I had taken my car to the car wash and I was sitting listening to the radio when I heard the news.

I do custom bass drum heads for a lot of the music industry here in Ireland. One brilliant one I got two and a half years ago was Brian Downey. His manager got in touch and said, 'I believe you do personalised drum heads.' Brian ended up coming out to me and we had a great chat and had a couple of photographs together. His new band is called Alive and Dangerous. It was great to see them.

When I was captain of my golf club, I arranged a tournament that was half players from Dublin and half from different places in Ireland so I called Dublin versus the Rest of Ireland. I arrived on the course at half seven in the morning and as soon as everybody arrived, I threw on 'The Boys are Back in Town'. I got some great laughs. And maybe some complaints from the local people as well.

LOCARNO
4 MARCH 1973, STEVENAGE, UK

I WAS THERE: MICK MORGAN
I only saw them once. The Locarno was rammed and they blew the roof off.

BROMLEY COLLEGE OF TECHNOLOGY
24 MARCH 1973, BROMLEY, UK

I WAS THERE: CHRIS GAYWOOD, AGE 14
I lived in Catford in south east London. Good bands were bringing out brilliant stuff all the time in the early Seventies – Bowie, Zeppelin and so on - music we had just never heard of before. Bromley Tech, where I latterly went to college, would put gigs on all the time. A band called Thin Lizzy were going to be playing there and a few of us went along. I can clearly remember - they were rubbish! There were about 50 people in the audience, if that, and the sound was appalling. They were just hopeless. They were a three piece band and had released two albums at that stage. And I remember thinking, 'Well, they're not going to last very long.' Phil did not stand out as a front man.

I subsequently saw them three or four times with Phil. By the time I saw them at Wembley in 1978 they were a totally different band. There seemed to be a change when they got the twin guitars. It was as if they had a rethink all round about how they were going to present themselves on stage. The sound was different and Phil's bass had a reflective mirror and he would have a spotlight shining on it which he reflected out across the audience. When they came on stage to play 'Jailbreak' they had the police sirens going off. That was a great night, a great gig. Phil Lynott had become the lead man that you think of as Phil Lynott. Before that, they were just three blokes on a stage.

TOWN HALL

30 MARCH 1973, CHELTENHAM, UK

I WAS THERE: KEITH THOMPSON, AGE 17

Tickets were 70p in advance and 85p on the door! This was the original three piece line up of Eric Bell, Brian Downey and Phil Lynott. Gigs at Cheltenham Town Hall happened every month and I was a regular fixture. If memory serves me correctly, The Sensational Alex Harvey Band were the opening act that night. After hearing them I have to admit I wondered if Lizzy would be able to top that! But I shouldn't have worried because they were amazingly good. It was raw but packed with great riffs and hooky songs and Phil was incredibly charismatic. He really knew how to connect with the audience.

Keith Thompson first saw Lizzy in 1973

I remember them doing 'Whiskey in the Jar' because that was the song that had been in the charts for several months prior to this tour. It was the only song in the set that Phil played a six string guitar on. He bust a string early into the song but didn't seem to care. Ironically, Thin Lizzy returned to the same venue on 2nd October that same year and in a weird time slip moment Phil broke a string in the same place. Maybe it was a regular occurrence? I don't know.

I WAS THERE: PETE REYNOLDS, AGE 16

I went to seven Reading Festivals in the Seventies and caught Thin Lizzy in 1975 and again in 1977, topping the bill on Saturday evening in a wet and soggy arena. By then they were a larger band and had become a slick outfit with a massive following. They were also due to top the bill on the Saturday night in 1979 but were replaced at short notice by The Scorpions – not a bad substitution!

However, the gigs that I remember the clearest are those at Cheltenham Town Hall in March and October of 1973. I was 16 and the March concert was only the second concert I had ever been to, having seen Uriah Heep and Magnum at Colston Hall in Bristol a few weeks earlier. Like many teenagers in the Seventies I used to listen to Radio Luxembourg under the bed clothes late at night and there was a show hosted by Kid Jensen called Jensen's Dimensions. He would play tracks from an LP called *Shades of a Blue Orphanage* by Thin Lizzy, so by the time 'Whiskey in the Jar' was a hit I was fairly au fait with them. The support act that day were The Sensational Alex Harvey Band, someone else I loved to bits. Thin Lizzy weren't such a big act back then and the band were happy for us kids to wander back stage and chat to them. As I recall, Phil let me have a bottle of Pepsi and I also came away with two old plectrums and a bit of broken guitar string! That gig was 70p.

Lizzy were back in October of that year and I was there again. Once more the band were happy to mingle and I still have my ticket for that concert, autographed by Brian Downey, Eric Bell and of course Phil Lynott.

Peter Reynolds saw Lizzy at Cheltenham Town Hall

I managed to persuade them to add 'Randolph's Tango' back into the set list. I really liked that follow up to 'Whiskey' and it remains the only time I have talked a major band into playing something that was not on the play list. It had been dropped as clearly it was not going to be a successful single. Interestingly the October ticket was only 60p but the support act, Sundance, were not as well known as SAHB so I guess the support act cost less.

TECHNICAL COLLEGE

13 APRIL 1973, MAIDSTONE, UK

I WAS THERE: DAVID USMAR, AGE 22

Back in the 1970s, Maidstone Art and Tech College used to put on 'dances'. We saw some great bands there. Thin Lizzy were on in April 1973. I think they played there more than once. I was going out with my now wife. These dances were one of the highlights of living in Maidstone. We were so lucky back then. Small venues with audiences under 2,000 people made it an intimate experience and they hosted some great bands.

David Usmar remembers Lizzy's visit to Maidstone Tech

LAKE COUNTY HOTEL

21 APRIL 1973, MULLINGAR, IRELAND

I WAS THERE: JIM DOLAN

I saw them in a pub in Mullingar, County Westmeath. They were trying out 'Whiskey in the Jar'.

LOCARNO

22 JUNE 1973, SUNDERLAND, UK

I WAS THERE: PETER SMITH

It's a Friday night and I'm in the upstairs bar of Sunderland Locarno ('the Mecca', as we called it). There's a tall black guy standing next to me. He's chatting away to everyone in a strong but soft Irish accent. He seems a friendly guy and he has the appearance of somebody who might be in a band. An hour or so later the night's group take to the stage. They are called Thin Lizzy, and the guy from the bar is the front man. None of us have heard of them; someone tells me that John Peel plays them quite a bit and that they have an album out called *Shades of a Blue Orphanage*. They play well; the front man has great stage presence; the guitarist is good and the drummer impressive. I find out later that the tall guy is called Phil Lynott and the other members are Eric Bell on guitar and Brian Downey on drums. Roll on a year. I'm watching *Top of the Pops* and Thin Lizzy are on my TV playing an Irish-folk sounding tune 'Whiskey in the Jar' which has a great guitar riff. Next day I go out and buy the record. My journey with Lizzy was beginning.

The next time I saw Thin Lizzy was on 22nd June 1973, again at Sunderland Mecca. By now they had released *Vagabonds of the Western World* which featured live favourite 'The Rocker'. Support came from local band Beckett.

Over the next few years Thin Lizzy played Sunderland a few more times, hitting the stages of the Mecca and the Rink. They also appeared down the bill at the Reading Festival a couple of times. Each time I saw them they got stronger and tighter, but they also seemed to miss out on that 'big break'. I must have seen them five or six times between 1972 and 1975.

THE GREYHOUND

22 JULY 1973, FULHAM, LONDON

I WAS THERE: BILL HINDMARSH

I was there in the audience - with Gary Moore! It was a great atmosphere, sticky and hot and the crowd were primed, boozy and reactive. The closing number of the set was 'Whiskey in the Jar' - very heady! There were rapid demands for 'more!' from everyone there. 'The Rocker' as the encore closed a very fast moving whirlwind set. This was the first and last time I saw Thin Lizzy with Eric Bell.

I WAS THERE: DOM BRACK

I saw Lizzy play in the Greyhound on Fulham Palace Road in 1973. They were just a pub band then, although Phil had a glint in his eye and you knew he was special. Then in '76 I saw them across the road at the Hammersmith Odeon and the world was soon going to be theirs for the taking. And then I was back at Hammersmith for the farewell tour, when it was all over really. So you could say I saw the rise and fall of the greatest band and frontman I ever saw!

NAG'S HEAD

(POSSIBLY) SEPTEMBER 1973, WOLLASTON, UK

I WAS THERE: NIGEL RICHARDS

In the early 1970s a pub in the village of Wollaston in Northamptonshire used to put bands on in the upstairs function room. You entered by going up an outside fire escape and paying at the door. The man who ran the venue was known as Big Bob and he was friends with John Peel, the DJ who used to decide which bands

The Nag's Head in Wollaston where Thin Lizzy played and John Peel DJed. Nigel Richards saw Thin Lizzy at the legendary venue

played there. It was a small room, holding maybe about 100 people with a tiny, low stage at one end of the room and a bar at the other.

I used to go over there on Friday nights with some mates to see what were usually unknown or little known bands. One night, an Irish band called Thin Lizzy were playing. None of us had heard of them but we thought we'd go anyway. They were a three piece band consisting of drummer, bassist and guitarist, who at this point was still the original guitarist, Eric Bell, who was sporting a startlingly red bubble perm hairdo. They had the standard back line of the times of a Marshall 4 x 12 each and a Marshall 100 watt head.

I remember the bass player played a Fender Precision Bass and the guitarist a Fender Strat - I was just becoming a guitar player myself and was a little obsessed with who used what. At the time we thought that they were okay but not the best band we had seen there. We'd also seen Skid Row there, another Irish band fronted by Gary Moore, so comparisons were inevitable. I remember them playing some Hendrix covers and some other original songs which seemed solid enough.

My most clear memory is after the gig. I was sitting on the edge of the stage chatting to the band while my mate tried to purchase something combustible from their bass player who was adamant that they only had enough of said material to get them back to London.

(The exact date of Lizzy's appearance at the Nag's Head is unknown. John Peel regularly DJed at the Nag's Head. He met Lizzy on a ferry from Dun Laoghaire to Holyhead and they 'urged me to listen out for them.... Throughout the first half of the Seventies, they provided a welcome antidote to much of the pretentious hogwash that bedevilled the age.' He went on to champion the band, as he did many others during his career. Lizzy went on to do eleven sessions for Peel's BBC Radio 1 programme.)

I did loads of gigs with Thin Lizzy around the time of these things but don't remember a great deal about them. **John Peel (1999)**

WINTER GARDENS

21 SEPTEMBER 1973, PENZANCE, UK

I WAS THERE: ROB TREWHELLA, AGE 16

I first saw Lizzy as a three piece when I worked at the Winter Gardens, collecting glasses for £1 a night. The first band I saw there was Status Quo, and not long after I saw Queen. I remember going upstairs to collect my £1 pay for picking up glasses and the three of them were sat in the corner having refreshments. I grabbed a promo pic of them but didn't get it signed. I later saw Lizzy at the Reading Festival – twice!

LOUGHBOROUGH UNIVERSITY OF TECHNOLOGY

6 OCTOBER 1973, LOUGHBOROUGH, UK

I WAS THERE: TONY HOLT

I was in my final year as a Chemical Engineering undergraduate. They played the Freshers Hop and were on with Ace. Tickets cost all of 75p. To a standing ovation they played 'Whiskey in the Jar' - twice!

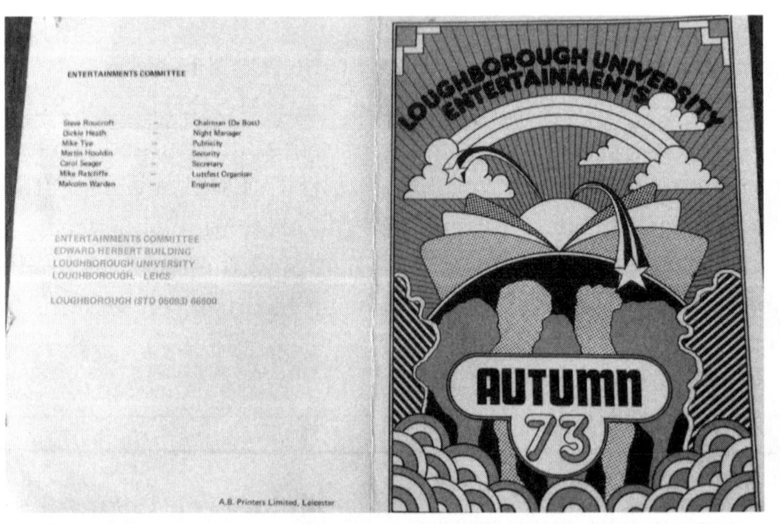

Tony Holt got to see Lizzy for just 75p

THE GREYHOUND, FULHAM PALACE ROAD

14 OCTOBER 1973, LONDON, UK

I WAS THERE: KEITH PARFSON

I was very tall for my age and in those days, you didn't need ID to get in anywhere, just the judgement of the person on box office. I was five foot eight when I started at high school and six foot three by the age of 13, which was very handy for getting into venues and meant I had a great view wherever I stood. I fell in with a group of sixth formers and would listen to records at various people's houses. I was very much a fan of the hard rock triumvirate of Purple, Zeppelin and Sabbath, all of whom I was fortunate enough to see.

The first time I saw Lizzy was at the Greyhound on Fulham Palace Road, 100 yards from Hammersmith Palais. It was a free gig in a fairly big traditional pub that had a large bar room with a gallery with a rail around so you could watch the band in relative comfort. They played 'The Rocker' which became and remains one of my 'go to' rock songs. I remember them playing 'Vagabonds' and I thought they played 'Whiskey in the Jar', but my mate is not sure.

I remember Phil Lynott changing from bass to rhythm for that one song, because as a three piece they needed the rhythm guitar in it. Eric Bell was amazing and Brian Downey completely solid. And Phil - what could I say that hasn't already been said about him? He was majestic, he owned the stage and the audience.

Keith Parfson started going to Lizzy shows around London

MARQUEE CLUB

13 NOVEMBER 1973, LONDON, UK

I WAS THERE: KEITH PARFSON

My father always gave me tacit support when seeking out live music. Dad used to go to a place called The Bag O' Nails from 1942 until he went in the army in June 1944, where the blind pianist George Shearing often led a jazz jam session on Sunday afternoons.

After the Fulham Greyhound gig, we looked for Lizzy all over. We saw them at the Marquee two or three times as they seemed to play there every month. I lived in Neasden and the number 8 bus used to take us along Oxford Street on its way to Old Ford in the East End, ideal for Wardour Street. Me and a mate who was my age started going up to the Marquee a couple of times a week. We often stopped off at The Shakespeare's Head in the downstairs dive bar on Carnaby Street for a couple of early ones.

The Marquee was a great venue. One of my mum's friends was on the door and would nod us through. You walked in with the cash window on the left and you then were led down a dark corridor through doors and into the room with the stage behind you, so that you emerged from stage right as it were. In front of the stage were two rows of cinema-type seats. Me and my mate Peter used to stand behind the seats so that we were six to eight feet from the stage. We'd take it in turns to get the beer or go to the loo.

The band were always excellent, so professional and absolutely exciting from start to finish! And I was only ten feet from Phil and his Rickenbacker. It had a funny shaped machine head with a little cut out and he used to hook this over an amp or speaker while leaning on it doing those exaggerated splits. I saw Lizzy a few more times but, as good as they were, they could never match what I saw back in the early days.

Incidentally, unbeknownst to me at the time, the Bag O'Nails that my dad used to visit was just around the corner from the Marquee.

The band were always excellent and exciting from start to finish!

VAGABONDS OF THE WESTERN WORLD
RELEASED 9 NOVEMBER 1973

Vagabonds of the Western World featured 'The Rocker' which was to become an enduring highlight of Lizzy's live set for the remainder of their career.

CAERLEON COLLEGE
5 DECEMBER 1973, NEWPORT, WALES

I WAS THERE: DENNIS STALLARD

Dennis Stallard remembers a raw version of 'The Rocker'

I was studying at Caerleon College when I saw Thin Lizzy there in 1973. They were supported by Blackfoot Sue with their one big hit, 'Standing in the Road'. It was my first date with my wife to be and we had a few drinks in the local before going to see Thin Lizzy and Blackfoot Sue in the main hall. It was a great night, although I don't think Phil was too happy that a lot of the students were calling out for 'Whiskey in the Jar' and singing it when he was playing other songs. I remember a raw version of 'The Rocker' and a bluesy version of 'Broken Dreams'.

One of my friends had met a 'rock chick' (as she advertised herself in either the *NME* or *Sounds*) who jumped at the chance of seeing Thin Lizzy. There were stacks of chairs lined up and on the afternoon of the gig he moved some of them so that they covered an alcove where the coconut mats were stored and so he and this rock chick could spend the night together. They emerged from under the chairs at about 10am the following morning!

A guy on my course had argued with his girlfriend in the local pub. He told her not to go to the Lizzy concert. She turned up at about 10pm and a fight broke out between the two of them by the entrance hallway. The guy was thrown out by the doormen and decided to punch his way out through a door with safety glass and chicken wire in it. As you can imagine, he cut both his hands to pieces and there was blood everywhere. I remember talking to him a few days later and he couldn't remember any of the music.

IRISH TOUR
DECEMBER 1973, IRELAND

I WAS THERE: BILL HINDMARSH

Lizzy were concluding their Irish tour at the end of 1973 and had added an extra date in Portrush. On New Year's Eve 1973, Gary Moore received a visit from Thin Lizzy's manager asking him if he could 'step in and close the Irish tour as Eric had left Lizzy, or been sacked!' Gary agreed this without going through his manager, who had evaporated. Gary was barely existing on the money he was earning from gigs.

Gigs scheduled for 1 and 2 January 1974 were cancelled.

RED ISLAND
4 JANUARY 1974, SKERRIES, IRELAND

Gary Moore played his first gig with Lizzy, deputising for Eric Bell.

NATIONAL STADIUM
16 JANUARY 1974, DUBLIN, IRELAND

I WAS THERE: BILL HINDMARSH

During January I was persuaded by a girlfriend to accompany her to Dublin 'for the last date of tour'. As it turned out I was there ten days and saw at least two gigs. They also put in an appearance at Portrush after the last date of tour. I got to spend most of my free time with Lizzy's roadcrew and much rehearsal practise took place. I recall it all as a really wild education. I fell in love with Dublin too.

Bill Hindmarsh saw Lizzy several times

There was a perceptible freedom and expansiveness about their music at this time. Gary could be relied upon to know their music and understand their personalities and he contributed through his own innovatory leanings. In Ireland this even included doing Lizzy versions of Stevie Wonder songs he and Phil loved - a kind of open jamming!

TOP RANK

13 FEBRUARY 1974, CARDIFF, UK

I WAS THERE: RICHARD RHODES

I was just 18. I was into rock music right from the start - Black Sabbath. Deep Purple. All the usual suspects. And then Thin Lizzy came along. That was the first time I heard a twin guitar sound, although of course it's been replicated many times since by Iron Maiden and various other groups.

There were two theatres in Cardiff - the Capitol, which was the largest, and the Top Rank, which was a smaller, more intimate club-type of venue. And that's where I saw Thin Lizzy, with the Brian Robertson and Scott Gorham line up. I went with some friends who were all into the same kind of music. There was seating available but I was standing up, just two or three yards away from Phil Lynott. They were brilliant. What has stayed with me is the intimacy and the accessibility of that show. And they were good to watch too - visually as well as musically brilliant.

ROUNDHOUSE

17 FEBRUARY 1974, LONDON, UK

I WAS THERE: ALAN R PRICE

I saw Thin Lizzy at the Roundhouse in 1974, supported by Ducks Deluxe, Heavy Metal Kids and Kokomo, and again at Reading Festival on 23 August 1975. I was in the sixth form at school, with all that involved, in the mid-1970s. I lived in Finchley, north London, so the Roundhouse was just a short hop on the Northern Line, being a stone's throw from Camden Town underground station. The Sunday afternoon gigs at the Roundhouse were legendary: 'Float up to the Roundhouse on a Sunday afternoon,' as Mott the Hoople sang. It cost a quid for four bands and about six hours of music. I also saw Pete Townshend there, among others. The hippy character William Jellett, nicknamed 'Jesus', who used to dance like a mad thing, was a regular.

Alan Price (in white) saw Lizzy at the Roundhouse

Reading was a blast, in spite of the rain later on, but the line-up was fantastic, including the Kursaal Flyers, SNAFU, Alain Stivell (a John Peel favourite), Supertramp, and the headliners Yes, who were my favourite band at the time.

My recollection of the performances themselves is a little hazy - for many reasons! I remember particularly the atmosphere, the experience and the sheer excitement of the whole thing as an adolescent exploring a whole new world. My overriding memories of Thin Lizzy are of a 'lads' band, pelting out high-energy rock, with this amazing beanpole of a front man, playing bass and looking like a swashbuckling warrior from another galaxy, all backed up by screaming guitar work by two amazing guitarists.

Lizzy had this amazing beanpole of a front man, playing bass and looking like a swashbuckling warrior from another galaxy

---

VILLAGE BLUES CLUB, THE ROUNDHOUSE

16 MARCH 1974, DAGENHAM, UK

I WAS THERE: DAVE CHITTY

I first saw Lizzy at the Roundhouse in Dagenham in 1974 and met Philo at the bar. I went on to see them several times around the London area. I've seen Limehouse Lizzy at several places too, the last being the Dagenham Roundhouse in 2018!

LEAS CLIFF HALL

10 APRIL 1974, FOLKESTONE, UK

I WAS THERE: JULIA YOUNG

Julia Young first met Phil in 1972

My story starts in 1972. I'd watched Lizzy on *Top of the Pops* on a Thursday. I'd not seen or heard of them before. The next night, Friday, I went to a club in London called the Speakeasy and as I came out of the ladies, I heard someone say in a lovely Irish accent, 'Would you like to come to a party?' As I turned around, I saw it was Philip and recognised him from the night before. I told him I'd have to go ask my friend as she was in the restaurant area. I took his hand and led him to where my friend Jan was.

Jan agreed to go as well, and in the end there were five of us crammed into my little Triumph Herald – me, Jan, Lizzy's tour manager Frank Murray, Peter Green from Fleetwood Mac and Philip. I don't know how we all got in it to be honest. After going down a one way street, I drove to the party behind the Hilton.

From then on, I started to see Philip. He and Frank would come to Jan's flat in Bounds Green from time to time and we also went to many gigs, from the Greyhound to bigger gigs like Cambridge Corn Exchange, where I was at the back of the stage when Philip sang 'Happy Birthday' to me. One gig was Folkestone, where I must have managed to borrow a camera and took pictures, which I still have.

Philip gave me many bits and pieces which I still have. The one thing that got lost when I moved was the green velvet jacket that he gave me and which he wore that night I saw him on *Top of the Pops*. I was seeing Philip on and off, but what with touring after they got more popular, it started to get less.

I knew him in all for six years. The last time I saw him was at *Top of the Pops* in 1976. I then got married in '77 and didn't see him anymore. My friend Jan was still working in the music business so would bump into him now and again. In fact, she saw him about a month before he passed away. He said we would all have to meet again. Who knows what might have happened if we had? I was so shocked when he did pass away. I really thought he would pull through.

After going on the internet many years later, putting my pictures on Facebook and making many friends who love Lizzy, I also found out about the statue in Dublin and wrote to Philomena telling her about Philip and I. I used to visit Dublin twice a year to go to the *Vibe* and the birthday bash. I was lucky enough to be able to call Philomena a friend until she passed away. I realised then how Philip was so like her. They were both jokers with great senses of humour.

LOCARNO

14 APRIL 1974, BRISTOL, UK

I WAS THERE: CHAD GIBBONS

Admission was £1. The flyer is wrong, because it wasn't the Climax Blues Band who supported them but Trapeze. There's a bootleg CD on YouTube called *Gary's Jig Bristol 74* and I remember shouting out 'Rocker' before the band started and on there you can hear Phil answer, 'Sometime later.' It's my claim to fame. There were 'Little Darling'

Chad Gibbons was at Bristol Locarno

badges which I seem to recall had John Peel dressed as a schoolgirl, St Trinian's style.

Mr Moore was in the line up and I always thought it seemed more of his showcase than the band's gig. I'm sure he did stuff with his teeth and as well as lots of solos. Then there was a drum solo and some dry ice and then they were gone. I was hoping for more off the *Vagabonds* album but in hindsight this was only a short lived line up. I did catch them again at Bath Uni the following year on the *Nightlife* tour. That and *Fighting* represent my favourite Lizzy era.

GARY MOORE LEAVES
APRIL 1974, LONDON, UK

I WAS THERE: BILL HINDMARSH

Living in North West London meant we all were near neighbours - Gary, Phil, Brian and myself. This involved some socialising and musical appreciation! The first I knew of Gary leaving Lizzy was from a chance meeting on Belsize Park Avenue, when Phil and Brian were travelling somewhere by car and I was walking along towards Chalk Farm. Phil told me and could read my surprise at this news. I recall him saying, 'We've had to get two fookin' guitarists to replace him!' and laughing, but I could tell he was saddened.

In May 1974 Thin Lizzy embarked upon a German tour with John Du Cann and Andy Gee in the line up, replacing Gary Moore. The line up was temporary. Two permanent guitarists were being recruited.

SCOTT GORHAM AND BRIAN ROBERTSON JOIN THIN LIZZY
JUNE 1974, LONDON, UK

Phil said, 'Let's go in, let's learn some songs, let's have a jam session and see what happens.' It was on the day that I did the jam… that he asked me to join the band. **Scott Gorham (talking to *Australian Musician*, November 2021)**

He was American and he had long hair. It was nothing to do with the guitar playing. Phil was thinking about world domination, about getting to America. **Brian Robertson**

LAFAYETTE CLUB

5 JULY 1974, WOLVERHAMPTON, UK

I WAS THERE: SCOTT GORHAM

Until that first show, no one had even talked about what we were actually going to look like on stage. So we get to the Lafayette Club, at which there were about eight paying customers, and Brian Downey on drums counts us in. And Phil and Brian Robertson, they're flying. Back and forth and around the stage. 'Wait a minute! Nobody told me we were supposed to do that shit – what the fuck's going on?' And I just cowered back to my amps. Finally, in the middle of a song, Phil walked over, grabbed me by the collar, dragged me to the front of the stage, and said, 'Don't fucking move from there.' He wanted a frontal attack. No one was going to be sitting back in the shadows in this band.
Scott Gorham, (talking to *The Guardian*, 22 October 2020)

MARQUEE CLUB

19 AUGUST 1974, LONDON, UK

I WAS THERE: PHIL SPALDING

I and my friends followed Lizzy around all the unis, colleges and pubs. I was at the Marquee the first and second times they first played with the twin guitars. I watched them up until Wembley '78, by which time I was in the 'business' so I got in for free.

MECCA

25 OCTOBER 1974, SUNDERLAND, UK

I WAS THERE: PETER SMITH

I next saw Lizzy at the 1974 Reading Festival, halfway down a varied bill which featured Georgie Fame, Procol Harum, Trapeze and Greenslade, and was headlined by Traffic. The classic twin guitar line-up was now in place: Philip Lynott, Brian Downey, Scott Gorham, and Brian Robertson, and they had released *Nightlife*. The attitude and presence were there; some of the songs and the success took a little longer. I saw them back at the Mecca on 25th October 1974 with support from Quicksand.

NIGHTLIFE RELEASED 8 NOVEMBER 1974

Lizzy's fourth studio album was the first to feature Scott Gorham and Brian Robertson and included 'Still in Love with You', a song that was to form a staple of Lizzy's live set and the lead guitar for which was performed by Gary Moore before he departed the band.

LIVERPOOL STADIUM

9 NOVEMBER 1974, LIVERPOOL, UK

I WAS THERE: PETER FINNEY

Finding Lizzy led me to make lifelong friends I've known since school in 1973. I saw Lizzy on every tour from 1974 to their final *Thunder and Lightning* tour in 1983. I only ever saw them in Liverpool and looking back I can't believe I never made the short journey to Manchester to see them there too. I have made a couple of visits to Phil's grave and on the last occasion, Philomena was there and invited my friend and I back to her house to look at all of Phil's stuff - his jukebox, his gold discs and awards, etc. She was lovely and thanked us for taking the time to come and pay our respects to Phil. This was a very humbling experience.

HAMMERSMITH ODEON

5 APRIL 1975, LONDON, UK

I WAS THERE: KEITH PARKER

A mate and myself saw them several times, mostly at the Hammersmith Odeon. It goes without saying they were superb live. Sometimes bands have a bad night due to the excesses of drink and unmentionable substances but if any of them were under any kind of chemical influences, it never showed during any gig I ever attended. I'm not sure how old I was when I attended my first Lizzy gig, with a mate I met in our respective first jobs, but I was very much into T.Rex, Bowie, Atomic Rooster and many of the bands that came through from the Sixties. I purchased 'Whiskey in the Jar' and played it to death.

APOLLO THEATRE

1 MAY 1975, GLASGOW, UK

I WAS THERE: PAUL FOY

The first time I saw Thin Lizzy was when they supported Bachman Turner Overdrive. I tagged along with friends who were going. Lizzy went down a storm that night and I went out and bought *Nightlife* and then *Fighting*. We then saw Lizzy a couple of times at the City Halls, once supported by City Boy, and once by Graham Parker and the Rumour. We saw them just as *Jailbreak* was about to be released, and that was when we bumped into Brian Robertson. We told him we came from Clarkston, where he was brought up, and that our big brothers had been at school with him, and he invited us to come backstage after the show and meet the band. Next time we saw them it was more difficult to get tickets as 'The Boys are Back in Town' had been a hit and their Apollo shows were usually sell outs. After Brian Robertson left, I saw them with Snowy White and Gary Moore on guitar. Both were great, but I missed Robbo's guitar solo during 'Still in Love with You'. I also missed seeing his soft toy mascot, Derek the Dog, who sat on an amp at the back. Phil Lynott would always introduce Derek as a member of the band, and there would usually be a roadie hidden behind the amp to lift Derek up and shake him about when the spotlight was on him.

I WAS THERE: JACKIE YUILL, AGE 17

Thin Lizzy came to my attention when 'Whiskey in the Jar' was getting a lot of airplay in late '72 and early '73, but my first chance to see them was in May 1975 when they were supporting Bachmann Turner Overdrive at the legendary Glasgow Apollo. I went with my friends Janice, Ian and Johnny. We had decent seats in the stalls, at the end of the row and just a few rows back from the stage. I can't remember Thin Lizzy's set apart from loving every minute of it - BTO, not so much. At the end of the show, the lights went up and we decided to leave through a door at the side of the stage. This led to a lane where the band's equipment was loaded and unloaded. On the way out, we noticed a narrow passage which looked like it went below the stage so we decided to investigate. It led to a tiny dressing room and in it were Phil, Scott and Brian Downey!

My friend Ian was 16, a guitarist with his own band who went on to have some success in the Eighties, immediately started chatting to Scott. One of us asked where Robbo was and Phil told us that he had gone 'home with his mammy'. We told them how much we'd enjoyed the show. Phil said they had just finished recording their latest album, *Fighting*, and to make sure we went out and bought it when it was released. (I did). I got my programme autographed and then it was time to leave to catch our last bus, one of the disadvantages of living out in the sticks.

Jackie Yuill saw Lizzy supporting Bachman Turner Overdrive

FREE TRADE HALL

2 MAY 1975, MANCHESTER, UK

I WAS THERE: MARTIN RIGBY

I saw them perform 'Whiskey in the Jar' on *Top of the Pops* in 1972 or '73, and when I was 15 going on 17 in the mid Seventies I'd go to Wigan Casino rock night on Saturday evenings. This ran from 7pm until midnight and they'd then turf us out and let all the Northern Soul all-nighters in! The rock nights featured bands such as Judas Priest and UFO, who went on to bigger and better things. They also had a DJ who always played 'The Rocker' (long version) off *Vagabonds of the Western World*. I ended up buying that album and their earlier albums. (The band I played in at the time were called Vagabond. Not very inventive.)

When we spotted Lizzy were on tour supporting BTO at the Free Trade Hall, we decided to go. It was the first of four times I saw them in 1975 and 1976. It was promoting the *Nightlife* album. They were good, not great, and weren't on stage for long.

CLEOPATRA'S

12 JUNE 1975, DERBY, UK

I WAS THERE: PAUL FOX

I saw them on the *Nightlife* tour here. They were fantastic.

I WAS THERE: VIV TAYLOR

I was there with Jim Taylor. I was 16 and they were awesome.

I WAS THERE: GARY ROOTS

Phil Lynott was sitting at a table near the bar with a couple of the band members (I can't remember who) with a bottle of whisky. He was chatting to the crowd before the concert. The queue was right round the corner near Zanzibar's and the place was rammed. It was an amazing show!

MR GEORGE'S

15 JUNE 1975, COVENTRY, UK

I WAS THERE: GERALD CLEAVER

One of my best friends, Larry, was trying to persuade a group of friends to travel the eight or so miles on a Sunday evening from where we lived in Leamington Spa to Coventry. The reason for going to Coventry was to see a band called Thin Lizzy. Nobody wanted to go since we all had to work the next day, and no one had heard much, if anything about them other than 'Whiskey in the Jar'. Larry was raving over an unknown but now classic album called *Vagabonds of the Western World.*

Thin Lizzy had issued *Nightlife* at this time, which had also not charted. Because no one who could drive was prepared to take us to the gig, in desperation Larry offered to take us all - on his motorbike! He said he would take and return as many as wanted to go, even if he had to ride his bike to and from Coventry for each of us. This would have meant four trips to and from Coventry to get us all there, and four more afterwards to bring us back home. Clearly ludicrous, but the idea worked as one of the car owners agreed to drive us all. None of us had bought tickets: in those far off days it was rarely necessary to book in advance other than for top acts. The gig was at Mr George's, a night club whose main claim to fame was booking Spot, ie. the Sex Pistols on Tour, at the height of their notoriety.

What can I say? For a band I didn't know, Thin Lizzy played one of the best gigs I have still ever attended, in a small nightclub to a small but enthusiastic audience. They had good songs, good musicians and a super live act. In those days, especially if you hadn't had a hit, you worked all the time. Thin Lizzy were well rehearsed and used to putting on a show to audiences who may not know them. They were really exciting. At that time, it was the soon to be classic line up of Lynott, Downey and the two lead guitarists Brian Robertson and Scott Gorham. A really super night out.

ROUNDHOUSE

22 JUNE 1975, LONDON, UK

I WAS THERE: PAUL RYAN

Paul Ryan saw Lizzy with his girlfriend Jackie

I loved the band and that style of music – it all started with a Jimi Hendrix concert in 1967 for my 15th birthday. The Roundhouse in June 1975 was an awesome concert. I went with my girlfriend Jackie of four years, now my wife, and remember having to walk miles as the parking was so crap. I was particularly drawn to the band as my father was from Dublin. 'Whiskey in the Jar' and 'The Boys are Back' are two of my all time favourites.

CARDIFF CASTLE

12 JULY 1975, CARDIFF, UK

I WAS THERE: BILL HINDMARSH

Lizzy were third on the bill for this show. I hitchhiked to Cardiff from London the night before and slept rough not far from the castle. On waking, I made my way to the castle and found a place by an entrance where I might sit and watch the comings and goings. No sooner had I got there than a car arrived, the window was lowered and Phil was grinning at me. The door opened: 'Get in!' Again, I became Lizzy's guest. I was labelled 'ligger'. It didn't keep me from enjoying all the bands or from joining 10cc's after show banquet!

Phil was grinning at me: 'Get in!'

HARLOW FREE FESTIVAL SPURRIERS PARK

19 JULY 1975, HARLOW, UK

I WAS THERE: GORDON SCOTT

I saw Lizzy at the Harlow Free Festival in July 1975. They were promoting the *Nightlife* album. They played many of their hits and the versions of 'Still in Love with You' and 'The Rocker' that they played were awesome. The crowd were going crazy.

I also met and spoke with Phil a few times in his last days. I worked for a garden maintenance company and we used to look after his garden in Twickenham. When I told him I played drums, he showed me around his home studio. His mother Philomena was a lovely lady. She always brought us out coffee and biscuits, and sometimes homemade cake.

I WAS THERE: GRAEME SELKIRK

Graeme Selkirk crewed a couple of Lizzy shows

I saw Lizzy on a couple of occasions, the first whilst working as sound man for East of Eden when we were supporting them at an open air gig in Harlow, Essex. East of England's (very accomplished) fiddle player at that time was one Joe O'Donnell, from Dublin. Joe was sitting chatting backstage to Phil Lynott and introduced me. Phil immediately came across as very charismatic and friendly and was speaking in glowing terms about the States, having recently been there on the band's first North American tour. I also seem to remember Brian Robertson somewhere in the background looking menacing!

After East of Eden had performed to a good reception for a support act, and after the obligatory 'test 1-2s' had been carried out, Lizzy took to the stage to a rapturous reception. Phil really knew how to get the crowd going. I've always considered him to be what a real rock star was all about.

The second occasion was in 1977 at Edinburgh Odeon, by which time the band had had a few hits and the production was considerably larger and more polished. Again, I was there in a working capacity - I was helping a friend retrieve some amps that had been hired to the band for the gig. Phil Lynott was oozing charisma and star quality once more. Gary Moore was in the band at this point. How he could play like he did and run around the stage with a Les Paul round his neck (they aren't exactly light) amazed me.

It was very sad when Phil died but you have to admit he lived the rock star life. No regurgitating hits in his mid-seventies for him!

ROCK ISLAND FESTIVAL INSEL NONNENAU FESTIVAL

9 AUGUST 1975, GINSHEIM, GERMANY

I WAS THERE: STEVE KUHNER

I was in the United States Air Force, based at Frankfurt am Main airbase. The show was in a little town outside of Frankfurt. Concert tickets only cost 8 to 10 bucks at the most. They were pretty cheap. Thin Lizzy played by themselves. There was no support act. It was in a convention centre auditorium, no bigger than a school gymnasium.

When they started to play, me and the guys that I went with were standing right there at the front. I had my elbows on the stage and I was so close I could've reached out and grabbed Phil's mic stand. We were smoking hash and Phil leaned over and said, 'Let me have a hit of your hash pipe,' so I let him smoke off my hash pipe. Then he saw us taking straight shots out of a bota bag, which is made for drinking wine but which we had filled with Jim Beam whiskey. He laid his bass guitar down to me and motioned, 'Yeah, let me have a bit of it.' I put the strap over his bass and he swung it up and around, took a big long draw of it. He said, 'Oh my God it's fucking whiskey.' He almost threw up!

The setting was really cheap. There was no major light show but they had four police lights sitting on top of the speakers which did the job when they played 'Jailbreak'. Phil could really connect with an audience. In between songs, he would talk to us like we were his best friends. He didn't seem even the slightest bit intoxicated or inebriated. He orchestrated the entire stage. He was the guy in charge. I have to rate it in the top ten concerts I have seen and I've literally seen thousands.

READING FESTIVAL
23 AUGUST 1975, READING, UK

I WAS THERE: PETER SMITH

In 1975 I was back at Reading and so were Lizzy, this time a little further up a bill headlined by Yes, Wishbone Ash, and Hawkwind. I may have seen them once or twice more. I have vague memories of a gig at Sunderland Top Rank, perhaps with Status Quo, or maybe Quo played the Mecca while Thin Lizzy played the Rink on the same night - or vice versa! What I do know is that Lizzy were gigging constantly throughout those years and played in the North East many times. They were a great live band and I guess I took them for granted. I was lucky enough to be able to see the band honing their craft and developing into a class rock act.

FIGHTING RELEASED
2 SEPTEMBER 1975
UK CHART POSITION 60

The first Lizzy album to crack the charts, and featuring the singles 'Rosalie' and 'Wild One', *Fighting* did not fare so well with the critics. Esteemed metal writer Geoff Barton described the album in *Sounds* magazine as 'adequate' with a 'lack of any real energy or aggression'. Barton then saw a Lizzy show where he witnessed a Phil diatribe against rock critics before Phil smiled and said, 'This next song is for Geoff Barton. 'Still in Love with You'.'

To promote the *Fighting* album, Lizzy went on what was billed as the *Rocktober* tour around the UK, supported by String Driven Thing and City Boy.

CITY HALL

10 OCTOBER 1975, NEWCASTLE, UK

I WAS THERE: ROBERT BRUCE

My wife and I always say that if we could get one band back together to see them again, it would be Lizzy in their heyday, doing anything between *Fighting* and *Black Rose*.

Like a lot of people, I knew about 'Whiskey in the Jar', I'd heard 'The Rocker' and I'd seen them on *Top of the Pops*. I'm a big Status Quo fan and I'd seen Slade and Quo at the City Hall. Seeing Lizzy at City Hall on the *Fighting* tour was just a life changing thing. It was a great concert with great sound. The twin harmony guitars were just a revelation. I then saw them on the first leg of the *Jailbreak* tour, which was only about six months later. There were probably only getting 400 to 500 people to see them on those tours. But with 'The Boys are Back in Town' in the charts, there was a big, big difference in the size of the crowd for the second leg of the *Jailbreak* tour. It was sold out. Those shows were the 'classic' Lizzy line up, with Brian Robertson and Scott Gorham. Clover supported them in November and Huey Lewis, who went on to be Huey Lewis and the News, played a bit of harmonica. He and Phil became quite pally.

It was the live energy and the sound of a Lizzy concert that made them so special. Phil was the perfect rock 'n' roll front man. He engaged with the audience as soon as he came on. There was bags of eye contact. That twin harmony guitar sound was quite a different thing in British music and Thin Lizzy always looked the part live with the double bass drum kit and the Marshalls. You walked into a concert hall and you thought 'wow'.

I've met Scott a few times and he's an absolutely lovely bloke. The first time I saw them, in 1975, I met them backstage and I've still got my ticket signed on the back by Phil, Scott and Brian Downey. Seven or eight years ago, a pal was doing merch for Lizzy and he got me to meet Scott in Carlisle and we probably got to talk to him for 45 minutes. He was absolutely tremendous, particularly when he knew I'd been a Thin Lizzy fan for so long.

LIVERPOOL STADIUM

11 OCTOBER 1975, LIVERPOOL, UK

I WAS THERE: MARTIN RIGBY

The next time was when they were headlining on the *Fighting* tour. Now demolished, Liverpool Stadium was a great venue albeit better known for staging boxing matches. Lizzy were on fire at this gig. Phil Lynott had his black Fender Precision bass with a mirrored scratchplate and personal spot light and would use it to pick out people in the audience, mainly girls I suspect! He also used the saying he probably used at all the gigs, 'Are there any girls out there with a bit of Irish in them? Are there any girls out there who'd like a bit of Irish in them?' It sounds pretty un-PC when you say it now.

I saw them next at Reading Festival but this is a bit hazy. It was raining and we'd been drinking for three days solid so I can't remember much about them. The last time I saw them was back at the Stadium on the *Jailbreak* tour. Again, they were on top form and Phil had the same mirrored scratchplate and the same Irish patter.

I never saw them again after that. In hindsight I'm not sure why. I bought the next couple of albums but then kind of moved on to other music.

UNIVERSITY OF SWANSEA

17 NOVEMBER 1975, SWANSEA, UK

I WAS THERE: MIKE WILLIAMS

I first saw Thin Lizzy at Swansea Students Union Hall. I was 16 or 17. I was an apprentice fitter and turner - like Phil! Being the cheeky tyke I was, I was right down the front and Phil gave me a bottle of Guinness. The energy and passion were electric. At that stage I went to see various bands - Alex Harvey Band, The Who - all in Swansea. But Thin Lizzy were my band. They sang the songs that meant something. The passion, the chords, the whole aura around all of the members.

I saw Lizzy again at Cardiff's Capitol Theatre and remember the raw energy and the power chords. I knew every word and every quip and responded wholeheartedly. Then I saw them at the Hammersmith Odeon. They were more polished now, and the Thin Lizzy emblem was glittering.

I recall seeing them headline Reading as well. It was a warm hot sunny Sunday night and a crowd of us sneaked in. We had plastic wrapping in the boot of my car which we coloured in with felt pen, flashing them at the Hell's Angels on the door.

I've been to the *Vibe* and went to the Phil Lynott Experience at the O2 Arena. My finale came when I paid £100 to meet and greet the boys without Phil in 2012 or so at Cardiff, which was money well spent.

When Phil died, I felt so guilty. I was living in Fulham, not far from Kew. I regularly visit Dublin and Crumlin. I have Irish roots and my partner's dad is from Dublin. My favourite Lizzy song ever is 'Still in Love with You.' It's so poignant. It meant so much, and still does.

DERBY COLLEGE

21 NOVEMBER 1975, DERBY, UK

I WAS THERE: PAUL FOX, AGE 16

I got their autographs. We helped them out with their equipment and chatted to them at the end of the day. I only understood the American. I don't remember much else as I was under the influence of a great deal of lager. Great gig though!

Photo Paul Fox

Paul Fox got Lizzy's autographs

A bootleg of this show includes Lizzy playing an unfinished version of 'Cowboy Song' which Phil christened 'Derby Blues'.

UNIVERSITY OF LEEDS
17 JANUARY 1976, LEEDS, UK

I WAS THERE: PAUL WHISTON

My whole music experience started at the age of around 15 when I was introduced to the likes of Tommy James and Duane Eddy by an older friend, although I'd always been brought up on Fifties and Sixties rock and roll by my parents. I loved Adam Faith, Bill Haley, etc. I cut my album-purchasing teeth on *Every Picture Tells a Story* as I've always leaned towards flat gravelly-voiced singers. 'Whiskey in the Jar' got me hooked on Lizzy in 1972 and led me to *Vagabonds of the Western World.*

The stand out feature for me has always been Phil Lynott's voice and vocals. I started university in Leeds in 1974 and went to as many gigs as I could afford. I saw Queen in November that year but the highlights were Lizzy in January and November of 1976. Watching them live was amazing, especially 'The Rocker'! They remain my 'go to' soundtrack in the car, and it's such a shame we lost Phil so young.

CIVIC HALL
25 JANUARY 1976, WOLVERHAMPTON, UK

I WAS THERE: STEVEN NICKLIN

Going to an all boys' grammar school in 1970 focused the mind on two things - footy and music. The first decision I had to make was T.Rex or Slade. I chose T.Rex and my first single was 'Jeepster'; the lyric of 'you've got the universe reclining in your hair' still resonates to this day. From glam I progressed to prog and the purchase of Hawkwind's *Space Ritual*, the whole sound and experience of which was astonishing, followed by a Hawkwind concert in 1973. I still listen to that album today. Other concerts followed up to late 1975, including the best I ever attended - Bowie on his final *Ziggy* tour - at venues across the West Midlands.

By late 1975, and now in the lower sixth, my friendship group had started to go to pubs. It was on the juke box of the Vic (the Queen Victoria lounge in Dudley) that I really listened to Phil's vocals and lyrics on 'Whiskey in the Jar' for the first time. That Christmas I was at a friend's house where, having listened to several albums, he produced *Fighting*. The title track, 'Suicide' and 'Rosalie' (still my favourite track by Lizzy) were fabulous and I bought my own copy the very next day. It was at the same friend's house, during the Christmas holidays, that we became aware that Lizzy were touring and coming to the Civic Hall in Wolverhampton. After a few phone calls to friends to see who wanted to attend, we were straight onto the bus into Wolverhampton to get the tickets.

We were on the second row and the concert was just fabulous. I can still remember standing on the seats, almost touching Phil whilst they blasted out much of the *Fighting* album. It was one of the few times I heard them play 'Little Darling', which is in my top five Lizzy tracks. They had really just started on the dual lead guitar sound but Robbo and Scott with Brian and Phil were, for me, the best line up. Phil's performance was magnetic. I never managed to get that close to the stage again.

After that '76 concert, I bought *Jailbreak* and remember Lizzy appearing on *Top of the Pops* with 'The Boys are Back in Town' during that long hot summer. It became a bit of an anthem.

TOWN HALL

15 MARCH 1976, BIRMINGHAM, UK

I WAS THERE: COLIN MASON

Glam rock was my thing in '72 but I loved 'Whiskey in the Jar', which of course is more than can ever be said about what Phil thought of it! I remember at one particular gig, him asking what we wanted to hear and many people shouting for 'Whiskey'. 'No, no, no, no. Not that fucking song, I hate it.' I only ever remember them playing it once in all the times I saw them, and that was the very last time I saw them with

Phil in March 1983 at Birmingham Odeon.

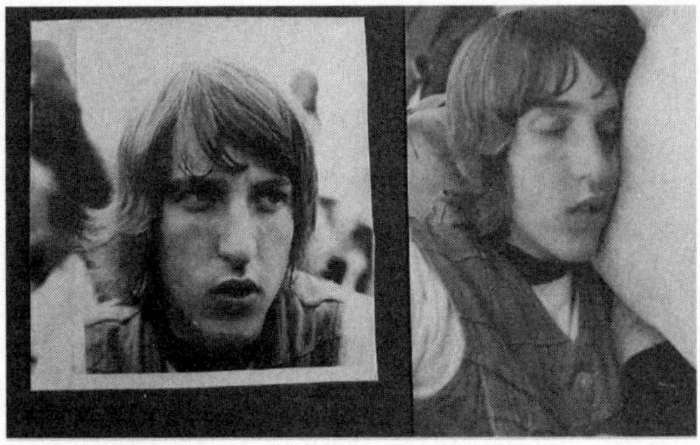

Colin Mason first saw Lizzy at Birmingham Town Hall

After 'Whiskey' I bought the *Nightlife* and *Fighting* albums. The twin guitar sound really appealed to me and guitars harmonising with each other still is one of my favourite musical sounds. When Scott Gorham and Brian Robertson joined the band in late 1974, that quickly became my favourite Thin Lizzy line up.

The first time I saw them play live was at Birmingham Town Hall, just a couple of weeks before *Jailbreak* was released, which of course rocketed the band to stardom. I felt very pleased with myself that I had 'discovered' this band before any of my gig-going friends – and, indeed, before most of the rest of the world!

I had a seat in the front row of the balcony, which in those days extended right around the sides of the stage, so I was sat right on the side of the stage. I had a little instamatic camera with me with those flash bulbs that had four flashes in a cube and which you rotated for the next photo. I got some great photos – it looks like I was actually on stage with them!

Keith Deacon got up close at Birmingham Town Hall

I WAS THERE: KEITH DEACON

I first saw Thin Lizzy at Leicester University around the time 'Whiskey in the Jar' came out. It was a small gig and you wouldn't have imagined how big they would get. My next gig was at the Birmingham Town Hall in 1976 for the *Jailbreak* tour. My friend Pat Murray and I travelled from

Leicester early in the day hoping to see the band before their gig. We saw them entering the hall with their roadies but we didn't get a chance to speak to them. The gig was amazing and we got to stand right in front of the stage, which is where I took the photos from. The first song was 'Jailbreak', which had the crowd buzzing from the start. We were so lucky to witness a brilliant gig but because it finished late, we missed our last train home and had to sleep on a couple of benches at Birmingham New Street station.

CITY HALL

18 MARCH 1976, NEWCASTLE, UK

I WAS THERE: COLIN THOMPSON

After catering college, I worked in County Durham. We stumbled one night into Newcastle and they were playing at the City Hall. I don't know how it had passed us by. It was sold out but we managed to wangle a couple of tickets from a tout outside. We saw them several times after that in various venues, including one really bad one in Kirkcaldy. A bit like the Faces, for a brief moment in time Thin Lizzy were the best band in the world.

For a brief moment in time Thin Lizzy were the best band in the world

---

FREE TRADE HALL

19 MARCH 1976, MANCHESTER, UK

I WAS THERE: JEFF JONES

I first got into Lizzy listening to the *Nightlife* album via an older rocker friend. I was lucky enough to see them on the *Jailbreak* tour at Manchester's Free Trade Hall. It's a shame that venue has gone as the acoustics in there were amazing and I saw many great bands there. Watching Philo playing bass has led to my love of bass playing. I loved his collaboration with the Greedies. I last saw Lizzy a few years ago aka the Black Star Riders. It was a good gig but it didn't float my boat. No Philo, no Lizzy. He went far too early, but that's what happens if you go down to Chinatown.

GUILDHALL

23 MARCH 1976, PORTSMOUTH, UK

I WAS THERE: PHIL CARTWRIGHT

I hadn't really heard of them as I was a big Status Quo fan, but when I saw Phil Lynott and the rest of the band I was blown away. Graham Parker and the Rumour left the stage and it was into the bar for a couple of beers which every 16-year-old did back in the Seventies! When the lights went down and the flashing blue lights and sirens echoed around the hall, the air of expectation was great. Then the opening chord of 'Jailbreak' rang out and – wow! - you just knew you were in for a great night.

Phil Cartwright was just 16 when he saw Lizzy

Rushing down the front as was the normal practice, I was about ten feet away from Phil and, my god, what a personality that man was. With his black leather trousers and I think a blue shirt, he was using his trademark

Fender Precision with the mirror scratchplate, picking out all the good-looking girls with the mirrored light reflection - and he could certainly pick 'em! The man could whip the crowd into a frenzy.

By the time they got to 'The Rocker', which was the last song, he was dripping with sweat and done in. I think we were as knackered just watching them. I've seen a lot of bands since, but Lizzy will always have a special place in my heart.

UNIVERSITY OF ABERYSTWYTH

25 MARCH 1976, ABERYSTWYTH, UK

I WAS THERE: ANDREW SUTHERLAND

It was '76. Punk had come into being and I did not like it. I've always been a fan of rock music and I'd seen Lizzy on *Top of the Pops* or *The Old Grey Whistle Test* and heard them play 'Whiskey in the Jar'. I must have then seen an ad in one of the music rags I used to buy then - *NME*, *Sounds* or *Disc* – saying that Thin Lizzy were playing at Aberystwyth University with a support band called Graham Parker and the Rumour.

Andrew Sutherland and his then girlfriend (now his wife) were at Aberystwyth

I asked a couple of my friends if they'd like to come with me but they all declined, so I got my girlfriend (now my wife) to come with me. I had a Mk1 Ford Escort so we drove the 35 miles to the venue and bought our tickets. My wife says we still have the tickets but I'm not sure where. I remember the beer was sold in plastic mugs and we watched the support band but weren't too impressed.

Finally Thin Lizzy came on stage. We pushed and shoved and finally got to the very front. Phil Lynott was within arm's reach of us. My wife said that Phil looked at her and gave her a smile, which made her day. Their set seemed to be over so quickly but they were excellent and we really enjoyed it. We have been huge fans ever since.

JAILBREAK RELEASED 26 MARCH 1976 UK CHART POSITION 10, US CHART POSITION 18

The album that was to return Lizzy to the eyes and ears of the music buying public. *Jailbreak* spawned two UK hit singles, 'The Boys are Back in Town' (which reached number 8 but also number 12 in the USA and number 1 in Ireland) and 'Jailbreak', which reached 31 in Britain.

I WAS THERE: TREVOR RAGGATT

I am a child of the Apollo programme. Precisely the right age to have been inspired by stories of 'giant leaps for mankind'. Precisely the right age for that enthusiasm to have been further stoked by teatime viewings of the original *Star Trek* series and delving into my brother's *Marvel* comics. And precisely the right age for the rise of classic rock in the early and mid-1970s.

I had eagerly absorbed my brother's musical tastes, whether Cream, Hendrix, Deep Purple or the Doobie Brothers, so when he arrived home from the record shop with a new LP it was cause for great excitement. The LP's largely silver and black cover showed a *Marvel*-style robotic sentinel poring over a viewscreen from which exploded a lurid, colourful band of rebellious adventurers. I was hooked on the basis of the cover art alone. When the semi-gatefold sleeve was opened to reveal that those adventurers were escaping from an inferno of explosions as they busted out of a prison built from futuristic sky scrapers, there was no turning back. This was my new favourite album. And I hadn't yet heard a note!

The period from 1975 to 1976 was a remarkably creative one for Thin Lizzy. Despite a punishing touring schedule both in the UK and the United States across those years they still scaled the creative heights. First, they had crystallised their line up, their sound and their image with the *Fighting* album. Then in the course of 1976 alone they released not one, but two seminal albums in *Jailbreak* and its' follow up, *Johnny the Fox*. Both showed a band at the top of their game, with Phil Lynott's songwriting and charismatic vocals taking centre stage and the intricate, intwining guitar lines of Scott Gorham and Brian Robertson creating a unique harmonic structure to the sound. All this was driven along by Brian Downey's subtle, driving drums - simultaneously loose yet precisely controlled.

And then there are the songs themselves. Now let's get one common misconception out of the way right at the start of things. The title track isn't one of rock and roll's great lyrical clangers. Honest. The album opens with a huge sustained power chord which coalesces into a driving rhythm, propelled forward by two angry, distorted Les Pauls. A flourish of wah-wah introduces the opening words... 'Tonight there's gonna be a jailbreak, somewhere in this town...' 'Oh yeah? You might try at the jail then! Arf arf arf!'

But here was another reason for an impressionable pre-teen to be caught under this album's spell. A story written across the rear sleeve revealed that *Jailbreak* was a loose concept album. In a distant future, a totalitarian government oppressed their citizens. Each was told what to think, what to believe and, most crucially, what music to listen to. Locked into a state of literal and psychological house arrest, all were imprisoned whether in their homes, their work or their thoughts. The whole town was a virtual prison and there would be a jailbreak somewhere in this town! See? Finally breaking free from their shackles, four young men had holed themselves up at the city media complex and were broadcasting songs of rebellion to the population. A true 'revolution in the head'.

There were songs of defiance, lost love, street gangs hanging down at Dino's Bar and Grill, mythic warriors fighting for their freedom and cowboys riding on the range. These were lyrical wells from which Lynott would drink deeply across his career but, somehow, it was in *Jailbreak* that all these themes seemed most perfectly encapsulated.

Across the entire album the quality of the songs presented never falters. Perhaps some of the album tracks have paled in the shade of the singles - not least of all that ubiquitous good-time anthem, 'The Boys are Back in Town'. However, each has nuggets of pure gold to mine, whether it is the sunny Californian brio of 'Angel from the Coast', the Van Morrison-tinged 'Running Back' or the deceptively jazzy rhythms of 'Romeo and the Lonely Girl'. Each is a song that rewards each new listen. And for me each song has passed the test of time. Today *Jailbreak* sounds just as fresh and exciting to these ears as it did then.

It is sad to think that, only a decade later Thin Lizzy were no more and their charismatic leader had passed on, his body having finally succumbed to years of abuse from alcohol and drugs. However, over all those years, *Jailbreak* and *Johnny the Fox* have been albums I have carried with me in my heart. There is a part of me that hopes that somewhere up there, riding lonesome on some celestial range, Phil's spirit is looking down and smiling.

ALBERT HALLS

30 MARCH 1976, STIRLING, UK

I WAS THERE: JACKIE YUILL

After seeing them at the Glasgow Apollo, the next time I saw them was at the much smaller Albert Halls in Stirling, a venue not usually known to host rock concerts. This time I was accompanied by Ian, Janice and my friend Erin. We arrived in Stirling an hour or so before the concert and went to the bar at the Station Hotel for a pre-show drink. We were sitting at a table at the window when a purple Transit van pulled up and the four members of Thin Lizzy got out and went into the hotel. When we left the bar, we stuck a note on the windscreen asking them to dedicate 'Suicide' to us.

The support band was Graham Parker and the Rumour, who were excellent, but the audience was rather subdued, applauding politely at the end of each song and remaining in their seats throughout the performance. Thin Lizzy came on stage and opened with 'Jailbreak'. The audience stayed seated, so the four of us got up, went down to the front of the stage and started to dance and soon everybody was on their feet.

It was a fantastic show. I remember Phil picked us out and directed the beam from the reflection of the spotlight on his mirrored bass on us a few times during the show. Then we heard Phil announce, 'This one is for Big Ian, Janice, Jackie and Eric,' - you'd have thought, as an

Irishman, he'd have got Erin right, but we didn't care - and they played 'Suicide' just for us!

At the end of a brilliant show, we again managed to get backstage. This time there was a bouncer standing outside the open door who wasn't for letting us in. We told him that we had a bus to catch so we wouldn't stay long - and then heard Brian Robertson say in his distinctive Glasgow accent, 'Let them in, they've got a fucking bus to catch!' We were allowed in just as Brian Downey was pulling a pair of jeans on over his red underpants!

Phil recognised us and thanked us - and gave me hug and a kiss! (Swoon, I wish I'd been more forward in those days). They were all so friendly and chatted for a while and signed our programmes and all too soon, it was time to head off to catch the last bus home.

The next morning, I rang the Station Hotel and asked the receptionist to put me through to Phil Lynott's room. I was gobsmacked when I heard a sleepy Irish voice say 'hello'. I told him who I was and that we'd met after the show. He said he remembered. It could have been a lie but who cares? He said he was glad we'd enjoyed the show and that the band were going to be at Bruce's Record Shop at lunchtime, so 'pop along and say hello'. I said I would, but I knew all too well that there were no buses into Stirling till later in the afternoon and anyway, I didn't have the bus fare. Am I the only girl in the world who has stood up Phil Lynott?

I saw them every time they played at the Apollo until their final gig there in 1983. They always put on a brilliant show and always had the audience jumping and left our ears ringing. Sadly, I never met them again.

SKINDLES HOTEL

3 APRIL 1976, MAIDENHEAD, UK

I WAS THERE: BOB WELLS

I saw Lizzy many times in the golden period of '74 to '79. At Skindles in Maidenhead, I was in awe of Robbo's playing. Just before they went on, we were asked to stand back from the front to make way for the thunderflashes at the start of 'Jailbreak'!

I WAS THERE: STUART LANGSBURY, AGE 21

They did a few smaller venues before the main *Jailbreak* tour later that year, when the album took off. I was standing next to the stage when they came on to 'Jailbreak' with lights flashing and smoke and fire crackers, one of which exploded right next to me! Phil looked down at me and put his thumb up, I guess to make sure I was okay. The gig was amazing. At 21 years old I had found my band and I went on to see them another 20 times. After the gig, I was sat at the hotel bar and Phil came up to me and asked was I the dude he tried to blow up? He apologised and bought me a drink!

'*THE BOYS ARE BACK IN TOWN*' RELEASED

17 APRIL 1976

IRISH CHART POSITION 1

UK CHART POSITION 8

US BILLBOARD 12

We owe it all to two DJs in Louisville, Kentucky. They fell in love with the fucking song and played it incessantly until other stations in the surrounding area picked up on it.... Had that song not kickstarted the sales of the album, then the band was over. **Scott Gorham**

In April and May 1976, Thin Lizzy toured the USA and played 37 gigs in 38 days, supporting acts ranging from Aerosmith to Rush.

ROXY THEATER

4 MAY 1976, NORTHAMPTON, PENNSYLVANIA

I WAS THERE: MARK A MAHAL

I had the pleasure of seeing Thin Lizzy in concert on two occasions. The first was as a headliner at the Roxy Theater. This was a small and intimate venue where we sat front and centre, approximately 20 feet from Phil Lynott's mic. They exploded on stage with 'Jailbreak' and continued to blow the crowd away throughout their entire 17 song set. This was during a time where, although it was stipulated on the ticket that violators would be ejected for smoking and alcohol, the theatre was quite festive both in performance and audience 'participation'!

The US tour was scheduled to continue into July, with Lizzy booked to support Rainbow. But Phil had contracted hepatitis and flew home to be admitted to hospital in Manchester. A scheduled gig at Hammersmith Odeon in July went ahead as Phil decided to do the show against medical advice.

HAMMERSMITH ODEON

11 JULY 1976, LONDON, UK

I WAS THERE: GARY HURST

I was 15 years old and didn't have a favourite band as such. I'd started buying albums in 1970 and was listening to Jimi Hendrix, the Beatles, Jethro Tull, Yes, Genesis, Pink Floyd, Black Sabbath and Deep Purple. Thin Lizzy were brought to my attention by a work colleague in the summer of 1974. They said they were going to see a band that evening that they thought I would like, at The Winning Post in Twickenham, a band called Thin Lizzy. I said, 'Oh yeah, 'Whiskey in the Jar'. Not really a fan.' The colleague came into work the next day waxing lyrical about how good they were and how 'Whiskey' was not really representative of the band's sound. They were much rockier, plus they had a gorgeous guy with long hair playing guitar! Step forward Mr Gorham.

I was convinced enough to go out and buy their then latest album, *Nightlife*. I thought the album was brilliant. I guess it can be described as a somewhat smooth and soulful record. Certainly, the first two tracks lull you into thinking that. Then 'It's Only Money' kicks in, which is much rockier and a sign of things to come in the future. The only other real rocker on the album was 'Sha La La'. Other tracks I really loved on it were 'She Knows', 'Still in Love with You', 'Banshee' and 'Philomena'. I really liked the twin guitar sound and Phil's voice. The album just sounded so different to anything else I had in my collection. The overall quality of the album was enough to make me want to get the next album and then I was hooked... for the rest of my life!

My first Lizzy gig was at the Hammersmith Odeon and they were amazing! Starting with the taped intro and then the flash bombs going off as the band hit the first note of 'Jailbreak', it was simple but effective. I was transfixed. The band went through a great set with the only slow number being 'Still in Love with You'. I remember buying a Lizzy t-shirt in the foyer after the gig, thinking I must have a souvenir of the occasion. Little did I know it would be the first of many Lizzy gigs in the coming seven years, and the first of many t-shirts - that I still have! I also remember walking out into the street after the gig, my ears ringing and me shouting at my friend about how good the band were and what a fantastic gig it was.

It was exhilarating. Phil was so charismatic. It was difficult to take your eyes off of him. He made you feel that you were part of his gang. The band and the audience were 'in it' together. It was similar to supporting your favourite football team. 'Baby Drives Me Crazy', near the end of the set, typified this when Phil got the fans singing along. Many bands do it, but no one did it quite like Phil.

Phil made you feel you were part of his gang

I WAS THERE: GRAHAME RIDLEY

For most of 1976 I was 15, and that hot summer really was the stuff of dreams. Since my indoctrination into the world of live music (care of my mum buying my brother and me tickets to Paul McCartney in 1973 - I'm still a massive fan), I hadn't seen much live music but a few of us had a band together at school and my mate Steve and I played guitar. Steve had some mates a couple of years older than us and they invited us to go to the Marquee in London to see Eddie and the Hot Rods. I had no idea who they were but what an amazing, loud, sweaty experience (the Hot Rods were recording a live EP that night). How I got in I'll never know, because when I was 15, I looked about 12!

A few days later, and Steve was concerned that his ears were still ringing and maybe he shouldn't go out to see Thin Lizzy that night. I was already jealous that he was going, as I'd been introduced to the *Jailbreak* album round his house and loved that record. I bit Steve's hand off when he offered me the ticket and together with another schoolmate Trev, we met four of Steve's older mates at Ealing Broadway Station where, while waiting for the train to depart, one of them proceeded to light up the biggest joint I'd ever seen. I declined to partake and there was never any pressure to do so, they were cool guys.

Half an hour later we were outside the Hammersmith Odeon. The buzz around the place was electric, oozing excitement and anticipation. After one of the older lads had been to the bar and got the drinks, we took our seats in the back row, downstairs.

As we sat chatting, the lights dimmed. Seconds later, we heard a massive power chord as Lizzy came on and the place erupted. Everyone in the whole place was on their feet and for a few seconds I was only able to hear the roar of 'Jailbreak'. I hoisted myself up onto the small timber-topped wall that was behind my seat and sat gazing towards the stage over the heads of the audience, witnessing the energy.

The spotlight reflecting off of Phil's bass whipped across the dark silhouettes of the crowd, catching me in the eyes… this was nothing like the record! Phil seems to feed from the crowd, aiming the head of the bass across the crowd like a machine gunner! Every so often I could see sticks darting up from behind Brian Downey's kit as Phil's charisma filled the entire theatre. Brian Robertson was there, cigarette in his mouth and black Les Paul slung low, with Scott Gorham, armed with his Sunburst Les Paul Deluxe and his hair flowing around him. Could these guys really look any cooler? That gig cemented Scott as one of my all time favourite guitar players and that night remains one the greatest gigs I ever attended.

I bought *Jailbreak* and then *Johnny the Fox* and *Nightlife* with my Saturday job money, and got *Live and Dangerous* the moment it came out, pretty much wearing it out in the following years.

After spending much of July 1976 recording *Johnny the Fox* in Musicland Studios in Munich, in October Lizzy embarked upon a European tour.

OLYMPEN

2 OCTOBER 1976, LUND, SWEDEN

I WAS THERE: TOM KRISCHAUSKY, AGE 18

I consider Thin Lizzy the best ever rock band after seeing them on this evening. I had already been a fan for three years. The sound was perfect and so was the concert. I still have the scarf I bought as a souvenir.

FRIEDRICH EBERT HALLE

9 OCTOBER 1976, LUDWIGSHAFEN, GERMANY

I WAS THERE: MIKE BOBBITT

They were warming up for Robin Trower. A whole bunch of us GIs were going for Trower, and about ten were going to trip on acid. I had two 35mm cameras with me so that was out of the question. I managed to get dead front centre, up against the stage and back in the good old days of general admission. When Lizzy opened, the sirens and police lights were both in high gear and then an enormous blast of flash pots went off at the front of the stage. I was blinded for several minutes.

When my vision returned it was all hell broke loose on stage. These guys tore up the stage. I took a few pics. Phil was practically standing over me. Maaan, let me tell you that guy could perspire! I was drenched in his flop sweat. It kept getting in my cameras!

None of us Americans were familiar with Lizzy. That was until after the show, when we were all raving about them at the barracks the next couple of days. I was a changed man. I listen to music differently because of that concert. Those two harmonious guitars were glorious. I was not aware of the songs they played until this year when I found out Bill Lordan, Trower's drummer, had recorded the show! I ended up trading front row professional pics of the Robin Trower Band for a copy of the show. The recording is a little rough, but as a record of the greatest show ever it was well worth it 44 years later!

I WAS THERE: HUME HAWKINS, AGE 16

I lived in Heidelberg, Germany and went to school there because my dad was in the services. We could just hop on the train to Ludwigshafen. Lizzy were opening up for Robin Trower and we'd been listening to *Bridge of Sighs*. But I'd been listening to *Jailbreak* to close for a year multiple times every day. It was good Trower was there but I was there to see Thin Lizzy.

Hume Hawkins remembers Lizzy as the best concert he ever saw

I didn't listen to German radio much. When you went to school in Germany, you all lived in the same small housing area so you went to each other's houses to listen to records, or people carried boom boxes around with them. I can tell you exactly where I was when I first heard Van Halen. I can't do that for Lizzy, but it was probably at somebody's house. I wasn't too familiar with their earlier stuff at that point. *Jailbreak* was my introduction to them. My brother had seen them open up for Bachman Turner Overdrive a year earlier, and he didn't know who they were when he saw them because he was there to see BTO.

It was a general admission thing like most European concerts. We got there and stood in line and ran as fast as we could to the centre of the stage. I ended up third row, pretty much dead centre and sitting just a little bit to Phil's left. I can't tell you what the set list was but they played 'Emerald', which I love, and 'Cowboy Song'.

To this day I tell people that this was the best concert I ever saw. I guess my age and my anticipation at seeing them play the songs from *Jailbreak* was overwhelming. I was just about to sit there and probably watch Thin Lizzy play most of *Jailbreak*.

They were first on. The lights were turned out and it was pitch dark. Time was going by and we were looking at the stage to try and see what was going on, because we could hear noise. You assumed that they were coming onto the stage but we couldn't see anything. Then we started hearing chains rattling to signify prisoners making a jailbreak or something and we thought, 'This is cool.'

And then pyrotechnics blew outlining the stage - just bright, bright, bright white lights - and the lights from the stage came on simultaneously and there were explosions right at the front of the stage. We had been sitting there with our eyes wide open peering into the dark and then that happened, so for seconds afterwards we could see nothing apart from that large explosion in our eyes.

We were waiting for our eyes to clear up so that we could see what the hell was going on. When they did, the smoke was all still there and all you see was the neck of Phil's bass sticking out of the smoke and 'Jailbreak' just tearing your face off. Then the smoke cleared and there they were and it was loud, really loud. It's the most memorable concert moment of my life.

It's the most memorable concert moment of my life

They played the songs I wanted to hear and somewhere along the line Phil introduced everybody. I had no idea that Scott Gorham was an American! Phil was just one of those people you stayed focused on, what he said and what he did, because he was just so charismatic. Listen to the battle between Brian Robertson and Scott Gorman at the end of

'Emerald'. Brian Robertson's guitar is the one that I prefer, but obviously Scott Gorham is a great player too.

I never had the opportunity to see them again. But 45 years later, I still listen to *Jailbreak* and *Johnny the Fox*.

PHILIPSHALLE

11 OCTOBER 1976, DUSSELDORF, GERMANY

I WAS THERE: BILL HINDMARSH

I happened to be in Germany and so I was able to get to neighbouring Dusseldorf where again I was able to 'lig' the gig. This concert was supporting Robin Trower. The highlight for me was seeing the guys from the band again. There was much talking and catching up in the dressing room beforehand. Lizzy were on exemplary form and were very well rewarded with the cheery applause from the Dusseldorfers. Robin Trower's sound in the large hall made my ears ring and spoiled what was otherwise a great performance and I left early. But much fun was had afterwards at Lizzy's hotel, where the bar closed before the band went to bed. A wild night indeed!

JOHNNY THE FOX RELEASED
16 OCTOBER 1976
UK CHART POSITION 11
US CHART POSITION 52

Johnny the Fox featured the live favourite 'Don't Believe a Word', but the album fared less well commercially than its predecessor because there was no stand out track to match 'The Boys are Back in Town' from *Jailbreak*.

The *Johnny the Fox* UK tour took in 25 shows in 28 days and was sold out in advance. Lizzy were supported by Clover, featuring Huey Lewis.

PAVILION

24 OCTOBER 1976, HEMEL HEMPSTEAD, UK

I WAS THERE: RORY EAMES

I went to a Catholic school. I was 14 or 15 and sat in the cloakroom because I had been excluded from school assembly when an older boy said, 'Have you heard that song by Thin Lizzy called 'Whiskey in the Jar'?' I went to the Reading Festival in 1975 and saw them there. And then in '76 they were playing Hemel Pavilion on the *Johnny the Fox* tour. It was a Sunday night. You could get really close to the stage there. They came on and started with 'Jailbreak' and it was unbelievable. We were so close to Phil you could almost touch him. I was sold big time.

I saw them loads of times after that. One time, I was working in London and it came on the radio that there was going to be a concert at the Rainbow and the first ones there would get tickets for £1.50. It was the recording for the *Live and Dangerous* album. I was working in Shepherd's Bush and I dropped my tools and shot up to the Rainbow and got two tickets. I was second or third in the queue so our seats were really close to the stage. They were unbelievable live.

I saw them at Reading again in '77, at Milton Keynes Bowl, at Wembley twice and loads of times at Hammersmith - 16 times altogether. I've seen The Who, the Stones and Pink Floyd, but there was something about Lizzy live. And Philip's songwriting was so clever. He was a poet, and he had that rapport with the crowd as well. He could really win the crowd over. They had a lot of bad luck as a band - Brian Robertson getting into fights, Phil getting hepatitis, Gary Moore walking out.

People continue to say that *Live and Dangerous* wasn't live but you had to have been there to realise just how good they were live. They were one of the first bands to use remote mics and they were accused of miming as a result.

I was sad when Phil died but I wasn't shocked. I watched him slowly get worse. But he'd still be playing now if he was alive. He was one of a kind.

DE MONTFORT HALL

25 OCTOBER 1976, LEICESTER, UK

I WAS THERE: MARK SMIGGY SMITH, AGE 17

1976 was a year of change. It was my seventeenth birthday in the January which meant I could learn to drive. Before the great heatwave of that year, *Jailbreak* was released and in the autumn *Johnny the Fox* came out. 'The Boys are Back in Town' was the catalyst for wanting to see the band, especially once I'd heard the B-side, 'Emerald'. It ignited all sorts of imagery in my head. On a rainy October night in '76, I drove Phil Rachael, Steve Chesterton, Chris Barlow and myself to De Montfort Hall, Leicester, my first concert. This is what I wrote in my diary afterwards:

What a concert, the first I'd been to, and I bet it'll be the best. The first group were not bad, (Clover), but not brilliant. But when Lizzy came on it was amazing. The music was loud, my god was it loud. They opened with 'Jailbreak' and then went into 'Massacre'. Fucking hell, we just went wild. I've never been so happy. I just didn't care about anyone or anything, just the music. It was the most exhilarating thing ever. The music, backed up by the lights, was just amazing. The heat was tremendous, but you didn't worry about it, you don't when you're in the middle of two thousand writhing bodies, swayed around the hall by the music. Brian Downey's drum solo was magic. Scott Gorham and Brian Robertson's guitars were completely amazing, and Phil Lynott was like a god, with everyone following him. Phil got everyone singing, stomping and freaking about. We stood at the front, right next to the speakers and they nearly blew my head to bits. Phil's guitar was soaked in his own sweat and the band really took off. They loved us and we loved them. They played 'Jailbreak', 'Massacre', 'Boys are Back

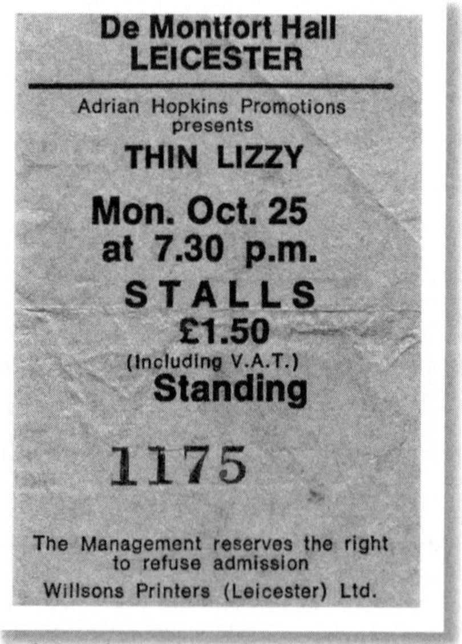

Mark Smith saw Lizzy for the first time in 1976

in Town', 'Johnny', 'Fool's Gold', 'Borderline', 'Still in Love with You' and 'Emerald'. (The one we all sang along to was 'Baby Drives Me Crazy'). Some I didn't know. The speed of the music was terrifying. My whole body ached and sweated, the only thing that stopped me from collapsing in a heap was the sheer intensity of the music. Intense is the right word, it was as if you could reach out, take the sound, and squeeze it. Phil (Rachael) said he could see the steam rising off me. I was soaked to the skin in sweat, my clothes were smelly and wringing wet. Breathing was virtually impossible and like sweaty fire. The atmosphere was amazing, nothing can compare with the early part of this night. Nine to ten thirty. Three encores. My body was just a container of fibrous enjoyment.

The latter part was the complete reverse feeling. Me knocking someone off his motorbike. He broke his ankle. Ruth towed us home. Dented car.

The atmosphere at De Mont almost tore the building down. My words, now or then, could never do it justice, as much as I have tried. It was if the earth tipped on its axis. I can still conjure up everything about that '76 night in my head - the sights, the sounds, even the smell. The 'greasers' that we ended up dancing with in the mosh pit, the chaos and pandemonium. It was anarchic. When it came to the encore the crowd was split fifty – fifty between 'Whiskey in the Jar' or 'Emerald'. The timeline at that point contained us newbies to Lizzy and also those that knew all the old stuff. At that point I hadn't heard 'Rocker', so was calling for 'Whiskey'. I didn't really know why I was shouting, because I didn't know how any of this worked. Phil played us all magicly and the band stepped up with a blistering rendition of 'The Rocker'. Cue more mayhem.

(After the crash my Vauxhall Viva was forever known as Wimpey - We Injure More People Each Year).

EMPIRE THEATRE

28 OCTOBER 1976, LIVERPOOL, UK

I WAS THERE: MARK RUMENS

I was a young art student at the time and went with a mate who was a big fan. I wasn't - but that soon changed! It was the Robertson/Gorham line up and an absolutely blinding gig at the Liverpool Empire. I was sat upstairs but Phil looked so big and was such a great front man it was like you were looking straight at him. Robertson and Gorham were sublime together and the band was note perfect. There was just something about the twin lead guitars and Phil's stage presence. And being a drummer at the time, I loved Brian Downey's rock solid drumming. He's still one of the most underrated drummers.

Mark Rumens caught the *Johnny the Fox* tour

WINTER GARDENS

29 OCTOBER 1976, MALVERN, UK

I WAS THERE: DAVID LEA, AGE 14

Some boys in the year above organised a minivan. We lived about 20 miles away. I didn't really know these boys that well, and one year older seems a big deal at that age, but I really wanted to see Lizzy. It was my first ever gig. I'll always remember the start with the sirens, when they opened with 'Jailbreak'. I've seen hundreds of bands since then, but the first one is always special. Just to see Phil Lynott and Scott Gorham live was awesome.

FREE TRADE HALL

29 OCTOBER 1976, MANCHESTER, UK

I WAS THERE: MARTIN SHORT

Back then the scene was much more vibrant than it is now because you had a college circuit running. I saw Lizzy twice at the Free Trade Hall in Manchester. The gig I remember the most was the '76 one. I remember the power of that band and how they got the crowd going. The stage makes you look big anyway but I was down the front and remember thinking how big Phil Lynott seemed larger than life. He was dressed all in black, and the back plate on his bass was a mirror, which was unusual.

The spotlight kept hitting him and he kept blasting the reflection out into the crowd. I've heard since that he would hit one of the girls with a beam of light from his guitar and the roadies would spot them and go down and say, 'Do you fancy a party after?'

The Free Trade Hall was built for the Hallé Orchestra. Acoustically it was stunning. It had a balcony and it was all seated, but when the main band came on the stalls just used to get up and move to the front. You didn't stay seated in the stalls for rock bands. Bands preferred it over playing the Apollo in Manchester in the 1970s because the Free Trade Hall was a better venue by a country mile - for atmosphere, for acoustics, for the way it was set up, everything - and you could get more people into it. Sadly, the Free Trade Hall closed because the council in Manchester decided the upkeep of the building was too much for them. They wanted to knock the whole bloody thing down but campaigners managed to get the frontage listed. It was an absolute disgrace. It should still be there as the premier hall in the city. The Free Trade Hall, with its wood panelling, makes the Apollo feel grubby. When AC/DC toured the UK with Bon Scott they always used to start or finish at the Free Trade Hall. They would stay with Phil's mother at her hotel in Ardwick and base themselves there for the tour.

APOLLO THEATRE

30 OCTOBER 1976, GLASGOW, UK

I WAS THERE: EVELYN HUNTER

They came blasting onto the stage to sirens and an explosion to the start of 'Jailbreak'. It left me coughing for over ten minutes as I was near the front - but it was a great night! I had great views of Robbo, with his cig attached to his guitar and drinking whisky on his home turf, and Phil, who was sex on legs. I couldn't see much of Scott. He was all in red but his hair was so long and covering his face most of the time. I wish I could have seen them live again, but if I put on my records I'm right back there.

If I put on my records I'm right back there

I WAS THERE: KAY HODGSON, AGE 15

I saw Lizzy at least three times at the Glasgow Apollo. Once I was seated in the box right next to the stage and couldn't believe my luck. The guitarists were amazing and Scott Gorham, with his long hair and tight jeans, was a feast for the eyes, let me tell you! It's just the songs that got me hooked. 'The Boys are Back in Town' is a perfect rock song, especially for a teenager, and the guitar playing, including the bass of course, would bring me out in goosebumps live.

I WAS THERE: NICK HIGHAM, AGE 15

A good pal had got me into rock music and we had already been to a couple of rock gigs. 'The Boys are Back in Town' really seemed to be the song of the summer of '76 and I loved it. It was just the sort of thing for an adolescent boy - heroic endeavour, redemption, girls. We even had a local hangout called Dino's! Thin Lizzy came on tour to Glasgow and played at the Apollo. I went and was smitten. I thought them great, not as 'heavy, man' as Led Zeppelin and not as raucous as Black Sabbath. I chased up every album they ever made, going right back to *Shades of a Blue Orphanage*.

They toured again the next year and I saw another fantastic gig at the Apollo, just a real show. Me and Jim had also seen a load of other rock gigs at that time - Black Sabbath, Tangerine Dream, Hawkwind, Deep Purple, etc., but Lizzy were the best. I don't remember it, but Jim swears we managed to meet the band and get backstage.

By 1980 I had moved to Manchester and saw them again at the Manchester Apollo on the *Black Rose* tour. I had been on a gap year to Australia in the meantime and heard *Black Rose* as a demo in a record shop there in Perth. I liked it but by the time I saw them in Manchester, the magic had gone a bit - my musical mind had been blown by punk, reggae and Two Tone. I had stopped dressing as a rocker-hippie in my Afghan coat and flared denim and had taken to wearing black suits a la John Cooper Clarke.

Thin Lizzy were and remain my favourite rock band, and 'The Rocker', 'The Boys are Back in Town' and 'Whiskey in the Jar' still take me back to those days. But time had moved on and they looked more and more like dinosaurs (although not as bad as Rush) compared to The

Selecter, The Specials, etc. and their highly politicised music. Reggae also was becoming a big thing in my life.

Lizzy is just about the only Seventies rock band that I find at all listenable now. Perhaps it's nostalgia on my part but maybe they had something a bit more. *Spinal Tap* ruined rock!

I WAS THERE: SEAN TEMPLETON

Thin Lizzy was my first gig ever. My mum took me and I struggled to see as I was only nine or ten. But I remember the music and volume and I am forever glad to have seen Phil in the Apollo of all places.

I WAS THERE: STUART CUNNINGHAME, AGE 14

My first ever gig was Thin Lizzy on the *Johnny the Fox* tour in 1976 at the Glasgow Apollo. A friend who ended up being my best man got me into them. Phil was the consummate front man and the twin lead guitar thing was new to me.

I saw them a few times more, largely at the Apollo. The Apollo was built as a cinema and at one time was Europe's biggest. It held three and a half to four thousand people on three levels and was regarded as the best rock venue on the planet at the time. Everybody wanted to play Glasgow, just because of the atmosphere and the crowd. When the lights went up you saw how tacky the Apollo was. The seats were all bashed and broken with holes in them but the atmosphere of the place was just unbelievable. The urban myth was that when rock bands were playing, you could see the middle balcony moving up and down, but of course what you were seeing was people headbanging in unison.

I saw Lizzy again on the *Bad Reputation* tour and when they toured the *Live and Dangerous* album. That show was a bit disappointing. They just played the album as it was. Even the patter was the same. They could have stuck the album on the PA and mimed to it and no one would have been any the wiser!

Then I saw them on the *Black Rose* tour with Gary Moore. Gary Moore did his *One night in Dublin* thing, when they unveiled the statue of Phil in Grafton Street, and the songs he did with Thin Lizzy only needed the one guitarist because he was so good.

I saw them again on the *Chinatown* tour. The last time I saw them was

1982, with John Sykes. I thought he took Lizzy back to what they were like in the Brian Robertson days. He was very similar looking with long blond curly hair, and he did all the licks that Brian Robertson did. It was almost a throwback to five or six years earlier and Lizzy at their best.

They blew my teenage brain to bits! **Bobby Gillespie, Primal Scream**

USHER HALL

31 OCTOBER 1976, EDINBURGH, UK

I WAS THERE: JOHN HALL

As I trudged through the rain on a wet Scottish evening, little did I know that what I was about to witness was a set which would be regarded as another classic moment in rock and roll. It was 1976 and I was at university in Edinburgh. A great place to be a student, but as I look back now, for me this was the beginning of the end of rock and roll as I knew it. Punk had broken in the summer and soon would be everywhere. Many of the bands I had worshiped would not be considered cool any more or would be on hiatus. Fortunately, in the autumn of '76, many of them were still active and even yet to reach their peak. So it was with Thin Lizzy.

I had seen Lizzy in Sunderland in '73 when Eric Bell was in the band and 'Whiskey in the Jar' had charted. My friend Pete had met Phil Lynott in the bar. It sounds really cool, and it was, but at the time we took it for granted. But now, following the success of 'The Boys are Back in Town' and 'Jailbreak', Lizzy were big.

We always played 'The Boys are Back in Town' on a Friday at about 6pm as we consumed our first beers of the weekend and got revved up for the night out. The three of us headed to the Usher Hall in the West End of Edinburgh, a nice - if aging - theatre and a mainstay on the UK circuit. One of my friends was Irish, from a suburb of Belfast, and this was a special night for him. We would also go and see Rory Gallagher at the same venue a couple of months later.

They opened with 'Jailbreak' and they were loud. I had seen of lot of gigs but I was surprised at the volume and how heavy they seemed.

You didn't get that sense from listening to the albums. While I knew the famous songs, 'Emerald' and 'Massacre' made a big impression live, along with 'Still in Love with You' - an epic and emotive song which was so much better live than the original studio version.

I would also have said they played 'Cowboy Song', although setlists from the period would prove me wrong. 'Rosalie' was great too, a Bob Seger cover that the band would make their own. Overall, it was a great gig by a band at their peak, although it would take eighteen months or so before extracts from the final gig on the tour at the Hammersmith Odeon would be immortalised on *Live and Dangerous*, arguably one of the greatest live albums of all time.

CITY HALL

1 NOVEMBER 1976, NEWCASTLE-UPON-TYNE, UK

I WAS THERE: PETER SMITH

1976 was Thin Lizzy's year. Suddenly Lizzy went from being the club band you could see all the time to rock heroes who were selling out concert halls and theatres up and down the country. They performed 25 concerts during the UK tour, all of which were completely sold out. I saw the Newcastle gig which was powerful, energetic and a celebration of Lizzy's recent success. The crowd welcomed the band back as conquering heroes and Phil was becoming the ultimate rock frontman, who could command a crowd like no one else at the time. A simple thing, like reflecting light off his mirrored bass front plate so that it cut across the concert hall and dazzled us all, seemed fantastic at the time.

Phil told us stories, got us to sing along with him and led his two fantastic guitar compatriots Scott and Brian and drummer Brian in some perfect rock music. 'Emerald' and 'The Rocker' were my favourites, and when they played 'The Boys Are Back in Town' we just knew that the song was about Phil and the guys, but we also felt that it was about us and that we were all 'boys' together. A wonderful, uplifting performance. We were so proud that this band, who we had followed through the clubs, ballrooms and festivals, was taking on the world and was doing it with rock songs which we could relate to.

Oh, and I forgot to mention the length of Scott's hair, which I was so jealous of. I never quite figured out why mine stopped growing at a certain length, and never quite reached my waist!

I WAS THERE: COLIN PETERSEN

The second time I saw Thin Lizzy they'd changed drastically and had the twin guitars with Scott Gorham and Brian Robertson and much better material. Some people will argue the *Bad Reputation/Live and Dangerous* tour was better but I loved the *Johnny the Fox* album, which is what the 1976 tour promoted. I've seen some great bands over the years but that has to be in my top ten gigs. The energy from the band was unbelievable and the City Hall was bouncing that night. I think everybody was sweating buckets by the end of the evening.

Colin Petersen was back at Newcastle City Hall in 1976

I WAS THERE: BRONIA GLENDINNING

I saw Lizzy with Phil three times in a row in the Seventies, including the *Johnny the Fox* tour. I took my camera with me on the third occasion and took two photos of Scott, who was my idol. His hair is what did it for me, and the way he positioned his legs when playing his guitar. I also managed to get a photograph of Phil in one of his iconic poses. I remember Phil asking if there were any of the girls wanting any more Irish in them. At the time I thought that that was really quite rude – but funny. Brian Robertson with his cigarette stuck in his guitar is the other thing I remember. One year later I had run off to Scotland with a married man and my concert going was sadly at an end. I have only in the last few years rekindled my love for Lizzy by going to see tribute bands and investing in a DAB radio and an Alexa!

I WAS THERE: COLIN DOTCHIN, AGE 20

I saw them in '76 and again in '77, barely a year apart. My cousin Kevin Harper would have been with me as we went to all the concerts together. Phil had a spotlight on his bass with a mirror badge on it shining back at the crowd. It was truly amazing. I loved the beautiful stereo sound of the twin guitars. For the encore, which was 'The Rocker', Phil wanted everyone down the front so we ran at the bouncers who were trying in vain to stop us. What Phil wanted from a crowd, he got. They were both truly memorable concerts after a day on the drink in Newcastle. And afterwards, my mother would have picked us up. Rock and roll, eh?

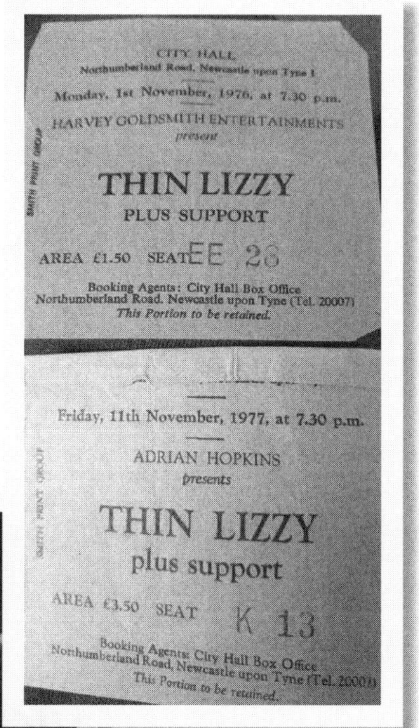

761101 Colin Dotchin saw Lizzy twice in 12 months

UNIVERSITY OF LEEDS REFECTORY

6 NOVEMBER 1976, LEEDS, UK

I WAS THERE: ANDREW VOLANS

As a student at Leeds, I was on the Events team as stage crew. This got me into all the gigs and so I got to meet a superb selection of bands and their touring crew. My first gig was Lynyrd Skynyrd. It was all great fun, and one of the bands I worked with was Thin Lizzy. The gig was at the Refectory at Leeds University, the same place where The Who's *Live at Leeds* was recorded. We always wanted The Who to return. It was a constant rumour. When they did play again, I was invited to get tickets as I'd been on Ents, but due to the grown up world I was on duty as a hospital consultant and couldn't get away to take advantage of the invitation. I got the CD instead!

After we had set up the stage for Lizzy, they let us stay while they did their sound check. They used Pink Floyd's *Wish You Were Here* to check the PA – it was like listening to the album through a fantastic hi-fi! Sitting there with this fantastic 3D sound image, we played a bit of frisbee with the band, including Phil. He was a lovely man, such an Irish charmer. He had me arrange for an uncle to get in past security to see the gig from the balcony.

It was a fantastic gig and one that sticks in my memory and brings a smile to my face when I think of it. I was on stack security, stage left, and my ear defenders were working overtime. During the gig Phil did his seductive, 'Does anyone have any Irish in them? Do any of the girls want a little more Irish in them?' and the screams were deafening. We never found so many knickers around the stage at the end of a gig.

We never found so many knickers around the stage at the end of a gig!

VICTORIA HALL

7 NOVEMBER 1976, HANLEY, STOKE-ON-TRENT, UK

I WAS THERE: ANDREW BROOKES, AGE 15

I heard Thin Lizzy for the first time back in 1973 whilst listening to the Sunday chart rundown. I wasn't overly drawn to them as I was still into the glam rock scene dominated by Slade, Sweet, Suzi Quatro, T.Rex and Bowie and I never bothered to check out the Lizzy albums, wrongly assuming 'Whiskey in the Jar' was representative of their sound. But 'The Boys are Back in Town' drew me in and I quickly sought out the *Jailbreak* album and was hooked.

I was fortunate to be able to go to see Lizzy four times over the years – twice at the Victoria Hall in '76 and '83 and twice on the *Black Rose* tour, at Trentham Gardens and New Bingley Hall. Each time I was accompanied by a couple of school or college mates. I saw the classic line up of Lynott, Gorham, Robertson and Downey and Lizzy never let me or the audience down. Lynott's cocky swagger and cheeky rapport typified a charismatic presence that allowed the superb musicians around him to ease in to their groove and shine.

I was so sad when Phil Lynott died - a troubled character but one hell of a showman who held the audience in the palm of his hand. I wish I'd seen them more but at least I can say I saw them at their peak.

COVENTRY THEATRE

9 NOVEMBER 1976, COVENTRY, UK

I WAS THERE: NICK BETTERIDGE

The first time I saw Lizzy was in support of the *Johnny the Fox* album at Coventry Theatre. Lizzy were riding high on the back of the *Jailbreak* album and it was a great show. After that I saw them at Birmingham Odeon and then Stafford New Bingley Hall on the *Black Rose* tour, back in Coventry for the *Chinatown* tour and back at the Odeon for what was sadly the venue for the last gig for me with Lizzy, on the *Thunder and Lightning* tour. On some tours I saw more than one show and it was always a privilege to see them. Phil was the ultimate showman and second to none. He always had the audience in the palm of his hand. What charisma he had, especially when catching a spotlight on his mirror scratch plate. Lizzy were unbeatable live.

HAMMERSMITH ODEON

14 NOVEMBER 1976, LONDON, UK

I WAS THERE: CRIS MARTIN

As an eleven-year-old, I was more accustomed to pop music but hearing 'Whiskey in the Jar' on the radio and seeing Lizzy on *Top of the Pops* confirmed me as a fan and rock music lover from then on. I bought all the earlier albums, the *Vagabonds* album being a particular favourite. *Nightlife* was a bit of a disappointment but I was blown away by both *Fighting* and *Jailbreak*. In 1975, I decided that I wanted to be a guitar hero - even though I couldn't play a note!

The first live performance I witnessed was one of the gigs recorded for inclusion on the *Live and Dangerous* album. I remember that first gig, the anticipation, the smell of cigarettes and alcohol, the lights dimming and the band hitting the stage. I wasn't used to the incredibly high audio volume that they performed at. Suffice to say, it left an indelible mark on my young psyche and left my ears ringing for days.

I saw them many times after that, Wembley Arena being a notable gig. Robbo was kitted out in white corduroy pants, and I remember the stack of Marshalls with the cabs facing backwards! What a gig. Then the slow trudge back to the tube station for the long journey home with tired legs and ringing ears.

The 1977 gig at Lewisham Odeon was great as it was just around the corner from where I lived at the time. I smuggled in a portable Philips cassette recorder and a microphone to record the gig. Sadly, the tape was wiped. I saw them with Gary Moore, which was an incredible spectacle, He was one of the best guitar players ever. The *Chinatown* tour with Snowy White was a bit disappointing, probably because he wasn't a naturally flamboyant kind of guitarist and had a lot to live up to.

Phil projected an extraordinary persona live. I remember being caught in the spotlight reflecting off his mirrored bass scratchplate and feeling like I had somehow been physically touched by him. Amazing times.

In 1983, I was quite an accomplished guitarist and my aim was to get a crack at joining Lizzy. I had recently joined NWOBHM band Thunderstick and was waiting for my chance to audition. Sadly, that never came to pass.

Thunderstick were booked in at John Henry Rehearsal Studios in London in 1983 and next door Gary Moore and his band were rehearsing for their tour. I met Gary, Ian Paice and Neil Murray (who I became friends with) in the canteen. It was very surreal seeing these rock gods sitting around a table sipping tea! I also met Robbo backstage at the Marquee Club in London after his first London gig with Motörhead. He didn't seem too happy at the time, unfortunately. I never got to see the John Sykes line up of Lizzy.

I also saw Grand Slam several times at the Marquee. It was always a packed house and I was amazed they never got signed. Phil's passing was a huge blow. Myself and a friend went to the church service in London which was incredibly sad. The end of an era. Phil and Lizzy left a big impression on me and my music.

NATIONAL STADIUM

18 NOVEMBER 1976, DUBLIN, IRELAND

I WAS THERE: ALAN LONG

I have been a Thin Lizzy fan for more years than I care to remember. The second youngest of five boys, my older brothers were very much into Pink Floyd, Led Zeppelin and of course Thin Lizzy so they were being played in the house all the time. My brother had two tickets to go and see Lizzy in the National Stadium in Dublin, which was one of only a few places where bands played in the mid Seventies. When his mate couldn't go to the gig my brother asked me if I wanted to go and off we went. I was hooked. I went out the following weekend and got *Jailbreak* and I was off. I went out and bought *Fighting*, and then *Nightlife*, and my mother had her eardrums blown away.

In January 1977, Thin Lizzy embarked upon a huge North American tour supporting Queen, who were themselves established as a headline act following the success of 'Bohemian Rhapsody'. Brian Robertson was unavailable having injured his hand in a bar room brawl so Gary Moore replaced him (temporarily) on guitar.

We really learned a lot from opening for Freddie and the boys. They were in a different league to us. **Brian Downey**

LOUISVILLE GARDENS

21 JANUARY 1977, LOUISVILLE, KENTUCKY

I WAS THERE: MARK SNEED

I saw them live three times, all in Louisville, Kentucky. The first time was on the Queen tour. They were amazing, although Robbo wasn't there. Gary Moore is certainly more accomplished than Robbo, but I was a fan of the Robbo/Gorham line up. My local paper detested hard rock and nobody got great reviews. Louisville Gardens held about 6,500 people for a sold out rock show, and I'd guess the Queen show was sold out. The local newspaper reviewed the show and said Robbo was on guitar. If it was Robbo, then he had cut his hair! This was the tour where he messed up his hand right before leaving the UK and Moore stepped in. I vividly recall 'Warriors' because the lighting during the long intro to the song just mesmerised my 14-year-old brain.

CIVIC CENTRE

25 JANUARY 1977, OTTAWA, CANADA

I WAS THERE: CLARK CRAIG, AGE 15

Queen were the headliners. It was my first big concert out of my town and we went on a bus tour from Kingston to Ottawa. I was a bigger Lizzy fan than I was a Queen fan at the time. I remember buying *Johnny the Fox* a few months before the concert. Brian Robertson had an arm injury for the first part of the tour and Gary Moore was filling in on guitar.

Clark Craig's first rock concert was the Lizzy-Queen double bill

CHICAGO STADIUM

28 JANUARY 1977, CHICAGO, ILLINOIS

I WAS THERE: CHUCK GUZIK

My interest in Thin Lizzy came about from seeing them on *Don Kirschner's Rock Concert* and *The Midnight Special* in 1976 or '77. I was 15 years old and had been playing guitar for about two years after being classically taught on the organ from the age of 10. I had already been listening to UFO and Led Zeppelin and just stumbled across Thin Lizzy on that Friday night when both those shows aired. My first thought was, 'Wow – raw power!' I loved the sound and the aggression shown on stage

Chuck Guzik almost didn't go to see the Queen show – until he saw who was support

and the whole experience was like 'I have to do this' somehow, some way! All four guys were just large and the sound was an orgasm for the ears. I remember Phil in spandex and all black, and even the bass with a silver pick plate which reflected the lights - and Scott Gorham's long hair! Brian Downey was just powerful behind them.

I grew up in the inner city of Chicago, Illinois in an industrial area with steel mills everywhere. It was a nasty area really. I started to identify with the bands out of the very same type of areas in England - Uriah Heep, Sabbath, UFO. My entire neighbourhood went to concerts two or three times a week, and tickets were seven to ten dollars. When the DJ on the radio said Queen were coming to Chicago Stadium, I almost didn't go because I'm not much of a Queen fan although I've grown to respect them over time.

I worked at a record store part time where they would list the opening acts for the shows that were coming to Chicago. That's when I saw Thin Lizzy as the opening act for Queen. I rushed down to a Sears department store on my bike and grabbed whatever was left in the way of tickets. Queen were huge then and I figured just to get in was okay as I could then walk around inside the venue and get close for Thin Lizzy. The show was in a cold weather month, with lots of snow and very cold temperatures. Chicago Stadium was a huge cavern that hosted hockey and basketball pro teams - and the circus too!

When we went for the show, I figured to leave after Thin Lizzy for some ridiculous reason. The minute the fog machines started, the huge Thin Lizzy logo lit up and they hit the low E chord which rang out as they took the stage and I was hooked for life. I got the same chills writing this as I did on that night. It was so powerful! Watching Phil walk around and up to the mic stand and the two guitarists bouncing around was phenomenal! Two Les Pauls! I had the red sunburst Les Paul just like Scott Gorham (and still have it). I got it from being a Rush fan but felt even better knowing that these guys used them as well. 'Massacre' still sticks out in my mind as the song I will always remember. I was right at the front of the barricade they had up close to the stage for that song. Security asked me to return to my seat - which didn't happen!

Another thing that impacted me was the first time I felt the double bass drums of Brian Downey in my chest! You could literally feel each time he used them, and I loved that then and love it today.

After Thin Lizzy finished, I was going to leave but was talked into staying for Queen and I'm glad I did. The next day, I bought *Johnny the Fox* and *Jailbreak* and started to figure out how to play as many Lizzy songs as I could. I got pretty successful in the clubs and concerts around Chicago over the years and always played a handful of Thin Lizzy songs. One time, I smiled ear to ear when someone told me my stage presence reminded them of the Thin Lizzy guitarist with the long hair. I then got interested in Iron Maiden and was stunned at the influence Lizzy had on them. The double guitars and the large presence of the bass player, Steve Harris? That's all Phil!

I WAS THERE: JOHN REGAN, AGE 19

I got to see most of the great acts of the Seventies as they came through the US, mostly in Chicago, but I also travelled for the right shows at what now seems like the best era ever for live rock. I saw Thin Lizzy back up Queen at the Chicago Stadium. I grabbed tickets early for this one, since I had attended Queen's *A Night at the Opera* tour the previous year at the Auditorium and it was amazing. For this show, Thin Lizzy were doing *Jailbreak* and Queen were doing *A Day at the Races*.

John Regan saw the Lizzy-Queen double header

Thin Lizzy completely dazzled the audience almost into a frenzy. I don't think anyone expected what they got. It didn't take long before Phil had the crowd going crazy. It must have only been halfway through the first song. You don't get to see many do that in your lifetime.

Freddie Mercury came out in a one piece pink leggings-type outfit. Queen were playing what I would say was their weakest offering of music, especially after the last tour, and people booed and were actually throwing things. They stopped playing and warned that the show would end if it didn't stop. It did stop and the show went on, but to this day the Thin Lizzy performance will always be one of my favourites. It's like Huey Lewis stated. He said Phil was the most professional musician he ever worked with. Phil could hold the audience in the palm of his hand!

MAPLE LEAF GARDENS

1 FEBRUARY 1977, TORONTO, CANADA

I WAS THERE: THOMAS VACCARO, AGE 18

I was lucky enough to see two of my favourite bands on the same bill, all for $6.60 in Canadian dollars. As much as I loved Queen, I was there to see Phil and co. and they did not disappoint. They were great that night. Rest in peace, Phil. You are missed.

Thomas Vaccaro saw Lizzy and Queen for less than seven Canadian dollars

COLE FIELD HOUSE, UNIVERSITY OF MARYLAND

4 FEBRUARY 1977, MADISON, MARYLAND

I WAS THERE: DAVID CRAIG MAULER, AGE 17

I saw Lizzy in a small (14,000 seat) venue with Queen, and I remember how powerful Phil's voice was. They were very tight and I was very impressed with how they performed. But my abiding memory is that

I was almost crushed going through the door at what was a general admission show. The concert venue was at the facility where the Maryland Terps played college basketball. Being a general admission show everyone was rushing to get in to get the best seat. As it was a college, the entrances had school doors that had a removable beam between the doors! I was lodged against that beam as the crowd rushed the door. Luckily, I got one side of body around the one side of the beam and was flushed into the arena. My girlfriend at the time was next to me and got through the door a lot easier.

Not long after that some people were crushed and died at a Who show in Cincinnati.

David Craig Mauler saw Lizzy supporting Queen

MADISON SQUARE GARDEN

5 FEBRUARY 1977, NEW YORK, NEW YORK

I WAS THERE: JOHN DE NOIA

I saw Lizzy four or five times in NYC, but always at different venues. I saw them at the Academy of Music on 14th Street. I also saw them at Madison Square Garden when they opened up for Queen. That was a fantastic show. And I saw them at the Ritz on 11th Street when they did the *Chinatown* tour. Phil was spot on. They were just a fantastic group that could rock you out and also hit you with some great ballads.

PROVIDENCE CIVIC CENTER

10 FEBRUARY 1977, PROVIDENCE, RHODE ISLAND

I WAS THERE: MICHAEL MOONEY

This was a general admission show. I had only heard 'The Boys are Back in Town' and didn't know anything about them, but I was so captivated by their live performance, and just blown away by the energy coming off the stage. I remember Philo reflecting the spotlight from his mirrored Fender Precision Bass and how memorable each of the songs was. I only found out years later that it was actually Gary Moore on guitar filling in for Brian, because he had cut his hand in a fight. Of course Queen came out and they were truly "royalty" on the Day at the Races tour, but Lizzy always remained my 'first'.

I WAS THERE: RON THATCHER

'Jailbreak' was being played a lot on the radio. Everyone I knew loved that song so when I went to this concert, I was really wanting to see this band even though I only knew that one song by them. Well, I gotta tell you they tore the stage up, one song after the other. For them to rock the place with what was mostly unheard material was something to experience. I was right up front and Phil and the boys moved around that stage like crazy. It was only a short set because they were an opening act, but for weeks after the concert everyone - and I mean everyone - was talking about this band that played first. I started buying their albums, buying *Live and Dangerous* several times over because I wore out each copy.

Ron Thatcher plays in a Lizzy tribute band called Cold Sweat

I also started learning to play guitar. I've been told by people who hear me play that I sound like Gary Moore, which is a real compliment. I now play in a tribute band called Cold Sweat. We have a black singer/bassist who sounds so much like Phil. I turned him on to Thin Lizzy and he's amazed at Phil's lyrics, as am I. I always thought Phil was very deep, and far better than a lot of songwriters.

I could go on forever, as will Thin Lizzy's music….

CIVIC CENTER

11 FEBRUARY 1977, PHILADELPHIA, PENNSYLVANIA

I WAS THERE: TEODORO LOPES

It was general admission and tickets were $7.50. As the arena doors opened, Grant and I ran to the exact spot we wanted to be, directly in front of the sound mixing board. We almost got trampled to death taking our first ten steps entering the place. I'll never forget that when Grant bought these tickets, we were both extremely disappointed. We both questioned, 'Why not play at the Tower Theater or the Spectrum or even Robin Hood Dell East?' Why the dreary, cold and acoustically dead Civic Center? 'Ah man, this isn't going to be very good.' Not once did we think or even consider that just maybe the sheer talents of Thin Lizzy and Queen would see us all through. No, we looked at this as a 'glass half empty' scenario.

But all bands are not created the same and, simply put, this was the best show I have ever attended at the Civic Center. Thin Lizzy came out and just tore the roof off the place. They rocked Grant, myself and the rest of the crowd to a frenzy, like a great opening act should. They played all their hits from their six albums and a few more. The reception was so great for these guys that they blessed us with a two song encore. A fantastic and exciting band, I knew I would see these guys again in a heartbeat.

I WAS THERE: MARK A MAHAL

My second Lizzy show at the Philadelphia Convention and Civic Center, where they opened for Queen, was an entirely different experience. The difference in the crowd energy between 600 people at the Roxy and 12,000 in the Civic Center was palpable. The night belonged to Queen but Thin Lizzy certainly made their presence known on that winter night.

Lizzy made their presence known on that winter night

SPORTATORIUM
19 FEBRUARY 1977, HOLLYWOOD, FLORIDA

I WAS THERE: STUART BARNETT, AGE 12

I was there to see Queen but knew about Thin Lizzy. I snuck a tape player in and recorded all of Thin Lizzy, but the batteries were dying and so the recording made Queen sound real speeded up. Like a 12-year-old would, I just recorded over the tape so the recording was lost forever.

Stuart Barnett taped the show

SAM HOUSTON COLISEUM
26 FEBRUARY 1977, HOUSTON, TEXAS

I WAS THERE: TONY WEAVER

Even though they had just come out with *Johnny the Fox* the songs off of *Jailbreak* received the best reaction from the crowd. When they played 'Cowboy Song', which mentions Texas in the lyrics, the crowd cheered the loudest. I know Phil had issues with drugs around that time. However, he and the band were very tight that night. Speaking of the band, one of the guitar players, Brian Robertson, wasn't able to make it so Gary Moore filled in. They were on the verge of stealing the show. But Queen opened with 'Tie Your Mother Down' and just blew the crowd away. Both bands were great and this was one of the better shows I've seen.

I WAS THERE: JAMES FRAZIER, AGE 17

They opened for Queen. It was Gary Moore instead of Robbo and they kicked ass. I was told that Queen were upset, because Lizzy kicked ass the whole tour.

LOS ANGELES FORUM
2 & 3 MARCH 1977, LOS ANGELES, CALIFORNIA

I WAS THERE: GILBERT BUSCH

I was living in California when *Jailbreak* came out. The first time I saw them was in Los Angeles on the *Johnny the Fox* tour. Then I saw them the following year in Los Angeles on the *Bad Reputation* tour, and on the *Chinatown* tour in 1980. The *Johnny the Fox* tour was amazing. I don't think I've ever seen a band with such an energy and a raw sound, and I saw Zeppelin in '73 and Tull in '74. One of my favourite live albums out of anybody is *Life*. It's up there with Deep Purple's *Made in Japan* and UFO's *Strangers in the Night*.

SOUTHERN ALBERTA JUBILEE AUDITORIUM
16 MARCH 1977, ALBERTA, CANADA

I WAS THERE: BRIAN SMOLIK

Brian Smolik was blinded by the reflections off Phil's bass

I saw Thin Lizzy when they toured with Queen. This venue is fantastic for a concert. It's small and intimate and the sound is stellar. I had waited in line to get the first tickets sold and ended up in the first row, centre stage. I was a huge fan of both bands and was stoked for this show. Initially I was disappointed that Robbo would not be playing, but that thought quickly left my mind when Gary Moore hit the first notes of the night. Lizzy were on fire and played a fantastic set. I got blinded a couple of times as Phil reflected the stage lights off of his bass into our eyes! What a fantastic frontman and musician. Gary Moore was playing his ass off, and sporting some sparkly sneakers! Queen also played great that night, but in my mind Thin Lizzy was the better of the two. I was, and remain, a huge Thin Lizzy fan.

BRIAN ROBERTSON QUITS
26 MARCH 1977

UK music magazine *Sounds* announced that Brian Robertson had left Lizzy. This was confirmed by a press statement from the band in May 1977.

Thin Lizzy guitarist quits

BRIAN ROBERTSON will not be rejoining Thin Lizzy as guitarist when they return from their US tour next week.

Robertson missed out on the tour when, a few days before it was due to start in January, he cut his hand in a brawl at London's Marquee club. Gary Moore, Thin Lizzy's guitarist in early 1974, was brought in as a last minute replacement but repeated statements from the band's publicist scotched rumours that Robertson would be out for good.

But in Lizzy's absence, Robertson has been working on a solo project and doing some informal session and live work wi Jimmy Bain, former bassist wi Ritchie Blackmore's Rainbow.

He now feels that he cann continue his solo career or his wo with Bain within the confines Lizzy. He and Bain will be e panding the band — unchristen as yet — and will be doing li dates when they've finish rehearsing.

Gary Moore will now repla Robertson full-time, and will fulf his present role for forthcomi recording commitments and U and European dates planned f later this spring and summer.

Sounds broke the news about Robbo

BRIAN ROBERTSON REJOINS
20 JULY 1977

Less than two months after officially leaving, Robbo was officially back in the Lizzy line up.

STORA SCENEN, LISEBERG
9 AUGUST 1977, GOTHENBURG, SWEDEN

I WAS THERE: ÅKE MOANGE, AGE 16

In the summer of 1977, I visited my uncle in Gothenburg, 510 miles south of my home, as I didn't have much to do during the summer holidays. I went down by train and while I was there, I saw that Thin Lizzy would be playing there in August at Liseberg, Sweden's biggest amusement park. As we never had any good concerts at home, I stayed more or less the whole summer so that I could see Lizzy before I went home.

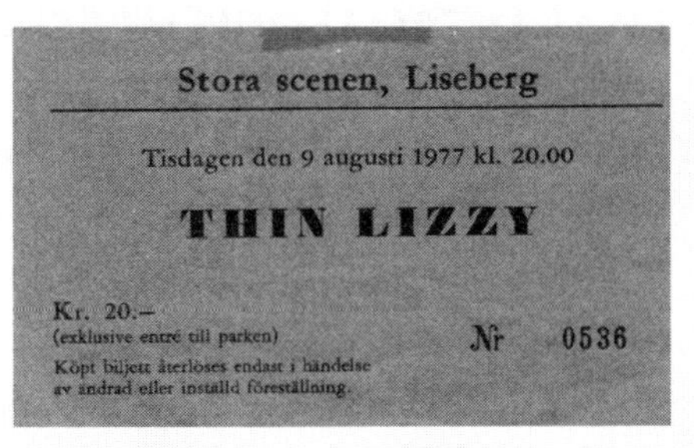

Stora scenen, Liseberg

Tisdagen den 9 augusti 1977 kl. 20.00

THIN LIZZY

Kr. 20.–
(exklusive entré till parken)
Köpt biljett återlöses endast i händelse av ändrad eller inställd föreställning.

№ 0536

Ake Moange saw Lizzy in Gothenburg

They didn't have any support act and it was the real Thin Lizzy for me, with Gorham and Robertson on guitars. They started with a keyboard intro to a song I never heard before, 'Soldier of Fortune', from the forthcoming *Bad Reputation* album. This was followed by 'Jailbreak' and I was in seventh heaven. They had some stage effects like explosives and lights of course. They also played 'Dancing in the Moonlight' and 'Bad Reputation'. Brian Downey had a drum solo in 'Bad Reputation' which ended with a beat on the big gong behind him. They closed the show with 'The Rocker' and I was left totally stunned. It was just such a fantastic night.

JAZZ BILZEN FESTIVAL

14 AUGUST 1977, BILZEN, BELGIUM

I WAS THERE: MARC HAUWE

I saw them very early on, in '76, and then at the Jazz Bilzen Festival, which was the first European festival to be played over three days. The PA system at that time at Jazz Bilzen was 10,000 watts and Thin Lizzy brought their own 10,000 watt PA system. Holy crap! They didn't want to play an encore. A lot of people started throwing bottles, cans, etc. I can still see a bottle hitting a guitar as a roadie carried it from the stage. Bottles and cans were banned from the festival from the very next day. And I saw them at the Pink Pop Festival in the Netherlands, where Lizzy's roadies caught me while I was having fun with a girl in a car. They started rocking the car to 'help' me!

MORAN'S HOTEL

19 AUGUST 1977, DUBLIN, IRELAND

I WAS THERE: LEONIE MCDONAGH

I saw them in Moran's Hotel near me. Up and coming groups played there and it only held 250 people downstairs. The place was jammed. It was an impromptu warm up before Lizzy played in Dalymount Park. A poster was put up in the hotel that morning and then it was word of mouth. Thin Lizzy played and grabbed the drummer out of Horslips to play with them. The Boomtown Rats filled in until they arrived.

I knew Phil's mam well enough to talk to her. I used to meet her in the pub. She was a lovely, lovely woman - a real lady. I live near where Phil is buried in Howth. I visit the grave when I am out that way. Gone too soon.

It was Phil's idea to do the impromptu gig but he decided to cancel when he saw a crowd of people outside Moran's, fearing their licence might be at risk. When he discovered that The Boomtown Rats were planning to play the show instead, he fetched his bass guitar from the car, accusing the Rats of 'robbing my fucking gig'.

DALYMOUNT PARK

21 AUGUST 1977, DUBLIN, IRELAND

I WAS THERE: MARK O'ROURKE, AGE 13

Thin Lizzy started in Crumlin which is just south of Phoenix Park in Dublin. I grew up in Dublin in the Seventies, on the north side of the park on the North Circular Road, about four miles away. My first Lizzy gig was in the summer of '77, at Dalymount Park on Phil's birthday. I was 13 years old and wanted to go but no one would sell me a ticket, which I had saved up to buy by having a paper round.

Mark O'Rourke was at Dalymount Park in Dublin

Every shop told me that I had to be 16 and none of my older mates would take a chance on buying the ticket for me in case they were refused admission as well.

I decided to just sit outside and enjoy the day. If I couldn't see them, I could at least hear them for free.

It was a gloriously sunny day and just as the turnstiles were about to close one of the guys asked me to get him some cigarettes from the local shop. When I came back, he asked me why I was sitting around outside so I told him why. He asked me if I was a Bohs fan (Dalymount was - and still is - the home of Bohemians Football Club). To prove I was, he asked me who my favourite player was and I told him - Gerry Ryan, who later signed to Derby County and Brighton. He allowed me into the venue for free and told me, if the police caught me, to just say that I climbed over the back wall via a well known telephone pole.

When people ask me who was the first band that I ever saw live I always say Lizzy, which is wrong. It was in fact Graham Parker, and I have lost count of how many times I have seen them over the years. Lizzy were introduced to the crowd with the words 'the boys are back in town!' They played the usual set for the period - most of *Live and Dangerous* – and started with 'Soldier of Fortune' and ended with 'The Rocker'.

I remember the smell of cannabis for the first time, and how loud Lizzy were. I stopped in at my uncle's house in Cabra on the way home, about a mile away, and he told me that you could hear every note Lizzy played as clear as day in his back garden.

My second and favourite Lizzy gig was on the *Black Rose* tour at the RDS in the summer of 1980. Gary Moore took them to another level and was never equalled in my honest opinion. I heard the album for the first time in my mate's parents' bathroom when a pirate radio station in Dublin got a test pressing and played the whole album. The bathroom had the best reception!

My least favourite Lizzy gig was at Slane Castle in '81. U2 were crap (The Edge spent most of the time puking from stage fright), Sweet Savage with Vivian Campbell were great and Rose Tattoo stole the show. For me Lizzy were a bit flat. The drugs had overtaken the band by then.

I WAS THERE: ALAN LONG

Next up came a concert in Dalymount Park in Dublin, home of one of Dublin's League of Ireland teams, Bohemians. In August 1977, it was a day long outdoor gig with the Boomtown Rats, Graham Parker and the Rumour and others. We hit the pub about 10.30am and left about 2pm to bus our way across Dublin to the northside for the gig. I remember Geldof mouthing off about one thing and another, but Philip and the boys were just great. Everybody left the stadium on a musical high. It took us almost two hours to get home on the bus and we sang Lizzy songs all the way.

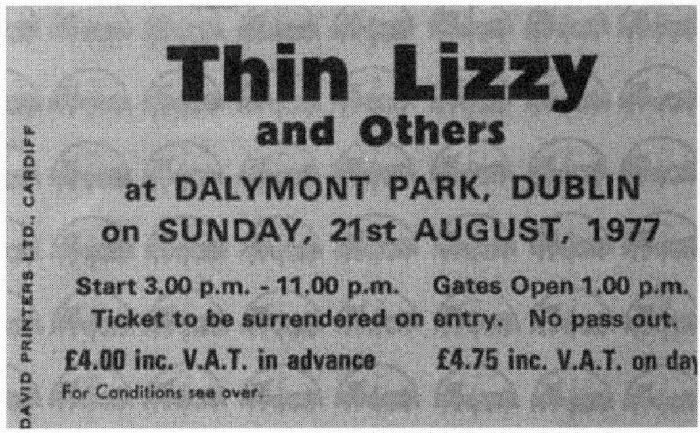

Thin Lizzy played Dalymount Park the day after Phil's birthday

I WAS THERE: BRIAN O'CONNOR, AGE 17

I came across Skid Row when they were playing in a local hall. It would have been around 1969 and I was only very small at the time. The talk all week was that there was a big band coming to play. Brush Shiels was pretty instantly recognisable even at that age, and Phil looked a million dollars. The next time they caught my attention was when they were on *Top of the Pops* with 'Whiskey in the Jar'. After that I started getting their albums.

In 1977 they were appearing in Dalymount Park. Myself and my friend Frannie Copeland got a lift up to Dublin with his brother. It was the first time either of us had even been in Dublin by ourselves. It was a big thing, and we had to pull all sorts of strokes with our

Brian O'Connor was at Dalymount Park with his friend Frannie

parents to get them to let us go. We were dropped off about ten o'clock in the morning so we walked around Dublin. We didn't know where Dalymount Park was but eventually we found out. We went to a bar and I said to my friend, 'I'll go in and see if we can get two pints. You wait outside.' So I went in, at 17 years of age, and said to the barman, 'Can I have two pints of Smithwicks please?' He said, 'Yeah, no problem,' and he gave them to me. We couldn't believe it – he'd given us two pints! We drank the pints and headed up to Dalymount Park.

It was described somewhere as one of the longest days. It was the first real rock concert in Dublin. Thin Lizzy were topping a bill with Graham Parker and the Rumour, Fairport Convention and The Boomtown Rats. By the time Thin Lizzy were coming on stage, it was around ten o'clock and it was time for us to catch the last bus home, so we had to make a decision. Do we take the last bus home to Wicklow or do we stay for the concert? We saw people there from Wicklow and we said, 'Someone will take pity on us. We'll stay!' The concert went on until after midnight. I'd never experienced an atmosphere anything like that before in my life.

I saw them at the Simmonscourt Pavilion in 1980 on the *Chinatown* tour and then Lizzy played the first ever concert at Slane Castle, in 1981, with U2 and Hazel O'Connor. We went up on the Friday and were camping in Bettystown. In the morning, we headed for Slane in a convoy of cars. Little did we know that U2 were going to become so famous. Mama's Boys were supposed to start the concert, but to this day no one knows if it was Mama's Boys or if it was someone else who played.

I saw Thin Lizzy twice more at the Simmonscourt Pavilion. Before every concert one of the great discussions would be, 'Who's going to be the sax player for 'Dancing in the Moonlight'? You would have the guy from Supertramp maybe, or the guy from Madness.

You got to know what Phil was going to do. You'd hear the riff for 'Cowboy Song' and you'd know that he was going straight into 'Jailbreak'. But the concerts were never really long. He might play ten songs and an encore, so an hour and 20 minutes, perhaps an hour and a half. They weren't like a Queen or Supertramp concert, that would go on for hours.

When Gary Moore left the band, it was like, 'What the fuck's he at? Why's he doing this to us?' He was always the bad one. It was never Phil. He'd get someone else in.

I was very shocked when I heard he had died. I had a great sense of sadness. A girl said to me, 'Oh sure, he was only a druggie anyway,' and I lost my cool and just tore into her. I said, 'Listen, that's the most insensitive remark I've ever heard in my life. I don't want to hear you talk like that ever again.'

Myself and Frannie, who had gone to Dalymount with me, went to the do in Dublin on the first anniversary of Phil's death. His mother was there, along with all the band members and Brush, and all different bands played. It was a great celebration but it was also very sad. They still have it every January, but the first one was the most poignant.

The whole thing about Lizzy and Philip was that there was a great sense of Irishness about them, a great sense of 'there's an Irishman and that's what an Irishman can achieve.' There was great pride in the way he always talked up the Irish. He'd always say, 'Anyone here from Ireland?' and when all the women would scream, he'd say, 'Would you like any more Irish in you?'

You had Rory Gallagher a little bit earlier, but Phil and Thin Lizzy were the frontrunners for Irish rock for my generation. They were the first Irish band to really look up to. You just felt very attached to them.

I WAS THERE: CHRISTY CORCORAN, AGE 16

At the age of 12, I was working in a petrol filling station and one day Eric Bell pulled in. All I could see was his bushy hair and his guitar case on the back seat. I asked him for his autograph and he said he wasn't Eric but to this day I'm convinced it was him. Dalymount Park was just pure excitement, from the moment I got my ticket until the day of the concert. It was the first time I went to a concert. I was only allowed to go if my older brother looked after me. I was so in awe of Phil Lynott. I was hynotised by him. I just kept looking at him all night. It's just the best concert I was ever at. When you play the music now it is still fresh. When they talk about reforming Thin Lizzy, I say it is like baking a cake without the main ingredient.

I WAS THERE: JOHN MCCAUL

I liked Thin Lizzy ever since the Lynott, Bell and Downey trio charted in early 1973 with their inimitable take on the Irish traditional standard 'Whiskey in the Jar', set in the southern mountains of Ireland, often with specific mention of the counties of Cork and Kerry. The song first gained wide exposure when Irish folk band The Dubliners performed it internationally as a signature song and recorded it on three albums in the 1960s. In the US, the song was popularized by The Highwaymen, who recorded it on their 1962 album, *Encore*. Belfast man Eric Bell's solo got me straight way – I was hooked.

I was, of course, disappointed that the follow ups failed to chart but that all changed with 1976's 'The Boys are Back in Town', culled from the iconic *Jailbreak* album.

I had finished grammar school in June 1977 and by the time of the Dalymount Park concert, I was getting ready to go to university and had both *Jailbreak* and *Johnny the Fox*. John Masterson, a schoolfriend, and I decided to go to the Thin Lizzy-headed gig. The line up appeared good because Graham Parker and the Rumour were also scheduled to perform. We bought our tickets from Carlin Records, Newry for the princely sum of £4.75.

The concert was on Sunday. On Saturday, the two of us met up at the bottom of the Dublin Road in Newry and stuck out our thumbs. Along came two other guys I knew vaguely, so we decided to stick together when we got to Dublin. All four of us managed to get a lift when a minibus driver took pity and told us to jump in.

We were dropped off in Dublin's city centre and made our way in the general direction of Moran's Hotel, where we knew there'd be music on offer. (We even had time for a game of pool along the way.)

Unexpectedly, more Newry lads joined us and a good night was had by all.

However, at the end of the evening, one of us suddenly realised that we had nowhere to stay the night. One of our group decided that we should go to Phoenix Park. He said there was a bus depot there and maybe we could find a bus which was unlocked, which proved to be the case. We found an open bus and managed a few hours' sleep.

We rose early and went to eight o'clock Mass - ostensibly to keep warm

- then made our way to Dalymount Park, having only a hazy idea of where it was. We arrived at 2pm and made our way toward the front, only to meet up with yet another contingent of Newry music fans.

We missed the announcement of the full line-up: Stepaside, The Radiators from Space (featuring the late Phil Chevron, of subsequent Pogues fame), Fairport Convention (a rather odd choice, I thought), The Boomtown Rats (who I hadn't heard of at that stage), Graham Parker and the Rumour (featuring elements of Brinsley Schwarz) and, of course, Thin Lizzy topping the bill (on Phil's birthday).

I was really impressed with The Boomtown Rats, especially when they showcased their version of the old Nat King Cole and Rolling Stones standard, *Route 66*. Geldof was full of self confidence, telling us at every opportunity how brilliant the Rats were and that they'd just got on Radio 1's playlist with 'Looking After Number 1'. I immediately believed him and have been a fan of the band ever since. Needless to say, I thought they were excellent.

Fairport Convention washed over me. I knew they had a fine pedigree but I didn't know any of their songs. Graham Parker and the Rumour were a different matter. I'd heard the *Pink Parker* EP and seen them on *Top of the Pops*. They had released three albums by this stage – *Howling Wind*, *Live at Marble Arch* and *Heat Treatment* – which, in later years, found a place in my collection. The band featured the late John Earle who Lizzy later borrowed to play the iconic sax solo on 'Dancing in the Moonlight', the new single.

The Thin Lizzy line up was the Lynott-Gorham-Robertson-Downey combo which, in my estimation, was their best. The setlist, of course, was brilliant. *Bad Reputation* was the new release and *Live and Dangerous* had yet to be recorded. However, I knew the rest of the songs well and, it seems, so did the crowd. At one stage, someone shouted up, 'Happy birthday, Phil', to which Philo responded with a 'thank you'. A group of people to our left then chorused, 'Who's the special guest?' Again, Phil heard this and replied, 'Jimmy the Weed!'

The gig ended in darkness and we slowly made our way towards the exit gates, the bass line from 'Dancing in the Moonlight' still ringing in my ears. Any number of people seemed to be going to Newry, so we had no bother getting a lift home.

When *Live and Dangerous* was released in 1978, I was first in the queue. The track list was broadly similar to what I had experience at Dalymount. To this day, I listen to it frequently.

I look back on the gig with fondness. I'm still a fan of Thin Lizzy, Graham Parker and the Rumour and The Boomtown Rats and have most of their CDs in my collection. University gave me a great opportunity to see live bands. I saw Thin Lizzy, Graham Parker and the Rumour and The Boomtown Rats on separate occasions since (even getting Geldof's autograph in December 1977) but nothing really compares to my first festival of music, especially to Thin Lizzy in all their live splendour.

Unfortunately, the Lizzy performance was not recorded for posterity.

I WAS THERE: JOHNNY REYNOLDS

I started playing music professionally around 1985. I love Phil Lynott and Thin Lizzy - they were a big influence on me musically. My first live concert was Thin Lizzy live at Dalymount Park, Dublin in 1977. It was the turning point for me regarding wanting to play music. It was such a jaw-dropping experience to see Phil and the band power through that concert. I will never forget that magical and life changing concert. I went to see them four times after that. Phil and Lizzy will always be fondly remembered as the ground breaking Irish rock band of the Seventies and early Eighties.

I WAS THERE: KEVIN BERGIN

When Phil moved over and stayed permanently in London, he got a flat that was like a doss house where everybody turned up. I wasn't really into that drugs scene so I only saw him the once, about 1973, and we only met up intermittently after that. But in 1977 he had a big concert on at Dalymount Park and he said, 'Come over, Kev. We'll bring you round the back and you can come in with the roadies and stand there.' That was the last real time I saw him properly. I could tell at the time that he was a troubled man. I used to try and contact him after that but never got anything back. Then my grandmother passed away so I didn't really have the connection anymore, so that's when it ended. But from about 1964 up until 1973, I used to see him quite regularly.

17TH NATIONAL JAZZ BLUES & ROCK FESTIVAL

27 AUGUST 1977, READING, UK

I WAS THERE: KEITH DEACON

The last gig I saw Lizzy at was the Reading Festival in 1977. I went with three mates - Phil Crouch, Steve Hickingbottom and Neil Joyce – and we camped the whole weekend. It only cost us £7.95. I managed to get a photo of the hot air balloon advertising Thin Lizzy. I had run to where it was landing in the field but fell over and was then covered in mud. Not good. Lizzy were headlining on the Saturday night. The sound wasn't brilliant but we watched it in the pouring rain and mud. As always, they played a great set and showed that they were now a top act.

Keith Deacon was at the Reading Festival and remembers the mud

I WAS THERE: MERRILYN LUCAS

We saw Lizzy quite a few times. As each album came out, we'd book to see them. I joined the fan club and was proud to be fan number 12 - one of the first! The first time I saw them was in Oxford. I remember the blue swirling police lights and the sirens. We were a married couple in our early thirties so not in with the youngsters with long hair and leather jackets. We then booked tickets to see them at the Hammersmith Odeon through the fan club, when they made the live video, and had front row seats. I won tickets for Reading Rock Festival, which got us into the back stage enclosure. I have a couple of photos that my husband took. I also have a *Black Rose* album which Phil signed for me after seeing that tour and all my albums, a few fan letter booklets and two of Philip's books of lyrics.

I travelled to the *Vibe* a few years ago on my own, but met friends there who I am still in touch with on Facebook. There was no one quite like Lizzy, and Phil was the best front man. We liked the early years when Brian Robertson played with the band. Sadly, he was propping up the bar when my husband took the photos at Reading.

Merrilyn Lucas won tickets to get backstage at the Reading Festival

I WAS THERE: MIKE ROBERTS, AGE 19

I first encountered Thin Lizzy on kids' TV after school. They were a three piece and played 'Whiskey in the Jar'. I thought they were brilliant, but they disappeared more or less straight away. Then in 1977 I went to the Reading Festival. Thin Lizzy were to headline on the Saturday. On Saturday morning, whilst I was wandering around the empty arena, Lizzy suddenly appeared on the stage and played a couple of songs as a sound check. Only a few people were there so most of the crowd missed it. Their headline act that night was superb. Then in 1983 they headlined Reading again, on the Sunday night slot. I was in the sound tower to the left of the stage. The view was excellent, the sound brilliant and they played 'Emerald', my favourite Thin Lizzy track of all time. Including that '77 soundcheck I like to say that I saw them two and a half times!

I WAS THERE: MARK 'SMIGGY' SMITH

The official car park was full, so we had to park over the Thames and up the road. We pitched the tent on the banks of the Thames and went back to the car for the rest of our kit and to buy some beer. After eating, we went to the arena, where we got wristband tickets put on us, which had to be kept on all weekend. We left to feed our faces and got back to the arena prepared for the knee-deep mud. We got some beer and wine and settled in for Aerosmith, Graham Parker and the Rumour and Thin Lizzy. The first two were exceptionally good but the third? Well, they were better than at De Mont.

I WAS THERE: KEITH THOMPSON, AGE 17

Next time I saw Thin Lizzy was when they headlined Reading Rock Festival in 1977. This was the now expanded band with Scott Gorham and Brian Robertson. Rain had turned the site into a bit of a bog and I was knee deep in mud, determined to hang on for Lizzy. By the time they hit the stage a decision had been made to decrease the volume levels due to complaints but nonetheless Lizzy were triumphant that night.

I WAS THERE: PETER SMITH

Thin Lizzy returned to the Reading Festival for a triumphant headlining Saturday night performance. This was the year when the festival site became a mud bowl, with a lake of mud in front of the stage. We needed a great band and a great performance to cheer us all up, and Thin Lizzy gave us that. They played a classic set including 'Jailbreak', 'Dancing in the Moonlight', 'Still in Love With You', 'Cowboy Song', 'The Boys are Back in Town', 'Don't Believe a Word' and 'Emerald', closing with an encore of 'The Rocker'. This was Thin Lizzy at their very best. The classic line up of Lynott, Gorham, Robertson and Downey couldn't be beaten.

Phil would say, 'Are there any cowboys out there?', which would always receive a massive roar from the crowd, and then 'this is for all the cowboys...' (cue the quiet guitar intro to 'Cowboy Song') before he sang 'I am just a cowboy, lonesome on the trail,' the full band came in, the familiar twin guitar riff started and away we would go. You just couldn't beat it.

Their status as one of the world's best rock bands was even more evident amidst all the mud and chaos of the festival.

BAD REPUTATION RELEASED
2 SEPTEMBER 1977
UK CHART POSITION 4
US CHART POSITION 39

Bad Reputation is viewed by some Lizzy fans as their best album. It contained the single 'Dancing in the Moonlight (It's Caught Me in its Spotlight)' which reached number 14 in the UK singles chart and number 4 in Ireland.

THE GARDENS

24 SEPTEMBER 1977, VANCOUVER, CANADA

I WAS THERE: BRAD LILLIE

I saw Thin Lizzy every tour they did in Vancouver, BC. Seeing Moore, Robertson and Sykes with Thin Lizzy on different tours was absolutely amazing. Phil always had a way to fill that side of the stage with extremely talented guitarists. Damn, they were great.

THE PALLADIUM

22 OCTOBER 1977, NEW YORK, NEW YORK

I WAS THERE: MARIO CORD, AGE 16

I saw them at the New York Academy of Music on 14th Street which was renamed the Palladium. I was in high school. I remember Phil on the middle with the two guitarists on either side. He was a great showman clad in leather pants. They were tight and had a great sound. His singing was excellent and the two axemen took turns playing solos. The drummer was in the back pounding out a steady rhythm. They were very professional and well rehearsed. I went to the concert with my best friend John Tyrcha and enjoyed it very much. 'The Boys are Back in Town' is my favourite song of theirs.

UPTOWN THEATER

5 NOVEMBER 1977, CHICAGO, ILLINOIS

I WASN'T THERE: JODI PAULSEN

My guitar tutor saw them in Chicago. He said he went down to the hotel and Phil Lynott was running around with a hair dryer in his pants!

The UK *Bad Reputation* tour kicked off in Newcastle and saw Lizzy play 28 dates in 37 days, including four London dates.

CITY HALL

11 NOVEMBER 1977, NEWCASTLE, UK

I WAS THERE: DAVID FRAZER, AGE 14

I saw them several times but the first time was the most memorable. After the show I managed to get backstage to meet the band with my friend Craig. The band were very friendly and gracious and signed autographs. It took a while for someone to translate what Craig was saying from Geordie into Irish so Phil could understand Craig's name!

ODEON THEATRE

14 NOVEMBER 1977, EDINBURGH, UK

I WAS THERE: GAVIN HOGG

I was 12 when 'Whiskey in the Jar' came out but I was well into my music. I queued up to buy *Tubular Bells* when it came out! I bought the album *Shades of a Blue Orphanage* and thought that was fantastic. Wishbone Ash had the same twin guitar concept as Thin Lizzy and I was getting into them. I saw Lizzy at the Edinburgh Odeon. It was the *Bad Reputation* line up with Brian Robertson and Scott Gorham. Phil's guitar had the mirrored back and he kept reflecting the lights onto the audience, mostly to spotlight the women. I remember the comment, 'Are there any women in the audience with any Irish in them? Would you like some?' He was a lad!

I WAS THERE: KEITH MCSHANE

The first Lizzy tour I saw was the *Bad Reputation* tour, in Edinburgh. Lights down. Are you ready? Boom! Smoke bombs! Audience reaction? Totally excited. Into 'Bad Reputation' and the hits. You don't stop clapping your hands. Mirror balls for starry effect for 'Cowboy Song' leading into 'Boys are Back in Town.' Crowd going mental. Near the end a never ending 'Baby Drives Me Crazy' with spotlight beaming off Phil's mirror pickguard as he was looking for a chick.

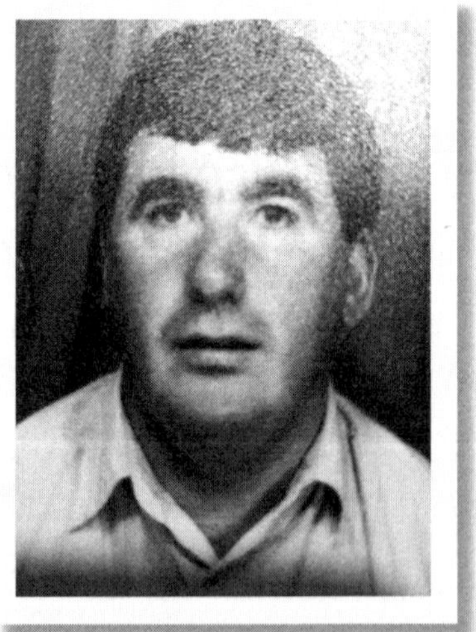

Keith McShane saw Lizzy a number of times

EMPIRE THEATRE

17 NOVEMBER 1977, LIVERPOOL, UK

I WAS THERE: GERARD SHELBOURNE

I first heard the band with the single 'Whiskey in the Jar' and started taking an interest in the band's music with the *Fighting* album and then *Jailbreak*. The release of *Bad Reputation* was my chance to get to see the band live and by then I had convinced a few friends to also buy tickets for the show.

I saw them a couple of times at Liverpool Empire, the first time with Radiators From Space as support. I remember Phil telling the audience the reason behind the mirrored bass was due to a girlfriend leaving him. The only item she left behind was a budgie cage and mirror, so each night thereafter he would hang the mirror off the bass guitar which then evolved into the version he was famous for!

I recently lost my son, and the music played at his funeral was 'Whiskey in the Jar' and 'Dancing in the Moonlight'. A verse from 'Southbound' was read out.

COLSTON HALL

22 NOVEMBER 1977, BRISTOL, UK

I WAS THERE: KEITH BOLLING, AGE 18

I saw Thin Lizzy twice, the first time the 'classic' line up; it was just like the *Live and Dangerous* album, with Lynott with his mirror bass and twin guitars from Robertson and Gorham. I'd been a few concerts by then but Thin Lizzy were just great. Afterwards we queued up for autographs and got to their room but were then told they'd had enough. I can remember them all slumped on chairs smoking and drinking. At that age to get within touching distance of a rock group was pretty epic.

The second time I saw them, with Gary Moore in 1979, they were just okay. Having seen them not much more than a year previously, it had less impact. Gary Moore had replaced Brian Robertson and I knew his solo stuff. In a weird way his guitar work, which was of virtuoso quality on the *Black Rose* album, was almost too good and didn't quite slot into the Lizzy set up. Phil Lynott looked tired as if he was going through the motions. That second concert was on at the same time as Kate Bush was playing Bristol and I now wish I'd seen Ms Bush!

About five years later I was with my dad and a relative who used to have the odd beer with Brian Robertson's dad, and he said Brian was struggling with drink and wasn't playing much, which I thought was pretty sad.

Brian Downey was a great drummer - really tight. His live playing on the 'Bad Reputation' song was cracking and I always liked that song because of his drumming. He was underrated. They were a great band.

I WAS THERE: MARK WILLIAMS

It was the summer of '76 and I was fully into my Quo phase... and then it happened. I saw it on *Top of the Pops*. 'The Boys are Back in Town' he sang, this cool lanky black dude, with the obligatory Afro, with his band weaving their harmonised celtic magic. I was hooked. Me and my school mate discovered them at the same moment, and we became obsessed. We began buying all the albums, and the back catalogue when we could afford them, starting with *Jailbreak*, that summer's hit album, swiftly followed by *Johnny the Fox*. We narrowly missed out on tickets for that tour, having left it too late. Damn!

Bad Reputation was released and we got tickets. It's the first gig I went to that I would class as a real gig. We sat patiently through the Radiators From Space but were not impressed. Eventually the lights went down, the amp lights shone through the dry ice and they strolled on and went straight into 'Soldier of Fortune'. Phil's bass mirror scratch plate aimed beams of light at the audience – so cool! – and 90 minutes later it was all over. The obsession had only been heightened.

Over the years, the albums were released, the band rolled into town on each tour and we were there every time. We even saw The Eric Bell Band and met Eric, and Wild Horses and met Brian Robertson. That was two heroes ticked off the 'meeting' list!

Then, on the *Chinatown* tour… I met God. We hung around after the show, and eventually were ushered backstage (as you frequently could be in those days) and there we met them, including my hero… all six foot one of him! The band were so friendly and welcoming, and I was so relieved, as they say 'you shouldn't meet your heroes!' There was no fear of that here. And after a quick chat and some autographs, off we all disappeared off into the night, thoroughly satisfied.

I WAS THERE: KELLY RAVEL

I wasn't a fan until I got to be invited to all their shows as a guest – I was a Bowie fan. But I used to be a freelance interviewer for the BBC in my early 20s and so I got to interview Thin Lizzy in my home town of Bristol when they played the Colston Hall in 1977. It was a fun interview. Phil did all the talking but the others were all smiling. He was such a fun guy, sweet and kinda shy. We remained friends for years. I saw him every time they came to Bristol from 1977 to 1982. Every time he was there, he would say he had searched half of Bristol looking for me. What a lovely guy he was. I was honoured to be given his *Black Rose* album and be invited to the after show get together. In the early Eighties, when my boyfriend was in a band, Lizzy's support didn't turn up at the Colston Hall and Phil asked me if my boyfriend's band would fill in and support them.

I was working in Paris when on my return flight to London I saw they were at Hammersmith so I called by to their dressing room. Phil and Gary Moore were in there, strumming. Phil looked so sick I was worried about him. That was the last time I saw him.

CITY HALL

23 NOVEMBER 1977, SHEFFIELD, UK

I WAS THERE: BRIAN BANNISTER

I was the youngest of five children, with a father who loved music of all genres and a brother who was nine years older than me and playing in a local rock band. Warrior were influenced by the great twin lead bands of that era, Wishbone Ash and Thin Lizzy, so I had those amazing guitar riffs and one-of-a-kind vocals thrust into my eardrums from an early age. One of Warrior's favourite tracks to play was 'Jailbreak'. It always went down a storm, although their home-made pyrotechnics would not get through health and safety checks today.

I began collecting Lizzy vinyls whilst working on a record stall on Chesterfield Market and was soon hooked. My first Lizzy gig was at Sheffield City Hall. I remember Phil's charisma and the awesome sound that had my ears ringing for a week afterwards. I saw Lizzy several more times and saw Phil join Gary Moore on stage for 'Soldier of Fortune' on Gary's *Back on the Streets* tour, an unexpected but brilliant treat.

I last saw Gary Moore the year before he died, at the *Hard Rock Hell Festival* in London. He still had the same blues feel he'd always had. And in the late Eighties we'd seen Eric Bell at a really tiny club in Bolsover. I very nearly walked out when he pretty much ruined 'Whiskey in the Jar', playing all the right notes but definitely not in the right order!

In 2008, we decided to have a fancy dress 'music awards' party and asked our guests to dress up as someone from the music world. I wrote to the Thin Lizzy fan club to ask if they had any posters I could decorate the house with. The following Sunday, the phone rang about 10pm and my wife answered. She seemed somewhat stunned as she passed me the phone saying, 'It's Philomena.' Sure enough, it was Phil's mum, calling me and saying how she appreciated the letter and would like to help but could someone collect some 'bits' from her home in Dublin. Luckily, my wife's cousin lived close to Dublin and just happened to be a Lizzy fan too, so he was delighted to be able to help. He took along his two musician sons and friend of theirs who played in a Lizzy tribute band called Renegade. Philomena let them play Phil's bass and gave them lots of memorabilia, including a framed photo of Phil for me.

This was the start of a lovely relationship between these boys and Philomena. She was so kind to them, asking them to perform at several events she and Smiley organised over the following years, including the *Vibe for Philo* that I was thrilled to be invited to. Philomena was so appreciative of the love and support for her son and his music, and particularly the fact that I had taken time to send a letter.

I WAS THERE: KEVIN FERGUSON, AGE 20

The first album I bought was *Jailbreak* and I was already a huge Thin Lizzy fan before I went to see them at Sheffield City Hall. My friend and I caught the train as neither of us had a car and the City Hall was close to the station. The concert was truly awesome. The concert was loud

Kevin Ferguson saw Lizzy at Sheffield City Hall

and Phil got the crowd going, using his guitar scratch pad to turn the spotlight back onto the audience. 'Jailbreak' really got things hopping, especially with the lighting and smoke effects, and the crowd were rowdy but exceptionally well behaved. I saw no sign of trouble and only a lot of smiling happy faces. We crashed at a friend's place. Next day, I caught the train home and my ears were ringing so badly I couldn't hear the conductor asking for my ticket. It was three days before my hearing returned to normal, but I loved every minute of the experience.

How big of a fan am I? I have every album and, better still, my adult children are big fans too.

I WAS THERE: KEVIN DRISCOLL

I had heard some of their songs round at people's houses when I went to parties, but it was when I was driving home from a night shift one time and 'Suicide' came on the radio that I thought, 'Crikey, this is brilliant.' The radio said that they were playing at the City Hall in Sheffield that Saturday and my mate, who was a big Quo fan, was always going on about them. I said, 'Do you fancy a ride up on Saturday to see if we can get in?' There were loads of people outside, and ticket outs, so we went round the side to the box office. It was open but there was nobody in it.

We walked in and a man said, 'Can I help you?' and I said, 'Is there any chance of any tickets for tonight's gig?' He went off, came back and said, 'How many do you want?' They'd had some returns and we were two rows from the front of the stage, right in the middle. It was the *Bad Reputation* tour and they opened up with 'Soldier of Fortune'. It was an absolutely brilliant gig. As we were driving home that night I said to my friend, the absolute Quo nutter, 'What did you think of that then?' and he said, 'Best band ever.'

ST GEORGE'S HALL

24 NOVEMBER 1977, BRADFORD, UK

I WAS THERE: GLENN DAY

I got hooked on Thin Lizzy when I was 18 and my mates at work bought me 'Whiskey in the Jar' on vinyl 45 rpm for my birthday. I first saw Lizzy at St George's Hall in Bradford. It was the iconic Robertson – Gorham line up. The standout song was 'Still in Love with You' and everything was played with such precision it was just like listening to the record.

Glenn Day (right) and his wife were invited by Phil's mum Philomena (centre) to visit her shrine to Phil

I WAS THERE: JOHN CES HESELTINE

From 1973 until 1976, I was a 10cc fanatic, with Status Quo thrown into the mix. But one day I heard a song on the radio… something about some boys being back in town. I thought that it sounded good, but really didn't get too excited about it. But I heard it again, and again, and then I couldn't wait to hear it yet again, flicking from radio station to radio station just hoping to hear a few lines from it.

I found out it was from an album called *Jailbreak*. I was only 15 so I begged my parents for double pocket money so I could buy the album. Thankfully, they gave into me and I jumped on the bus into town to buy it. *Jailbreak* was soon in my hands. I was absolutely blown away by it, and couldn't get over 'Emerald'. I played it to death for months. Then I heard that a new album called *Bad Reputation* was coming out and that Lizzy were going on tour - and coming to my home town of Bradford. Needless to say, when the tickets went on sale I was in the queue.

When the lights went down and 'Soldier of Fortune' started up, I became addicted to Thin Lizzy for the rest of my life. Even today I still listen to them on a daily basis and watch the live concerts.

Phil Lynott and Thin Lizzy have been a massive part of my life growing up. Now, at the age of 61, the memories of seeing them live twice and the friends I made through their music will stay with me forever.

FREE TRADE HALL

25 & 26 NOVEMBER 1977, MANCHESTER, UK

I WAS THERE: PETER TINDALL

I saw Lizzy 14 times on different tours in Sheffield, Liverpool, Stafford and mostly in Manchester. My brother John and I followed them for a long time. My first tour was *Bad Reputation* at the Free Trade Hall in Manchester and the last time I saw them was Reading Rock Festival in 1983. My favourite track is 'Opium Trail' and my favourite tour was probably *Black Rose* or *Renegade*. I loved them live. I still have all my tickets.

THE DOME

28 NOVEMBER 1977, BRIGHTON, UK

I WAS THERE: PETER THOMSON

I had loved 'Whiskey in the Jar' but in 1975 Lizzy had yet to enjoy a follow up hit. I first saw them at that year's Reading Rock Festival. They were far from the headliners, playing an afternoon slot, but so too were Supertramp and other luminaries of the next few years. I was impressed by that Reading gig, as were many others.

With the release of 'The Boys are Back in Town' and a flurry of other hit singles, not to mention the albums, I was delighted that a proper rock band was punching above its weight against punk rock. I couldn't wait to see them again and acquired tickets for their 1977 Brighton Dome gig. We arrived to find our seats were where the mixing desk had been installed,

Peter Thomson saw Lizzy in Brighton and London

whereupon a steward quickly descended on us to apologise and move us to complimentary seats in Row F. That experience set them on a pedestal for me. I had seen most touring acts of that time, including Queen the previous autumn, but none had the polish, stage presence or visual spectacle of Thin Lizzy.

GUILDHALL

29 NOVEMBER 1977, PORTSMOUTH, UK

I WAS THERE: CLAIRE JACKSON

I followed a local covers band in Portsmouth who played many Thin Lizzy tracks. 'The Boys are Back in Town' was their signature tune and, as a 15-year-old, I was hooked onto live music and transitioned from my teenybop taste of David Essex to Thin Lizzy. I bought all their albums and first saw them live at Portsmouth Guildhall with my bestie, Suzie. I met the band afterwards - I had a bit of a crush on Brian Robertson.

I had gained a bit of a reputation for being 'lucky' at meeting my favourite people, having met David Essex amongst others. On December 16th, 1978, Suzie and I went to the Electric Ballroom in London to see The Greedies, the Lizzy/Rats/Pistols collaboration where we met Bob Geldof and Scott Gorham.

Claire Jackson first saw Lizzy in '77 and got backstage in '79

I WAS THERE: STEVE PAGE, AGE 15

There was music in my life from a very young age. My parents were regular Prom goers and saw the big stage musicals - *South Pacific*, *Seven Brides for Seven Brothers.* I still have all my dad's 78s. I went to classical concerts and I had three brothers - the two older ones were into rock so we had anything from Bowie to T.Rex to Sammy Hagar, Blue Oyster Cult, Rainbow, Led Zep and Deep Purple.

I discovered Lizzy on the back of *Jailbreak* and then *Bad Reputation*. I was lucky enough to get tickets for Portsmouth Guildhall and went with my younger brother and my then girlfriend. I had the cut off denim with all the badges, jeans and lace up DM boots - you get the picture. There were no seats and the unappreciated support band - Radiators From Space – got pelted with beer. The atmosphere began to build to show time but, this being my first time at a live rock concert, I wasn't sure what to expect.

The lights went down and all hell broke loose, with everyone charging for the front. The lights came up and we were four or five back from the stage as Lizzy exploded into 'Soldier of Fortune', with the dry ice clearing to reveal Phil just 20 feet away from me. From that moment, I was hooked. The power and the charisma of this black Irishman mesmerised the whole audience. 'Opium Trail' was dark and thunderous. How could it get any better?

WINTER GARDENS

30 NOVEMBER 1977, BOURNEMOUTH, UK

I WAS THERE: MARTIN BATCHELOR, AGE 17

I can honestly say this was the best concert I've ever been to. As a 17-year-old I was mesmerised by how fantastic they sounded. Seven encores too! I went with a friend, a work colleague who'd got me into Lizzy. I had borrowed his copy of *Johnny the*

Martin Batchelor saw Lizzy deliver a knockout show

Fox which blew me away and I went out and bought it for myself soon afterwards, followed quickly by *Jailbreak*. After the concert, I bought *Bad Reputation* and when *Live and Dangerous* came out, I got it straight away. In my opinion it's the greatest live album of all time.

Live and Dangerous is the greatest live album of all time

ODEON THEATRE

2 & 3 DECEMBER 1977, BIRMINGHAM, UK

I WAS THERE: JEFF COLLINS

I'll always remember the start of this show, when the dry ice swirled around and Phil sang the opening line of 'Soldier of Fortune'. I can still see Brian and Scott walking out of the dry ice fog as the twin guitars kicked in. From that night Lizzy became one of my all time favourite bands.

I WAS THERE: DAVE PEAKE

A few of us from school had got tickets. The place was jumping and I was transfixed by Robbo. The next time I saw them was on the *Chinatown* tour, Snowy White's first. They were still a great band but some of the magic had gone. And then I saw them do a blistering set in '83 with John Sykes, when they had got some of their mojo back. What a shame it was to be the last tour as Lizzy. I got to see Phil again with Grand Slam with the young Lawrence Archer. I think they were destined for great things, but that was sadly cut short.

I think myself lucky I got to see them.

Dave Peake was transfixed by Robbo

DE MONTFORT HALL

5 DECEMBER 1977, LEICESTER, UK

I WAS THERE: MARK SMIGGY SMITH

I failed to get tickets for this gig and was so mortified I even entered a competition in what I considered the inferior (to the *NME*) *Melody Maker* to try and win tickets. My diary entry for that day reads:

Chris Moore and Tessa came to my room. 'Do you still want to go and see Lizzy?' 'Yes.' 'Right, you're going.' Tessa didn't want to go, so she let me have her ticket. I was speechless. We went in my van and the concert was brilliant, as usual. Some songs from *Bad Reputation*, *Jailbreak*, one from *Nightlife* and two or three I didn't know, plus the usual singalongs and stompers that we all knew.

CAPITOL THEATRE

8 DECEMBER 1977, CARDIFF, UK

I WAS THERE: DAI BARRY, AGE 14

I saw Lizzy play the very last concert at Cardiff's Capitol Theatre. The following week they started work on turning it into a bingo hall. I went down to Cardiff on the train with two friends. We met a couple of other friends there who we didn't know were going. It was a great gig with an amazing atmosphere. Phil opened the show with, 'I hear you have a football team around here,' which went down well with the crowd. During the show loads of joints were being thrown on the stage and Phil picked one up and put it behind his ear to another loud cheer.

Nobody was sat down. They were either shaking their hair and heads or playing air guitar to the duelling guitars of Scott and Brian. 'Emerald' was a big crowd favourite and Phil had the crowd singing and repeating his lines to 'Baby Drives

Dai Barry saw the last ever gig at Cardiff's Capitol Theatre before it became a bingo hall

Me Crazy'. It was an amazing sound. The acoustics in that hall were brilliant. They played the obligatory encore and the crowd were calling very loudly for another, but then the lights came on and so it was a sharp dash to catch the last train. We were all in awe and talked about the gig for a whole week afterwards.

I WAS THERE: NIGEL COTTRELL, AGE 15

Thin Lizzy were playing Cardiff so being 15 I did what I needed to do and skipped school. Hanging around the back stage door with my friend, we started to offer to help. We asked so many times that I think the roadies just gave in and so we started helping them lift the kit in. They opened one box and I saw it was the mirrored Lizzy sign, folded in half. It was a bit battered with some of the little mirrored tiles missing. Then we sat down as they started doing the sound check, with Robbo going for it on drums. Later I flashed the backstage pass that had been given to me and there they were in front of me. Phil signed my programme first, followed by the others. Great times. My pride and joy is my signed *Bad Reputation* tour programme.

Nigel Cottrell and his friend got to help on the load in and got his programme signed

HAMMERSMITH ODEON

10 & 11 DECEMBER 1977, LONDON, UK

I WAS THERE: ANDY BENNETT

Thin Lizzy were my first serious band after growing up on Slade and Sweet. My dad was into military band music, my mum Glen Miller and my sister liked pop music like Abba. Lizzy was my escape. I remember

Andy Bennett saw Lizzy several times

skipping school in Hammersmith to go and buy tickets. The twin lead guitars and Phil Lynott's voice were unique. I saw them on the *Bad Reputation* tour and each tour after that, to start with just at Hammersmith Odeon and then later at Portsmouth, Southampton, Brighton and even Norwich. I worshipped the whole band. I also saw Wild Horses, with Brian Robertson and Jimmy Bain, and Gary Moore in various places.

I was at college in Luton when I heard about Phil's death. I was devastated and played all the albums from *Johnny the Fox* onwards for about a month until my housemates starting hiding my albums. I was driving them mad.

We always thought Scott Gorham was as cool as Phil. He had that long mane of hair to his waist and always had a style where his jeans and shirt would match. He was often all in white or in red. He made guitar playing look so calm and effortless. One night on the *Black Rose* tour I was in the front row, straight in front of him. I put my hand up and he bent down and shook my hand. It was half way through a gig under the lights and his hand literally was cool. I was amazed and honoured!

I WAS THERE: KAREN DILLON, AGE 15

I've been a Thin Lizzy fan since I was 14. I played their music endlessly in my room. I had a crush on the boy next door. He was the same age, he was cute, had long hair (he was half Persian) and he was something of a rebel. When he asked if I'd like to go to a Lizzy gig I jumped at the chance. We went with a group of his mates - all dressed in double denim. This was my first gig apart from Rush and I was blown away by how good Lizzy were. In some ways they were my awakening. The sound was electric and I felt energised and alive, my shy young Catholic girl upbringing slipping away. We all dressed in double denim and had our Lizzy mirror badges pinned to our denim cutdowns. I played *Bad Reputation* in my room endlessly. Something about Phil's voice gave me comfort and lifted my soul.

A few years later, I was with a different boyfriend and we saw Lizzy at Wembley Arena for the *Live and Dangerous* tour. I loved it, but it didn't have the same feel as the previous gig because the boyfriend I went with wasn't automatically a fan. I absolutely loved 'Still in Love with You' and it made me think of my childhood sweetheart. But the boyfriend I went to the gig with turned up at my door the next day with the *Live and Dangerous* album, which I played endlessly.

I was devastated to read in the *News of the World* that Phil had died. I was pregnant with my daughter. I wanted to call her Sarah but my ex-husband had other ideas and we named her Amber. I wrote to Philomena after Phil passed and was gobsmacked to receive a handwritten reply. What a wonderful woman. There was no pretentiousness, she just loved her son until the day she died. I'm happy that they're now together.

Lizzy's music will live on in all our hearts

I WAS THERE: JOHN TRUMAN

I was living in Bexleyheath in South London. I was 13 and my ears were beginning to open up to things other than what was in the charts. I was listening to music round a friend's house and he had an older brother who was into what is now known as classic rock. The album that really jumped out at me was *Jailbreak*. I thought, 'What on earth is this?' I'd not heard anything like that before. I lapped up everything I could about them and started to buy the albums. I was smitten.

In December 1977 my parents somehow agreed that I could travel into central London with my friends to see Lizzy on the understanding that we stayed at the house of one of my friend's grandmothers, who lived around the corner from the Hammersmith Odeon. We travelled up on the bus on a Red Rover ticket. Brian Robertson was on guitar with Scott Gorham and I was blown away. They were playing the *Bad Reputation* album and it's still to this day my favourite album. It brings back such memories and the songs are so strong and the melodies amazing.

Every time Lizzy played London, my friends and I would travel into London to see them, so we saw Gary Moore on the *Black Rose* tour and then Snowy White and onto John Sykes in the Eighties with the *Thunder and Lightning* album. I must've seen them easily a dozen times, if not more. The gigs themselves were always brilliant. Phil Lynott was just a complete and utter showman. I was even at the Rainbow gig in '78 which I've still got the ticket for where they videoed the performance of the *Live and Dangerous* tour. I think the ticket cost £1.50. We had really good seats.

LEWISHAM ODEON

13 & 14 DECEMBER 1977, LONDON, UK

I WAS THERE: STEVE CAVALLI, AGE 18

I first heard Lizzy on the radio with 'Whiskey in the Jar' in 1972 and bought it. I was 13. I started work in 1975 and the following year bought *Jailbreak* and began following them properly, buying all their albums. I first saw them at the Reading Festival in 1977, and saw them again at Lewisham Odeon in south east London, supported by the Radiators From Space. Both times they were fantastic, and Phil Lynott was one of the greatest frontmen ever.

Steve Cavalli saw Lizzy twice

I WAS THERE: AHMET ÖZ KELES-AHMET

We managed to get to the front, after the flash bombs went off, and Phil was sweating so much it was dripping down onto us!

I WAS THERE: DAVID HEWITT, AGE 14

I had bought *Bad Reputation* so I was familiar with the songs before the concert. I went with my older sister. We lived down the road in Greenwich. I arrived extra early and stood outside the main doors waiting to get in. I could hear them sound checking 'Soldier of Fortune'. Phil Lynott wore black leather trousers and played a black bass guitar with a silver scratch plate, which he used to keep reflecting the spotlight back into the crowd. And there was a drawbridge running into the crowd from the centre of the stage so Phil was performing up and down the bridge. Scott Gorham on lead guitar was amazing and had straight hair flowing down below his waist. It was a fantastic gig. They really blew the roof off.

David Hewitt (left) saw the *Bad Reputation* tour

KURSAAL BALLROOM

17 DECEMBER 1977, SOUTHEND-ON-SEA, UK

I WAS THERE: PAUL LANGRIDGE

Radiators From Space were the support. It was billed as the Boomtown Rats, but because they had a bit of chart action, Geldof felt he was too important to be a support act. No loss, really. Lizzy were mind-blowingly awesome. It was one of my first dates with my girlfriend, who is now my wife. My mate, Chip, had a girlfriend called Ursula. She wandered around the back of the theatre to have a smoke and ended up sharing a spliff with Phil! We saw Lizzy again at the Rainbow Theatre and that was good, but the Kursaal gig is still one of the best gigs I ever saw.

Paul Langridge and his girlfriend were at the Kursaal Ballroom

---

The Kursaal gig is still one of the best gigs I ever saw

Although the album *Live and Dangerous*, which was released in 1978, was culled from performances which included the Hammersmith Odeon show on 14 November 1976, a gig at the Rainbow Theatre on 29 March 1978 was filmed for a television broadcast but never aired.

RAINBOW THEATRE

29 MARCH 1978, LONDON, UK

I WAS THERE: LESLIE GILBERT

I was a teenage rock fan and I attended the *Live and Dangerous* concert. I was leaning on the stage and at one point Phil actually passed me his orange juice.

I recall the tickets were around £1 or £1.50, the idea being to fill the hall including the aisles (health and safety wasn't a thing then!). The concert was so atmospheric and crowded, and I believe it is often described as the best live rock concert of all time. The crush in the crowd was so hard that I experienced a lit cigarette going out on my bum cheek (dropped into my jeans), chest bruising for six weeks and a girl's naked breast bouncing on my shoulder from behind. As I left the concert I noticed that the first ten rows of seats were demolished and that the barriers from the mezzanine above had fallen.

In the Nineties my family become friendly with Philomena. We met with her a number of times and we were invited to the unveiling of Phil's statue and the tribute gig. It was very poignant.

I WAS THERE: PAUL BEARD

I saw Lizzy dozens of times from '76 to '83, including the legendary Finsbury Park Rainbow gig that was to become *Live and Dangerous*. I had loads of tour programmes but many years ago, the wife made me get rid of all of them plus my vinyl. I put them up on eBay. Most had tour ticket stubs stapled inside and a guy bought them all because he was collecting ticket stubs. He wasn't really interested in the tour brochures.

At another Lizzy gig I stood next to Bob Geldof, Paula Yates and Johnnie Fingers. I was too shy to speak to them.

I WAS THERE: STEVE PARSONS

I saw them at the Rainbow in north London and at the Corn Exchange in Bury and Camden. I always remember that you couldn't sit down when they did a gig. You'd always be up and dancing. Phil Lynott was very talented. He said, 'There was only one guitarist who could play lead on 'Whiskey in the Jar' and that was Eric Bell.'

PINK POP FESTIVAL

15 MAY 1978, GELEEN, THE NETHERLANDS

I WAS THERE: HANS REUSER

I saw Thin Lizzy at Pinkpop in 1978. I was 18 at the time. They were sharing the bill with Journey, Graham Parker and Mother's Finest. Lizzy were and are my favourite band. I now play as a bassist and singer in a band that covers six Lizzy songs.

Hans Reuser plays in a band that covers Lizzy

I WAS THERE: GARY HURST

In May 1978 I was lucky enough to travel to Geleen in The Netherlands with the Thin Lizzy Fan Club to see them perform at the Pink Pop Festival. Lizzy topped the bill and there were six support bands, including Journey and Graham Parker and the Rumour. Thanks to the fan club I was able to meet the band after the gig. I had a chat with Phil and Scott, both very friendly, and had pictures taken with Phil, Scott and Robbo. Brian Downey kept himself to himself and chatted to a roadie in the middle of an ice rink! The compere for the festival was the legendary John Peel and I managed to get a photo with him in the car park.

LIVE AND DANGEROUS RELEASED
2 JUNE 1978
UK CHART POSITION 2
US CHART POSITION 84

Possibly the most written about live album ever, after reports suggesting most of the album was overdubbed and therefore not live at all, *Live and Dangerous* captures Lizzy at their absolute best, including Phil's between song banter.

Gary Hurst met Thin Lizzy backstage at the Pink Pop Festival

Gary Hurst met John Peel at the Pink Pop Festival

Doing an 'in concert' album this way was cheating, slightly, but the album is about 55% live and the overdubs gave the poorly recorded performances a more uniform sound. **Tony Visconti, Producer**

BELLE VUE

8 JUNE 1978, MANCHESTER, UK

I WAS THERE: GORDON FURNESS

I was a 22-year-old British soldier stationed in Belgium. Lizzy were my favourite band - and still are! I was due to be posted to Hong Kong for two years at the beginning of August and begged my sergeant to let me have some time off to see them somewhere in England. Sergeant Lopata allowed me two days off - 8 and 9 June. I cut the application form out of the *NME* and posted my cheque off. But as the gig was in a week's time, I couldn't risk my ticket not getting to Belgium in time. I included a short letter on my blue writing paper asking for the ticket to be left at the box office for me to collect on the day.

On the day, an army Land Rover took me to the nearest railway station to the camp where I caught a train to Zeebrugge, changing at Antwerp, and then a four hour ferry to Dover, a train to Waterloo, the underground to Euston and a train up to Manchester. I then caught a bus to Belle Vue and sat at the front, asking the bus driver to tell me when to get off. I got off and followed the hordes of Lizzy fans to the venue. But when I got to box office there was no ticket for me!

Eventually, the duty manager was called. He went away and came back with my sheet of blue writing paper with the ticket attached. He asked for ID but I couldn't show him my army ID card as squaddies were warned to be careful about displaying their army ID due to the prevailing IRA threat on the UK mainland.

He was reluctant to give me the ticket until I told him word for word what was on the sheet of blue writing paper he was holding. What clinched it was my address in Belgium BFPO (British Forces Post Office) 21. He asked where that was. I told him Belgium and that I had been travelling all day to get there. He was gobsmacked that anyone would come alone, travelling all day from Belgium to see Thin Lizzy. He gave me the ticket and allowed me to leave my small backpack and leather bomber jacket in the office and collect these after the gig.

I was blown away by Lizzy's performance. They were at the height of their powers and it was the *Live and Dangerous* set. At the end of the gig, very sweaty but still reeling, I went to the office to collect my gear. Chris Morrison - or possibly Chris O'Donnell, I can't remember which - was in the office talking to the duty manager who said I must be Lizzy's most 'fervent' fan as I had travelled from Belgium for the gig.

Chris asked if I wanted to meet the band. I said, 'Yes please!' and he took me backstage where the roadies were packing all the gear away. I recall box after box with Thin Lizzy stencilled in silver onto black. Chris stood me next to a young girl who was also going backstage and said he would be back soon, and then he left. The girl talked to me about her favourite tracks off the previous album, *Nightlife*. I had all the previous five albums, which impressed her.

Ten minutes later Chris reappeared and let us to mingle in a room with around 20 people in it, including Phil, Scott and Brian Downey. There was a hostess trolley filled with booze. I asked the girl what she wanted to drink and got us both cans of Tennants lager. Brian Robertson wasn't there as he was in a huff and had already left with a couple of girls and a couple of bottles of whisky. I felt like a fish out of water.

There were no seats in the room and we stood overlooking where Scott and Brian Downey were sat on the floor, playing cards with a number of girls around them while the local news reporter was trying to get an interview. Phil was stood in the corner, talking to England and Manchester United winger Steve Coppell. Scott looked up at the girl and me and asked if we enjoyed the gig, to which we replied enthusiastically in the affirmative! Brian looked up and said 'hi'. I thought how humble and down to earth they both were. This put me at ease and I started savouring this unique experience.

All the while I was glancing across at Phil, waiting for my chance to talk to him. Eventually Steve Coppell and his gorgeous lady moved away and I immediately made a beeline towards Phil. I was speechless and he could see that. He smiled a big beaming smile and I asked, 'Do you like football?' It was the first thing that popped into my head because he had just been talking to Steve Coppell. He said, 'Yeah, who's your team?' I said, 'Man U,' which was also my dad's team. He said, 'Mine too!' We then talked for 15 minutes or more about Manchester United and the situation with Georgie Best leaving Manchester United, etc. I didn't know at the time that Phil was good mates with George Best.

Having packed all the gear away, the roadies started piling into the room and opening cans of beer. Everyone then moved onto a new disco in Manchester city centre. I just followed the crowd and no one batted an eyelid. Outside were two white limos for the band, managers and the duly selected dozen or so girls including the one I talked to earlier. She was quite cute!

The roadies and I jumped into taxis to the disco. We were all in the VIP lounge reserved for Thin Lizzy plus entourage. This was a dream come true for a young but switched on lad from a working class background. I remember somehow ending up in this small hotel in the early hours where the roadies were staying. The roadies took around half a dozen girls the band didn't want back to the hotel. I copped off with the young girl who I had first spoken to. I'm sure she would have preferred copping off with Phil, Scott or Brian Downey but she hadn't been selected. One of the roadies was sniffing round her but she wasn't interested. I reckon the fact that I had been in deep conversation with Phil at Belle Vue and a couple of times in the VIP lounge later clinched her interest in me, plus our first meeting and chat. She kept asking me how I knew Phil, like we were big buddies!

I caught the last ferry from Dover around midnight and slept in the ferry terminal in Zeebrugge, waiting for the first train back to Antwerp and then on to camp. I had some wonderful tales to tell my Army mates and my Sergeant.

ULSTER HALL

14 & 15 JUNE 1978, BELFAST, UK

I WAS THERE: STEPHEN BARRY, AGE 19

I bought *Jailbreak* shortly after leaving school in 1976 and it was awesome hearing Phil and the boys blasting it out. I went to see Lizzy a couple of times. The first time was in the Ulster Hall in Belfast and the gig featured a lot of the songs that ended up on *Live and Dangerous*. I went with my then girlfriend Maddie (now my wife). I would have been 19 at the time and Maddie 18. The Ulster Hall is such an amazing, intimate hall that served Belfast well through the worst of the Troubles in the Seventies, although plenty of bands gave Belfast a swerve. We were on the ground floor where there were seats, not that we sat for any part of the gig! We were quite close to the front, so had a great view of the show. It was my favourite Lizzy line up, with Brian Robertson and Scott Gorham on lead guitars.

Stephen Barry and girlfriend Maddie were at the Ulster Hall

APOLLO THEATRE

17 JUNE 1978, GLASGOW, UK

I WAS THERE: CRAIG STEWART

I first saw them in June 1978 in Glasgow with Gary Moore. I then saw them a couple of times with Snowy and a few times after with John Sykes, including Reading '83. Every gig was amazing in its own way. Seeing Gary Moore play with Lizzy was great and Phil wore a Scotland football top!

Craig Stewart first saw Lizzy at the Glasgow Apollo

I WAS THERE: ROBERT GOODWIN, AGE 16

I saw them on my 16th birthday. My mate who was with me had screen printed two t-shirts at school with a silhouette of the cover of the *Fighting* album. People in the queue were asking where they could buy them! It's the best gig ever and I've been to hundreds since then.

I WAS THERE: KEN ANDERSON

Ken Anderson met Phil in the local bookshop

I saw Thin Lizzy at the Apollo on the second night of their two sell out concerts in 1978, when they were probably at the height of their popularity. It was an awesome gig and the first one, I think, where fluorescent wristbands were sold. The place was awash with them. That very morning, I was downtown and as I walked into John Smith's bookshop I came face to face with Phil Lynott, who was exiting. He looked impossibly tall and cool in a pair of green strides and snakeskin boots. Totally starstruck, I couldn't think of what to say to him but came out with, 'I think you're gallus and I've got all of your albums.' Mr Lynott fixed me with a withering sneer and disappeared off down the road!

I WAS THERE: PAUL RAS

Phil was wearing a Scotland top. It was when the World Cup was being held in Argentina. He said to the crowd, 'Any Irish girls in?' and then, 'Would you like some more Irish in you?' It was a brilliant concert and it feels like it was only yesterday.

I WAS THERE: PETER LAMONT

They were always brilliant. The greatest nights were with the classic line up, including Robbo, and which I saw three times. I met Phil and Robbo on the third occasion. It was the night Phil wore a Scotland top, during Argentina '78. He was a big Man U fan and he explained his Scotland top thus, saying that if it was good enough for Gordon McQueen, Martin Buchan, Willie Morgan and Lou Macari, it was good enough for him!

Lizzy were explosive as ever. That night was the first time I heard 'Waiting for an Alibi', which of course wound up on *Black Rose* with Gary Moore.

I WAS THERE: JOHN CAMPBELL

I saw Lizzy three times at the Apollo. They were always on top form and the guitarists always seemed to be outplaying each other, with Gary Moore trying his best. I have fond memories of Phil in a Scotland top and the spotlight reflecting off the mirror on his guitar and shining back into the audience.

KING'S HALL

18 JUNE 1978, BELLE VUE, MANCHESTER, UK

I WAS THERE: TIM ROBERTS

I was aware of Lizzy in the mid Seventies from a distance whilst still at senior school. I remembered seeing them on *Top of the Pops* with 'Whiskey', 'Jailbreak' and 'The Boys…'. But it was when I was on a school coach trip across Europe in October 1977 that we seemed to have three songs on continuous loop on the coach – 'Dancing in the Moonlight', 'We are the Champions' by Queen and 'Black is Black' by Baccara. When I returned home, I immediately bought *Bad Reputation* with my milk round money.

I put it on my small Fidelity record player and, after the introduction of 'Soldier of Fortune' I was hooked on the band for life. The vocals and guitar playing just sucked me in and the balance between hard rock and more medolic tunes was great. As a wannabe drummer I had also found my hero in Brian Downey. I took the album to our local village youth club where we had an air guitar room and my friends were soon converted to 'Bad Reputation' and 'Killer without a Cause'. We got such a sweat on – in the moment!

It was back to the milk round money and I quickly bought the back catalogue of albums, joined the fan club and bought lots of t-shirts, badges and posters. So it was that, in late '77, *Jailbreak* became my favourite album. And remains so. The school youth club started to play 'Emerald' in the evening's heavy rock session which previously had all been about Status Quo. When the denim clad guys left the stage, it was just me and my t-shirt doing air guitar, with threatening looks from the Quo gang. Each week though, more and more joined me and soon the school had a good Lizzy following. I had a thing about playing the *Fighting* album before bed with the light off, especially the mood of 'Spirit Slips Away', a very underrated album.

My first gig was at Kings Hall, Belle Vue in June 1978 as part of the small number of *Live and Dangerous* concerts, the last ones with Robbo. I don't recall being aware of any infighting between the band at the time.

Me and three friends made a day of it, going over on the train from Leeds. The concert was the night before our Geography O level exam and we had no idea how we were going to get home. Our parents were less than impressed. We were first into the venue and spent well at the merchandise stand. When Lizzy came on one of my friends said I let out the biggest roar he had ever heard or seen. It was a top moment in my life and I still feel very lucky to have seen what I consider to be the best Lizzy line up. We ended up getting the paper train home in the early morning and so got to the afternoon exam – which I failed!

I WAS THERE: MICHAEL GREANEY

I remember someone telling me whilst I was still at school that Lizzy had released *Jailbreak*. I heard it on the radio so that weekend I went out and bought it and played it every night for months when I got home from work. There was no Google so to check for any back catalogue you had to go to the music store and look for it. As such I bought *Nightlife* (because I liked the album cover) and then *Johnny the Fox* came out, so I bought that. In 1977 This Lizzy announced a tour which took in Manchester so four of us bought tickets. Prior to the concert I bought *Fighting* so I now had the entire back catalogue of Robertson, Gorham, Downey and Lynott.

The concert was at Belle Vue in Manchester. I remember being close to the stage when the first explosion of 'Jailbreak' happened. There was a flash of light and smoke filled the stage and out of the mist appeared the band. The set was drawn from the last four albums, except for 'The Rocker'. (Lizzy had decided not to play 'Whiskey in the Jar' anymore.)

I was mesmerised by the look and sound of the band as they were much heavier than the albums and, as I stood outside, my ears were ringing and my heart was pounding. Although I had seen several bands previously, including Elton John and Nazareth, this was me taken even though I 'missed the last bus home' (now that should be in a Lizzy song).

I WAS THERE: MIKE GALWAY

I remember picking *Fighting* out of my friend's brother's album collection whilst I was at secondary school in 1976. Scott looked so cool on the cover! I had no doubts that they were a 'proper' rock band. They looked and sounded great, they rocked and they had hooks and appealed to both male and female fans. Owning *Live and Dangerous* was almost mandatory amongst my peers. It was a great album with plenty of fantastic photos to feast your eyes on in the gatefold and inner bags.

I saw them on every tour when they played Manchester from 1978 to 1983. Philip treated Manchester as his second home after Dublin and he always seemed to enjoy playing there. He was the ultimate rock star. Every gig I attended he would have the audience in the palm of his hand - clapping, stomping or coyote calling at his command. Whether flanked by Scott and Robbo, Gary, Snowy or John you were guaranteed a great night. Brian Downey was always fantastic and Darren added a splash of colour to the sound, which worked particularly well on the *Renegade* tour.

Being a big fan of the team from Trafford, he would hang a scarf with their colours on his mic stand. I'm a Blue but he obviously loved them so I could live with it. On the *Black Rose* tour, I went to both shows at the Apollo. On the second night I went with two mates. We had seats in the middle of the sixth or seventh row, although everyone spent the whole show on their feet. At one stage, Philip made eye contact with us and gave us the clenched fist. We all experienced the same thing and were buzzing on the bus home talking about it.

I was gutted when they pulled out of the Reading Festival in '79; they were due to headline Saturday night and were replaced at short notice by The Scorpions.

Although Snowy was a fine player he seemed a little reluctant to play the rock star on stage, whereas John certainly rose to the challenge on the final tour and was a great addition to the band.

In 1991 my only child was born, a beautiful daughter. My inspiration for her name came from Philip. I considered calling her Sarah but it could only be Roisin. She is my Roisin Dubh, my one and only true love.

I WAS THERE: RICHARD HUDSON, AGE 16

I'd bought *Johnny the Fox* and *Jailbreak* on cassette and was totally blown away by the songs that actually told a story with swagger, characters and drama. *Bad Reputation* was purchased on release, this time on vinyl - a much better format as you could get more information and pictures on the sleeve!

In those pre-internet days it was so much harder to find out about bands, but I often read *Sounds* magazine and saw that Lizzy were touring. I'd seen a few bands locally, but guessed (correctly) that the tour wouldn't come to my neck of the woods in Mansfield. But I was amazed to see in a local newspaper that a bus company actually ran trips to see bands, one of which was Thin Lizzy in Manchester! I have no recollection how much it cost, or how much pleading must have been involved with my parents to allow me to go, but I convinced them that all would be well and my mate John and I booked. We were just 16 years old.

Richard Hudson saw Lizzy at Belle Vue, Manchester

Even the bus trip was a revelation, 50-odd like-minded rockers all intent on having a good time. It was almost like being part of a tribe - a slightly crazy, hairy tribe, clad in denim, leather and Afghan coats and smelling of stale beer, fags and patchouli oil!

The venue was King's Hall, Belle Vue, Manchester, and I'd never seen a band in such a large space. The stage seemed huge, and whilst we weren't that near the front, we had a decent view. The support band was called The Drones. I'd never previously heard anything by them but they were okay, although the interval seemed to last forever.

Eventually the lights dimmed and accompanied by a huge cheer, flashing police lights, sirens and flash bombs, Lizzy simply tore into 'Jailbreak'. On the left was Robbo, the fiery young Scots guitarist, on the right, the effortlessly cool Californian Scott Gorham, and at the back was of course the fantastic Brian Downey.

Front and centre was Phil, pulling outrageous shapes from the off and pummelling his bass like his very life depended on it, with the spotlights glancing off its mirror scratch plate.

Not all the songs were familiar. I'd never heard 'Rosalie' for instance, but what a set, and all delivered with such style and passion – this was a band at the height of their powers, and for me their best line up. Phil had the crowd totally in the palm of his hand, effortlessly getting us on our feet, singing and clapping along, and the banter between songs seemed to come so easily to him. I've seen thousands of bands since, but nobody has the roguish mix of romeo/tough-guy/poet/rock star that made Phil the enigma that he was.

All too soon, the lights dimmed and the band were gone, but of course after we'd chanted 'Lizzy, Lizzy, Lizzy...' for a while, back they came to play a couple of (then unfamiliar) songs for an encore. Phil was wearing a Manchester City shirt – he was a big United fan, and back then there was often violence between the supporters of the two clubs, so this was quite a powerful gesture. For the last song, they were joined by Bob Geldof, Phil's friend and fellow countryman. 'Route 66' was gloriously ramshackle, a great way to end the gig.

The lights came up and we filed out and headed to the bus - I'm still not sure what I'd witnessed that night, but it left a lasting impression. On the bus, they had a raffle to win the newly released *Live and Dangerous* album... which I won! I still have it, and have of course bought the album in several different formats over the years, but I'll never part with the original.

After being dropped in town, we walked the couple of miles home (the last bus had long gone...), ears still ringing.

EMPIRE POOL

22 & 23 JUNE 1978, LONDON, UK

I WAS THERE: GARY HURST

At the beginning of June, the live album *Live and Dangerous* was released. Often cited as being the greatest live album of all time, it captures their stage performance brilliantly. The energy and power that Lizzy created on stage was amazing. The studio albums were great. They were always quite varied in that they included some slower songs and some mid-paced songs, but live everything was beefed up. It's an album that has stood the test of time and remains a perfect document of how brilliant a live band Lizzy were. The front cover photo, showing Phil on his knees in his leather strides, is an iconic image of the ultimate rock front man.

Another favourite gig for me was at the Empire Pool, Wembley. It was Lizzy's biggest gig to date with an audience of some 10,000. This was Lizzy at the height of their powers. I don't think it's an exaggeration to say that they were probably the best rock band on the planet at that time. All four members of the band just melded together in one hard hitting rock machine. They simply blew the roof off of Wembley. They even had a laser show. It wasn't spectacular, but everyone thought it was brilliant anyway. And the ticket price was just £4!

I WAS THERE: GREG HART

This was Robbo's last gig. They played embryonic versions of 'Alibi' and 'S&M'. Phil also dedicated 'Warriors' to 'Big Joe Jordan of Manchester United'. I was there and they were magic.

I WAS THERE: JS HOLFORD

I saw them from the VIP area at Wembley. I was only 12 at the time and wasn't really into them, but it was something for a bored boy to do. They used to come into my mum's pub in Pimlico. My mum became very good friends with Brian Robertson and he ended up giving her his gold disc for *Jailbreak*, which I've still got.

Photo Daniel Boss

Lizzy in action 1979

Photo Daniel Boss

I WAS THERE: PHIL ROSS

One of the oft repeated phrases about your teenage years is that you never forget your first. Usually, the context is a romantic one, but for me it also applies to the indelible impact of my first live gig - Thin Lizzy at the Empire Pool, Wembley, promoting their recently released (and now rightly revered) live double album, *Live and Dangerous*.

I was born on the border of Upper and South Norwood in South London. Just a few yards from my home, which was firmly in posher Upper Norwood, the administrative border ran right down the middle of the street. At the far end of the road was a modest looking detached house which had been owned by a drummer. One of his frequent house guests was Lonnie Donegan. When I was still a very wee lad, he sold it to another drummer, Alan Whitehead of The Marmalade. When he in turn moved on, there was a slight air of disappointment that the new owner was a taxi driver with a very quiet southern Irish accent. But when Thin Lizzy hit the charts with 'The Boys are Back in Town', rumours began to circulate that the drummer connection had not been entirely lost, as the taxi driver's cousin was one Brian Downey!

The combination of 'The Boys are Back in Town' and the resulting exposure on *Top of the Pops*, coupled with my street's tenuous claims to a connection to the band, really brought both Thin Lizzy and the charismatic Phil Lynott to my attention. I was 16 when one of my schoolmates suggested going to see Thin Lizzy in concert, and I was really keen. This would be an evening of so many firsts for me. All previous trips to London had been either with my parents or elder siblings, and as there is an eleven year gap between me and the next youngest, that pretty much meant I was travelling with responsible adults. This night, it would be four 16-year-old lads.

Changing from the British Rail trains to the Underground brought about a change from the dark suited office workers to the denim and band patches of the heavy rock gig goers. Hair in 1978 was still reasonably long; not so free flowing as the early Seventies but definitely not a short-back-and-sides affair. At each stop on the Tube, the haircuts got longer and longer, either in the straight and long Scott Gorham style or the wild and unkempt 'I've just got out of bed' look of Brian Robertson. Then followed the trek from the station to the venue, and the first of multiple encounters with ticket touts and merch vendors. All this, a whole new world for four grammar school boys living on the borders of South London and Surrey.

Next to assail the senses as we found our way to our seats would be something that was a regular part of many gigs around that time, the scent of 'herbal cigarettes', yet another sign for us that we were four young rookies in a wholly different kind of place. The support band were Horslips and I thoroughly enjoyed their musicianship and stage craft. However, the audience were definitely tensing for something, and whilst the venue hummed with conversation during the interval as the stage was being set for Lizzy, the collective air of expectation slowly lowered the hum of conversation to an expectant hush.

I've since learnt that the adrenaline rush experienced from a good loud rock concert is the same hit as you get when doing something risky like skydiving. Certainly, the wall of noise that erupted from the amplifiers, the on stage pyrotechnics and the roaring crowd hit me like a tidal wave, totally engulfing my senses.

The adrenaline rush at a rock concert is the same hit you get from skydiving

---

Every member of Thin Lizzy was a consummate performer. Those who state that Brian Downey was very solid rather than showy don't give him the credit he is due. And for all the strut and swagger of Scott Gorham, or the reckless abandon of Brian Robertson, your eyes were continually drawn to the man with the bass guitar and the voice that was like a velvet glove hiding a fistful of gravel.

This was my first live concert. There were lights, there were explosions, there were laser beams spelling out the words 'Thin Lizzy' and 'Live and Dangerous', and there were two great guitarists blasting out those heavenly riffs and striking all the poses, but who was I drawn to time and again? Who was the master of the pose, the gesture, the facial expression? Phil Lynott.

However, what really won you over was that you could tell that these were poses and that this was stagecraft. After a particularly exuberant pump of the fist, or an exaggerated swagger with the bass, Phil would look down and laugh to himself about how, in the nicest possible way, this was all a bit daft. Yes, he would be your rock god, but please, whatever you do, Don't Believe A Word!

After that night, I was truly won over. No longer did I use my full given name of Philip, I was Phil, and after many months saving, I possessed a Black Fender Jazzmaster bass, and my lifelong love affair with live gigs was begun. The blame for all this addiction I can lay squarely, and quite gladly, at the door of Phil Lynott and Thin Lizzy.

I have had the good fortune to witness many charismatic performers, but you never forget your first, and that puts Phil Lynott in a whole separate category all of his own.

I WAS THERE: RICHARD BROWN

A mate of mine used to work for Phonogram Records so we would go backstage after the gigs to meet them. I talked to Scott and Phil for a while and had loads of whisky and cokes because it was all free. And we talked to Gary Moore too. He was there at the party but wasn't playing on stage with them that evening.

Richard Brown was backstage at Wembley Arena

I WAS THERE: GRAHAME RIDLEY

Two years later, I found out that Thin Lizzy were scheduled to be playing at Wembley. It was the evening before my Economics 'O' level. None of my friends wanted to go as they said we really needed to be revising. I bought myself a ticket anyway and went on my own. By this time, they had lasers illuminating their logo on the back wall of the Empire Pool and Phil, Brian, Robbo and Scott were every bit as good as that time in '76.

To my lasting regret, I never got to see them again. Phil was a force of nature, one of the greatest front men I ever saw live, and that '76 gig I saw cemented Scott as one of my all time favourite guitar players. His solo on 'Dancing in the Moonlight' is surely one of the finest guitar solos ever played on a single. I bought a Cherry Sunburst Les Paul Deluxe for my 31st birthday. I own a fair few guitars but that is 'the one'.

I tell people that 'unfortunately, I only saw Thin Lizzy twice.' But I was very fortunate indeed.

I WAS THERE: ALISON RUSSELL

I saw Thin Lizzy many times with the different line ups, met them, was in the fan club and saw Grand Slam many times too. Phil was always lovely, a very kind man. He called me Spike because of my hair! The gigs were amazing. Thin Lizzy were my life from the mid Seventies until the end.

I discovered them in 1976. I lived in a country village and a guy I grew up with on the farm was DJing in the local village hall at a youth club. I walked by one night and heard 'Jailbreak' and that was it. I just thought, 'Wow, what is that? I have to know more.' I had to find out everything I could about Thin Lizzy. Then *Jackie* magazine had a poster of them, and I was young and Robbo was gorgeous, so music and Robbo sold it!

I joined the Thin Lizzy fan club. My membership number was 453. I wrote lots of letters to the fan club, one to find out if Robbo was married! (Very sad, I was so young.) Before Wembley, I had spent time at home in my early teens playing their albums and couldn't wait to see them live. They were the most exciting gigs I ever saw - the passion, the lighting, the smoke bombs. I always left singing and with chills down my spine.

The 1978 Wembley gig was fantastic. It's hard to explain how I felt - exhilarated and alive. I just had to hear them more and more. I was devastated when Robbo left Lizzy. I cried.

I WAS THERE: ANDREW SMYTH

Now when one of your favourite bands announces they are playing two massive shows at the Empire Pool, Wembley you know you have to be there! By 1978, Thin Lizzy were a huge draw. They had moved up the ladder from playing the Rainbow, and the Hammersmith Odeon to two nights at a much bigger (and soulless) venue.

My friend Robert and I managed to get tickets, three rows from the front, on the Friday night. The gig was smack bang in the middle of seeing Black Sabbath at the Hammersmith Odeon the previous Monday and David Bowie at Earls Court the following Friday. Being so near to the front took away the empty feeling I had about the venue. The band were only a few songs into their set when some knucklehead behind us started looking for a fight. But thanks to a quick intervention by security, the fool was thrown out and order was restored.

There was that rush of adrenaline when the house lights dimmed and suddenly the band appeared on stage with the siren blaring as the band kicked into 'Jailbreak'. Scott Gorham was to our right, with Brian Robertson to the left of the stage, with Brian Downey providing the backbeat on drums. And there, centre stage, was Phil Lynott, the charismatic frontman looking every inch the rock star. He knew it, and we knew it.

This being the first time I had seen the band, they did not disappoint. They delivered a classic set, which had us wanting more. After they played 'The Rocker' for the encore, you knew you had been treated to a gig of all gigs.

I WAS THERE: PETER THOMSON

I saw them again the following summer, this time at the soulless Empire Pool, Wembley, but they easily filled the void with their incredible sound. It was also one of the first UK gigs where a laser projector was used as part of the light show, to great effect.

Live and Dangerous was released the same month as the Wembley gig. Aware now of the contentious overdubs and edits, I maintain that it comes closest to what I heard and experienced. The album opens with 'Jailbreak', presumably for commercial reasons, but with a clumsy cut in at the start. They opened with 'Soldier of Fortune' at most performances at that time, and that's the missing piece. The best part of the album is where 'Cowboy Song' segues into 'Boys are Back', which signifies what we all went to Lizzy concerts for. That is Lizzy and Phil Lynott at their performing best.

I WAS THERE: IAN BOWLER

It was a banging night, which I remember fondly because it was my final day at grammar school. Two nights later, I saw Genesis at Knebworth, a great way to start my adult life at 16.

PLACE DE TOROS

6 JULY 1978, IBIZA, SPAIN

I WAS THERE: ANDY MCANALLY, AGE 15

The first time I saw Lizzy was in 1978 at a bullring in Ibiza. It was their *Live and Dangerous* tour. I was fourth in line to get into the concert. I was by myself and only 15 at the time. The boys came out of a pub across the road and walked right past me and into the bullring. I didn't have a camera, but there was another kid in front of me with his parents. They had a camera and Phil stopped to pose for some photos. I was mesmerised by the flashing lights during 'Jailbreak'. It was awesome!

Andy McAnally saw Lizzy twice

The second time I saw them was in Germany in 1983. I don't remember too much because I was older and alcohol was involved! They played as part of the *Monsters of Rock* Festival. I can't even remember what town it was. I think Motörhead and Whitesnake were on the same bill, and Jon Lord was doing keyboards for his old band mate, David Coverdale.

GARY MOORE REPLACES BRIAN ROBERTSON

30 JULY 1978

The band announced that Gary Moore had permanently replaced Robbo.

Thin Lizzy embarked upon another US tour, with Mark Nauseef on drums as Brian Downey returned to London to sort out personal matters. The tour was supporting other acts – Kansas, Journey, REO Speedwagon, Blue Öyster Cult, AC/DC and Styx.

CAL EXPO

18 AUGUST 1978, SACRAMENTO, CALIFORNIA

I WAS THERE: MLADEN VUKIC

I saw them at on a bill with The Cars, Marshall Tucker Band and Journey. Phil was at his best, lightning in a bottle. All the bands were at their peak but Phil just seemed to tower over the rest.

COW PALACE

20 AUGUST 1978, SAN JOSE, CALIFORNIA

I WAS THERE: JIM MOHR

The first time I saw Thin Lizzy was an accident that almost didn't happen. It was the summer of 1978 and I was a senior in high school. My friends and I were all big Kansas fans and they announced a show at the Cow Palace near San Francisco, so I had to get tickets. I actually bought three, but one friend decided he wanted to work that night to earn money for a new car.

I borrowed my mother's car, but on the way I ran out of gas. As luck would have it, two other friends from school saw me hitchhiking on the side of the road and gave me a lift to the next gas station.

The opener was The Cars on their first tour, and I had not yet heard of them. I did enjoy them and became a fan, but were nothing compared to what came afterwards. Next up was a band that I only knew superficially, as my stepbrother could play one of their songs on the guitar: Thin Lizzy. Needless to say, they were fantastic, as I had never seen a front man before with so much energy and stage presence.

Phil played his signature Fender bass with the mirror pick guard, which he used to reflect the sports lights onto fans, making eye contact with them and raising his hand in a first, acknowledging the connection with each fan as he did so. Although the only song I remember them playing was the one my stepbrother knew, 'Jailbreak', they made such an impression on me that within a year, I had all of their albums, with the exception of *Vagabonds of the Western World*, which it took me years to acquire.

PALMER AUDITORIUM

25 AUGUST 1978, DAVENPORT, INDIANA

I WAS THERE: JIM PUSATERI

I worked for a major Midwest concert promoter from about 1973 to '82 so I have more than a few tales of stupidity. In 1978 we were doing REO Speedwagon and Thin Lizzy at the Palmer Auditorium in Davenport, Indiana. I ran the stage and worked directly with the production folks for the bands and the sound and light companies. I was also responsible for the dressing rooms so I had a crew of people taking care of them, and I had other responsibilities prior to the day of the show. I'd done a ton of shows with REO so I knew the crew and it looked to be an easy show. I was (and still am) a huge Thin Lizzy fan and getting to meet and see them live? Well, let's just say I was stoked.

Lizzy arrived for the sound check and Phil and I got to talking. Gary Moore was in the conversation also. As we were talking, I saw my wife (now ex for many years) come through the stage door. She was a typical Seventies rock chick, with bleached blonde Stevie Nicks hair, lots of make up, tight jeans and stiletto heels. She walked up and I introduced her to Phil and he said, 'Are you looking forward to the show tonight?'

She paused and said, 'I am so sick of Thin Lizzy. That's all we listen to at home. He has all the albums, knows all the words to all the song and knows all the guitar parts.' While I was hearing this all I was thinking was, 'Where can I hide the body so no one finds it?' As she finished being a huge bitch, Phil got a big smile on his face, put his arm around my shoulder, squeezed me and said, 'I knew I liked you, now I know why. Will ya come out with me for a few drinks after the show?'

So that night I went drinking with Phil Lynott and Gary Moore - and learned how to roll what Phil called 'English joints'. The most welcoming and gracious man I have ever met.

BUSCH CAPE COD SUMMER MUSIC FESTIVAL, CAPE COD COLISEUM

3 SEPTEMBER 1978, SOUTH YARMOUTH, MASSACHUSETTS

I WAS THERE: HARRY KING

I was in the Bill Chinnock Band. Bill had just been signed to Atlantic Records and we were booked on the Thin Lizzy show in Cape Cod Coliseum to warm them up. I didn't get to hobnob with them backstage like we did with other names we were tagged with to promote Bill. I just remember we did the show and performed our best. Bill's band was a lot like Springsteen's, and probably not exactly the cup of tea that Lizzy's young crowd was looking for. But they were polite and tolerated us.

Then Thin Lizzy came on and I was so impressed by their amazing control of their audience and fans. Every gesture Lynott made was a cue for that huge audience, and they would respond with hand gestures, lighters and head bobs in such lockstep as I'd never seen. The music was infectious and the sound was superb. They put on a great show and everyone left happy. It knocked me for a loop and made our band all feel a bit inferior.

I was impressed by Lizzy's control of their audience and fans

---

FAIRGROUNDS STADIUM

10 SEPTEMBER 1978, LOUISVILLE, KENTUCKY

I WAS THERE: MARK SNEED

The second time I saw Lizzy was an outdoor stadium show and they were fourth billed behind REO, Foreigner and Steve Miller. To this day, I'm not sure who was on second guitar. I believe it was Moore, but this was a stadium show and I couldn't really see them. In those days there were no video screens. I also passed out at this show (I was drunk) and may have missed some of the set.

UPTOWN THEATER

23 SEPTEMBER 1978, KANSAS CITY, MISSOURI

I WAS THERE: MIKE FLANIGAN

Thin Lizzy were headlining. I was, and remain, a much bigger Lizzy fan than AC/DC but on this particular evening AC/DC blew them away. AC/DC came out on fire with a tremendous amount of energy and the crowd went crazy. It was a rowdy crowd and the band was feeding off of it. Angus pulled out all the stops and was like a Tasmanian Devil running around the stage and laying on his side on the stage and pinwheeling around in circles. As part of the encore, Bon lofted Angus onto his shoulders and carried him all over the floor, out to the lobby and up into the balcony, all while Angus was ripping into it with the band. It was amazing.

So Thin Lizzy had a tough act to follow, and their set was marred by overall sound problems. Phil Lynott's bass was very muddy and just didn't sound right. He may have even been out of tune. It wasn't good. Multiple times Gary Moore's guitar signal cut out while he was soloing and he was furious about it. I've never seen a gig where a musician was so angry, but it seemed to spur him on and he was playing unlike anything I'd seen before. I'd seen Blackmore, Iommi, Buck Dharma, Nugent, Van Halen… and what Gary Moore did have topped them all.

He was doing another solo and the guitar cut out again. He took off the Les Paul and literally threw it across the stage at a roadie, strapped another guitar on, finished the song and they walked off the stage. AC/DC was by far the better band but Gary Moore was the best guitar player!

PALLADIUM

1 OCTOBER 1978, NEW YORK, NEW YORK

I WAS THERE: FREDDY BAILEY, AGE 15

I first saw Thin Lizzy on a show called *The Soap Factory*. I don't remember what they played but they looked cool in black leather and I liked the song. Then I saw them on a show called *Midnight Special* which aired late night on Fridays at 1am, with Wolfman Jack hosting, so I knew of them but wasn't a huge fan.

Then my friend Bobby and I bought *Jailbreak*. We really liked 'The Boys are Back in Town' but also 'Jailbreak', 'Emerald' and 'Angel from the Coast'. Then more we started reading articles about and looking at pictures of them, the more we liked them. Then we bought *Live and Dangerous* from disc-O-mat. We stared at the pictures on the sleeve for hours. There were some really great concert shots on that album sleeve. We were blown away hearing them live – 'Cowboy Song', 'Don't Believe a Word' and 'Still in Love with You'.

We said, 'Next time they play NYC we will go and see them.' Bobby's mom came along to take some pictures as she had a really good camera. The bill was Blue Öyster Cult, Thin Lizzy and The Dictators. We went to the show early. It didn't start on time. We waited and waited and the crowd was growing restless. Finally, somebody came out and said that Blue Öyster Cult's truck had broken down 100 miles outside of the city and that they were waiting for their equipment to arrive.

The show was supposed to start at 8pm but Thin Lizzy finally came out at about 10.30pm and played a flawless set of hits. I thought I was going to see the original line up but when Phil Lynott introduced the band, he said, 'On guitar, Gary Moore,' who I had heard of although I wasn't familiar with his work, and, 'Mark Nauseef from New York City.'

We felt kinda cheated not to see Brian Downey and Brian Robertson, but it didn't matter. Gary Moore was on another level and completely blew us the fuck away. His vibrato was insane. I hadn't seen a guy play guitar like him at that show. He had a punk hair cut like Johnny Ramone and was wearing jeans and a leather jacket. This guy kicked ass. And Scott Gorham was excellent too. These two complemented each other so beautifully. They were masters of the twin lead guitar, a dying art form.

This band was so tight, loud and vicious you couldn't help but like them. Phil's lyrics and voice were great. He kept chanting 'Ireland' and asking the crowd how we were doing. They did 'Waiting for an Alibi'. I had never heard such guitar playing before. I can still hear Gary Moore's vibrato. Then they did 'Bad Reputation' and the solo Gary did had me tearing up. He was so aggressive and soulful. It was awesome to see. Everybody was on point. I remember a lot of green light during the show.

This band was so tight, loud and vicious you couldn't help but like them

Blue Öyster Cult came on and we left halfway through the show. They bored us to death plus it was late, something like 2.30am. We never saw The Dictators. By the time they came on it had to be 3.30am.

Bobby's mother developed the film afterwards. She had captured some great stage shots. We were in the second tier of the Palladium, right above the floor seats, so we had great seats. We could see the whole stage and everyone on it clearly. It was a magnificent show and one I will never forget.

I've been a Lizzy fan ever since. I wish I could have seen them again. There was a rumour they were going to play the *Dr Pepper Central Park Music Festival* concert series with Heart. I never found out if that was true, but I'm glad I got the chance to see Thin Lizzy. When I talk to most rock fans, they tell me they never saw them live and that I'm lucky. I smile and say, 'I know!'

Long live THIN FUCKING LIZZY!

Love live Thin fucking Lizzy!

MCNICHOLS SPORTS ARENA
6 OCTOBER 1978, DENVER, COLORADO

I WAS THERE: STEVE CAUDLE
I was there. They opened for Styx. I enjoyed the show and I took some photographs.

Steve Caudle took some photos of Lizzy in action

I WAS THERE: MARIO CORD

I saw them at the New York Academy of Music on 14th Street, later renamed the Palladium. I was in high school. I remember Phil in the middle with the two guitarists on either side. He was a great showman clad in his leather pants. They were tight and had a great sound. His singing was excellent and the two axemen took turns playing solos. The drummer was in the back pounding out a steady rhythm. They were very professional and well rehearsed. The concert was a very enjoyable experience.

PACIFIC COLISEUM

12 OCTOBER 1978, VANCOUVER, CANADA

I WAS THERE: STEVE NEWTON

Steve Newton saw Lizzy in Vancouver, Canada

I was a 21-year-old student at the University of British Columbia, or UBC as we liked to call it. I was working towards a Bachelor of Arts degree, with a major in English Lit, so I had to study a bunch of weird ass novels by guys like John Barth and Thomas Pynchon instead of my usual faves like King, Bloch and Matheson. This was just four months after Thin Lizzy had released their *Live and Dangerous* double album, which is widely believed to be the 'greatest live album of all time'. For the past five years – ever since hearing their first great LP, 1973's *Vagabonds of the Western World*, I'd been a huge Thin Lizzy fan. Back in '78, you could have dangled backstage passes for Led Zeppelin, AC/DC and the Rolling Stones in front of me and I would have said, 'Got any Lizzy?'

I'd seen Thin Lizzy in Vancouver the year before, opening for Queen on their *A Day at the Races* tour and they were stunning. I can't say that they blew Queen off the stage, because back then nobody blew Queen off the stage. But when I heard they were coming back in '78 to open for

Styx – who had just released *Pieces of Eight* - I was more than psyched. The thought of having to eat more Hamburger Helper as a result of buying a ticket didn't phase me in the least.

The night of the show I even got all dressed up, meaning that I put on my black *Bad Reputation* t-shirt, which sported the image of Thin Lizzy's latest studio album on the front. I always thought it was weird that co-guitarist Brian Robertson wasn't included on the cover, especially since he played lead on my favourite track, 'Opium Trail', but apparently he was being a bit of a knob back then.

Anyway, taking full advantage of the fact that most people at the gig were there for the headliner, I easily worked my way up to the front of the stage and rocked out about ten feet from my heroes. I was quite shocked to find that Robertson wasn't on stage, because I was primed to hear him and Gorham trade solos on the gorgeous ballad 'Still in Love with You', just like on *Live and Dangerous*. But he had been replaced, yet again, by off-and-on Lizzy member Gary Moore. Lucky for me, Moore was a complete madman on guitar, and his fierce performance helped make it the most thrilling arena-concert experience of my life.

Completely and utterly blown away by the opening act, I couldn't really give a rat's ass when the headliner hit the stage. I was still in kind of a daze from the sheer rockingness of Thin Lizzy and was wandering around the Coliseum concourse when I spotted a familiar looking longhair. Leaning up against a railing, smoking a Marlboro and watching Styx, was none other than Scott Gorham! I approached him in wide-eyed wonder - all 'I'm not worthy!' - and he was incredibly cool and friendly. I told him that there was no way a band like his should be opening for Styx, and he seemed to agree.

Though not a smoker, I asked Gorham for a cigarette just so I could have one as a souvenir, and he offered me his last one. When I happily took it – as well as the now-empty Marlboro packet to keep it in – he must have realised I was a pretty hardcore fan. He motioned me to follow him, and the next thing you know we're headed backstage. When we got to a security checkpoint he slapped a green all-access pass on my leg and we continued on our journey.

As we were walking along a long hallway, I noticed a guy strolling alone ahead of us and realised from the silver runners that it was Gary Moore.

I asked Gorham what happened to Brian Robertson, and I'll never forget his answer: 'Oh, this guy's way better!'

A few minutes later Gorham parked me outside the band's dressing room, told me to wait a minute, and then headed inside. Looking back now I like to think that, in his infinite kindness, he was seeing if it was cool to take me back and meet Phil. I'll never know for sure. But he came back out with a resigned look on his face, handed me a little Thin Lizzy mirror pin, wished me well, and told me I could just hang out backstage and watch the rest of the show.

I vividly remember Tommy Shaw and the other guys from Styx walking past me, all smiles and laughter, to play their encore, but I couldn't tell you what song it was. I was stuck in my Thin Lizzy moment, and have been ever since.

That little rectangle of glass with the pink-and-blue Lizzy logo has become one of my most prized possessions, and the green backstage pass has been permanently affixed to my vinyl copy of *Jailbreak*. Not sure what happened to the Marlboro.

I didn't meet Gorham again until 23 years later, in February of 2001. That's when me and my buddy Ferg drove down to Seattle to see the post-Lynott Lizzy – featuring John Sykes on guitar and vocals and Tommy Aldridge on drums – play at a club called the Showbox. The show was as good as it could have been without Phil – or Robbo, or Gary, for that matter – and afterwards I drunkenly waylaid the greying Gorham as he was heading to the band's bus. I told him about the '78 backstage incident, and this time he was the wide-eyed one. I gave him a big friggin' hug and thanked him profusely.

'You're the reason he became a rock journalist!' blurted out Ferg, although I don't believe Scott Gorham is entirely to blame.

In October 1978 Thin Lizzy toured Australia and New Zealand, playing six shows. Mark Nauseef filled in on drums for Brian Downey.

INTERNATIONAL SPORTS CENTRE
22 OCTOBER 1978, NEWCASTLE, AUSTRALIA

I WAS THERE: DAVID TAYLOR, AGE 14

I saw them twice on the *Live and Dangerous* tour, at Newcastle, New South Wales and then at Sydney Opera House. Thin Lizzy were my first ever concert. It was epic. I was only 14 and I remember it was super loud. At the Newcastle show, when the band hit the stage, Phil Lynott was up front near the pyrotechnics and the flashpots shifted forward. When the band hit the first note, people in the audience lost some hair. There were people in front of me putting each other's hair out!

I WAS THERE: DAVID HINDS

I first heard Thin Lizzy when 'The Boys are Back in Town' was released in 1976. Being a guitar player myself and, at the time, playing with top Australian hard rock band, Rabbit, I was immediately drawn to the twin guitar attack of Scott Gorham and Brian Robertson. I just loved the hard-edged sound and the guitar harmonies. Rabbit had a twin guitar line up, as did the next band I played in, Finch/Contraband, so I was particularly impressed by the way that Scott and Brian arranged their parts.

David Hinds was at the ISC to see Lizzy

I duly bought the *Jailbreak* album, and when *Live and Dangerous* was released, it blew my mind! From the moment I heard 'The Boys are Back in Town', Thin Lizzy became one of my all time favourite bands.

I only got to see them live once, on the Australian leg of their 1978 *Live and Dangerous* tour. The support bands were the local Jon English Band and Wha-Koo. But everyone was there to see Lizzy! The line up for this gig was Phil Lynott, Scott Gorham and the brilliant Gary Moore on guitars, and Mark Nauseef on drums, filling in for Brian Downey, who was out of action due to illness or an injury - I can't remember which. There was a big American-style police car red and blue light above the drum kit, obviously to be used in 'Jailbreak'.

The band hit the stage and it was like being run over by a freight train! Phil prowled the stage in his leathers, wielding his black Fender Precision Bass with the mirror pickguard like a weapon. Gary Moore was absolutely on fire, ripping into his lead breaks like a man possessed, and Scott Gorham was the ultimate rock god, with his long flowing hair and super cool stage persona. The way he and Gary worked together was brilliant. Mark did a brave job filling in for Brian Downey, but Brian's incredible drumming was definitely missed.

At one stage Phil delivered his classic line, 'Are there any young ladies here with any Irish in them?', which was met with squeals of delight from the girls in the audience. And then he delivered the punch line, 'Are there any young ladies here who'd like a bit more Irish in them?' That cracked the whole crowd up - classic Phil! Every song was delivered with maximum intensity, and we all left that gig feeling totally blown away, having seen one of the world's greatest rock bands at the height of their powers.

I am still a huge Lizzy fan, and all of their albums are in my CD library. We have sadly lost Phil and Gary, but the legacy of Thin Lizzy will forever live on in the annals of rock and roll. Long live rock and roll, and long live Thin Lizzy!

I WAS THERE: DAVID HUGHES

I loved Thin Lizzy from the first time I heard them. What always amazed me was how Phil Lynott could play the bass guitar like he did and sing as well. I also loved how the two guitarists could play in harmony. They were completely unique. When I saw them, there were four bands on before them, including Jon English and the Sports. When Thin Lizzy came on, they blew us all away because they were that bloody awesome. And my memory is that after Thin Lizzy played their set, the Charlie Daniels Band came on and finished the day off. They were bloody great too!

I WAS THERE: GINO PIN

I went to high school just about a mile away from the ISC, as it was known them, and after school and on the weekends, we would ride our bikes at the back of the stadium. There were just piles of dirt and other building crap that had been there since they finished the stadium. We knew how to get in the grounds for nothing!

When we heard the commotion and work going on, we were noses to the cyclone fence. We watched them finish setting up and later that afternoon, we snuck through the strategically located entrance which we used to get in to watch the footy and rugby league. A couple of the road crew saw us and yelled out 'oi!' and we bolted into the crowd. After that, it was a bit overwhelming for me - the sounds, the lights, the volume and the unusual smell of the place compared to footy days. I now realise that it was what they called 'happy cabbage' back then!

I WAS THERE: KIM BROWN

When Thin Lizzy toured Australia, they were engaged for a series of free 'super concert' gigs that were promoted by a national radio network. They appeared at the ISC along with a number of local Australian and Newcastle supporting acts. It was through my connections to the latter that I was fortunate enough to gain some backstage access. I didn't get to meet any of the band but did get in some shots with my trusty Praktica SLR camera from above and behind the stage, including of Phil Lynott chilling in the stands behind the stage. The programme and props were as per *Live and Dangerous* and the boys punched the material out both energetically and professionally, with plenty of star leaps from the guitarists and the obligatory police lights for 'Jailbreak' of course.

Photo Kim Brown

Kim Brown got some shots at the concert

I WAS THERE: MICK KING, AGE 13

As a 13-year-old I loved rock music so when I got the chance to see Thin Lizzy, I jumped at it. It was part of a tour called *Rocktober* and it was sponsored by a national radio station. On the bill were the Australian band The Sports and American band Wha-Koo. It was an overcast day and I remember there were a lot of bikies there and a lot of fighting and drinking. Brian Downey had a fill in drummer while Gary Moore was on guitar with Scott Gorham. I wasn't that familiar with their catalogue apart from 'The Boys are Back in Town', which I'd seen on music shows on TV, but by the end of the gig I had become a lifelong fan. I was blown away by tunes like 'Jailbreak', 'Don't Believe a Word' and 'Dancing in the Moonlight' and by the sheer power of it all. With the sparkling Thin Lizzy sign as a back drop it was rock heaven. I'm sure it influenced me to become a musician and especially a bass player myself. I will never forget watching Phil play. Even though I got grounded for three months for coming home drunk, it was all worth it!

I WAS THERE: ROB PARIC, AGE 16

I've seen lots of big names since but I still remember the greatness and enormity of this show. To say they had stage presence is an understatement. I've said for a long time that forever the highlight of my life was seeing Thin Lizzy. But actually? Phil Lynott was just it.

I WAS THERE: STEVE 'MAC' MCLENNAN

Phil Lynott was chasing one of the guys from Wha-Koo with a piece of four by two threatening to cave his 'fookin' head in'. Gary Moore gave me a tour badge. Mark Nauseef was on drums. Much as I was disappointed that the Brians weren't there, Gary Moore and Mark Nauseef were awesome.

Steve Mac McLennan was at the ISC show

I WAS THERE: STEVE RUSSELL

It was an outdoor concert. I don't remember a lot of detail, except that they were great. Phil Lynott was in top form musically and as a front man, and the dual guitar stuff was super tight. Being a guitar player myself, I was interested in seeing Gary Moore who I was aware of through some of his earlier stuff and I was really impressed by how well he fitted in, as well as his solos. It was the same line up, and presumably the same or similar set list, as preserved on the video of their performance at the Sydney Opera House on the same tour.

I WAS THERE: TREVOR DARE

Thin Lizzy were coming to my hometown in 1978 and I was very excited to see them live. They were awesome, so powerful and tight, and Phil was a fantastic frontman. I was a huge Brian Robertson fan and I was disappointed that Brian was not in the band on this tour but that someone by the name of Gary Moore was filling in for him. The crowd were rocking! After the gig I went to the local night club and Phil and Gary turned up signing autographs and giving out badges, so I go to meet them both. I even got a Thin Lizzy badge from Phil. I'll never forget that day.

Trevor Dare was at the ISC

MYER MUSIC BOWL

27 & 28 OCTOBER 1978, MELBOURNE, AUSTRALIA

I WAS THERE: ANDREW JACKSON, AGE 18

I met Lizzy on the Australian *Countdown* music show at ABC Studios and Phil and Scott signed my *Live and Dangerous* album cover. Then I saw them live at the Myer Music Bowl in Melbourne, Australia where they shared a bill with Wha-Koo and other American bands. They were sensational with the dual lead guitar, the drummer and the lead vocals and bass, so tight, powerful and energetic.

I WAS THERE: KIM VOLKMAN, AGE 17

In 1978 I was a lad of 17. I had just left high school and Thin Lizzy were my heroes. Of course, the biggest was Phil. I had all their albums up to that point and when I learned they were going to be playing in my hometown I was beyond ecstatic. It was a free concert put on by the radio station 3XY. The other bands on the bill that I remember were our own Sherbet and a band called Wha-Koo.

The Sidney Myer Music Bowl was an amphitheatre set in the park. I made my way there that night awash with anticipation. The bands before Thin Lizzy blew over me with little fanfare. I had positioned myself on the right hand side up in the wings, looking down on the stage. Then the moment came. Out of the darkness and the billowing smoke the red lights spun and the sirens wailed. The opening chords to 'Jailbreak' rung out in unison.

There they were - THIN LIZZY! Phil, Scott, Gary – and Mark (who did an admirable job). I could not believe it. The gig went in an ecstatic blur of light and sound. It is a gig that, 44 years on, is still etched in my memory.

These days, whenever I meet someone from Ireland, I always ask them, 'What is the best band to have ever come out of Ireland?' There is a right answer and a wrong answer. I think you know the right answer. Did I go on to become a bass player? You bet I did. I have Phil to thank for that.

Thin Lizzy played two outdoor shows at Sydney Opera House.

SYDNEY OPERA HOUSE

29 & 30 OCTOBER 1978, SYDNEY, AUSTRALIA

I WAS THERE: GRAHAM HIBBARD

As unlikely as it sounds, I was at home doing my maths homework at the kitchen table and one of my older brother's friends had just come back from late night shopping (a new thing for Sydney) and wanted to play the record he just bought. It stopped me in my tracks and I thought, 'Now that is real music!' It was love at first listening. Later that year, Thin Lizzy were the headline act for local AM radio station 2SM's *Rocktober* concert series featuring Thin Lizzy and who knows who else....

What a stage for the band, what a backdrop! On my way home I wanted to buy a Thin Lizzy singlet for the princely sum of A$7.99 but I only had A$6.99. I begged and pleaded with the seller, and counted and recounted my funds but no joy. Heartbreakingly, on my train ride home I counted the cash again... A$7.99!

I WAS THERE: SEAN FRIEL

They did two shows, one of which was filmed. My mother let me and my older brother go both times. She was born in Derry and grew up in Dublin. I didn't know much about the band at all. I was 13, possibly 14 and terrified by the massive crowd, all of whom seemed to have a bad attitude. These events were far too big to police. Rocking hard, the guitarist was constantly flicking picks out into the crowd. The songs I remember to this day are the ones that sent the crowd wild, 'Jailbreak' and 'The Boys are Back...'.

MCGONAGLES

19 DECEMBER 1978, DUBLIN, IRELAND

I WAS THERE: DAVID SWEENEY, THE VIPERS

I'd met Phil in Dublin the Christmas before we went on tour with them. There was a party for *Hot Press*, the local magazine, and Phil was playing at it with a few other people. If he got the chance, he'd get up on the stage anywhere and play. Phil was very self conscious. He just wanted to stay current, stay relevant so he was friendly with people who were in the punk scene. He hung out with Paul Cook and Steve Jones from the Sex Pistols and the three of them were part of the Greedy Bastards. We were a punk band ourselves and so he was keen to hang out with us. He would have been around 12 years older than us. This is my diary entry for that day:

I played at the *Hot Press* party. Jammed with Paul Cook and Steve Jones of the Pistols and did 'Pretty Vacant' and 'Route 66'. (Larry Mullen also got up. I didn't know him that well at the time). Scott Gorham was there. He was a really nice guy. Saw the original Skid Row with Phil Lynott play. Met Lynott later and he gave me a lecture on stardom and we were invited to the Greedies' gig in the Stardust.

In February 1979, Thin Lizzy were back on the road in North America, this time supporting Nazareth.

KIEL AUDITORIUM

11 MARCH 1979, ST LOUIS, MISSOURI

Lisa North saw Lizzy with her best friend Karen

I WAS THERE: LISA NORTH, AGE 19

I saw Lizzy open for Nazareth and then Journey in '79 - both stellar shows! I discovered them in '75. I was 16. I saw the cover of the *Fighting* album and was immediately smitten by Philip. I began collecting their albums on the spot and was forever impressed by Phil's charisma, voice and songwriting talent. I listened to Lizzy all the time from then on. I was 19 when I saw them live in St Louis. For the Journey show, I spent the night outside the Checkerdome in order to get a chance to get the best tickets. But it didn't work and I actually got nosebleed seats with my best friend, Karen. I tried offering someone in the best seats on the floor money just to see them open but it didn't work. My biggest memory of that show was when the sirens were blaring during 'Jailbreak'. I've been a lifelong fan since.

EVANSVILLE COLISEUM

12 MARCH 1979, EVANSVILLE, INDIANA

Kevin Greenwood saw Lizzy at the Evansville Coliseum

I WAS THERE: KEVIN GREENWOOD

I saw them in 1979 in a tiny venue in Evansville, Indiana. They were the opening act for Nazareth. I was a junior in high school. I and two classmates were driven to the concert by one of their moms. There were 2,000 to 3,000 people there. The stage was like one found in a high school and I was no more than six to eight feet away from Phil the whole show. It was great. Gary Moore was the guitarist. They were ultra-tight and Phil's vocals were on point. The light show, like most then, was rudimentary. There were police lights during 'Jailbreak'. Phil had a mirror pick guard on his Fender bass and during the show he reflected the spotlight back into the balcony, where a young couple were really making out and some extreme heavy petting was taking place. They didn't notice but the crowd - and Phil - loved it. I've seen about every rock act going and this show is still one of my favourites.

Nazareth, the headliners, were too loud. Uncomfortably loud. We were there for Thin Lizzy.

CIVIC CENTRE

16 MARCH 1979, CHARLESTON, WEST VIRGINIA

I WAS THERE: ROBERT NELSON

They were opening for Nazareth. My friend and I skipped school and caught the bus to town that afternoon and snuck backstage. We were so excited to see *them*, not Nazareth. Our plan worked perfectly and we slipped through the kitchen and into the arena. Nazareth was doing sound check and out came Phil and Scott. Wow! Phil was kicking a soccer ball around the empty hall, wearing a black leather jumpsuit and black boots. Scott had on jeans and a green jacket. Both were nice and glad to talk to two young kids. They let us take pictures. Being guitar players, my friend and I were quizzing Scott about gear. Phil continued his antics.

Then suddenly Phil boots the ball really hard and it sailed into the sound console. The sound guy screamed, 'I don't give a fuck who you are, you're fucking outta here!' We all ran to Phil's defence: 'You can't throw him out… blah, blah, blah.' Then he booted us all out. Phil and Scott went backstage and my friend and I were ushered out. As we parted, I asked Scott what the opening number would be. He smiled and said, 'Jailbreak'….

Straight off the back of the North American tour, Lizzy began the 30 date UK *Black Rose* tour. It kicked off in Brighton on 29 March 1979 and took in 30 shows in just 36 days.

BRIGHTON CENTRE

29 MARCH 1979, BRIGHTON, UK

I WAS THERE: RAY YOUNG

My wife Karen has enjoyed Thin Lizzy as much as me. We saw them three times at the Brighton Centre, all fantastic gigs and on all three occasions our ears were ringing for days after. We turned up at the venue one cold evening and were amazed by the number of trucks there were transporting the gear around. At another gig, the stage lighting was a couple of traffic lights on each corner of the stage, with the band's logo shining brightly at the back of the stage. At one point the stand holding the traffic light fell over into the audience.

I remember Phil flashing the spotlight reflecting off his mirror-faced guitar onto girls he liked who were then happily escorted back stage. We were lucky to see Snowy White, Gary Moore and Brian Robertson play with the band and of course Scott's fantastic guitaring and his near waist-length hair and Brian's mesmerising drumming, even though you didn't see much of him as he was surrounded by kit. Phil of course was the best front man any band would wish for, standing at the front of the stage, milking the audience's love for him and the band.

I played a cassette of *Bad Reputation* to death in my car, full blast with the windows open. Every track had a meaning to me and I still listen to it now. *Live and Dangerous* was the must have album of its day and 'Still in Love with You' remains as haunting as ever. And me being a drummer, 'Sha La La' featuring Brian was always special.

Thin Lizzy were so close to our hearts we named our daughter Sarah after one of their songs. The first lines were so true for us: 'When you came in my life, you changed my world....'

ODEON THEATRE

2 APRIL 1979, BIRMINGHAM, UK

I WAS THERE: COLIN MASON

In the Seventies and Eighties, the Odeon in Birmingham was the venue for live music, seating about 2,500 – although the audience weren't seated for long at a Lizzy concert. I saw them there in October 1976 on the *Johnny the Fox* tour and twice in December 1977 on the *Bad Reputation* tour and in1979 I saw the band four times, including twice in April at the Birmingham Odeon when Steve Jones of Sex Pistols fame joined them on stage, a collaboration that would later make it onto vinyl under the name The Greedies. They were initially called The Greedy Bastards but I guess with that name, their single 'A Merry Jingle' was never going to get any airplay.

I WAS THERE: MIKE BARBER

I had started to learn the guitar when I started senior school in 1977, aged 12, and began making lots of new friends. A few had older brothers who were into Lizzy so a few C90 tapes later I had recordings of *Jailbreak* and

Johnny the Fox and was getting into the band. The following year, I bought my first Lizzy album with my paper round money, the mighty *Live and Dangerous*. Hearing the chanting of 'Lizzy, Lizzy,' followed by the opening E chord on 'Jailbreak' had me completely hooked. I had to wait until 1979 to see them live for the first time, on the *Black Rose* tour, and it's one of the most memorable and influential days of my life. I went with my best mate Smithy. My mum had queued for hours to get the tickets for us.

I went on to see Lizzy a further nine times. The best experience was on the *Chinatown* tour. Me and Smithy went down the side of the Birmingham Odeon to try and get to see the band backstage after the gig, and to our surprise we did! Phil was awesome and had loads of time for us. We got autographs off the guys and I remember having a conversation with Scott about the sound.

DE MONTFORT HALL

5 APRIL 1979, LEICESTER, UK

I WAS THERE: COLIN WOOD

My very first gig was Lizzy at Leicester's De Mont for the *Black Rose* tour. The atmosphere was awesome. The gig was more than a sell out as many, many fans were climbing through upstairs windows to get onto the balcony. I was standing in the middle, about a third of the way back, so had a clear view of these fans. The band themselves were awesome and climaxed with Gary Moore playing 'Black Rose' as the encore.

I WAS THERE: MARK SMIGGY SMITH

My diary entry for this gig reads:

What more can I say, except that it was the best yet. Got right up to the front. Blinded and singed by magnesium flares, kicked in the head, fookin' sweated my bollocks off. Angie came too and, although obviously not getting off on the atmosphere during the first ten to 15 minutes, she soon fell into the swing of things. I must say that this is what I like best of all. The sound and the atmosphere just carry you up and away to another dimension where you couldn't care whether you lived or not.

GUILDHALL

6 APRIL 1979, PORTSMOUTH, UK

I WAS THERE: CLAIRE JACKSON

Suzie and I went to see Thin Lizzy at Portsmouth Guildhall and went backstage to meet the band, where we spent a good hour or so chatting, being moved on by the staff. We were asked to go on to a club and we accepted and ran out the back door. We were quickly ushered into the back of a car, to find Phil Lynott in the passenger seat and his tour manager, Gus, driving. I told them how the club they were planning to go to was a bit 'office girl', so it was decided to go back to their hotel. They were staying at the Centre Hotel in Southsea, in Room 003 – I remember Phil made a joke that it was a bit like James Bond. We spent that night partying with Phil, Scott, Gus and members of The Vipers, their support band. Phil said that Brian Downey always went home to his wife and Gary Moore was loved up!

The next day I got my friend Pat to phone Phil at the hotel. She was the mother of a member of the band I followed, and a big Thin Lizzy fan herself. (Her talking to Phil on the phone was her most cherished moment right up until her death.) On the phone, we arranged for guest passes to see the band in Bournemouth as Phil's personal guests.

COLSTON HALL

8 & 9 APRIL 1979, BRISTOL, UK

I WAS THERE: DUNCAN CRUTE

I had friends who were a couple of years older than me and my friend's brother, who was into music and bikes, had a particular album whose cover fascinated me. I said, 'What's this?' and he said, 'I think it's a band called Thin Lizzy.' The album was *Jailbreak* and his brother put it on. As soon as I looked at the cover I was hooked. I was 14 years old.

I first saw Thin Lizzy in 1977 with the Brian Robertson line up and that was a mind blowing experience. I saw them at the Colston Hall again in '79 on the *Black Rose* tour and we were lucky enough to get backstage. I went with a guy called Mike Patch who was in the same year at school. I said, 'I'm just gonna wait by the door and see if we can get in.' There was a queue but it wasn't massive. Back in the Seventies it was quite a done deal that you could go and do these sorts of things without worrying too much about security.

They let us in and we met the road crew and they gave us a photograph of the band. Then they let us into the room where all the guys and girls were – Phil, Scott Gorham, Brian Downey and Gary Moore. It was surreal. It was like, 'There's my hero.' He was massive. I'm five foot ten but I stood next to Phil and he was a big guy. And he was so pleasant and down-to-earth.

Scott Gorham was a big guy too. He had massively long hair and red eyes. He was in full on party mode. He was really nice and softly spoken but we didn't have a massive conversation. Gary Moore was sat on a leather sofa with two girls on either side of him and more interested in talking to them than to us, but he signed the photograph.

But I must've spent 20 minutes sat down talking to Brian Downey. As a drummer myself he was my point of contact. They were letting people in for about ten minutes and then moving them out and letting the next batch of people in, so we were on a rota. I watched two or three groups come in. I remember Brian said to me, 'Are you coming tomorrow night?' and I said, 'No, I just couldn't get tickets.'

I WAS THERE: MARK GRIFFITHS

I became a fan when I was a teenager. I really liked *Johnny the Fox* and listening to *Bad Reputation* on a Saturday really used to make my Saturdays. It's hard to discern which is the better album. Songs like 'Rocky' and 'Southbound' are equally great. I remember buying the 'Waiting for an Alibi' single, arguably the best thing they've ever done.

Mark Griffiths went backstage at the Colston Hall

My friend and I went to see them at Bristol Colston Hall on the Black Rose tour. By then the late Gary Moore had returned to the fold. They were outstanding live and Phil had charisma and knew how to work the crowd. We went backstage. Gary Moore was with his girlfriend. Brian Downey did not say much and neither did Scott Gorham but I am introverted so I didn't try to make conversation. I guess I was in awe of them. Phil raised his fist and I followed suit!

Many years later I played a lot of their songs in a covers band. They are one of the very finest rock bands to ever emerge. Their legacy will live on.

I WAS THERE: DAVID DAVIES, AGE 18

David Davies was at the Colston Hall in 1979

My favourite band for some four years had been Queen. The art work for the album *A Night at the Opera* had been skilfully embroidered on the back of my Wrangler jacket by my mother. But in reality I was yet to see any live band.

On my eighteenth birthday I found myself on a coach heading from Pontypool in South Wales to just over the Severn Bridge and into Bristol. I had a Thin Lizzy ticket in my back pocket and was more than a little excited. On to the coach stepped people I had not seen for two years since leaving school, now dressed in denim and studded belts and wrist bands, a far cry from the old school uniform. I sat with a close friend, Tony, who had been into Thin Lizzy and Queen for a while. Another friend, Hugh, had joined the ride. Now I had listened to *Johnny the Fox* and to be honest I had not been terribly impressed. In my defence, in that year's flood of quality music, an album had to be something incredibly fantastic to stand out. But I had loved the singles put out with the newly returned Gary Moore to the line up, 'Waiting for an Alibi' and 'Do Anything You Want To'. With their previous hits, I knew enough of their material to hopefully enjoy the show.

Arriving at Colston Hall and having paid 60p for a tour programme I could hear that support act The Vipers had already taken to the stage. Tony, the voice of experience, said that the support acts were usually crap and not to worry as we wouldn't be missing much. However, this being my first concert, I was desperate to get to my seat and check them out. I thought they were quite good.

Then the place was plunged into darkness and the 'Lizzy' chanting began. An adrenaline rush followed and suddenly the place was lit up with a thunderous explosion as Lizzy took the stage and smashed head first straight into the first number. Tony had got us brilliant seats right at the front and for the next couple of hours I felt we were very much a part of the action.

It was life changing. There was never a question of who was in charge. Phil Lynott dominated. He was a rock star. I watched as he lit up elated faces, sweeping the crowd with a beam of light reflected from his mirrored pick-guard Fender bass. The sheer power of the music, power which had not struck me from the studio album I had listened to, was now dancing around the stage with Gorham and Moore frequently changing sides of the stage amidst flashes and bangs, duelling and harmonising solos and riffs. A show - an incredible show - complete with a Downey drum solo. I was beyond satisfied.

Gorham and Moore frequently changed sides amidst flashes and bangs, duelling and harmonising solos and riffs

---

After the show we waited for the coach to arrive and were not far from the Bristol Hippodrome. Kate Bush had played there that night and her tour bus was parked just a hundred yards up the road. The word spread that Kate Bush was actually on the parked bus. Being rockers, all the boys from our coach ran up the road and were up against her tour bus, flashing the Vs at her and getting the same back from her.

I WAS THERE: SUZANNE WILLIAMS, AGE 16

The memories are very hazy but I remember it was a cracking gig and Phil had the crowd in the palm of his hand.

NEW BINGLEY HALL

10 APRIL 1979, STAFFORD, UK

I WAS THERE: JEFF COLLINS

In 1979 I saw them on the *Black Rose* tour at Stafford Bingley Hall, the cow shed. This was another absolutely brilliant gig and Gary Moore was on fire. Phil was using a wireless bass. Waiting for them to come back on for the encore, he began tapping a beat out on his guitar from the dressing room. The beat was fed through the PA, the crowd joined in and the band came crashing back to encore with 'Emerald'.

Jeff Collins saw Lizzy five times

I WAS THERE: GRAHAM WALTERS

I remember a smog coming off the stage and then they broke into 'Jailbreak'. It was always very crowded at that venue - we called it the cattle shed. I had been to see Motörhead the night before and got a very painful neck. I never tried headbanging again! Lizzy were fantastic, although the support band The Vipers got bottles thrown at them so they left the stage early. Lizzy did 'Black Rose' and most of the hits, and I remember hearing comments about Brian Robertson's punk trousers. Great show!

I WAS THERE: STEVEN NICKLIN

From '76 to '83 I saw Lizzy on every tour, mostly at the Odeon in Birmingham plus the *Live and Dangerous* tour at New Bingley Hall, Stafford. That was memorable simply for the energy of the crowd, Phil having us all in his pocket, with us watching the flash plate on his bass and wishing we could be playing one of the lead guitars. I didn't really like *Johnny the Fox* other than 'Massacre', but *Bad Reputation* was better and gave us 'Southbound', which is for me the track that sums up Lizzy best; great lyrics, wonderful harmony on the guitars and a story told.

I enjoyed *Black Rose* but *Chinatown* was better and I loved 'Killer on the Loose' and 'Hey You'. The final two albums had for me started to move the band to a harder rock sound. Had 'The Sun Goes Down' been released in the Seventies I would probably have appreciated it more. By 1981, my musical tastes had moved on. I still attended prog and rock band concerts through the Eighties but I had been introduced to *Breezin'* by George Benson and I was embracing funk, jazz funk, soul and more dance-oriented music, not to mention the whole electro sound.

All of that having been said, Lizzy stayed with me during the years my tastes changed and I still went to their concerts. Phil was just the best front man. You wanted to be him - simple as. Whilst never hitting the heights of Robbo and Scott, the Moore years were good and Lizzy maintained that harmony up to *Thunder and Lightning*.

Phil's passing was so sad and needless, and I still have the vision from the second row at Wolverhampton of him blasting out 'Rosalie' almost close enough for me to touch him. Lizzy are the band I have seen the most times and they will always be my favourite rock act. When I go out of this world, 'Rosalie' will be one of the tracks played at my funeral.

When I go out of this world, 'Rosalie' will be one of the tracks played at my funeral

---

I WAS THERE: DAVID SWEENEY, THE VIPERS

We toured with them in '79. I was still a teenager. We had moved back to London and we were doing gigs on our own and got a phone call at very short notice. 'Could you be in Brighton the next night to start the tour?' We were supposed to be on stage at eight o'clock. We frantically pulled everything together the next day and barely made it to Brighton in time. We got there about twenty past seven. Another band had already set their equipment up on the stage. But once Phil heard we were there he said, 'The Vipers are to go on stage.' The poor other guys had to take their gear down and we did the show instead. That must have been really disappointing for them.

The tour lasted a month and a half. It was like being in a theatrical production, because you're doing the same show every night. There's a cast of people – the road crew, the caterers, the management, the bands. It was an amazing experience. We went down really well in some places we played and in some places they didn't want to hear us, because the way we were dressed wasn't the way Lizzy were dressed and we had shorter hair. We weren't of the same genre.

The Midlands was a difficult place to play, and especially Bingley Hall, Stafford. There was a huge crowd of very rowdy Lizzy fans who just wanted to hear Lizzy. We only got a couple of numbers done before the singer got a full beer can in the face, so we just left the stage. Phil was like a father figure, and we were looking for him to explain to him what had happened. We went to our dressing room and he was in there with a girl. We surprised him! He was very understanding and told us about the time Lizzy toured with Slade, where he had got a lot of racist abuse from the crowds. He wanted people to realise that he'd been through it too, and that now he was on the other side of the coin, he was getting all this frantic, almost hysterical adulation from the big crowds.

Overall, the receptions we got were good. We played Bridlington and we went down very well with a rowdy Lizzy crowd. The Glasgow Apollo, which was quite a place on Sauchiehall Street, had an upper balcony that actually moved with the crowd – it wasn't very stable. The stage was about 20 feet high so people couldn't get on it and there was rat poison in the dressing rooms. But it was a great crowd and they weren't hostile to us. Most places were very receptive and we'd occasionally get an encore, but Phil didn't like that. If we got an encore, we wouldn't get a soundcheck the next night. But overall, he was fantastic. He would talk to us about fame and how to get places and what to do.

CITY HALL

11 & 12 APRIL 1979, NEWCASTLE, UK

I WAS THERE: PETER SMITH

There had been some to-ing and fro-ing between Gary Moore and Brian Robertson for a while, with Gary replacing Brian for a few spells. This time however, the disagreements between Phil Lynott and Brian Robertson had got to a point where the two could no longer work together. Brian left, and Gary Moore joined as his permanent replacement. Thin Lizzy was now Philip Lynott, Brian Downey, Scott Gorham, and

Peter Smith saw Lizzy at the City Hall

Gary Moore. This line-up recorded *Black Rose*, the ninth Thin Lizzy studio album.

Lizzy went out on a UK tour to promote *Black Rose.* The tour included two nights at Newcastle City Hall. Marie and I had tickets to see them on the second night, but then Kate Bush announced her first ever tour which included a concert at Sunderland Empire on the very same night. We decided that we had to forego the Lizzy concert (I can't remember if I sold my tickets or gave them away) so that we could go and see Kate Bush.

However, the pull of Thin Lizzy soon got the better of me, and I somehow managed to get a ticket for the first Lizzy concert on the Wednesday, although as the show was sold out, I can't recall how.

Lizzy were, as always, excellent. Gary Moore fitted in seamlessly; he came from the same musical and cultural background, was an old mate, and had played with the band before on many occasions. However, his stay with the band was short-lived; he walked out on them a few months later, during a tour of the USA. I was, however, extremely glad I'd had the chance to see this line-up.

The band felt fresh, tight and with a renewed energy. The audience were captivated, as usual. We were all on our feet, singing along from the off. It was a truly wonderful night.

BLACK ROSE RELEASED 13 APRIL 1979
UK CHART POSITION 2
US CHART POSITION 81

Black Rose received mixed reviews at the time but has since been described as 'Thin Lizzy's last true classic album'. The stand out title track, which showcased Moore and Gorham's guitar work, truly came to life on stage. The album also spawned three hit singles – 'Waiting for an Alibi' (UK number 9/Ireland number 6), 'Do Anything You Want To' (UK number 14/Ireland number 25) and 'Sarah' (UK number 24/Ireland number 26).

During the recording of the last album, Black Rose, Phil's complexion was ashen. There were a few days when he couldn't even get out of bed.... I tried to reach out to Phil, but like a lot of people who have an addiction problem, he said, 'Don't worry, I've got it under control.' **Tony Visconti, Producer**

ODEON THEATRE

16 APRIL 1979, EDINBURGH, UK

I WAS THERE: KEITH MCSHANE

I thought the *Black Rose* tour was up with the best of all the shows I saw. I can't remember if they opened with 'Are You Ready' or 'Do Anything You Want To' but it was fantastic seeing the kettle drums. I do clearly remember that next was 'Toughest Street in Town'. Gary Moore was jumping on the spot at the start of the song. And it was pure brilliance when they played 'Black Rose (Roisin Dubh)'.

GUILD HALL

17 APRIL 1979, PRESTON, UK

I WAS THERE: KEVIN SWIFT

I saw them ten times. And I played pool with Phil Lynott, Scott Gorham and Darren Wharton at the Crest Motel in Preston on their *Black Rose* tour.

Kevin Swift saw Lizzy ten times

I got into Lizzy very young. I bought *Bad Reputation* when I was 14 or 15, and because I played drums, the title track blew me away. 'Opium Trail' is fantastic too, and of course the track that hooked me was 'Whiskey in the Jar'. I once had a drum stick given to me by Brian Downey but I've since lost it and I'm gutted.

I saw Gary Moore, Snowy White, Brian

Robertson and Midge Ure all play with Thin Lizzy. The dual lead guitar was a new concept and the talent Lizzy had just orbited the band. Scott Gorham's long straight hair was how I wanted mine. I grew it half as long. They had a fantastic drummer in Brian and of course a fantastic bass player in Phil, who loved his role and the band. The Lizzy name above the stage lit up was amazing, and Brian's gong behind him being hit and the smoke bomb going off just enthralled me as a teenager.

I remember a girl groupie who had been on the whole tour with the band. She was a stunner. Not sure which band member had the pleasure, but I was shit jealous. Who wouldn't be at the age I was?

CITY HALL

18 APRIL 1979, SHEFFIELD, UK

I WAS THERE: TIM FREEMAN, AGE 15

It was sold out but it must have been the school holidays as I rocked up at Sheffield City Hall in the morning with a couple of mates and when the trucks arrived, we started humping gear in. We spent the morning getting flight cases off the trucks and up the little ramp at the rear of the hall, and then building the PA stacks. I was a skinny youth in trainers so they had me shin up the stacks to place the bullet tweeters on the top. After that, I hung around the guitar tech, passing him stuff and setting the amps up and then he gave me a tenner to go and buy all the PP3 nine volt batteries I could get hold of, so I nipped down to Boots and cleaned them out.

Tim Freeman was roadie for the day

It was pretty cool coming back in the stage door through the crowd that was already starting to gather and security just waving me through. Then it was the early afternoon and suddenly four of the guys wandering round on the stage were the band. Gary and Scott plugged in and started noodling and I stood next to them, watching in awe. Lighting rig guys were still working and we went and sat in the auditorium for the soundcheck. They jammed through 'TV' by the Flying Lizards and then The Cars' 'Just What I Needed', both of which seemed bizarrely fabulous at the time. Then we got an instrumental 'Parisienne Walkways' with Gary shouting the chords to Scott on the other side of the stage. It was just magic.

Most of the rest of the afternoon was spent dodging security and looking busy until the road manager dished out the backstage passes. Now we weren't going to get chucked out, I went into the foyer and spotted my mates who had tickets queuing up outside and did a bit of gloating, flashing the pass at them.

The support band were The Vipers, an Irish new wave outfit. They were pretty good but the crowd gave them a rough ride. I watched Lizzy's set partly from the stage and partly from in the audience. They were awesome, and Phil was outstanding.

I remember Gary and Scott playing timpani on 'Do Anything You Want To', the roar when they went into 'Don't Believe a Word', the blue flashing lights and sirens on 'Jailbreak', duelling leads on 'Róisín Dubh' and the singalongs to 'Cowboy Song' and 'The Boys are Back in Town'. They did 'Rosalie' and 'Emerald' in the encores and finished with 'The Rocker'.

At the end of the show, I tried to get backstage but security was a bit stricter and I found myself waiting inside the stage door with a girl who kept telling the bouncer that her brother was in the band. The bouncer was having none of it. We were there maybe 20 minutes before Gary appeared, saw the girl, gave her a hug and asked why she was out there waiting. She told him the bouncer wouldn't let anyone in so Gary gave the guy a bit of a bollocking. I asked him if he'd sign my programme, album cover and pass but he said he didn't have time. There was nobody else there! They chatted for a few minutes and left.

The bouncer must have felt sorry for me because he then let me in to the green room. Phil, Brian and Scott were in there and there was a buffet and drinks and we chatted. Phil was charming, and Scott asked how I'd got in so I told him about the day. And that's how I ended up with the three signatures on my gear rather than four. It was one to remember.

ST GEORGE'S HALL
19 APRIL 1979, BRADFORD, UK

I WAS THERE: ANDY WICKS, AGE 14

I've seen Thin Lizzy about ten times in total. My older brother was into Thin Lizzy and bought all their albums - I was more of a Status Quo fan. My friends included two brothers who lived just up the road and who were the same age as us. We used to go to concerts with them and the four of us would listen to music around each other's houses. *Live and Dangerous* was a big initial draw.

Andy Wicks saw Thin Lizzy 'about ten times'

I was only 14 when I first went to see Lizzy, but we still slept in the local pub. Being six foot tall and with no identity checks, it was easier to go and have a pint when you weren't supposed to. We first saw them at St George's Hall on the *Black Rose* tour. Gary Moore was a brilliant guitarist.

I also saw them twice at the old tram depot at the Queens Hall in Leeds. It was a horrible place but it was big and you could get many thousands of people standing in there. And we saw them when they headlined at Milton Keynes Bowl. They were pretty consistently great live, with the dual guitars. Phil was such an amazing front man, and larger than life. He was charming, he was cheeky, he was just great fun on stage.

I WAS THERE: BILL HINDMARSH

By now I'd had no contact with any of Thin Lizzy for a long while. Life and circumstances had brought me back to Yorkshire and various day jobs, with mixing local bands filling the evenings. Together with the drummer and bassist from one of these bands, I went to Bradford one evening aiming to enjoy some beers and a curry, and then sleep in the van so as to be early in the queue to buy Lizzy tickets the next morning.

For our sins the weather was cold, icy and snowing. We went anyway. I recall the van sliding sideways as we went down one major hill into

Bradford. The band's gear was in the back and the weight of the equipment had caused the double rear drive wheels to want to overtake the front. Fortunately, I was not driving. Also fortunately, the rear end brushed a kerb and lamp post and this was enough, along with the driver's efforts and our prayers, to set van back on its original course!

We had the beers and we had the curry. We kind of slept in the van. Most impressive of all was the sight of dedicated fans, in sleeping bags, around the base of St George's Hall in the snow, such was Lizzy's popularity. When we joined the queue in the morning, there were plenty ahead of us but we got tickets! I was touched and humbled to see this amazing support for and dedication to live music.

Come the day of gig, I was inevitably seeing the Thin Lizzy crew and especially Gary for 'hellos' and a catch up. When he learned I had a ticket, he immediately arranged a pass for me with the directive to me, 'Sell it!' Thin Lizzy played a storming set, received with great audience involvement and applause. My main recollection is of the kettle drums on either side of stage which both guitarists used on the opening 'Do Anything You Want To' – superb! It really was wonderful to hear the twin guitars. And for the first time I saw Phil use his mirror scratch plate to great effect.

I WAS THERE: MICK RYAN

I saw them three times. The first time was at Bradford. I remember going down to get tickets and over 100 fans had queued in the snow. I thought, 'I'm not waiting on that,' so I had a walk around town for a bit and then, walking back, I saw a mate of mine in the queue so I pushed in and got tickets. The most memorable moment of the show was when they wheeled out the kettle drums.

The second time I saw them was at the Queens Hall in Leeds on the *Renegade* tour. We got there late morning and there were only six folks in front of us. We saw Lizzy drive past us in a white Merc as they arrived for the soundcheck. When the doors opened, we got to the front barrier and stayed there through the support act. When Lizzy hit the stage – wow, what a feeling. Phil Lynott was just a couple of feet away. But it was absolute madness at the front so after a couple of songs we moved a bit further back where it felt safer.

The third time was also at the Queens Hall, on the last tour. We didn't do the barrier this time and we didn't stay until the end. As we left to catch the last train, Lizzy were playing 'The Sun Goes Down'....

In Dublin about 20 years ago, the girls went off shopping and we went to Tourist Information to get directions to see Phil. We went to the bus stop and were stood with our Lizzy t-shirts on, waiting for the bus we'd been told we needed to catch. A heavily pregnant lady spotted us and said, 'Hi lads, you going to Phil's grave?' We said we were and she said we should get off at the same stop as her. When we got off, she walked with us to the cemetery and told us she had been in the same class at school as Philomena, Phil's mum.

BRIDLINGTON SPA PAVILION

20 APRIL 1979, BRIDLINGTON, UK

I WAS THERE: TIM ROBERTS

I was more than happy about Gary Moore joining full time and we went to 10 *Black Rose* gigs around the north of England. This included having to go to the cities beforehand to buy the tickets, often travelling in thick snow. Queueing to get into the Bradford gig, Scott came down the line shaking hands with us. At the infamous Bridlington gig, we briefly met the band going through the stage door. There was a great Phil lookalike outside, the only real difference being the quality (or not) of his teeth. The Bridlington gig is remembered for no encore, allegedly because beer was spilt from above onto the mixing desk. We were stood on the balcony above the desk and never saw anything happen. I read recently that the real reason was a drugs raid, so I'm still not sure exactly what happened.

We continued to attend Lizzy gigs in the north of England and whilst they were always great, they never seemed to get to the level of '78 and '79. It was sad to see how Phil's appearance seemed to be worsening, albeit I had no idea at the time of the reason why.

We became regulars at Wild Horses gigs with Robbo and were allowed backstage and to a sound check. In Sheffield, we were allowed into the sound check but another group of guys weren't. They were at the concert later and it turned out to be some guys from Def Leppard! Robbo was very impressed with the Lizzy and Wild Horses stitching work we had done on the back of our jackets. I had a Wild Horses fan club t-shirt which I wore for years, even when it was dropping to bits.

In later years we went to see Gary Moore many times and met him on his tour bus but he wasn't particularly friendly. I put it down to tiredness but did get his autograph.

My wife bought me a great surprise present of going to Dublin to see the reunion gig they did when Phil's statue was unveiled. We had a great time. Watching the DVD from the event, it was lovely to know that we are in the crowd. My wife braved the mosh pit - but not for long! My t-shirt from the event shrank in the wash but it's been converted into a cushion cover and so still sits proudly in the house!

I have a Lizzy tattoo on my arm to recognise my lifelong commitment to the band. So many changes happen in your life - people come and go, careers come and go, places change - but music is a constant. Lizzy have always been there with me and always will be.

HAMMERSMITH ODEON

22 & 23 APRIL 1979, LONDON, UK

I WAS THERE: ALAN LONG

The next show was out of Ireland. I was a member of the Thin Lizzy Fan Club in London and whenever shows were happening in England we got the chance to purchase tickets through the fan club. So it was that in April 1979 myself and a friend headed to London to stay with an aunt in Watford and then off to see Lizzy in the Hammersmith Odeon with our tickets, A11 and A12.

It was stunning. We stood with our hands on the stage the whole show and were blown away by the sound and the noise. After the show, people heard our Dublin accents and were asking us whereabouts in Dublin we were from and whether we knew Crumlin, where Philip grew up. When we said Crumlin was about three miles from where I live, they were blown away.

I WAS THERE: ANDREW SMYTH

By the time we saw Thin Lizzy again, in 1979, it was at the Hammersmith Odeon, with Gary Moore on guitar, and a new album in the shops, *Black Rose*. Hammersmith Odeon is the perfect venue to see a band. No matter where you sit or stand, you always get a cracking view with an amazing sound. This time a group of us went and saw the band. It was a tradition to go to the Dirty Duck opposite the venue, where you could sink a few pints, and then go to the chip shop and stuff your face before getting inside the venue.

As soon as we got inside the venue, Robert and I would go straight to the merchandise stand. I wanted everyone to know I saw Thin Lizzy, so anything they had on sale, we would pretty much buy. We would then go to the upstairs bar for a quick pint, before the announcement that the band would be on stage soon.

Thin Lizzy always attracted a mixed audience, and made them feel part of the show. What I remember about this gig was Gary Moore, getting more and more frustrated with his guitar and throwing it across the stage to a hapless roadie! The set list was once again a mixture of classics and new material, this time from the *Black Rose* album. They finished the set with 'Emerald'. The football-like chants of 'Lizzy, Lizzy' echoed round the venue. As the house lights came on, you knew you had been treated to an evening you would not forget.

I WAS THERE: WAYNE NOBLE

Thin Lizzy first came onto my radar with the single 'Whiskey in the Jar', but it was the *Jailbreak* album that really got me into them. I suppose I was a Seventies biker teenager and their music sort of fitted into my lifestyle at the time. I got married when I was 19, and it was around this time that I went to these gigs with my brother-in-law. My wife was more into soul and reggae!

I saw them at the Hammersmith Odeon on the *Black Rose* tour with the awesome Gary Moore on guitar. He has been a hero ever since and I still refer to him as Jesus, only being surpassed by the God that is Dave Gilmour. I also saw them on the *Chinatown* tour. Snowy White had replaced Gary Moore by this time and, although a great guitarist, he could not match his predecessor. The lasting memory from these gigs was having the flash of reflected light momentarily blinding me from Phil Lynott's mirrored bass.

I WAS THERE: JOHN TRUMAN

At Hammersmith they had these walkways reaching out into the auditorium that the guitarist could walk down. And Gary Moore, because he was such a complete and utter arrogant show off as well as being an amazing guitar player, chose the middle one when it was his turn to take a solo. He ran down the walkway and lifted his guitar up as he was about to go into a solo - and nothing came out. It was completely silent.

A roadie ran on. Gary ran back from the stage, took his guitar from around his neck and literally threw it at this roadie. Now a Gibson Les Paul is a heavy piece of wood and it hit this poor roadie and virtually knocked him senseless. At which point another guy came on and passed Gary Moore another guitar and played on. But this poor roadie had to be dragged off.

I've been to the *Vibe for Philo*, which takes place on the anniversary of his death, three times. My sons are both huge Lizzy fans, and when I went over four or five years ago, I wrote a lengthy letter to Philomena, Phil's mum, to tell her what influence her son's work has had on my life. (I'm a guitarist myself.) I sent the letter to White Horses, the house that Phil bought for her and where he had a room.

I didn't expect to hear anything, but the phone rang in my house a couple of weeks later and it was her. We had a really lengthy phone call and she thanked me for what I had put in the letter and invited me over to go and see her. The next time the *Vibe* was on, my son and I visited her house. She showed us Phil's room, with all his albums and his jukebox and his guitars, and we took some photographs. She told some stories and she signed a copy of her biography of Phil, *My Boy*, for my son. We spent a fantastic afternoon there. She did that for so many people. People would come from all over the world and she never turned them away. She was always really, really humbled that Phil meant so much to so many people. And it was a pilgrimage for me.

I WAS THERE: MIKE NEWSHAM

I had a black rose made specially out of crepe paper by a pal's mother who made them for a hobby. It was immaculate and looked just like the rose on the album cover. I wore it all day leading up to a gig at Hammersmith Odeon. It was attached to strong wire that was attached to my Levi's jacket button. After the rush to the stage soon after the band came on, I detached the rose and threw it towards Phil's feet, knowing he would pick it up as I had seen him with an ordinary red rose in his guitar at a previous gig on the tour. I launched the rose airborne, but to my dismay the wire – crucial for the weight in flight – had stayed attached to my jacket button. The rose flopped down just before reaching the stage and was crushed underfoot and never seen again. But the gig was epic!

Mike Newsham had a black rose to give to Phil

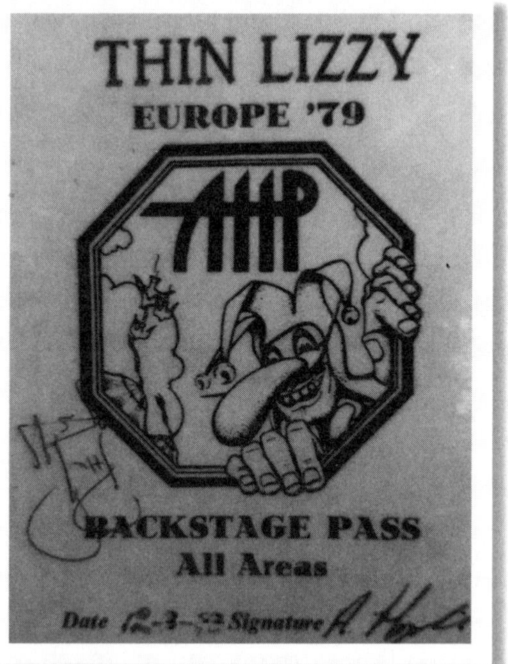

Mike Newsham's brother got backstage on a dodgy backstage pass

In 1983, my brother blagged his way inside Hammersmith Odeon on the *Thunder and Lightning* tour in March 1983 using my 1979 backstage pass. The doorman noticed the year but we told him to look at the date I'd written on the bottom and said Adrian Hopkins had said it was okay and had signed it.

GAUMONT THEATRE
25 APRIL 1979, SOUTHAMPTON, UK

I WAS THERE: CLAIRE JACKSON

We were taken to the Bournemouth gig by a friend, Steve Hopgood, and spent time backstage with the band afterwards before going home. Suzie and I were then at the Gaumont in Southampton on April 25th, again as guests and again spending time with them post gig. Gary Moore was particularly funny, cracking jokes and attacking me in a shower with a bunch of grapes saying, 'You can tell everyone you have been graped by Gary Moore.' The band kept asking me to stand with my back to the upstairs dressing room window and make the fans scream as they would see my silhouette and think it was a band member as I had long dark curly hair!

After going to see them as guests at Hammersmith Odeon on April 27th and leaving to go to the Fulham Greyhound to see another friend's band (I can't believe we got bored that quickly), I never saw the band live again or kept in contact. However, this brief encounter was enough for Suzie and I to take the plunge to move to London 'to work in the music industry'. This was always my goal, but as a woman in the late Seventies, as Phil said, there weren't many openings. I certainly wouldn't have made a roadie or an A&R 'man', but maybe I could try and do lighting! Both Suzie and I eventually worked for Virgin after Suzie mailshotted them when they opened the Megastore in Oxford Street.

HAMMERSMITH ODEON
27 & 28 APRIL 1979, LONDON, UK

I WAS THERE: GLENN GALLOCKER, AGE 15

Glenn Gallocker was only 15 when he saw Lizzy

I'd bought a lone ticket to see them at the Hammersmith Odeon but I was only 15 and lived in leafy Surrey so my transport options were limited. I discovered that my aunt knew a bloke who was a bouncer at the venue and he said he'd give me a lift there and back. When we got there, he suggested I watch the gig from the gantry above the stage, and he'd like to give my ticket to a 'poor young girl who couldn't get a ticket'. My 15-year-old naivety accepted this completely. It was only years later that I realised he'd probably sold it outside to a tout! Anyway, I saw the gig from the electrician's gantry, where I could also see the band backstage before the encore. It was a great view but I regretted not being out there with my fellow Lizzy fans, enjoying the atmosphere and perceived camaraderie.

I WAS THERE: ANDREW SWEET

I would have been about 15 or so and just getting into music and finding out which bands I liked. I'd listen to the radio a lot - Radio 1 or Capital – and not just through the day but the evening and night time shows too, like John Peel and Annie Nightingale. One of them played a track from *Live and Dangerous* and that was where the next week's pay from my Saturday job was going. There I was on the Monday after school, giving the guy behind the counter in Our Price my money, and then off home to play it on the record player I'd inherited from my grandad.

I wasn't disappointed. There wasn't a bad track on the album. Once I left school at 16 and got a bit more money, although being an apprentice it wasn't that much more, I could afford to go to gigs. Being in south west London, I was only two buses from Hammersmith Odeon, a popular stopping off point for bands on tour. Pre internet, the weekly music papers like *Sounds* and *NME* had to be scoured for news of concert dates and when tickets were going on sale. You either had to go to the box office in person or send a postal order through the mail, which for popular bands could be hit or miss in terms of availability. When the *Black Rose* tour was announced, my mate was volunteered to get tickets on the day they went on sale.

Then it was a case of waiting for the night of the show. *Live and Dangerous* was on the deck in the meantime. The night of the show meant a dash home from work to get ready and then onto the bus to meet my mate there. I don't remember the support act, but Thin Lizzy were on stage and lighting the place up with songs like 'The Boys are Back in Town' and 'Jailbreak'. Phil had a tremendous stage presence and a great rapport with the audience. At one point he had a Gretsch or similar metal-bodied guitar and was reflecting the spotlight back out to the audience. If I recall correctly, they either announced extra dates at the end of the tour or toured again very quickly. Sometimes bands did gigs pre the release of an album and then again immediately after its release.

EMPIRE THEATRE
3 MAY 1979, LIVERPOOL, UK

I WAS THERE: SALLY MORRISON, AGE 14

In early 1979 I was 14 years old and my friend Lynne and I had 'discovered' a band called Thin Lizzy. We bought the *Live and Dangerous* album and it was all we ever played - blasting out 'Rosalie' every time we got a chance. Both our boyfriends liked the band too so when we heard they were coming to Liverpool, of course we had to have tickets. We both turned 15 later in May so our boyfriends bought us the tickets for our birthdays. We were so excited and as the date approached, we decided we were going to try and meet the band! Crazy, right? We sat and made plans in Lynne's bedroom. We would bunk off school during the day and stalk the Liverpool hotels, looking for the band. We would then go home in time for our tea, so our mothers wouldn't suspect we had been off school, get changed and be back in time for the gig with our boyfriends.

Sally Morrison bunked off school to get the band's autographs

On the day we set off early. We had heard rumours that the band were staying at the

Holiday Inn so went there first. We naively thought that the doorman would tell us the truth, so we asked if Thin Lizzy were staying there. He just looked at us like we were crazy and said 'no'. Of course, we later found out that they were staying there.

Undeterred, we went up to the Liverpool Empire Theatre where they were playing that night. By this time, it was just after midday. We arrived at the stage door where a small group of other fans were also hanging around. We could hear the band playing inside! We guessed they were practising. We were so excited and determined not to leave until we saw them. I can't remember how long we waited. I do remember chatting with some lads and swapping stories of how we all got into the band and what Thin Lizzy meant for us. But then, without any warning, the stage door flew open and out walked... Brian Downey, Scott Gorham, Gary Moore and Philip Lynott! They seemed to be quite pleased to see this small gaggle of fans, waiting hopefully for autographs.

As Lynne and I were nearest to the door, we got to meet them first and got autographs off all four of them. I used to spell my name 'Sali' when I was 14 – I thought it was cooler – and I told Phil how to spell it. I also pointed to my cheek and asked Phil for a kiss which he duly delivered (a very chaste and embarrassed kiss) and I squealed with delight, vowing never to wash my cheek again! I can remember how happy I felt and my head was in a spin - our heroes were standing right there, smiling and being kind and gracious to us. When I look back, I wonder what it seemed like to them - two 14-year-old kids who definitely should have been at school. They didn't have to be nice to us, but they were.

We spent the rest of the afternoon with the other Lizzy fans and the heady excitement didn't wear off at all. We actually swapped addresses with these guys and kept in touch for a while. We managed to get home on the bus in time for tea, our parents none the wiser, and changed ready to be picked up by our (much older) boyfriends to go to the gig.

It was my first proper gig and I was mesmerised by the whole stage show. The thing I remember the most is when they did 'Jailbreak' and the police sirens and lights started up around Brian Downey's drum kit. We drank beer (underage drinking was more acceptable then) and I kept the bottle as a memento for a while. It's a day in my life that I will never forget.

I WAS THERE: PAUL HOWARD

I (Howie) went to this gig with my mates Ian (Pato), Dave (Murph), Phill (Catty) and Steve (Yikky). Ian managed to get his copy of the *Jailbreak* album signed afterwards. We saw Lizzy there twice but also Rush, Bad Company, AC/DC, UFO and The Scorpions Great times.

Paul Howard and his mates were at the Empire

I WAS THERE: PHILIP CURRAN, AGE 19

I wasn't really a fan but I liked what I had heard of them so I went along with a friend who was a fan and I'm glad I did - the sheer showmanship of the band was extraordinary. Phil Lynott exuded immense charisma and machismo as an entertainer, and able to cheerfully banter with the audience while using the mirror pick guard on his bass to reflect the spotlight back into the crowd. As I recall the audience was a good mix of males and females - not your usual all male hard rocker types. It was a very memorable and enjoyable show. I still have the programme and ticket stub. One funny thing I recall is Scott Gorham wobbling over in his platform boots!

Philip Curran recalls Scott wobbling over in his platform boots

---

Phil Lynott exuded immense charisma and machismo

May 1979 saw Thin Lizzy touring Europe again, playing 20 dates.

FALKONER TEATRET

10 MAY 1979, COPENHAGEN, DENMARK

I WAS THERE: JAN HVEDHAVEN

I heard Thin Lizzy for the first time when I heard the album *Live and Dangerous*. I was sold. This band - and especially Phil Lynott - was what I had been searching for. I was 17 years old and I knew that I wanted to become a rock musician.

This band was what I had been searching for

When I heard Phil, I wanted to become a bass player. I went to my first Thin Lizzy concert with my band, which was heavily influenced by Thin Lizzy. They had just released *Black Rose*. They opened with 'Do Anything You Want To'. Gary and Scott were playing the timpani in the intro and it was amazing. Then came 'Are You Ready' and off we went.

Lizzy returned to North America to tour in support of *Black Rose*.

LONG BEACH ARENA

30 JUNE 1979, LONG BEACH, CALIFORNIA

I WAS THERE: TONI KASS TREVIZO

They were not a major band here in the States when I first heard them. I was a dancer, and regularly appeared on a show called *American Bandstand*. I got to meet a lot of musicians and I was always interested in new bands coming to the United States. I heard of

Thin Lizzy, got the album and went to see them with my brother-in-law. I loved the melodic sound and the twin guitar styles, and Phil's vocals were so perfectly meshed into the guitars. 'Black Rose' was just overwhelming. I knew Gary was hard to work with but I still loved his playing. I'm a big Lizzy fan and also a Gary Moore fan. I couldn't rave about Lizzy enough to my musician friends, or my other friends.

4TH OF JULY ALL-AMERICAN ROCK & ROLL SHOW, DAY ON THE GREEN, OAKLAND STADIUM

4 JULY 1979, OAKLAND CALIFORNIA

I WAS THERE: STEVE RUSSEY

During my formative years, aged 12 or 13, I would lock into the cool amplitude modulation pop hit radio stations and eventually the much cooler frequency modulation rock stations and take in a variety of impressive sounds. One song that stood out was this tune about the 'boys' being 'back in town'. Even more enjoyable was that we actually had a 'Dino's Bar & Grill' in our realm. I was much too young to enter the establishment, but driving around town with Mom listening to the radio, it was always a fun bit of synchronicity if this great tune came on while we were driving by Dino's, especially if it wouldn't 'be long 'til summer comes….'

I never got to enter Dino's – it was bulldozed before I was 21 – but summer came in 1979 and so did Thin Lizzy! I recall 'Get Out of Here' from *Black Rose* getting moderate airplay that summer, and my being totally mesmerised by Gary Moore's fabulous guitar solo. Lizzy were on the line up at one of Bill Graham's famous *Days on the Green* at the Oakland/Alameda Stadium.

Phil, Scott and Brian hit the stage along with Gary Moore and they ripped into 'Jailbreak'. However, Phil's microphone did not work and in true rock and roll tradition he kicked it over in frustration. A tech rushed out and replaced it and the gig proceeded without further incident. The big question was, 'Are they going to do 'The Boys are Back in Town'?' It was perhaps their biggest hit over here in the USA, with 'Dancing in the Moonlight' their second biggest.

Sure enough, as that other gem of a tune, 'Cowboy Song', was winding up to its crescendo – 'the cowboy's life is the life for me…' - Thin Lizzy pulled off a moment of pure rock transcendence and – ZAP! - segued directly into 'The Boys are Back in Town'. The opening chord of that true rock classic had the stadium in hysterics, and I just experienced a spinal chill simply typing about it. My Thin Lizzy experience was complete….

Having spent the day beholding UFO, Nazareth, Journey, J Geils Band and The Rockets, I drove home with my circle of friends, basking in the glory of having witnessed this fantastic Irish rock quartet forge an unforgettable proverbial chapter in my personal rock music history book. Yes, later we were indeed 'dancing in the moonlight on that long hot summer night'.

RIP Phil and Gary, and thanks for all the great music!

I WAS THERE: JIM MOHR

The next summer, a Day on the Green was announced for July 4, at the Oakland Coliseum with Journey as the headliner. However, the band I went to see was Thin Lizzy! This show was alternately called the '4TH of July All-American Rock & Roll Show', which is somewhat ironic because half of the six bands were not American (although Thin Lizzy's 'candidate for the next president of the United States' is).

My friends were there to see other bands and had no interest in going down onto the field to get closer, so I went by myself and ended up about 30 yards from the stage.

Opening with 'Are You Ready?' I certainly was and Phil once again displayed his prowess as the ultimate front-man, and definitely earning the accolade from Huey Lewis as 'the best hard-rock performer of his time'. Although not as obvious as during the indoor show the year before, Phil once again used the light reflecting off of his pick guard to connect with fans. I knew every song and wrote them down in a small notebook that I brought explicitly for that purpose.

'Jailbreak' also played a special role at this show. At the end of the previous song ('Waiting for an Alibi'), Phil knocked over his mic stand and unknowingly broke something. They started playing 'Jailbreak', but when Phil started singing, nothing came over the speakers. As the road crew scurried to get a new mic in place, they continued to play the 'Jailbreak' intro for what felt like an eternity, but was probably closer to five minutes.

Following the *Day on the Green* show, and after a serious row with Phil, Gary Moore walked out of Thin Lizzy.

COLISEUM

6 JULY 1979, RENO, NEVADA

HE WASN'T THERE: GARY MOORE

Gary Moore failed to show in Reno and Phil, Scott and Brian played the show as a three piece. The show scheduled for 12 July in Wichita, Kansas was then cancelled due to 'illness', but four subsequent shows were performed as a three piece while a replacement guitarist was located.

Gary leaving the band halfway through a tour was the death knell for Thin Lizzy in America, it really was. We were still hugely popular in the UK and Europe, but the last semblance of trying to make it in America was blown out of the window. **Brian Downey**

THE BARTON COLISEUM

15 JULY 1979, LITTLE ROCK, ARKANSAS

I WAS THERE: DAVID GODSEY

I probably first heard Thin Lizzy on the AM radio in my car. I was immediately drawn to the power of their music, and the twin guitars and great lyrics. I set out to find their albums and (8-track) tapes - I was completely smitten! I loved the blend of Irish stories and classic American rock and roll and bought everything by them that I could.

In 1977, I joined the Air Force and they sent me to Little Rock Air Force Base, where in 1979 I heard that Thin Lizzy were opening up for Journey. They had Gary Moore as a guitarist and I loved his work on *Black Rose* so I just had to see them. But the concert came around and it turned out that Gary Moore was ill and would not be there and Lizzy would play as a three piece. Well, they came out and just killed it!

David Godsey got a book inscribed by Phil's mother

They were awesome, the sound was powerful and Phil was completely on his game. I loved how the powerful spotlight would bounce off the pickguard and he would point it into the crowd like a laser. I had seen a lot of concerts but this time was the only time the opening band did encores. In fact, they did two! I had the time of my life and actually met a girl in the crowd and kissed her without ever knowing her name! (Those were the days.)

I was driving home when I heard Phil had died. I just started crying. It hurt badly. I felt I had come to know Phil and the boys through their music. As the years have gone by, I have pursued their music even more. One day I read that Phil's mother was writing a book about her life with Phil and the band so I looked for it and found it on eBay. Someone in Ireland was selling it for, like, five bucks. Well, that was a no brainer – I had to have it!

I remember the day it arrived, I had a package from Ireland, and I opened it being excited to read it, and then being shocked to learn after opening it that I had bought the book from Phil's mother! She wrote me a nice note and had drawn on the book and given me her address and phone number! I just sat there speechless.

THE WAREHOUSE

18 JULY 1979, NEW ORLEANS, LOUISIANA

HE WAS THERE: MIDGE URE

Having been flown in by the band on Concorde, and with hardly any time to learn the songs, Midge Ure joined Thin Lizzy as the replacement for Gary Moore.

I thought I would try and learn the songs on the plane. But they flew me out on Concorde so I was in New York before I had written down all the chords for the second song. **Midge Ure**

JAI-ALAI FRONTON

22 JULY 1979, MIAMI, FLORIDA

I WAS THERE: JAE CEE, AGE 17

Riding to school in the back seat of my cousin's car he was always playing some music. Most of the time it sucked. But one day there was a change - bam! - and there it was, 'Fool's Gold' by Thin Lizzy. The line 'the vulture sits on top of the big top circus arena...' still gives me chills today. That's when I first heard them and I had to hear more. I saw them at the Jai-Alai Fronton in Florida in 1979. They opened for Journey and I left after Lizzy played, as I'm not much of a Journey fan. The memory of the spots flashing off Phil's black Fender bass is still vivid. Phil's charisma hit you like a brick. He was larger than life for sure. I was 17 and had been to my fair share of concerts by then and have seen quite a few since. No one compares to Phil Lynott!

WELSH AUDITORIUM

29 JULY 1979, GRAND RAPIDS, MICHIGAN

I WAS THERE: BILL MURPHY

I saw Thin Lizzy open for Journey. I was in the front row, centre. Phil Lynott was a force, to be sure. He was a sweaty rock god who spoke with a sly wink, tongue firmly in cheek. He used his black bass guitar with the mirrored pick guard to catch the spotlight and throw it back to sections of the audience, talking to them in turn.

'You up there!' he said, as he manoeuvred his mirrored bass guitar to reflect the spotlight to an upper seating area. 'And you over there! And you back there! Are you feeling it?' Then he launched into his famously hilarious question that is captured on *Live and Dangerous*. 'Are there any girls with a little Irish in them in the audience tonight?' he asked with a gleam in his eye, sweat dripping off his brow, and a broad smile on his face. 'Are there are any girls in the audience tonight who'd like a little more Irish in them?' The audience roared.

Drummer Brian Downey lived up to what one UK journalist wrote about him in one album review. He was 'as tight as a camel's arse in a sandstorm'. Scott Gorham looked to be having a great time. He was the guitarist who was closest to me from my vantage point. He spent a lot of time grinning widely. Overall, my impression of Lizzy that evening was they were tight, chockful of energy and having the time of their lives. *Black Rose* was killer material, especially the title track, and the audience went wild for 'The Boys Are Back in Town'.

Lizzy were the perfect opener for Journey because they got the audience powered up and eager to see the headliner. But Phil grabbed and held my attention. He was so unbelievably charismatic and the perfect front man. It was a hot, sweaty, non-stop party and I saw every drop of sweat fall from Phil's face.

Yup. Saw Lizzy live. Front row, centre.

COMISKEY PARK

5 AUGUST 1979, CHICAGO, ILLINOIS

I WAS THERE: THOMAS PYTEL

I hated 'The Boys are Back in Town' but my cousin had the *Jailbreak* album on 8-track (remember those?) and played me the album. The one

Thomas Pytel saw Lizzy steal the show

song that I liked was 'Cowboy Song' so when *Live and Dangerous* came out I bought it just for that. I was hooked. I couldn't wait for *Black Rose* to come out and when I just discovered Gary Moore was on that album, I fell in love with his playing right away.

We heard that Lizzy were coming to Chicago later that summer, third on the bill to Journey and Santana but over Eddie Money and Molly Hatchet. It was insane getting in that morning as it was general admission and I almost got killed in the crush. Drugs were flowing freely but no one seemed to mind. When Thin Lizzy came out, Phil rushed up and asked the crowd, 'Are you fooking ready?' They started off with 'Are you Ready' and 'Bad Reputation' and then did both the slow and fast versions of 'Don't Believe a Word'. We kept asking if the other guitarist was Gary Moore. We noticed that he wasn't doing any lead solos. Unbeknownst to us, Gary had gone AWOL the month before at Bill Graham's *Day on the Green* in Oakland, California. It was all Scott and he shone that day and carried Lizzy through the show.

When they got around to playing 'Got to Give it Up', Phil told the crowd of 66,000, 'This is a little disco for you.' The whole stadium started booing and got very loud doing so. As Phil was singing the intro to 'Got to Give it Up', the crowd kept booing and then, when he hit the opening chords, the crowd went nuts. Phil was so magical and charismatic, fist shaking and double fist shaking. He had the crowd in the palm of his hands.

When they did the 'Cowboy Song' and 'The Boys are Back in Town', the crowd really went crazy. 'Suicide' was next and Scott really looked so cool, right on the side of the stage in front of the Marshall amps. He really played well and his leads were spot on. Then they went into 'Sha-

La-La' and Brian Downey's drum solo did not disappoint the crowd as people were amazed at his playing.

The last number was 'Baby Drives Me Crazy' and it was at that point that Phil introduced Midge Ure. We were like, 'Who is he?' In the USA back then, we didn't get the news on the band so we really had no idea what had happened regarding Gary Moore. I was gutted that I didn't get to see Gary, but thankful that I was able to see Phil and Thin Lizzy. 'Suicide', 'Sha-La-La' and 'Baby Drives Me Crazy' all sounded very close to what was on *Live and Dangerous.*

Journey were the headliners and big at the time, Lizzy stole the show. Phil Lynott's stage presence is forever etched in my memory.

After the US tour concluded in August 1979, Lizzy were scheduled to play the UK's Reading Festival but the appearance was cancelled as the band were auditioning replacements for Gary Moore. With Midge Ure on keyboards and Dave Flett on guitar, Lizzy toured Japan in September.

ELECTRIC BALLROOM

1 DECEMBER 1979, LONDON, UK

I WAS THERE: PETER JOHNSON

After leaving Lizzy, Robbo formed Wild Horses with Jimmy Bain. Robbo was always bringing on guest stars. The Horses had already played a great gig when on walked Phil and Scott for the encore. The crowd naturally went wild. They played 'Suicide' and 'Are You Ready'. The chanting of 'Lizzy, Lizzy' wouldn't stop. Phil and Scott were the cherry on the icing of a three tier cake. Absolutely unforgettable.

APOLLO THEATRE

16 & 17 DECEMBER 1979, MANCHESTER, UK

I WAS THERE: DAVE HAMMOND

I was fortunate enough to see Lizzy live on five separate occasions, but my favourite show was definitely the one at the Manchester Apollo in December 1979. During one of the songs, Phil shone his mirrored bass guitar on me and my friend Nick and raised his fist at us. It's something I will never forget. We saw them on both the *Black Rose* and *Chinatown* tours and I still have the concert programmes. The line up of the band for our show was a bit out of the ordinary with Midge Ure (Ultravox) and Dave Flett (Manfred Mann's Earth Band) in the group replacing Gary Moore. The set list was drawn mainly from *Black Rose*, *Chinatown*, *Jailbreak*, *Bad Rep* and *Live and Dangerous*. And because the show was close to Christmas time, they added the Greedies' song 'A Merry Jingle' to the set list, but no Sex Pistols were on stage with them.

Dave Hammond, pictured here with Neil Peart from Rush, saw Lizzy five times

My favourite memories of Lizzy are from when my friend Nick and I used to go into town (Kettering, Northants) with a tape recorder, blaring out Lizzy songs as loud as we possibly could. In fact, we became known as the Lizzy lads by the locals. Another fond memory is of waiting outside the record store

Dave Hammond's fan club membership card

on release day for a new single or album as I was a member of the fan club, so we were the first to get info on new releases. Lizzy's music is the soundtrack to my life and I will be one of the people that makes sure it is always remembered by playing it as often as I can on my radio show here in South Africa.

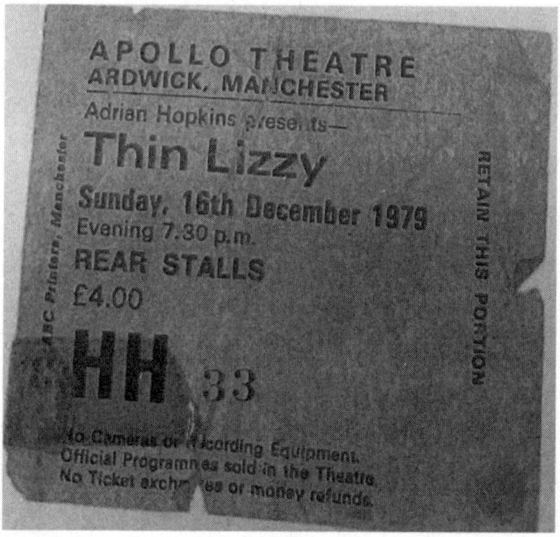

Dave Hammond's Apollo ticket

I WAS THERE: CARL HAMILTON

I was a young lad at the time and still at school. Lizzy were my favourite band, so when they came to Manchester we would always go to see them. Gary Moore was in their line up the first time I saw them. They were always outstanding live. Phil really knew how to get the crowd involved and he loved Manchester, and Manchester United, and spent a lot of time here, where his mum, Philomena, lived for over 30 years. Years later, she became a really good friend of mine.

Carl Hamilton with Philomena Lynott

Thin Lizzy are still to this day the best band I've ever seen. The songs, the energy and the sheer love of their trade all accounted for what was always a magical show. On one occasion, my friends and I went to a Christmas concert. As kids, we always waited outside at the side of the Apollo to try and catch the band coming out and maybe get an autograph.

Whilst we were waiting, a guy was holding a cassette tape in the air boasting about how he'd 'taped the whole fucking gig, and this tape will be worth a fortune in many years to come.' While our eyes and attention were on this guy, we were totally shocked to find Phil Lynott was standing behind him. We all thought Phil was going to beat him up for taping the show

Petrified, the tape holder turned round to face Phil. Phil held out his hand and said quietly, 'Give me that tape.' The tape, rattling with the guy's nerves, was handed over and we all stood in complete silence. Phil asked the lad for a pen, proceeded to sign the tape, and then smiled and handed it back, saying 'It'll be worth a lot more now.' The look on the guy's face, and the relief on the faces of us bystanders, was a picture I'll never forget. Phil loved the supporters and always took time to have a chat and ask if we enjoyed the show. A true legend.

NEW BINGLEY HALL

18 DECEMBER 1979, STAFFORD, UK

I WAS THERE: ANDY TUNSTALL

When Thin Lizzy were in their prime, I was 14 years old. In those days there was little 'heavy rock' played on the radio apart from Saturday afternoons on Radio 1 and, later, the *Friday Rock Show*. The main way to learn about such music was the music press (mainly *Sounds* for rock bands), looking at album covers, rare appearances on *Top of the Pops* and going to see the bands live. It wasn't massively expensive then, but living in rural Shrewsbury, which was too small to attract major bands, presented another issue – how to get to gigs. The answer was that 12 to 14 of us would club together and hire a minibus and driver, which worked out at a reasonable price per person.

Andy Tunstall (centre) was an aspiring bass player

However, as well as listening to music, we wanted to make it in the music business and I had been given the role of bass player in our early band, Pyramid. When I got hold of *Live and Dangerous* there was the obvious attraction of them being led by the bass player. The 12 inch vinyl double album was very well packaged, with lots of photos of the band from the 1977 tour featuring Lynott, Downey and Gorham plus Brian Robertson.

So I had high hopes when I saw Lizzy for the first time in December 1979 at Stafford Bingley Hall. They opened with 'Jailbreak', with exploding flash bombs and blue flashing lights, and it was pretty mindblowing. Whilst the very capable guitarists were doing their harmony lead bits at each side, Phil was bang in the middle, aiming his Fender Precision at the audience like a sniper's rifle or shining the spotlights off his pickguard into the faces of the audience - allegedly, the best looking girls he could see! He really made the show, a great front man with good banter between the songs in his cheeky way and a very good bass player. Overall, it was a great show.

I WAS THERE: KEVIN O'CONNELL, AGE 16

I had the privilege of growing up alongside the formation and subsequent growth of Thin Lizzy. As a young drummer learning my trade and attending my weekly lessons and subsequent grades, underneath it all was my hero, Brian Downey. Brian inspired me to stick through the learning of the 26 rudiments and all of those difficult and at times challenging moments in order to become the drummer that I became.

At the age of 16, I travelled from Suffolk to Staffordshire to see Thin Lizzy for the first time at Bingley Hall. The line up comprised of Phil Lynott, Brian Downey, Scott Gorham, Midge Ure and Dave Flett. They did not disappoint and I remember to this day just how on it Lizzy were, and the roadies dressed in their Santa outfits throwing out goodies to the crowd. At the end of the gig, Phil invited fans to stay behind to meet the band, but doing so meant missing all the last buses back to the train stations.

I WAS THERE: COLIN MASON

A new venue had opened up in Stafford about 30 miles from where I lived in Birmingham, the New Bingley Hall, or 'the cowshed' as most gig goers called it, because that's what it was - a county showground for farmers! But you could fit about 5,000 people in there so it became a big music venue for the Midlands. I saw Lizzy there three times, twice in 1979 and again in 1980. But it's the December 1979 gig which was a very special one for me. For whatever reason - perhaps it being a week before Christmas, perhaps because of a little over indulgence in the alcohol on my part (I'd turned 20), perhaps just because it was a superb gig - this gig was recorded in my little red book (later transferred to a spreadsheet which I still update after every gig I go to) as the best gig I'd ever been to - a long set and then six encores. I remember the band members coming on stage near the end of the show with large toy guns – the sort that fire tennis balls – but they were shooting out t-shirts and other merch into the audience. And those guns had a good range!

Getting to the New Bingley Hall was quite a feat for me and my gig buddies before any of us could drive. It usually involved a bus to the train station, a train to Stafford and then hitching a lift or walking three and a half miles. After this gig, me and a mate walked back to Stafford railway station only to find we'd missed the last train back to Birmingham. We settled down on a couple of benches on the station platform to kip - in December! - but a short while later an engine pulled in running light (no carriages, just the locomotive). We chatted to the driver. He was heading back to Saltley just a couple of miles outside Birmingham city centre. 'Can we get a lift in your cab?' I asked. 'Yeah sure,' was the reply. I can't see that happening nowadays.

I WAS THERE: LINDA DOBSON

I saw them at the Victoria Hall in Hanley at least twice, but I saw them three or four times altogether. I can only remember a couple of things, like once when Phil came out wearing a Father Christmas outfit.

Linda Dobson still has her Lizzy badge

In 1985, Phil and the TV presenter Dustin Gee were ill at the same time and there was a lot about Dustin on the news over the Christmas period, but I heard absolutely nothing about Phil until the awful news that he'd gone.

I WAS THERE: JOHN RYAN

Phil came on dressed as Father Christmas and started throwing records into the audience. Midge Ure was on guitar and dressed as a cowboy!

RAINBOW THEATRE

20 DECEMBER 1979, LONDON, UK

I WAS THERE: PETER THOMSON

My final experience of Thin Lizzy live was the 1979 Christmas concert they played. It was a bit like a greatest hits performance but all the old spirit was still there. My abiding memory is of the encore, where they performed 'A Merry Jingle' that had been released by the ad hoc supergroup The Greedy Bastards. Quickly shortening their title to The Greedies, to ensure radio and TV airplay, the single had been a hit during the previous weeks. Lizzy were joined on stage by Paul Cook and Steve Jones of Sex Pistols fame, and at least Johnnie Fingers of The Boomtown Rats. It was a suitably comic end to the Seventies, with Brian Robertson playing out with a paper bag over his head.

I eventually got to hear 'Whiskey' performed live a couple of weeks before Christmas 2017 by some bloke in a Dublin bar – how appropriate is that?

Overall, Thin Lizzy were a great part of my young life. I've seen many, diverse live performances and I can still say they were the best.

(Peter remembers this show as being at the Hammersmith Odeon)

MARQUEE CLUB

27 FEBRUARY 1980, LONDON, UK

I WAS THERE: KEITH THOMPSON, AGE 17

Fast forward to February 1980. I was now living in London. On this particular night I was out on the town with a friend and we walked past the Marquee Club. A band called Wild Horses were playing and although we had no idea who they were, we liked what we were hearing and remarked that they sounded like Thin Lizzy. It started to dawn on us that this was Brian Robertson's band and just at that point he announced that he had a few friends with him and on walked the rest of Thin Lizzy! They kicked off this impromptu set with 'Rosalie' and proceeded to take the place apart! To see them at such close range was unbelievable. They were a big influence on me as a young musician and they left an indelible impression.

Thin Lizzy began 1980 with an Irish tour in April. This was Snowy White's debut tour.

ANTRIM FORUM

5 APRIL 1980, ANTRIM, UK

I WAS THERE: STEPHEN BARRY

After seeing them at the Ulster Hall, we then saw them for a second and final time in the unusual setting of a leisure centre in the town of Antrim. It was a Saturday night. I recall that mine and Phil's team, Man United, had beaten Liverpool that afternoon, so that set me up well for a good evening! Once again Phil and the boys didn't disappoint. There were no seats. Maddie and me were joined by my good mate Davie, who happened to be suffering from an ingrown toenail and was in some considerable pain, not helped by revellers landing on it a few times!

Stephen Barry saw Lizzy at the Antrim Forum

CARLTON BALLROOM

10 APRIL 1980, KILKENNY, IRELAND

I WAS THERE: MICK MORTON, AGE 17

Back in 1980 Thin Lizzy were playing Kilkenny, one of the smaller venues of the Irish tour. I was just turned 17 and it was one of my first Thin Lizzy gigs but I looked like I was just turned 12! That morning the buzz around Kilkenny was great. The road crew had arrived around 10 in the morning and was rolling the equipment to the venue up a narrow lane, as no trucks could get up. I remember talking to one of the crew about the gig when a guy passed up by us with a dog. I knew he was a member of the drug squad and said as much to the roadie. The roadie was asking me did I know him and what was he like. I told him I knew of him but that I'd never had any dealings with him (well, this was Ireland in the 1980).

Mick Morton got a pair of Brian's drumsticks

The roadie asked me was I going to the gig later and I told him, 'For sure'. He said, 'After the gig is over, I'll be working on the stage. I'll have a few things for you.'

One of my friend's aunts had got the catering gig for the band and crew so four of us went backstage around three o'clock to help out. We got in to hear the sound check and try and meet the band. Phil wanted cabbage, bacon and spuds for the dinner and you could smell the cabbage and bacon all over the place. The Carlton was used as a venue for roller disco at the time, so Phil and a few of the roadies and myself and one of the boys got the skates on and did some skating. We were buzzing all day. We even got to talk with the band and listened to the sound check. We were then asked to leave as the band was heading for dinner.

Later on, after the gig ended, I waited for the crowd to go. The roadie was up on the stage. He gave me two of Brian Downey's drum sticks and Phil's plectrum and he said that he had a few '79 tour books if I wanted them. He gave me around 20 of them. I met up with some of my friends and went up to a chipper and we sold some of the books. A guy offered me £60 for the drum sticks. At that time, I was earning around £12 a week. Boy, was I tempted, but I'm glad to say I didn't sell them and I still have them today, 40 years on.

I remember meeting Brian Downey at a Brian Robertson gig in Dublin some years ago and was talking to him for a while, telling him I had a set of his drum sticks. He said to me, 'Ya fecker, I don't even have a set of them!'

CITY HALL

13 APRIL 1980, CORK, IRELAND

I WAS THERE: ALAN LONG

My next time of seeing them was April 1980 and the hometown of my father, Cork. Myself and my pal drove to Cork on a motorcycle and again stopped off with an auntie for bed and board. Snowy was in the band now, and Midge Ure was still hanging on from the USA tour. That was the famous show where everybody wanted Lizzy to play 'Whiskey in the Jar' and Phil, in his own true south Dublin accent, said, 'I don't know it, and Snowy doesn't know it, and Scott doesn't know it, but Midge does…' and away they went. We all went wild, singing to our hearts' content.

From Ireland, Lizzy went on a short Scandinavian tour.

FORUM

24 APRIL 1980, COPENHAGEN, DENMARK

John Naldal Jakobsen met Phil in Copenhagen

I WAS THERE: JOHN NALDAL JAKOBSEN

This was my first time of seeing Lizzy. It was a great show and Phil was the ultimate frontman. Afterwards me and a friend were lucky to meet Phil and the rest of the band outside the Plaza Hotel in Copenhagen. We took a lot of photos and Phil was very nice and a real gentleman. All in all, I saw Thin Lizzy four times and every show was rocking. They were a top class band and the music will always remind me of how good Thin Lizzy were and how brilliant Phil was as a songwriter and front man.

OLYMPEN

25 APRIL 1980, LUND, SWEDEN

I WAS THERE: JANNE STARK

Back in 1980 I was a member of a local music club called Rockslaget (the rock battle), in Karlshamn, Sweden. Besides having a big house with rehearsal spaces for bands (my band Overdrive rehearsed there) and a stage to play, they also arranged bus trips to concerts. on April 25, 1980 about 40 young kids from Karlshamn, Sweden got on a bus for the two hour ride to see Thin Lizzy at Olympen in Lund, Sweden. It was the *Chinatown* tour and they played my two favourite songs from the album, 'Chinatown' and 'Sugar Blues'. We were just starting up Overdrive, and those Thin Lizzy harmony guitars had a big impact on our sound. And now I play in a Danish/Swedish Thin Lizzy tribute band called Falling Hazard.

May saw Thin Lizzy undertake the UK leg of what was billed as the *World Tour 80*.

CITY HALL

1 & 2 MAY 1980, NEWCASTLE, UK

I WAS THERE: ANDY KING

I first seriously became aware of music during the glam rock era. Aged 10 in 1972, I became totally addicted to the likes of T.Rex, Slade, Gary Glitter and, most of all, Sweet. At Christmas 1974 my family went to stay with my mum's sister in Florida. She had emigrated there some years previous. My cousin Judith bought a cassette of *Paranoid* by Black Sabbath and so my journey into metal and hard rock began.

In 1976 I was enrolled at Brighton College boarding school (my dad's work had taken him to Iran). On the way to the school, my mum stopped at Woolworths and bought me a small cassette recorder to play my *Paranoid* album on (I couldn't take my glam rock records). Feeling sorry for me only having the one tape, she also bought me a copy of *Jailbreak* by Thin Lizzy. She later told me she thought I might like the cover. For the next year I played both albums ad nauseum.

At school I started guitar lessons. My teacher was a bit of a rocker and the first tune I learnt was 'Waiting for an Alibi'. I left school and enrolled in college. I got a part time job at a shoe store in Portsmouth and spent pretty much all my wages on Lizzy material. Within six months I had pretty much everything they had officially recorded and some bootleg stuff but still hadn't seen them live. It was time to change that.

I dropped out of college in 1980, borrowed some money from my dad and ventured on a Lizzy quest. I saw them ten times in May 1980, starting at Newcastle City Hall and followed by Dundee, Liverpool, Leeds, Preston, Sheffield, Stafford, Birmingham and Bristol. By the time I got to Bristol I had run out of money so after the show I went back home to my mum and dad's house in Prestwich, Manchester. As luck would have it, a couple of days later I ventured into town to see the Hazel O'Connor movie, *Breaking Glass*, and happened to buy a Bury Football Club scratch card - and won the jackpot of £1,000. Lizzy Part Two was back on!

I ventured to London to resume what I now call 'my little Lizzy holiday'. I saw them at Hammersmith Odeon on 31 May and then the Rainbow, Portsmouth, Oxford, Leicester, Coventry, Brighton, Southampton and Cardiff.

Andy King was a glam rock addict before Lizzy came along

By this time my dad was putting pressure on me to finish my degree so I caved in and spent the next two years in college, finishing my business studies degree. During that period my folks had moved to Hatfield. After finishing my degree, I moved to my parents and took up a job at BAE as a buyer. That's where I met my wife (she was my dad's PA) – we are still married 34 plus years later.

All things Lizzy took a back seat for a while and of course NWOBHM came around and I fell hook, line and sinker into that after someone bought me a copy of the *Axe Attack* compilation album. However, Lizzy brought out *Chinatown* and *Renegade* during that period and I found myself back in the Lizzy camp.

I had planned to do a quick revisit in 1982 but a bunch of shows got cancelled due to Scott Gorham being ill so they never materialised. I picked a few to attend in 1983. Little did I know it would be the final year of Lizzy. That year I saw them in January (Hitchin), February (Manchester and Portsmouth), March (Hammersmith twice), May (Ipswich) and finally ending my live experience with Lizzy at the 1983 Reading Festival.

I can't remember when, but Radio 1 ran a competition to win Phil's Fender Precision mirror bass. I think the DJ was Peter Powell. I won it, but later sold it for a ridiculous price to pay for my honeymoon.

I saw Phil with Grand Slam once at the Derngate in Northampton. I remember thinking at the time that Phil looked very ill and how he lacked any charisma.

I was due to go to dinner and get engaged to my now wife on 4th January 1986, the day Phil left us. I was so upset on hearing the news I cancelled our plans and rescheduled for the next day.

In 1996, I was on vacation in Los Angeles and, whilst walking down Venice Beach, felt the need to get my first tattoo, so got a black rose tattoo on my right ankle. The following year I got a black rose on my other ankle. Eleven tattoos later, most of which are in deference to the *Black Rose* album, I am done with needles.

When Lizzy reformed post-Phil, I vowed never to go and see them. However, Elaine and I had booked a cruise from Southampton in 2007 and just down the road at the BIC in Bournemouth, two of my other favourite bands - Styx and Purple - were playing, along with the reformed Lizzy. I cried like a baby.

Since 1981 I have been fronting bands as a lead singer. They have all been rock covers bands, some more successful that others. But all have the same in common – they all have a big splattering of Lizzy in them. It's funny how things have a way of coming full circle. In one of my covers bands was a guy called Benjy Reid – a classy guy and an amazing drummer. His career has taken him to now playing with the reformed Grand Slam.

Am I the number one Lizzy fan? I doubt it, but I loved them then and I love them now.

I WAS THERE: PETER SMITH

Gary Moore had no sooner joined Thin Lizzy than he decided to leave. The switching guitarists wasn't the only problem for the band at the time; Phil and Scott were increasingly using hard drugs. Moore's replacement was Snowy White, a fine bluesy guitarist who had played with Peter Green and Pink Floyd. This was, for me, the beginning of the end of Thin Lizzy. Snowy was an excellent guitarist, but it just didn't seem to work. His blues style, his quiet manner and his on stage persona just didn't fit with the wild rock image of the rest of the band, or his predecessors. Snowy White is an excellent guitarist, but he wasn't right for Lizzy.

Peter Smith was at Newcastle City Hall

The new line-up recorded *Chinatown*, which was good but not one of their best records. Thin Lizzy called at Newcastle City Hall for two nights and I went to the first night's concert. It was another enjoyable show, but it seemed slicker and less wild than previous Lizzy concerts. Sadly, the classic years had passed. The highlight of the concert was when former Lizzy guitarist Brian Robertson joined the band for the encore, playing on 'Emerald' and 'Rosalie'. Apparently, Robbo's new band Wild Horses had a gig at Newcastle

Poly the following night. The appearance of Robbo was apparently reciprocated the next night at the Poly gig when Phil and Scott joined Wild Horses on stage.

I WAS THERE: IAN JOHNSON

My love for Lizzy began back in 1978 when a school friend lent me *Jailbreak*. It was the first rock album I had listened to and it changed my music loves forever. I started getting all their albums and by the time *Black Rose* was coming up for release, it was like Christmas was coming early. I first saw them on the *Chinatown* tour.

I arrived at Newcastle City Hall full of excitement, bought tour t-shirts from the lads selling t-shirts outside and then bought an official t-shirt and a programme inside. Come showtime and the lights went off and Phil's booming voice came over 'Are you ready?'. The pyrotechnics exploded and there they were - Thin Lizzy. What a gig and what a first gig to see.

ODEON THEATRE

4 MAY 1980, EDINBURGH, UK

I WAS THERE: KEITH MCSHANE

It was always great knowing Thin Lizzy were coming to Edinburgh, this time for the *Chinatown* tour. It was always a great opening at a Lizzy concert and I don't remember seeing or feeling this level of excitement. They played all the usual stuff alongside promoting the album, but by this time Snowy White was in the band. His playing was fabulous but his stage presence did not fit with the band. He's a musician's musician.

EMPIRE THEATRE

7 MAY 1980, LIVERPOOL, UK

I WAS THERE: SIMON MATTHEWS

Like many fans, it was Thin Lizzy playing 'Whiskey in the Jar' that got me into their music but what really cemented my fandom was the release of 'The Boys are Back in Town', along with the album *Jailbreak*. a key part of their success was down to the dual lead guitars and, of course, the flamboyance and song writing ability of the late, great Phil Lynott. But like so many great rock bands, they really excelled when they took to the stage. I was fortunate enough to see them play at the Liverpool Empire when Snowy White was on second guitar, alongside the always magnificent Scott Gorham.

Simon Matthews saw Lizzy with Snowy

I think most fans would agree that this was not one of the greatest line ups, but that gig was one of the best I've ever seen. Snowy basically stood and played whilst Phil and Scott raced around the stage, jumping on the monitors, etc. and Brian Downey laid down a great heavy beat from his kit, all under an effective light show. Phil took advantage of the lights by reflecting them off his mirrored scratch plate on his bass guitar.

One of the most memorable moments was when a few kettle drums out at the front of the stage were played by the band to dramatic effect, something I'd never seen before and have never seen since.

Sadly, I never saw them play live again, but I bought their albums and followed their careers, including solo releases, and to this day, I'm still a fan. My 'go to' albums are either of their live double albums, which help me to relive that amazing gig in Liverpool.

I WAS THERE: PAUL SMITHAM

I was an over excited 15-year-old seeing my all time favourite band but came away slightly disappointed. The band played mainly material from the as-yet-unreleased *Chinatown* album and I wanted to hear all those marvellous classics from the past. I bought *Chinatown* on its release months later but I still think it's one of their weakest albums. I am proud to have seen the great Mr Lynott – I just wish I had seen the band earlier as I love all the music with Bell, Robertson and Moore. There were a few class tunes in there, but for me the last three albums went off the boil a little.

QUEENS HALL

10 MAY 1980, LEEDS, UK

I WAS THERE: MICHAEL SOMERS

I was introduced to Lizzy by my friend Graham Hanley. I first saw them on the *Chinatown* tour in Leeds and Manchester. In those days we would queue for hours beforehand so that we were amongst the first few in, and then it was a run to the front as soon as the doors opened. Lizzy were brilliant and although Snowy White didn't look the part his playing was great. The next time I saw them was on the *Renegade* tour, again in Leeds and Manchester, and again they were excellent. *Renegade* is a very underrated album.

When they announced the final tour, I saw them in Leeds and Bradford. The St George's Hall was a smaller venue and had better sound. My mates and I had to make it to the Reading Festival. Lizzy's previous guitarists did guest spots and it was an awesome gig but a shithole of a place!

Lizzy are one of the best bands ever. Phil Lynott was a great bass player, poet and musician, and I so wish I was queuing outside the Queens Hall again. Great memories.

GUILD HALL

11 MAY 1980, PRESTON, UK

I WAS THERE: NIGEL EUBANK

I got to hear about the gig in music press at the time, but having unsuccessfully tried to get tickets for only one other gig at the time (Queen at Manchester Apollo), I was still unsure how you actually went about it. I determined that I wasn't coming home empty handed this time so I rode my motorcycle the 10 miles or so to Preston at five in the morning. I was on shift work at the time so I was used to early starts. I queued up. I wasn't at the front of the queue, but I returned with tickets in hand.

The day of the gig arrived and I got the bus to Preston early. I walked up to the Guild Hall mid-afternoon. Not much was happening. I looked up at the windows in the Guild Hall and who should walk past? Only Phil Lynott with a trail of very excited fans behind him. Phil had let a few lucky fans in early. Me and my mate were in the wrong place at the wrong time. We could have screamed.

7pm came soon enough. The doors opened and for the first time in my life I set foot inside a concert hall (little did I know that it was the start of a journey for me). We had seats but went to the front of the stage for a look. I was amazed at all the gear.

I can't remember the support act. I wasn't interested. I just wanted to see *Live and Dangerous* - actually see it. It was the only Thin Lizzy album I had at the time. My first impressions of live music? 'Bloody hell, it's louder than my hi-fi!' (I was proud of my Technics stack.) Then it was Lizzy's turn, the main event. The lights went down, chants of 'Lizzy,

Lizzy, Lizzy' filled the hall and then... BOOM!!! 'What the fuck was that?' The whole stage exploded and they were there.

If I thought it was loud before, I'd heard nothing yet. The bass was incredible, hitting me in the stomach. It's the feeling I look forward to to this day. It was all mesmerising. It had me under its spell.

Of course, Thin Lizzy were superb and Phil was a true showman and knew how to handle the crowd. Most of the songs I knew, but don't ask me to repeat the set list as I couldn't tell you what they played apart from opening the show with 'Jailbreak'.

CITY HALL

12 MAY 1980, SHEFFIELD, UK

I WAS THERE: JOHN COCKERHAM

The first time I heard their music was by going to see a covers band in a working men's club in Kippax near my home town of Leeds with my cousin and other pals. Despite my getting very drunk, their take on Lizzy songs stood out.

John Cockerham saw Lizzy twice

After listening so many times to the *Live and Dangerous* album, we got the opportunity to see Lizzy live at the height of their popularity in 1980 and travelled down from Leeds to see them at Sheffield City Hall as part of their *World Tour 80*. The band was Phil Lynott, Scott Gorham, Brian Downey and Snowy White. They were brilliant, with Phil at his strutting and charismatic best. This remains to this day the best live concert I have ever seen.

This remains to this day the best live concert I have ever seen

---

I continued to follow Lizzy right through until Phil's passing in 1986. After that I would still listen to their music - the initiation for any new car was playing *Live and Dangerous* at full volume! – but the band themselves fell off my radar… until 2011, when for my 50th birthday, my beautiful wife Karen took me to see Thin Lizzy at the Manchester Apollo as part of their European tour. This time Lizzy were Scott Gorham, Brian Downey, Darren Wharton, Vivian Campbell, Ricky Warwick and Marco Mendoza. Not quite the same as in 1980, but brilliant all the same.

NEW BINGLEY HALL

13 MAY 1980, STAFFORD, UK

I WAS THERE: COLIN MASON

Two more gigs followed in 1980 - back at the cowshed on 13th May for what was a below par performance due to Phil having a bad throat infection. But being the soldier he always was, they still put on a decent show. He was back in full voice less than two weeks later at the first of two gigs they were scheduled to play at the good old Birmingham Odeon in May. I went on the 22nd and also had a ticket for the following night at the same venue. I never went, which may have had something to do with the fact I was getting married shortly afterwards. I only went to three gigs that year, two of which were Thin Lizzy; I suspect two in two nights may have been pushing my luck a bit at that particular time. (Incidentally I'm still happily married to the girl I married back in 1980 and I go to more gigs now than ever!).

I WAS THERE: STEVE MURTAGH

After seeing them support Slade back in 1972, I then got tickets to see them again in December 1979, at Stafford Showground, but got snowed in so missed the show. The next time I managed to see Lizzy was in 1980 at Stafford Bingley Hall, or 'the cow shed' as it was known locally. I had already got a lot of their music and had four mates with me who I had got into the music of Lizzy. It was a packed house, and they had obviously honed their trade. I remember someone shouting out for them to do 'Sarah', and Phil telling them to 'fuck off' off as he wanted to forget that!

He had a mirror on the front of his guitar, and a spotlight was trained on it. He had a great way of putting the reflection onto girls in the audience and boy did they love it. He was a smooth sod! Scott Gorham and Gary Moore were in the line up and produced an amazing sound. They did all the rockers, all the hits, and for the second encore did 'The Rocker'. The place erupted again. We were all deaf for a few days after the show.

Phil was a showman. He left us before his talent was fully appreciated.

I WAS THERE: STU HUNTING

It's early 1980 and I'm 13 years old, in the kitchen at home with a pleading look in my eyes. Two older kids have just asked my parents if they can take me to see Thin Lizzy in May? It's a yes!

A couple of months later I was walking into Stafford's New Bingley Hall, surrounded by rockers in leather and smelling of patchouli oil. The underlying smell of the Bingley Hall's 'day job' as a cattle market was unmistakable. Support band The Lookalikes seemed to come and go then everything went dark. Sirens started, then police lights and smoke. The smoke cleared and there was Phil, centre stage and the place went wild. That moment changed so much for me. My life since has been completely dictated by music, a love that really began that night.

I WAS THERE: ANDY TUNSTALL

I was back at New Bingley Hall in May 1980, only this time Snowy White was on the second guitar (I'd seen him playing with Pink Floyd on *The Wall* tour earlier in.the year) and Darren Wharton was on keyboards, which added a nice dynamic. Newer songs such as 'Chinatown' were a welcome addition, but the biggest addition as far as I was concerned was that I was taking a girlfriend to a gig for the first time! She enjoyed it too – who wouldn't with such a marvellous show?

I never saw them again and they gradually disappeared from public view, splitting in 1983. Phil and Gary Moore were seen on *Top of the Pops* doing first 'Parisienne Walkways' and then 'Out in the Fields'. Then we heard of Phil's sad and untimely death in 1986.

I once auditioned – unsuccessfully - as the bass player (not the singer) for a Thin Lizzy tribute band. More recently I saw the documentary *Songs for While I'm Away*. I really recommend that for anyone who doesn't know the whole Lizzy story, and for the excellent concert footage I remember so well.

COLSTON HALL

24 MAY 1980, BRISTOL, UK

I WAS THERE: DAVID PENBERTHY, AGE 17

I'd been immersed in rock music at a very young age. My neighbour Jenny Drew used to blast out Hawkwind and Quo every Sunday afternoon on her hi-fi. We talked, breathed and lived rock 'n' roll. Nothing else existed. Then I was desperate to fly the nest and live. I'd found a six month scheme in Taunton working in the youth and community centre, and after a few week of settling in I realised that Bristol had the Colston Hall and the Locarno. I started organising mini bus trips to watch all the groups. I put a small margin on the other tickets and that way I saw bands like the Clash, Stiff Little Fingers and the Undertones for free. When *Live and Dangerous* came out, Phil and the boys became my iconic nirvana. I had the t-shirts and the vinyl. I even had 'Whiskey in the Jar' on a demo.

I remember opening up the *NME* or *Sounds* and checking the dates. Lizzy were programmed at the Colston Hall and my life stopped. My best mates were two brothers who rode Motoguzzi bikes and we decided to queue overnight to get front row tickets. It was December when tickets went on sale. At that age you go in just your jacket and jeans. We slept outside the hall all night and it was minus something awful. I was blue with the cold. We made regular visits to the public toilets to use the hand dryers to survive. But we were successful in our quest and had super places.

David Penberthy was at the Colston Hall

The line up was with Scott and Snowy. Eric Bell came on to play 'Whiskey in the Jar'. I felt it was just for me. I had one of Scott's plectrums and spent the night dancing until I was incapable of moving. The show was fantastic, with flash bombs. Phil was a living god for me.

I WAS THERE: ROGER TULLY

The Eric Bell Band were playing at the Granary Rock Club in Bristol the same night that Lizzy were playing at the Colston Hall. Towards the end of Lizzy's gig, Phil shouted out, 'What song do you want to hear?' and then joked, '"Whiskey in the Jar"? No, Scott can't play the intro.' Then the haunting intro started and Eric Bell walked on stage - and the crowd went mental! After the gig, me and my mates rushed over to the Granary to watch the Eric Bell Band and, you guessed it, Phil came on stage to return the favour and play bass on 'Whiskey'. I was near the stage and Phil actually pushed past me to climb on stage.

APOLLO THEATRE

26 MAY 1980, MANCHESTER, UK

I WAS THERE: NICK HARNEY

Nick Harney was at Manchester Apollo

In 1978 I was 13 years old and heavily influenced by my 17-year-old cousin Barrie, a talented drummer and avid Thin Lizzy fan. I used to love going to his house where he would let me play on his silver Tama Rockstar drum kit. It was there that he introduced me to the recently released *Live and Dangerous*, which in later years I would play repeatedly, specifically 'Baby Drives Me Crazy' where Phil would introduce the band and the hairs on my neck would stand on end listening to Scott Gorham's band intro solo!

I was in my first year at secondary school and resisting the urges of my peers to follow the punk rock trends of the late Seventies and then the start of the acid house movement on my doorstep in my home town of Manchester. It wasn't long before I persuaded my grandmother to buy me my first drum kit - a humble re-covered (in fireguard copper) Premier kit which I promptly re-covered again in something a little more pleasing to the eye. Soon afterwards I formed my first band, which attempted a few heavy rock tracks rather badly, including tracks from *Live and Dangerous*.

In 1979, I was 14 years old and an avid fan. 'Do Anything You Want To' was released and I attempted to replicate the intro drum riff. My fellow band members refused to cover the song but did agree to cover 'Waiting for an Alibi'. When we played it live, I missed the countdown cue (which in hindsight I should have set myself) and our bass player launched into the opening riff on his own. I let him play a couple of bars and then joined in, making it sound like we had planned a non-original version all along!

In 1980 my dream came true. The Thin Lizzy *World Tour* was announced! But I hadn't realised that queuing early at the box office was required when the tickets were released, and I was devastated to see that it was a sell out. I was told I might be able to score a ticket with a tout on the night but that it was likely to set me back several times the face value. My allowance from the parents was minimal.

Then I heard that an older guy at school had a few tickets for sale. I approached him and he reluctantly pulled a crumpled blue ticket from his pocket labelled 'rear stalls'. Excited, I asked him how much he wanted for it to which he replied four pounds and fifty pence - face value. I begged him to hold it for me until the next day, and that night I begged my parents to let me have the money. I collected the ticket the next day and that was it - I was finally going to see Thin Lizzy live!

On the day I couldn't contain my excitement. After arguing for several weeks with my parents about how I would be getting to and from the gig, I found out that Barrie also had a ticket and so he would take me to the gig. Donning a Levi's jacket (freshly embroidered with the Thin Lizzy logo) and ripped jeans, I arrived at the Apollo. The first thing that hit me as I entered was the aroma of patchouli oil and, over the top of it, occasional wafts of marijuana making their way through the smoky haze. My cousin headed to the bar with me closely in tow. He handed me a pint of lager which at 15 years of age was a fairly big deal.

I really don't remember the support act but I do remember the amazing vibrations of a live band which hit me as we made our way to our seats, two thirds of the way towards the rear of the concert hall. It was around 9pm when suddenly the lights dimmed which prompted the crowd to roar. The next minute – boom! – a few flash bombs and they were on and rocking into 'Are You Ready'. The rest of the gig is now a blur but I do remember Lizzy hitting all of my favourites. Exiting the Apollo and buzzing with post-gig excitement, I was unable to speak and had severe ringing in my ears. My voice came back the next day and the tinnitus didn't go until the day after but – wow, it was worth it. I had scored a programme from the merchandise stand. I subsequently studied every inch of that for the next several years.

I WAS THERE: PAUL MULDERRIG

I saw Thin Lizzy 20 times. The first time was on Bonfire Night 1977 at Lancaster University on the *Johnny the Fox* tour. I remember scrapping in the hall and in the street outside... but what a night! I was near the front at Hammersmith Odeon in 1978 when the *Live and Dangerous* video was filmed. On one occasion I slept in the doorway at Manchester Apollo to get tickets, and on another occasion we blagged our way in for nowt at Preston Guild Hall.

Paul Mulderrig was at Manchester Apollo amongst the 20 shows he saw

HAMMERSMITH ODEON

28 – 30 MAY 1980, LONDON, UK

I WAS THERE: DAVID ROWE

It was the *Chinatown* tour at Hammersmith Odeon and I was up in the circle. The show had started and a woman in a red ball gown and a man in a tuxedo came along my row to occupy the seats next to us. They had obviously come from some function, and without sitting down the woman kicked off her high heels and started banging her head and playing air guitar with the best of us!

I WAS THERE: ANDREW SMYTH

By 1980, Thin Lizzy had another album in the shops, and another new guitarist, Snowy White, who had taken over from the departed Gary Moore. The new album, *Chinatown*, was a hard one for me to swallow, as a massive fan of the band. It was patchy and weak in my opinion, with only 'We Will Be Strong' and 'Killer on the Loose' being the stand out tracks. Even though the album was a disappointment, I still saw the tour at the Hammersmith Odeon. I came away from the venue feeling that the band were going through the motions. The atmosphere inside was lacking as well. It felt rather flat, and I hoped that when I saw them live again, it would be different, and that they would be firing on all cylinders!

ROYAL DUBLIN SOCIETY
7 JUNE 1980, DUBLIN, IRELAND

I WAS THERE: ALAN LONG
June 1980 in Dublin at the RDS was the most special day for me of all my Lizzy shows. I worked as a milkman for a lot of my life, and one of my customers just happened to be Jim Fitzpatrick, who was living on Sandyford Road in Dublin at that time. Being a Lizzy fan, I was also a big fan of Jim and his work.

On the day of the concert, I was at the RDS at about 2.00pm for a 6.30pm show, such was my love for the band. As myself and some others were sitting around chatting, who should walk up to the entrance but Jim Fitz. He was heading into the sound check, so I called him and he came over for a chat. I asked was there any chance I could go in with him? He walked over to the doorman, said a couple of words and then waved me over. I almost died.

In we went and the band were all up on the stage doing their checks. Philip saw Jim so came down to greet him. Jim introduced me to Philip and I just stood there with my big mouth open. I was stunned. But I had my camera with me and got some very special shots of all the lads wearing Irish rugby jerseys, as Ireland had just won the Triple Crown. That has to be the highlight of my life.

I WAS THERE: JUSTIN HEALY
I'm a musician and the reason I'm a musician is because of Thin Lizzy. I first heard Lizzy in late '78 when I was about 11 and I was intrigued. I was loving the Stranglers and the Sex Pistols and all the punk stuff but when I saw Lizzy on TV, I was absolutely amazed. 'This is an Irish band

on *Top of the Pops*?' And then I found out they were hugely successful internationally but were only from up the road from me - I was living in Sandymount, only walking distance from Crumlin – and that really knocked me out. Then I got *Black Rose* for Christmas and I was amazed by the punky energy of that album. On St Stephen's Day (Boxing Day) I went straight out and bought *Live and Dangerous*.

My brother's girlfriend worked in the Gresham Hotel on O'Connell Street in Dublin. She gave me tickets for 10cc and I was going, 'That's great.' A few weeks later she said, 'I don't know whether you'd be interested in Thin Lizzy?' She'd been given the tickets by a band member. I went to the 10cc gig and it was all seated. It was a pretty subdued affair but I didn't know what to expect from a live concert so I thought 'this is great'.

A few weeks later, I went to the Lizzy gig and I didn't know what to expect. In my mind, it was going to be the same as 10cc. It was going to be seated and it was going to be subdued. But I went to the gig and there was a real sense of anticipation. It was jammed full of dangerous looking hairy guys. I said to my friend, 'I'm going up the front.' He said, 'No way am I going up there. See you - good luck!' so I went up on my own.

I got right up to the very, very front, right in the middle. I was the first person in the audience. I still didn't know what to expect. I was looking round and the whole crowd was chanting 'Lizzy, Lizzy' and clapping like on *Live and Dangerous*. The lights went out and everything just went black. Everybody was screaming and I was like, 'What the fuck is this?' I was looking around and all I could see was a few little red lights from the amps. I didn't even see the boys walk on.

'Are You Ready' was the opening number. The lights, the PA, the flash bombs and that first power chord all came in in that millisecond – bang! – and the fucking place exploded. It was such a powerful moment it frightened the living shite out of me. I thought they'd killed me. I actually thought I was dead. I ran back to the end of the hall and caught my breath and I was thinking, 'Jesus!' But I calmed down and then 'fuck this'. I had been blooded and I went straight back in.

It frightened the living shite out of me

I fought my way back through all the crowd to where I was before. I was literally standing right under Phil, looking up from just feet away. He was standing with his legs bent over the two monitors, looking out at the audience, and he had a massive grin on his face. He was always so glad to be home. He was in the same position as when the flash bomb had gone off.

That concert was amazing and the sound was great. I walked the mile home from the Simmonscourt Arena. By the end of that mile, I knew that was what I was going to be doing for the rest of my life. I was 13, and I didn't know how I was going to do it, but I knew that I was going to be a musician. And that's what I've done from that day to this.

DE MONTFORT HALL

11 JUNE 1980, LEICESTER, UK

I WAS THERE: TIM CHAMBERS, AGE 15

Tim Chambers saw Lizzy at De Mont

I discovered Thin Lizzy thanks to my friend's brother. We used to sneak into his room and listen to his Queen collection but one day there was a new album, *Jailbreak*. Wow – this was a lot heavier than Queen, and in my opinion better. I was sold. That Christmas, I got *Live and Dangerous* and after that there was no looking back. After bugging my grandad to go and see them live (me being a young 15-year-old) off I popped to Way Ahead Records in Nottingham to buy tickets. I wasn't allowed the coach travel package as a condition of me going was that I was dropped off and picked up. There were four of us - myself, Paul, Stef and his brother Andrew.

The show was amazing and it was great seeing all these rockers in denim and leather who were so much older than us in our brand new Levi's jackets. So my cut off battle jacket was born. Most of the evening was a blur but I was caught up in the atmosphere, which was electric. It's amazing how quickly you could pick up the words to some of the songs. After the gig, we were stood somewhere at the back and waiting to be picked up when who should appear from a rear exit but Phil. Talk about being starstruck!

He spent about ten minutes talking to us about the gig and thanked us for coming and then he was ushered away. If I wasn't sold on them before I was then. My love affair with Lizzy had begun. I've seen Thin Lizzy a few times since, but sadly without Phil and to be honest it wasn't the same. In my opinion Lizzy are the most underrated rock band ever.

COVENTRY THEATRE

12 JUNE 1980, COVENTRY, UK

I WAS THERE: SCOTT GILL

It all started around mid-1979. I was 17 and had been a massive ELO fan for years but I also liked Queen, Boston and Supertramp, etc. I started to look for something different to listen to. It was a midweek evening when my brother's mate came round on his Suzuki GT185 (we were all bikers) and brought with him a double cassette of *Live and Dangerous*. I had heard of Thin Lizzy but regarded them as 'heavy metal'!

My brother was learning guitar at the time so we plugged the cassette recorder into his practice amp. As soon as I heard 'Emerald' I was totally blown away. We all were. I couldn't believe how incredible a band could sound live, and the drumming was sharp as a razor, never mind the twin-pronged dual lead guitar of Scott Gorham and Brian Robertson. When 'Sha La La' came on, I thought I'd died and gone to heaven. We decided there and then that we had to see this band live.

I bought most of their back catalogue but was very disappointed by the studio sound on everything up to *Chinatown*. It was as if all the producers were telling the band, 'Very nice but can we shove the drums way back in the mix and tune down those guitars?' (I'm a drummer, by the way). It didn't put me off seeing them live. We found out they were playing at the Coventry Theatre and managed to get three tickets for the front circle for myself, my brother and a friend who was learning bass guitar. We were living for that night for about three months.

We got the bus into town, had a few beers and then got to the theatre, which was mobbed. We eventually found our seats and sat through a very boring support act called The Lookalikes.

After an interval and more beer, the lights went out and the cheering started – 'Thin Liz, Thin Liz – and then the traffic light on the stage which had been red and which had been on amber for what seemed like hours suddenly turned green. The roar of the crowd was deafening and we all stood chanting. Then the stage erupted and the band launched into 'Are You Ready'. By this time Scott Gorham was the main man and was clearly enjoying his role, backed up by the talents of Snowy White.

Chinatown had a superb drum sound and the band played most of the album along with a chunk of *Live and Dangerous*, including 'Sha La La', which I finally witnessed live! I remember a mate of mine running on stage and nicking Phil's plectrum. That would never happen now. Eventually, after two encores, we filed out, ears ringing.

After 42 years this is still the best concert I've ever attended, and I've been to a few.

After 42 years this is still the best concert I've ever attended

---

BRIGHTON CENTRE

13 JUNE 1980, BRIGHTON, UK

I WAS THERE: IAN LIDBETTER

My wife Terri and I first saw Thin Lizzy at the Brighton Centre in 1980 and we were hooked. Soon after, I joined the fan club and we bought most of their albums. We went to see them again at the Brighton Centre in 1983. We're still massive fans. We've become fans of Limehouse Lizzy. They play like Lizzy and are keeping Thin Lizzy's music alive, but no matter how good they are they will never replace the great Phil Lynott.

GAUMONT THEATRE

14 JUNE 1980, SOUTHAMPTON, UK

Post gig in Southampton, Phil is hit by a bottle, knocked out and has his head gashed over his eye.

SOPHIA GARDENS

15 JUNE 1980, CARDIFF, UK

Andrew King first saw Lizzy in Cardiff in 1980

I WAS THERE: ANDREW KING

I saw Thin Lizzy on three of the 12 times they played in Cardiff with Phil, twice in the sadly lost Sophia Gardens and once at its replacement, St David's Hall. Lizzy shows always had a reputation of being frantic and wild affairs and we were never disappointed in Cardiff. Sophia Gardens was a shed-like standing venue and long needing an overhaul and an upgrade, but it was so full of character to many people. I always enjoyed concerts there. I was working locally to Sophia Gardens in the Eighties so managed to get tickets for most of the shows put on there – when I could afford to attend!

It was a standing only venue so getting in the queue early was essential for bagging the best spots at the front when the doors opened. Then it was just a quick sprint to the barrier and a wait for the show to start. Lights down at showtime would invoke a mad push forward from the 2,000 odd people behind you. It was always a challenge to keep your spot but I usually managed it, and before I knew it, the show would be over in what seemed a blur and it would be time for me to make my way out and home on the train dripping in sweat.

The first time I saw Lizzy was in June 1980 on the *Chinatown* tour. Phil came on and sang one song with support band, The Lookalikes. This was Snowy White's first tour replacing Gary Moore and it was a totally frantic affair.

I WAS THERE: DAVID DAVIES, AGE 18

Twelve months later I saw Lizzy again on the *Chinatown* tour at Cardiff's Sophia Gardens. There was less movement in the show as Snowy White had now replaced Gary Moore. The show was no less exciting but I must say I preferred Moore. Phil had a black eye and explained to the crowd that he had got it from a bottle-wielding husband of some woman he was trying to get it on with after the last gig!

I was a whole lot more Lizzified by now, having bought all their albums. I knew every song and this added to the enjoyment. The gig came to an end with Phil explaining he was going to do something special, since we had travelled to a cancelled gig a few weeks earlier. I clearly remember the crowd screaming out for 'Whiskey in the Jar', but this ageing brain cannot remember if they played it. I do remember Phil bringing on the roadies who took centre stage playing sweeping broom guitars, and Phil beckoning to the guitarist from the support band to come on. He soloed but he had a look of discomfort written on his face. It was another brilliant live performance.

In September 1980, Lizzy undertook an eight date Japanese tour and then moved on to Australia and New Zealand.

CAPITOL THEATRE

9 OCTOBER 1980, SYDNEY, AUSTRALIA

I WAS THERE: TRACEY GÜLIN, AGE 16

I saw Lizzy twice, the first time on the Opera House steps in Sydney when I was 14. A bunch of us caught the train to Circular Quay for the free concert. I remember getting up on my friend's shoulders right near the front left hand side of the stage, and another friend catching a little Thin Lizzy mirrored brooch that Phil threw into the crowd. The second time was at the Capitol Theatre in Sydney on the Chinatown tour. I went with my boyfriend. I remember being blinded by a reflection from Phil's guitar and getting a tap on the shoulder from security asking if I wanted to go backstage and meet the band. I naively asked if my boyfriend could come too (to which the answer was 'no') and he wouldn't let me go by myself!

I WAS THERE: GRAHAM HIBBARD

I was still under age for their *Bad Reputation* tour but bought tickets to see them with a mate at the Capitol Theatre when they came back to Australia. On stage was a set of traffic lights that were red during the support band (badly named The Motivators, which they weren't). During the break the officials made announcements that everyone must remain in their seats, and not to move away from our seats as per the brochure, etc. It was gut wrenching to consider sitting in our seats. My mate and I felt it was better to be there than to not be there, but not by much. With the threat of eviction from the venue if we moved, the idea of missing the show was worse than not having gone at all.

The lights dropped. The traffic lights turned green and we both ran to the front of the stage - agreeing that we would rather die than stay put. There was a large explosion as a part of the pyrotechnics and there was damage to the monitors on stage, followed by some furious gestures from Phil. Some busy roadies had it all sorted in a song or two.

I didn't ever get to see them live again. In dim dark Australia pre the internet, I was unaware of the *Life/Live* tour. Had I known about it I would have travelled to London for a show or two.

I WAS THERE: SIMON VANDERZIEL

My brother saw the free gig at the Sydney Opera House in 1978. There were over 100,000 at that gig and he said it was staggering. I wasn't at that concert as I was away. But in 1980, we both saw the concert at the Capitol Theatre in Sydney, a warm and characterful location. The boys played brilliantly. The combined guitar work really added a wonderful feel to the music. Somehow the leads had an Irish lilt which came through even though neither guitarist was Irish. Watching and hearing them play for the first time made my throat swell and tears well in my eyes. Everyone left with a huge smile on their face.

Many years earlier, when I was 12, I had seen Frank Zappa and, around the same time, Status Quo, so I knew good gigs, but there was something deeply personal about Thin Lizzy. It was rock music for the outsider in all of us, even though it was not unconventional music. It was not as technical as Jeff Beck or as overwhelming or horizon-reaching as Led Zeppelin. It wanted to speak directly to you, to get inside you. I think this is what makes Thin Lizzy so much more than just another rock band. It always fed your soul and enlivened your spirit.

There is a yearning in me for the Irish side of my family's history, but that is not the reason why Thin Lizzy had that effect on me. It was their honesty as a band.

CHINATOWN RELEASED 10 OCTOBER 1980
UK CHART POSITION 7
US CHART POSITION 120

***Chinatown* was Thin Lizzy's tenth studio album and spawned two singles, 'Chinatown' reaching number 12 in the Irish charts (21 in Britain) and 'Killer on the Loose', which reached number 5 in Ireland and 10 in the UK.**

SOUTHERN CROSS HOTEL

20 OCTOBER 1980, MELBOURNE, AUSTRALIA

I WAS THERE: LORAINE LUXA

My dad ran a hotel in Melbourne called the Southern Cross. It's since been demolished but in those days, there were only two hotels to choose from, the Hilton or the Southern Cross. The Southern Cross was a bit more groovy as it was right in the heart of the city, whereas the Hilton is 20 minutes out from the city. Deep Purple stayed at the Southern Cross. Alice Cooper, Deep Purple, Queen all stayed there.

Thin Lizzy stayed at our hotel for a week while they did one concert at the Festival Hall in Melbourne. They were in the lobby and I went up to them and said, 'Can you sign my copy of *Live and Dangerous*?' Phil Lynott might have been a bit stoned. He wasn't drunk because I couldn't smell anything on him, but he and Scott were a bit away with the fairies. They were nice. They weren't, 'We're Thin Lizzy.' There were no fans there. They didn't trash the hotel room or anything. They were just normal everyday people – but dressed as rock gods, because Phil Lynott was always walking around in his leather pants and open white shirt.

FESTIVAL HALL

20 OCTOBER 1980, MELBOURNE, AUSTRALIA

FRANK CANTELMI, AGE 19

I was 19 and went with two of my friends, Albert and Valado. We were in a band together. I saw them in my old home town of Melbourne, Australia on the *Chinatown* tour. The line up was Phil, Scott, Brian on drums and Snowy White on guitar. They started with the song 'Are You Ready?'. It was a great show, and probably my first real concert where the band was from overseas. I had discovered Lizzy through a music show in Australia called *Countdown* which played the film clip of 'The Boys are Back in Town'. I thought 'wow' and loved them instantly. I went out and bought the cassette of *Jailbreak* and have loved them ever since.

Thin Lizzy concluded their *World Tour 80* with 26 American dates.

PARADISE THEATRE

2 DECEMBER 1980, BOSTON, MASSACHUSETTS

I WAS THERE: MICHAEL MOONEY

The second time I saw Lizzy was a few years later on the *Chinatown* tour at the Paradise Rock Club in Boston. I had got there early and was having a drink at the bar with new keyboardist Darren Wharton. It was really difficult to understand his accent. Then Phil entered the club and came up behind us and said 'hello' and that he needed Darren in the dressing room. That's as close as I ever came to meeting the legend. Of course, to a younger me, he wasn't a legend yet. It's only in hindsight that they achieve that status.

In later years I got to hang with Smiley Bolger and Brian Downey and even visited Philomena at her home and spent the whole day there. I consider myself blessed for having had all these experiences.

RITZ THEATRE

5 DECEMBER 1980, NEW YORK, NEW YORK

I WAS THERE: DAVID PLASTIK

I was 14 years old when I heard 'The Boys are Back in Town'. I first saw Lizzy at The Ritz in NYC on the *Chinatown* tour with Snowy White on guitar. I had never been to The Ritz before so I didn't bring my camera, which I regret. Tickets were $10 on the door. It was a great show.

I next saw Phil in NYC where he took part in an all star jam originally billed as Carmine Appice and Friends. His 'friends' was a reunion of the original Vanilla Fudge line up and Ted Nugent, Rick Derringer and Phil Lynott all took part in the end jam. I was excited to get some good photos of Phil which I hadn't expected.

In 1983 I saw them with John Sykes at the Reading Rock Festival, another great show, and in 1984 and '85, I was back visiting England and caught Grand Slam at a small club in London.

In 1986 *Rolling Stone* used one of my photos for his obituary.

WARFIELD THEATRE

19 DECEMBER 1980, SAN FRANCISCO, CALIFORNIA

I WAS THERE: JIM MOHR

In May 1980, I joined the army and was sent to a year-long Korean course at the Defense Language Institute, not far from where I grew up. That fall, a Thin Lizzy show was announced for December 19th and I went to the local record store the very first day and end up with front row tickets!

Then disaster struck. One evening I was going out to get pizza with a couple of my army buddies and we took a shortcut that led us down a small hill. It was dark and I had had a little to drink. I took a misstep and ended up breaking my ankle just days before the show. Fortunately, as a Christmas present, I was taking one of the friends who went with me to my first Thin Lizzy show two years earlier, so he drove.

When they came out, I saw that Scott was also in a cast, and Phil called him 'the bravest guitarist in the world'. I could really relate to that, as I also knew the problems one had moving around in a cast. By that time, Thin Lizzy songs had been so ingrained in me that the only one I didn't know beforehand was 'Memory Pain'.

They played two encores. During the first one people rushed to the stage, and although we were front row, it was a little difficult with me on crutches. During the second encore, 'Rosalie', someone with a guitar slowly walked out from the left side of the stage and started playing with them. It took me a moment to recognize Neal Schon of Journey. He's a huge Thin Lizzy fan.

SCANDINAVIUM

6 FEBRUARY 1981, GOTHENBURG, SWEDEN

I WAS THERE: STEVAN TOMULEVSKI

My friend's brother played *Live and Dangerous* for me in 1979 and I was totally sold on Lizzy. I saw them four times between 1980 and 1983. I also saw Phil Lynott solo twice. When they came to Gothenburg in 1981, we waited to see them at the Hotel Rubinen. They signed autographs before they went in. Phil autographed a five krona note, tore it in half and put one half in his jacket. They had remote-controlled curtains in their hotel room and I remember how Philo stood at the window with his hands in the air and showed when the blinds went up and down.

CONCERTGEBOUW DE VEREENIGING
13 FEBRUARY 1981, NIJMEGEN, THE NETHERLANDS

I WAS THERE: QUIRIEN GRUL

When I was six, our family of six kids moved to the village of Odijk, near Utrecht. We became friends with the family of three boys and a girl across the street. In the first years of high school the two oldest boys, Mike and Pat, went off to boarding school in London. When they returned around the age of 16, Pat ended up in my class at high school. We would spend time together listening to music in our rooms. I was getting into hard rock at the time that the NWOBHM emerged. When Pat brought over *Chinatown* is when I really got to know Lizzy.

In 1980 Lizzy were scheduled to perform in Amsterdam but the concert was cancelled because Phil got sick, but in 1981 they played the Concertgebouw in Nijmegen. Five of us took the train. There was no support act so the whole venue was packed with diehard Lizzy fans.

The first song they played was 'Are You Ready', there was a look of surprise on Phil's face when the crowd went crazy and made a huge noise at the end of the song. He gave a big smile and you could see the band excited to give it their all.

We were right at the front, on the right side of the stage, just in front of Scott. Phil would go up and down the stage from left to right. He was sweating his pants off and when having his typical pose, slight bent forward and his guitar neck straight ahead, the sweat was falling down from his face. My friend put out his hands to catch the sweat and made Phil laugh. At the end of the song, he walked over to our side of the stage again and gave my friend his plectrum. So cool!

In the years after the concert, I bought all of their albums. I saw Lizzy twice more after Phil died and these were great shows too. In 1994, I and a bunch of friends went to Dublin for the *Vibe for Philo*. The pre-vibe in a very small pub was especially great. Now, 40 years later, I only wish I had seen them a lot more times but they just did not come to Holland that much. I just can't get enough of the energy and all of the fantastic songs with such rhythm, melodies and lyrics, along with the soft and charismatic tone of Phil's voice. As the years pass, I realise more and more how unbelievably fantastic Lizzy were.

GLOUCESTER HALL

28 JULY 1981, ST HELIER, JERSEY

I WAS THERE: GARY MALOREY-VIBERT

The story is that the support act was a local band called Legend who had a great following in Jersey and that Thin Lizzy were not happy that Legend were more popular than them and so tried to sabotage Legend's set. There was something Phil Lynott said during the concert which I use to this day. He said, 'Of all the crowds I have played to....' We were expecting him to say 'you're the best' but instead he said, 'You have been one of them.'

BEAU SEJOUR LEISURE CENTRE

30 JULY 1981, ST PETER PORT, GUERNSEY

I WAS THERE: MANDY SANGAN

I was there while they were warming up and right in the front during the concert. They threw plectrums and drum sticks into the crowd. I saw Phil Lynott walking around our town, St Peter Port. He was very tall. I tapped him on his back and he looked around and then down and saw me. I said, 'Can I please have your autograph?' and he replied, 'Hey man, it's not my signing day today!' On reflection, I think he was drunk or stoned - or both!

I WAS THERE: NICK WINDSOR

It was the night before Princess Diana and Prince Charles got married so the whole Island was buzzing with outdoor gigs and various celebrations in the main town of St Peter Port. I was 20 at the time and a massive fan of Thin Lizzy ever since hearing John Peel interview Phil Lynott in 1976 about the release of *Johnny the Fox*. The gig was all the more memorable as I was one of the guitarists in the support band, Limbo, a latin/funk rock originals band at the time.

The night before the gig I happened to see Phil Lynott in a night club. You couldn't miss him. He was taller than anyone else in there, dressed in a long black leather coat and with two blondes, one on each arm. You couldn't have scripted it any more rock 'n' roll. I approached him, tapped his shoulder and said, 'Hi Phil, looking forward to supporting you guys tomorrow night,' or words to that effect. He was really polite, asked what kind of music we played and said he was looking forward to hearing us. Then he glided off into the disco haze and faded into the shadows of the club.

Next day, Limbo were at the venue eager and early to set up and sound check. Snowy White had recently joined and initially I was disappointed because I loved Brian Robertson's playing and didn't think he was easily replaceable. But when Snowy sound checked, his bluesy flavour and touch was something else. Better still, he was a really nice guy, he had a go on my Les Paul and said it was a nice axe. To a 20-year-old fan it was a cool gesture and he told me of his travels in Sweden and his recent gig doing *The Wall* with Pink Floyd.

After Brian Downey and Darren Wharton had sound checked, Snowy came on and sound checked with some really tasty tones, rattling off a couple of Lizzy riffs in the process. He didn't hang around though, very coolly did what was required and left the stage. Phil also kept his sound check short and sweet. Then Scott Gorham got up and was the complete opposite, shredding like crazy through Lizzy riffs and basically saying 'I'm here'. While he was up there doing this, I got the chance to play frisbee with Phil and a couple of the roadies down on the floor. I was in awe to be in the same room as him, let alone throwing frisbee with the coolest frontman ever. After Scott had exhausted his lick library, the band then all got up and soundchecked one number – 'Chinatown', if my memory serves me correctly. During our soundcheck, I stayed on after we'd finished and jammed a few Lizzy licks hoping I might get earmarked for future vacancies... it was worth a punt!

Being our home crowd, when we walked out to pick up instruments the roar of that 2,000 plus audience was amazing. Tiny for Lizzy, massive for us. By all accounts we sounded great. The stage sound was certainly good but obviously we were never going to be as loud as Thin Lizzy. They were spectacular, and seeing them at full tilt with Phil and his iconic reflecting mirror scratch plate in action was awe inspiring. When meeting the band after the gig in the dressing room, Brian Downey and Snowy White were the most talkative.

Phil told us as he headed to their dressing room that he'd enjoyed our set and that he'd told the soundman to give us a good sound and raise the volume. He was a genuine star, ultra-cool but totally solid in his soul. Scott Gorham went straight to the dressing room. I believe he and Phil weren't in good shape, as I've since read that they had certain substance abuse issues, which is sad. It didn't seem to affect their performance at all. To many who were there, it's still the best gig they've seen locally - or ever.

I WAS THERE: PAUL POULLAIN, AGE 16

I was only 16 at the time and in awe of them. My main memory of the evening is that, as the concert started, the lights shone off Phil's guitar into the crowd. It was the start of a power performance of non-stop adrenaline and a night I will never forget.

CORNWALL COLISEUM

2 AUGUST 1981, ST AUSTELL, UK

I WAS THERE: TOBY MEDHURST, AGE 17

I went with my brother and a friend. We were early and before the gig saw a limo coming down the hill and going round the back of the concert hall. We followed it and out stepped Phil. We were the first ones in. Afterwards we hung around and met the whole band - it was amazing! I then saw them again at the same place a few months later and couldn't believe I was the first one in again – and that I met them all again afterwards!

Toby Medhurst caught Phil on film

ROCK AT THE BOWL
MILTON KEYNES CONCERT BOWL
8 AUGUST 1981, MILTON KEYNES, UK

I WAS THERE: ANDREW SMYTH

Thin Lizzy had decided to play an open air gig at the Milton Keynes Bowl. The Police had played this new venue the previous year, and it was a sell out, so my friends Kevin and Ian and I decided to get tickets to see Lizzy. (The previous Saturday, I had seen Motörhead, Ozzy Osbourne and others sell out a show at Port Vale FC.) Sadly, ticket sales for the Bowl were not brilliant and the concert not a sell out. Ian Hunter was one of the support acts, but the rest of the line up was weak and the weather on the day pretty miserable. Despite this, Thin Lizzy put on a brilliant and professional show, playing all the classics you wanted to hear.

Andrew Smyth met Phil backstage at Milton Keynes Bowl

Towards the end of the set, we decided to see if we could get backstage. We did not have a pass, but it was worth a try. Well, we managed it but were met by a security guard who advised us that, as we had no pass, we would have to leave. I said we only wanted to meet the band, say 'hello' and be on our way and that, if the security guard walked in the opposite direction, he would never know we were even there! He agreed. We then waited outside the portacabin that was serving as their dressing room until they came off stage. To be honest, they had faces of thunder when they did. Rumour has it their set was cut short by the council.

Once the band had calmed down, we were invited in by their manager. We were told the bar was off limits, but we said 'hello' to the band and got our programmes signed. There was a spare seat next to him so I decided to have a chat with Phil. What did we talk about? Manchester United of course, as we were both red devils! I even managed to get two photographs taken with him. I have no idea how long we stayed, but they were in no hurry to ask us to leave. The band were so friendly, and we chatted about everything, even my seven night stint at Earls Court watching Pink Floyd perform *The Wall*. That did raise a few eyebrows, and a few laughs!

When we finally did, it was handshakes all round and then a trip for us back to London Victoria, if we could find a coach going back that way. Thankfully we could. What a brilliant day.

I WAS THERE: JEFF COLLINS

A photographer friend gave me a press pass so I was allowed into the small press area in the front of the stage. Sadly, the roll of film I shot got lost but I had a great view! I saw them again in November '81 back at the Birmingham Odeon on the *Renegade* tour but I felt the line up with Snowy lacked the power I'd witnessed before.

I WAS THERE: STEVE DRISCOLL

Paul Young and the Q-Tips and Judie Tzuke were amongst the support. I remember Lizzy being loud and tight and Phil being the consummate showman. I'm also pretty sure that Phil and Judie sang a duet towards the end, backed by the rest of Lizzy. Other than that, my only other clear memory is of the constant queues for the portaloos!

I WAS THERE: MIKE HOLLAND

I had seen Lizzy in Ballybunion, at the Oisin Ballroom in Glin, at the Olympic in Newcastle West, at the SFX in Dublin, upstairs in the Parkway Hotel and in Club Marche at the Greenhills Hotel in Limerick, as well as several times in 1979 and '80, but this was the first time I had ventured abroad to see them. *Rock at the Bowl* was my first outside concert and it was a stunner of a summer's day.

Lizzy gigs always started with blue and red flashing sirens on stage and a big red flashing Thin Lizzy sign, with smoke, a big burst of guitars, a

Mike Holland saw Lizzy at Club Marche in Limerick before seeing them in Milton Keynes

thump of drums and straight into 'Jailbreak'! They burst on stage - Scott Gorham and Gary Moore on guitars with Brian Downey on drums and Phil with a little bit of mischief or double meanings in his sayings, which always brought a laugh or a big cheer from his audience. They had so many great songs, from 'Baby Drives Me Crazy', 'Cowboy Song', 'Whiskey' or 'Dancing in the Moonlight' through to Phil's mellow side and the songs he wrote for his daughters, 'Sarah' and 'Cathleen', or my personal favourite, 'A Child's Lullaby', from his *Solo in Soho* album, which I often hummed and sang to my own children.

Bob Geldof did *Live Aid* in '85 and Philip was heartbroken not to be asked to play, but Lizzy were gone. But like Queen, who were also teetering at the time, it could have been the beginning of something big.

I was working in Holland when I heard on the BBC World Service that Phil had died. It was my JFK moment. I took the day off and played his records all day and night. Phil's song 'King's Call' talked about him doing the same and getting drunk the night Elvis died. If I'd drunk alcohol, I'd have got drunk when Phil died.

I've been to the *Vibe for Philo* with my sons and my pal, Phil Snowe. Philip wrote three books of poetry and I remember the first one was £2 in Easons. I didn't buy it because I thought it was too dear and it's now a collector's item. I've been to his grave and met his mum at the house, White Horses. If he'd lived, I'm sure he'd still be touring like the Rolling Stones, or placed on a pedestal as being one of the greatest songwriter poets of our time. I'm so glad I saw him… lots!

I WAS THERE: TREVOR TUCKER

Myself and two friends went to see Lizzy at the Milton Keynes Bowl. After a very long day, we headed home and stopped off at a service station on the M1 at two in the morning to get something to eat and drink. When I walked back to the table where my friend Nicky was sitting, in a trembling voice she said 'it's Phil'. Sure enough, it was my hero standing in front of me. We had a great chat and he was just amazing, a perfect gentleman. I'll never forget that moment.

ICE RINK

10 AUGUST 1981, KIRKCALDY, UK

I WAS THERE: KEITH MCSHANE

Lizzy were on a small stage as this was at an ice rink. Phil opened with, 'What do you call this place?' He couldn't pronounce it or found it difficult and, as the crowd roared the name of the town, Lizzy burst into 'Are You Ready' and then 'Jailbreak'. They released 'Trouble Boys' that summer, which they played at this gig. Then Phil spoke to the audience about Scott dating Kirsty MacColl. Everyone was laughing and cheering because they started to play 'There's a Guy Works Down the Chip Shop Swears He's Elvis.' Phil also broke the A string on his bass, asking if we believed it was a C. And he dived into his audience!

I WAS THERE: ALAN MAICH

It was an unusual gig at Kirkcaldy Ice Rink with the stage set up at the end of what was the rink. I'm sure Snowy White was in the band then. Here is an extract from the local press:

> The night Thin Lizzy rocked Kirkcaldy Ice Rink and raised the roof… It was the night rock legends Thin Lizzy came to town. The noise

made by the Irish rockers at the Ice Rink led to complaints by nearby locals, meaning it was one of the last gigs to ever take place at the venue. It was the first leg part of a low-key Scottish tour which also took in Aberdeen, Inverness and Irvine.

I can recall it was a great show with all the hits played. Phil fell off the stage at one point. My ears were ringing on the way home.

I WAS THERE: STUART CUNNINGHAME

They did a mini tour of Scotland in 1981, which was a warm up tour for the Slane Castle gig. At the Magnum Leisure Centre on the west coast of Scotland, they were supported by a band called Red Ellis, who me and my mates knew because they played in pubs in Glasgow and had a Brian Robertson lookalike on lead guitar. Shaggy blond curly hair was the rock thing in those days. It was a sports hall with a capacity of three or four hundred and a wee stage and the gig was very up close and personal.

A few days before we had been to see them on the same mini tour at Kirkcaldy Ice Rink. At both gigs they announced that it was going to be a very short set of 45 minutes to an hour, basically bedding in some new songs. My abiding memory of that gig is that Phil was off his face and so out of it that at one point he fell off the stage and had to be pushed back on. He rambled on incessantly between each song about the background to the song and it wasn't terribly entertaining. People were getting a bit bored with it all and just walking out.

MAGNUM CENTRE

13 AUGUST 1981, IRVINE, UK

I WAS THERE: JAMES PETTICREW, AGE 16

As a pimply-faced 16-year-old, I first saw Lizzy in the rather odd surrounding of the Magnum Leisure Centre in Ayrshire, Scotland. It sticks in my memory because it was my first rock concert, and I went with a crowd of mates who assured me I would love Lizzy. I remember that, surprisingly for Scotland, it was stiflingly hot in the sports centre. They kicked off with 'Are You Ready' and from the moment I heard the first explosive notes, I became a diehard Lizzy fan and have remained one ever since.

Phil captured me with the sheer force of his personality and performance. Scott's guitar was mesmerising, and Brian battered that drum kit like a demon on speed. The thought did cross my mind that Snowy White looked a bit detached from the rest of the band. His playing was top notch but he seemed to me to be a square peg in the Lizzy round hole. We left the sports centre, exhausted, sweaty, and desperate for the next time that the boys would be back in town again.

James Petticrew first saw Lizzy at the Magnum Leisure Centre in Irvine

---

Brian battered that drum kit like a demon on speed

I WAS THERE: CRAIG STEWART

The next time I saw them was 1981, just after Snowy joined, when they did a low key 'greatest hits' tour. They played a couple of Scottish dates and I was at Irvine's Magnum Centre. Despite some of the haters, I thought Snowy was great, if a bit stoic on stage, but there again so was Scott when he first joined. As a live guitarist you can't really fault Mr White, and Scott was stunning. He'd taken on way more than he used to when Gary was around and stepped up brilliantly well. (I play in a Lizzy tribute and I'm our Scott - he's always been my favourite Lizzy guitarist anyway.)

Thin Lizzy headlined the first ever rock festival at Slane Castle in County Meath.

SLANE CASTLE

16 AUGUST 1981, COUNTY MEATH, IRELAND

I WAS THERE: BEN HANNIGAN

I hung around with Phil and the lads back in the Clontarf days, which were great. Everything was just taking off. I travelled with them on gigs. When Eric Bell left and Robbo and Scott came in, things changed and they became a fantastic rock band. I've seen them many times, mainly backstage. The last gig I was out front for was the *Thunder and Lightning* tour. If I could go back and see just one gig again it would be Slane.

I WAS THERE: COLIN DEAN

In 1975 I was handed a mixtape in school by a very good mate. It had Lizzy, Sabbath and Purple, etc. on it and it was my introduction into the world of heavy rock. I was 12 at the time and hadn't got an older brother to take me to gigs. The very first album I bought was *Jailbreak* in '76, a classic of high energy heavy rock, but it wasn't until 1981 that I saw Lizzy live, at the very first Slane Castle festival. After that, I saw them in Dublin in '82 and again in '83 at the RDS on the *Thunder and Lightning* tour. I also saw Phil on his solo tour at the SFX Centre in '82 and at the same venue with Grand Slam.

Colin Dean was at Slane Castle

I WAS THERE: JUSTIN HEALY

My mother passed away in the June of '81 and Lizzy really, really helped me at that time because I took solace in the music. I had a ticket for Slane and I was holding onto that for dear life. I would listen to Lizzy every day. I would get up in the morning and listen to Lizzy before I went to school. I would come at lunchtime to listen to them and I would listen to them in the evening.

I went to Slane with my friend. We arrived in Slane village and walked down to the castle grounds. It's a natural amphitheatre and it was like 'wow' - it's just an amazing place. It was a beautiful day, and you don't get many days in Ireland where the sun is splitting the stones. You could see the stage and the mirrored Lizzy logo as the stage backdrop. U2 were on the bill. Some people were there just to see them. The story goes that U2 insisted that the Lizzy logo be covered over while they were on stage which resulted in a delay in Lizzy coming on. I heard that Paul McGuinness, U2's manager, went into Lizzy's caravan and was talking to Phil and saying, 'We need to cover it over,' and Phil agreed. I would've given him a kick in the arse. But that's Phil for you. He supported all these young bands over time. I don't think any other headlining band would've done that at an outdoor concert.

Listening to the live recording of the Slane concert really brought it all back. I remembered a lot of what Phil said to the audience even though it was 40 years ago. On the first song I can remember Scott giving his backline tech a really, really nasty look and I thought that was surprising because he's always so cool and smiling. But when you listen to the concert, his guitar tech had given him a guitar that was out of tune so he obviously wasn't impressed. He couldn't be tuning it mid song. At the end of the song, Scott handed the guitar to the guitar tech and the guitar tech gave him a guitar that was in tune. When you come on big, you can't have delays and gaps between the songs. Phil had to fill that gap so he was having a bit of banter with the Dubs – the people from Dublin - in the audience, because there were people there from all over Ireland. When I heard that on the recording, it all came back.

I WAS THERE: ALAN LONG

I met my wife Helene in April of 1981, when I had just turned 21 years of age. I had my ticket already bought for Slane Castle and was planning the trip with some friends. Snowy was doing okay in the band, but in hindsight he was not the best choice. Brian Robertson was a far younger and more vibrant player and it was a shame that line up could not have stayed together for a little while longer.

Slane turned out to be the last time I would see them live. I had a ticket for the RDS in April 1983 for the farewell tour with John Sykes but, alas, my future mother-in-law passed away three days before the show, so I ended up giving my ticket to my brother Paul, who had taken me to my first show in 1976. We went full circle.

It is hard to describe what you feel at a Thin Lizzy concert. I feel very sorry for all the young people who I hear say I never got to see them live, as that was the only way to really experience Lizzy at their best. Just like the album says, Live and Dangerous. Philip had a great way of connecting with the crowd. He was always very honoured to be playing to a crowd. Listen to any of his shows - he never stops thanking people for coming: 'Thank you very much, 'til we meet again, thank you.'

I own every vinyl album that Lizzy recorded, and I enjoy the first albums as much as the later ones as I know where Philip is talking about in his songs. He was a poet as well as a songwriter and a singer. There will never be anyone like him again, as it is all so different now.

Until we meet again, Philip, stay safe.

In November 1981, Lizzy embarked upon the UK *Renegade* tour to promote the album of the same name.

Photo Andy Small

Lizzy in action 1983

CORNWALL COLISEUM

11 NOVEMBER 1981, ST AUSTELL, UK

I WAS THERE: NICK HALLAM, AGE 17

Living in rural north Devon wasn't easy for us, but thankfully two things came to our rescue - the Cornwall Coliseum and the Concert Travel Company. The Coliseum was the only venue in the southwest where all the major rock bands performed in the Eighties, and a local bus company saw a gap in the market and offered a service, picking up from towns and villages along the way.

The Coliseum was on the coast at the bottom of a narrow steep road. We often thought that the truck drivers must have hated that tour venue! But we were very thankful for it, seeing the likes of Motörhead, Rainbow, Whitesnake, Iron Maiden, and of course Thin Lizzy there. The venue claimed to have had the UK's longest bar! Everything was big back then - big speakers, big lighting rigs, big sets. We often used to look at the trucks in the car park. The more trucks, the more excited we got. It usually meant a bigger, more spectacular show! And louder. There were no dB restrictions back then.

We saw Thin Lizzy on their *Renegade* tour. What an absolutely incredible experience for a 17-year-old. I don't remember much of the actual concert, but I do remember meeting the band afterwards. We had a bit of time before the coach left, so me and my best mate Alistair decided to queue up at the back of the venue to try and see the band.

The dressing rooms etc were a bunch of tatty portacabins stacked two high. We walked up the external staircase, concert programmes in hand, and were beckoned into the top room of the portacabin. The band were sitting on sofas, signing programmes and shaking the hands of a moving line of young sweaty gig goers. I was petrified. I had never met a famous person before. Within seconds, I was stood in front of Phil Lynott. I was lost for words but thankfully he did all the talking.

I struggled to understand what he was saying with his broad accent and gravelly voice. I heard him clearly though when he offered me a drink. I was so excited. There was a massive bin of ice and cans of beer. He delved in the ice and pulled out a can of coke. He clearly realised I was underage. I was a tad disappointed, but it was still something that Phil

Lynott had given me! I kept that can of coke for months.

Sadly, the Coliseum closed in the late 1990s and is now demolished. The end of an era. But what great, great memories.

I WAS THERE: CHRIS PUTTOCK

I saw Thin Lizzy three times at the Cornwall Coliseum, which has since sadly been pulled down and which claimed at the time to have the longest bar in Britain! The best of the three gigs was the 1981 show. I travelled down from Plymouth by coach, all excited and ready for an evening of rock. On arrival, the priorities were the loo, the bar and then the merch!

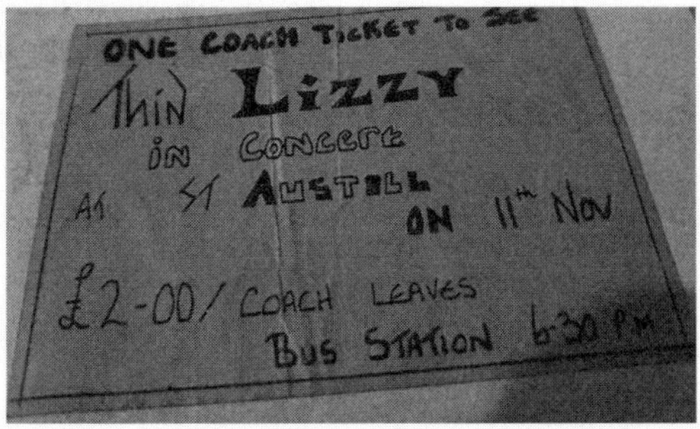

Chris Puttock saw Lizzy at St Austell

When Lizzy came on, the crowd surged forward and to my surprise I found myself near the front. And halfway through the concert, I was at the very front – the one and only time that's happened to me. Phil came to the front of the stage, so I chanced my luck and touched his foot. He looked down and pretended to stamp on my hand, a huge grin on his face. He winked at me and went back to the band. The rest of the gig was fantastic and I left hot and sweaty and with a huge grin on my face.

BRIGHTON CENTRE

14 NOVEMBER 1981, BRIGHTON, UK

I WAS THERE: STEVE PAGE

Another concert that stood out for me was on the *Renegade* tour. I took my younger brother and then girlfriend, and a couple of other friends. It was their first time but I knew what to expect. They opened with 'Angel of Death'. Again, there were no seats and I went for the front. This time I made it! Phil was leaning right over me, in that classic pose. It was unbelievable. We had to run for the last train out of Brighton and, on our journey home, we were high on adrenaline. What a night.

A couple of tracks from *Renegade* became very personal; the title track, because a very dear friend, a biker, died in the year of the album's release, and 'It's Getting Dangerous'. I was in a very dark place and the lyrics became an anthem that got me out the other side. They still do.

I cried my eyes out when we lost Phil. I was deeply saddened and I still am. It's only now we all realise how lucky those who saw Lizzy live were. When the next tour or record was released, the anticipation was electric. I saw them on every tour right up until the end. The line up and sound changed, but it didn't matter. It was still Phil up there.

APOLLO THEATRE

16 & 17 NOVEMBER 1981, MANCHESTER, UK

I WAS THERE: NICK HARNEY

My next Lizzy gig was the following year for the *Renegade* tour. Curious about the new keyboard player Darren Wharton, I managed to buy tickets to the Manchester Apollo gig for my mate Ian and I; this time we scored front row seats through a Jewish school friend with a very well connected father! We arrived at the Apollo, or more specifically the Apsley Cottage, early for a pre gig pint. As we approached the pub, walking past the road crew trucks we arrived at the stage door to hear the rumblings of the band doing their sound check. This was awesome (as they would say on the other side of the pond) – we were going to be in for a loud one!

A few hours later, the lights dimmed and we jumped out of our seats to rush to the edge of the stage. Immediately the sound of the new keys came though as they opened with 'Angel of Death'. Still awaiting the vinyl copy of *Renegade* I had ordered through the record club, I knew right then that this was going to be an exciting new chapter for Lizzy with Darren on board. What happened next, though, just blew my mind.

The band were over halfway through their set and rocking through 'Bad Reputation'. Scott Gorham, without a doubt my idol at that time, still sporting longish hair and wearing a cool black-with-white-stripes shirt, jumped down off a monitor onto my left hand, which was mirroring Brian Downey's drum beat on the stage floor. I felt no pain but Scott was clearly mortified that he might have seriously hurt me! He bent down and grabbed my right hand, trying to pull me up on stage. The crowd, however, surged forward and so I was trapped between the crowd and the edge of the stage. Scott's hand gradually slid away and I glanced round at Ian, whose eyes were out on stalks as to what had just happened. What I noticed was that Scott's hand was ice cold. At the time, I found this unusual as they had been playing for well over an hour but I just put it down to him being one cool dude. At the sheltered young age of 16, I hadn't considered the possibility of any side effects of drug use….

For days, months, years and decades I was reeling at my handshake with my true 1980s idol. I saw the band again at the Apollo early in 1983 for the *Thunder and Lightning* tour, not knowing that was to be my last encounter with Thin Lizzy as we knew it with Phil Lynott at the helm. This was again a great gig, but having only rear stall tickets I felt a little detached after my front row experience of a couple of years earlier.

I WAS THERE: TANIA BRIDDON, AGE 17

Tania Briddon remembers a surprise appearance by Gary Moore

I saw Thin Lizzy on the *Renegade* tour at Manchester Apollo. My lasting memory is of Gary Moore playing 'Parisienne Walkways'. He was not expected to be on stage and that first guitar note as he walked out on stage still gives me goose bumps when I remember it. The Thin Lizzy concert was very much about the music. There weren't huge screens or lots of pyrotechnics and smoke machines. It was just rock and roll.

I wasn't a huge Thin Lizzy fan but a huge music fan. My friend and I went to live gigs as often as we could afford - Rush, Styx, The Scorpions, Whitesnake, The Who and Deep Purple to name a few. We'd meet up with the same people from all over the country, pretty much for every gig, on the platform at Crewe station. Neither me nor my friend could drive at the time so the train was our only option, and they used to put on special trains just for the rock fans. The platform used to be packed with leather-clad teenagers with the smell of patchouli oil.

RENEGADE RELEASED
20 NOVEMBER 1981
UK CHART POSITION 38
US CHART POSITION 157

Renegade was Lizzy's eleventh studio album. Darren Wharton was recognised as a permanent member of the band (he'd played on previous albums) but his photograph wasn't on the album sleeve. 'Hollywood (Down on Your Luck)' was released as a single but didn't make the UK top 40, although it did reach 24 in Billboard's 'Top Tracks' chart to reflect the airplay it was getting on US radio.

ODEON THEATRE
20 & 21 NOVEMBER 1981, BIRMINGHAM, UK

I WAS THERE: COLIN MASON
I have recorded a brief 'rating' of all the gigs I've ever attended, ranging from 'terrible' to 'absolutely fucking brilliant'. Most of my Thin Lizzy gig ratings are up at the top end of the range. However, this one only rated a 'good but....' There's a note in my records saying 'completely new set' and the set list was very different to the previous times I'd seen them. They were promoting the *Renegade* album with Snowy White on guitar and Darren Wharton on keyboards – definitely not a classic Lizzy line up, and certainly not my favourite line up or album.

I WAS THERE: JOHN HOPE
I first got into Lizzy when a friend played their album, *Shades of a Blue Orphanage*. I bought all their albums and saw them live about six times – at Birmingham Odeon, Stafford, University of Warwick. I met the band

backstage once. It was when Phil got charged with a drugs offence, I had a t-shirt printed - 'Phil is innocent'. Phil laughed when he saw it and put his arm round me and told me I was sound.

I WAS THERE: HELEN DK

I was three rows from the stage, on Scott's side. I still remember the sweat running down Phil's chin and the fact that I couldn't hear for two days afterwards!

I WAS THERE: PAUL WHITEHOUSE

Paul Whitehouse visited Dublin a couple of years back

We started high school in the summer of '76. It was an exciting time to be young, with some great bands around. One of our mates was a couple of years older than us and in '78 he was going to a gig to see a band called Thin Lizzy at Birmingham Odeon. He came back from the gig saying that they were his new favourite band and when we next went into Brum, he bought *Jailbreak* and *Live and Dangerous*, which he would always play when we went round to his house. I first saw them on *Top of the Pops* and other TV shows at the time, so we said we were Lizzy fans too.

My first time seeing them was on the *Renegade* tour and we saw Phil scrubbing a ciggie at the back of the Odeon during the soundcheck. I went on to see them about five times in the next couple of years, the last time at Reading Festival. It was only after his sad passing and as the years have passed that I have come to appreciate just how great live they were. The albums are a great legacy.

I WAS THERE: ROBERT SHARMAN, AGE 20

There was none of this internet shit back in the Eighties. If you wanted to see a band you read *Sounds* or *NME*, which both came out once a week. My best mate Neal Wood and I would debate which band we could go and watch, jump on the bus from West Bromwich into New Street and then run around the corner straight into the Odeon box office and ask, 'Have you got any tickets for sale for…', depending on whoever was mentioned in *Sounds* that same day. We got front row tickets for ZZ Top, Foreigner and (my proudest moment) both nights of AC/DC's *Back in Black* tour.

Bingo! The plan worked. We stood next to the old HMV, which was also the slope to the stage door. Darren Wharton came across the road from the Midland Hotel where we assume they were staying. I was surprised how young he looked. Then the rest of the band came over, one by one. I recall Scott was quite arrogant but he signed my albums. Then Phil came over. The kid in front of me wanted him to sign his five pound note. Phil said, 'Are you sure?' 'Yep,' said the kid, so he did. What a nice guy Phil was, chatty and pleasant.

HAMMERSMITH ODEON

25 - 28 NOVEMBER 1981, LONDON, UK

I WAS THERE: PETER CRAMMER, AGE 16

I first witnessed Lizzy on the *Renegade* tour with my cousin, who was in the Hell's Angels Windsor Chapter, and I followed them until Phil's untimely death. In 1983 I witnessed the 'All Star Jam' where Robertson, Bell, Moore, Gorham and Sykes all took the stage, much to the crowd's bewilderment. I can still recall that day vividly, as Phil controlled the audience and had it in the palm of his hand. Lizzy stand peerless as the greatest rock band I ever witnessed and Phil, an outstanding frontman, remains my all time hero.

I WAS THERE: ANDREW SMYTH

The band had announced they would be playing another massive tour in November 1981, as their new album *Renegade* had just been released. With a brand new stage show, a stable line up and a keyboard player - Darren Wharton - added to the line up, everything was looking up for the band. The new album was an improvement on *Chinatown*, and so I decided to go to see them for two nights at Hammersmith Odeon, my favourite London venue and one they liked playing.

On the Tube to Hammersmith, I was filled with anticipation. It's always nice to have good seats in the stalls amongst a sell out crowd, and you knew that with Thin Lizzy, they would air new songs and play all the material you were thinking about. These shows were as good as any I saw. A stable line up made a difference, and with a good album in the shops, the future for the band looked very promising.

GAUMONT THEATRE
30 NOVEMBER 1981, SOUTHAMPTON, UK

I WAS THERE: GARY POWELL

After leaving school in 1978 I was working in a factory where a couple of the lads were Lizzy fans. The first album I purchased was *Black Rose*. Different venues seemed to have different sets for the gigs, which I guess may have been something to do with the size of the stage. On the *Renegade* tour in Southampton, the lighting guys were hanging in circular cages above the stage, controlling the lights. I'd have loved to have seen Gary Moore and Brian Robertson playing in Lizzy, but Snowy White and John Sykes were brilliant.

I've seen Limehouse Lizzy a couple of times. Close your eyes and the vocals are very close to Phil Lynott.

I WAS THERE: ALISON RUSSELL

Jailbreak and *Johnny the Fox* were ground breaking albums. No one else had done anything like this. Philip was a story teller and Robbo played a guitar with so much emotion. Scott and Brian Downey also were a great part of it too. I was sold on day one. I saw them on the *Live and Dangerous*, *Chinatown*, *Black Rose*, *Renegade* and *Thunder and Lightning* tours. On the *Chinatown* tour, I got dragged over the front barrier at the Gaumont when Gary was mid solo and Phil looked down at me in a concerned way. He just told the roadies to let me go and I was soon back enjoying the gig.

For the *Renegade* tour I wrote to Katherine at the fan club asking if I could meet the band. She said to just go to the backstage door and ask for Gus Curtis (their tour manager). When it got to the encore, I said to my friend, 'Now we have to go to the back of the Gaumont. We did, and we hammered on the back stage door. Some guy answered and asked what we wanted. I explained and he shut the door in our face. I tried again and insisted I speak to Gus. Then Gus came to the door and he was so lovely and took us back stage. I remember walking past their stage clothes all hung on hangers on a rail. I was so nervous. Gus said, 'Wait here, girls.' I thought we would get to a party, but it was just a room with Phil, Scott, Brian, Snowy and Darren sat in there, looking knackered!

But Phil just got up and said, 'Hello girls, did you enjoy the gig?' and then offered to sign photos. I had my Phil Lynott poetry book that I had bought through the fan club. He asked me what my favourite song was, I told him it was 'Massacre' and they all signed that page. I had ridden my Kawasaki ZZ250 to the gig and Phil commented on my blue bike leather jacket. I was on a high all the way home....

SOPHIA GARDENS

1 DECEMBER 1981, CARDIFF, UK

I WAS THERE: ANDREW KING

They came back for the *Renegade* tour in December 1981, this time supported by Sweet Savage. This was a rescheduled date after Phil had got into a fight. Because the show had been cancelled and then rescheduled, the crowd were well up for it and more boisterous than usual. I had been

Andrew King saw Lizzy when they returned to Cardiff in 1981

given a 35mm camera, so was able to take some photos from my prime position at the front. Lizzy played an amazing show which lasted for over two hours. As the band played the last encore, the roadies started unplugging their amps and equipment, eventually leaving just the drums and PA mics. The show had run well over the scheduled finish time and, as a result, I missed the last train home north from Cardiff and now had a 12 mile walk to look forward to. Thanks, boys....

PLAYHOUSE

3 DECEMBER 1981, EDINBURGH, UK

I WAS THERE: CRAIG STEWART

The *Renegade* tour was next in Edinburgh, and I met Scott and Phil after the show briefly. They both had time for a hello and a handshake. It was the first time I'd seen Phil up close, and he was way taller than he looked on stage and a huge presence.

I WAS THERE: JOHN PROW

I saw Lizzy on the *Renegade* tour. I went with a workmate - and it was a great gig!

I WAS THERE: KEITH MCSHANE

My second time of seeing them that year, and Darren Wharton was coming to the fore. This time they opened with 'Angel of Death' and I can remember the red flags flying and cages moving up and down. It was a good show but Snowy let the image down a bit as he stood and played whilst Phil and Scott were all over the stage. Of course, the whole theatre became more ecstatic in the greatest hits territory.

APOLLO THEATRE

8 DECEMBER 1981, COVENTRY, UK

I WAS THERE: SCOTT MCKENZIE GILL

Scott Mckenzie Gill was underwhelmed by the *Renegade* album

The *Renegade* album was released in 1981 to mixed reviews. It was probably the band's most commercial album to date, with another terrific drum track but it sounded a bit too polished, as if it was looking to the American market. The killer track was 'Angel of Death', which started with a menacing keyboard piece that reminded me of the beginning of Rainbow's 'Tarot Woman'. The other songs were pleasant enough but there were no real showstoppers. Still, we were looking forward to the coming tour, which saw Darren Wharton becoming officially part of the band and which proved to be Snowy White's last tour and album. I was to see them twice on this tour, firstly in Coventry.

Live they rocked, starting with 'Angel of Death' and playing most of the new album plus tracks from *Chinatown*, and a few old crowd pleasers like 'Emerald', 'Jailbreak', 'Cowboy Song', etc. They were superb but it felt a little forced. I came away a little disappointed. I had tickets for Leicester but that was the same. I felt the band needed a severe kick up the rectum. For various reasons, this was the last time I saw them live. After that, life got in the way for a while.

Thunder and Lightning was inspired, with John Sykes in the fold and a harder edged sound all round, with some blinding music, the high spot being 'The Sun Goes Down' with its superb guitar solo. 'Cold Sweat' was another highlight, with a pounding heavy drum sound from Mr Downey.

I will always be a Lizzy fan. They were a special part of my growing up and the original Thin Lizzy still sound fresh today. I have a huge Thin Lizzy playlist on my Spotify account. That way it doesn't wear out!

CITY HALL

9 DECEMBER 1981, SHEFFIELD, UK

I WAS THERE: MARK SYKES, AGE 16

I saw them at Sheffield City Hall on the *Renegade* tour. I went with my uncle and a school friend. I was at the front! It's so sad that Phil died so young.

Mark Sykes caught the *Renegade* tour

In 2006, I was working away in Brentwood in Essex. After eating, I used to go to a bar. I kept looking at this bloke thinking, 'I know that face.' Weeks later, I heard him talking to another customer about Thin Lizzy and then it clicked - Brian Robertson! It was a blast, chatting with him most nights. He has Phil's silver earring, which he showed me.

CITY HALL

10 DECEMBER 1981, NEWCASTLE-UPON-TYNE, UK

I WAS THERE: PETER SMITH

The *Renegade* tour was scheduled to call at Newcastle City Hall on 27th October 1981 but the concert was postponed until 10th December.

Lizzy were supported by Sweet Savage, a metal band from Belfast, who included Dio and Def Leppard guitarist Vivian Campbell.

Lizzy went out on tour again in 1982, and were scheduled to play at Newcastle City Hall on 25th March 1982. This one was also postponed – until April - as Scott Gorham was suffering from exhaustion. This was the last time I saw the band with Snowy White. Both gigs were excellent, but I felt that the classic Lizzy years were past.

DE MONTFORT HALL

14 DECEMBER 1981, LEICESTER, UK

I WAS THERE: CHRIS BIRT

A friend rang to say he had two tickets to see Thin Lizzy at Leicester's De Montfort Hall that Friday night. Being a rock music fan, I'd always liked the hits and I thought that Phil looked cool. Well, that Friday night changed my outlook on music. It was the *Renegade* tour with Snowy White, Scott Gorham, Brian Downey and this front man who just had the crowd in his hand. I can honestly say that they were the best live rock band I've ever seen. They just blew me away - two blazing guitars, a drummer who was fantastic and this Irish bass player who had every woman in there purring! I've been a fan ever since and I've got everything the band has ever done.

GAUMONT THEATRE

16 DECEMBER 1981, IPSWICH, UK

I WAS THERE: KEVIN O'CONNELL

It was December 1981 when I next saw Thin Lizzy live, on their *Renegade* tour. The line up had changed to Phil Lynott, Brian Downey, Scott Gorham, Snowy White and Darren Wharton. Once again, Thin Lizzy did not disappoint and, by now, I was used to seeing Phil torment the crowd (particularly the females) with the reflections from his bass guitar. The texture of the Lizzy sound had changed with the addition of Darren's keyboards. Snowy was a little less energetic on stage, while Scott was his lively self and Brian was at the back commanding the tempo and direction of each song.

JIM'LL FIX IT

9 JANUARY 1982, LONDON, UK

Thin Lizzy appear on the TV show *Jim'll Fix It,* performing 'Hollywood (Down on Your Luck)' with grandmother May Booker on keyboards.

Lizzy started 1982 with a European tour, playing mainly Scandinavian dates and one German show.

VEJLBY-RISSKOV HALLEN

8 FEBRUARY 1982, AARHUS, DENMARK

I WAS THERE: JOHN NALDAL JAKOBSEN

The night before the concert, Brian Downey was involved in a fight in a nightclub and he was not able to do the concert. So Thin Lizzy used the drummer from the support band, The Lookalikes. He had no time for rehearsal but he did well. It was the last time I saw Thin Lizzy.

I WAS THERE: JAN HVEDHAVEN

The second time I saw them was in Aarhus, with Snowy White. Brian Downey had been in a bar fight the night before and they had to replace him with the drummer from the support act, The Lookalikes. They had only had the afternoon to rehearse but it went quite well. Of course, there were some mistakes but it was still a great concert.

Mike Mesbur filled in on drums for this and two other shows on the tour, with Mark Nauseef taking the drummer's stool for the others.

OLYMPEN

9 FEBRUARY 1982, LUND, SWEDEN

I WAS THERE: LASSE HANNSON

Lasse Hannson saw one of the best three concerts of his life

I got to see Lizzy twice, on the *Renegade* tour in Lund and then in Copenhagen on the *Thunder and Lightning* farewell tour. I'm sorry to say me and my friends were wasted on that gig so I don't remember much about it (we were young and stupid) other than it was my wife's (still my girlfriend at the time) birthday and I had given her the ticket as a birthday present! But I remember the gig in Lund. We were blown away by the fantastic opening of the show. The stage was dark, the *Renegade* flags were waving on both sides of the stage, there was smoke and there was the keyboard intro to 'Angel of Death'. Then the flash/smoke bombs exploded and off we went. We were never to be the same again. One of the best concerts of my life.

DRAMMESHALLEN

11 FEBRUARY 1982, DRAMMEN, NORWAY

I WAS THERE: FRANK SØRENSEN, AGE 15

Lizzy were Frank Sørensen's first ever concert

I saw Lizzy on the *Renegade* tour in Norway in February 1982, my first ever concert. I was there with a friend and his father waited outside for us in his car. I don't really remember that much, but they started with 'Angel of Death' with the red flags as a back drop. As a 15-year-old kid this was a great event.

I had first heard Thin Lizzy two years earlier when I was at a friend's house after school. He played *Chinatown* and I was instantly hooked by the twin guitar sound and by Phil's voice. Lizzy have been my favourite band since that day. They always will be. I've been to a couple of the *Vibes for Philo*, had the privilege of shaking hands with Philomena Lynott, and met both Scott Gorham and Brian Robertson at the Sweden Rock Festival.

February 1982 saw Lizzy on the Irish leg of the *Renegade* tour.

ROYAL DUBLIN SOCIETY
20 FEBRUARY 1982, DUBLIN, IRELAND

I WAS THERE: JUSTIN HEALY

A friend who was there was complaining about the sound, but the sound was always bad at Simmonscourt unless you were down at the front. And I was at the front. Having seen them twice I'd been blooded. The opening of the concert was great. It was so simple, with the opening drone of Darren's keyboard for 'Angel of Death' and then the follow spot hit the *Renegade* flag which was being blown across the stage by a fan. It was very, very powerful and very effective. That was a great set.

From Ireland, Lizzy embarked on another European tour, taking in shows in France, Spain, Portugal and Germany. They were then touring the UK again, although many dates on the tour were postponed from March to April because Scott was suffering from exhaustion.

APOLLO THEATRE

22 APRIL 1982, OXFORD, UK

I WAS THERE: SIMON GILBEY

My journey with Lizzy began a long time ago, in the summer of '78 when *Live and Dangerous* was released in the UK, making me 13. My friends at school were still in the back end of punk mode or listening to Eddy Grant. I'd spent four years living in Canada where my cousin Ricky taught me to drum along to the likes of Alice Cooper and Grand Funk Railroad, so when we arrived back in the UK the Sex Pistols were not my thing.

The release of 'Rosalie' hit me - bang! I can still remember hearing it for the first time, in my dad's works van. I managed to get a bus into Reading at the weekend and bought the single. I spent the next month playing along with Brian Downey until I got the album. That was then my life - after school on my drum kit playing along to the whole album back-to-back. It was a good two hour session for a 13-year-old. I think it stopped me getting into a lot of trouble.

In '79, Lizzy were scheduled to play the Reading Rock Festival. I begged and begged, but got a stern 'no' from my mother. I was told that, until I was taller than her, I wasn't going to Reading. Two years later I was a lanky six foot and on my way to Reading. But not to see Lizzy.

I had to wait to see them live, but they were always there on the turntable and always on when I was messing around with bikes in the garage - *Bad Reputation*, *Chinatown* and, of course, *Live and Dangerous*.

In 1982 the Oxford Apollo was my then favourite place to see bands - Motörhead, April Wine, Def Leppard and Whitesnake, just to name a few. Then the boys came to town on the *Renegade* tour. It was a long, long wait from getting my ticket to the day of the gig but there we were, me and a mate who could drive, clad in our smelly old leather jackets with cut off denim waistcoats, three rows back from the stage and sharing the night with a few hundred other long-haired patchouli oil-smelling fans.

They came on and – bang! - it went off. We rushed the stage and, all of a sudden, I was there, at the front of the orchestra pit, right in front of Phil. The orchestra pit at the Apollo is literally that, about four feet from the stage and edged with a knee-high wooden surround. Having the weight of a load of head bangers behind you whilst not trying to fall in that pit is a pure skill, believe me.

Having the weight of a load of head bangers behind you whilst not trying to fall into that pit is a pure skill

---

We rocked hard and the big man sweated over us. We were that close! Halfway through the set Phil got a drink from a speaker cab, came over to the mic and said, 'Here's a lad that needs some Irish in him,' lent over the pit and handed me a whiskey and coke. 'This is 'Emerald'.'

ODEON THEATRE

23 APRIL 1982, BIRMINGHAM, UK

I WAS THERE: COLIN MASON

My rating for this show was back up to 'excellent'. Whilst still classed as the *Renegade* tour, the set list included much more of the earlier material as well – 'back to *Live and Dangerous*' according to my notes! This gig had been delayed by a month due to Brian Downey damaging himself in a fight in February, while Scott Gorham was missing due to 'personal problems'.

I WAS THERE: MARTIN DAVIS

I live in Tipton in the West Midlands, a couple of miles from Phil's birthplace in West Bromwich. I don't go back far enough for the heady days of Robertson, Moore and Bell (not in the live setting, anyway). Having said that I will be 60 at the end of this month. Where does all that time go?

I first got into Thin Lizzy while at secondary school in the mid Seventies, when I was in my early to mid teens. One of my classmates

Martin Davis saw Lizzy three times at Birmingham Odeon

lived opposite the school gate and, rather than stay for school dinners, we used to bring sandwiches and go to his house at lunchtimes. His mum and dad were both at work so the house was empty. We would put on Thin Lizzy, Status Quo and Black Sabbath albums while he played along on his bass guitar which he plugged into an enormous Marshall amp in the corner of his living room. It was quite funny watching the ornaments dance their way across the mantlepiece above the gas fire because of the vibration, and we had to keep a wary eye open for any that might fall. I can only hope that his neighbours were at work too!

I saw Lizzy play live three times, all at Birmingham Odeon. It should've been four, but on one occasion my friends turned up at my front door to collect me as I was frantically scouring a drawer in search of my ticket. They waited as long as they dared but it was nowhere to be found. I had to sit at home crestfallen while they enjoyed a fabulous night out. This was in the days before electronic receipts, etc. and I didn't think my chances of convincing the people on the doors that I had actually bought a ticket were very high. The ticket turned up a few months later, tucked in the pages of an old diary!

I did manage to attend the *Renegade* and *Thunder and Lightning* tours. There is a large Irish Community in the Digbeth area of Birmingham and they certainly made their presence known at the Odeon. The atmosphere was always electric as a result. It was a great concert venue and I've seen a lot of bands there who later went on to fill arenas and stadiums. The ground floor really channelled the sound… and by heaven it was LOUD!

The *Thunder and Lightning* tour was incredible. The band were still at the height of their game, which made the loss of Phil so much harder to bear. We felt that he still had so much more to offer and it was heartbreaking when we heard the news that he'd gone. I know some bands go on to become mere pastiches of themselves but Lizzy went out on top. It was just a shame that it took such tragedy for that to happen.

I remember coming out of the Odeon after my last gig on that tour with my bottom jaw still down by my knees! I was completely blown away by what I had just seen. I never saw some of the classic line ups, but I have to say John Sykes was simply stunning. I vowed that I would willingly make a pact with the Devil to get a bootleg of his performance of 'Still in Love with You'. I've absolutely no idea how I would've gone about that in those pre-internet days but that was going to be my mission!

Fortunately, I didn't have to sell my soul. I simply parted with £7.99 at John Menzies when the *Life* album was released a few months later, answering my prayers. I know the *Live and Dangerous* purists will be horrified, but *Life* is how I remember Lizzy the best, being a relatively late arrival at the party.

I can't quite remember why, but my sister's future husband gave me his copy of the 'Whiskey in the Jar' single on the Decca label sometime in the mid Seventies. When I got married in 1995, I passed it on to my best man as a gift for services rendered. He'd been one of those friends waiting awkwardly in my living room while I was looking for my gig ticket over a decade earlier.

DOMINION THEATRE

30 APRIL & 1 MAY 1982, LONDON, UK

I WAS THERE: CHRIS WHILE

As this was only my second gig ever - the first one being the Scorpions in '82 - the booming sound of Darren Wharton's keyboard to start off 'Angel of Death' almost blew the wind out of me. There were these cage-type lighting pods that were moving around with techs inside them, flashing the silver beams that cut through the smoke of a thousand lit cigarettes. It was 1982 and the Dominion Theatre in London.

It was supposed to have been recorded for a VHS tape, but sadly the tape got mangled at some point, and only snippets still exist on YouTube. But what a gig! We were sat up in the circle and while everyone around us was sitting down, we were up and bouncing around head banging. At one point we swore Phil raised his hands to thank us for rocking instead of just sitting.

Thus a legend was born in my mind, and although Thin Lizzy were on the home stretch, they were gods of music to me.

I next saw them at the Hammersmith Odeon on the *Thunder and Lightning* tour, the final farewell (that lasted a good while!) tour in 1983.

During that gig, the version of 'Still in Love with You' that appeared on the B-side of 'Thunder and Lightning' was recorded. I still say you can hear me yell during one of the quieter breaks!

Great gigs and great times for this young man as I was. A lifelong Lizzy fan, and so sad still at Philip's loss.

Viva Lizzy!

I WAS THERE: ANDREW SMYTH

They had no album to promote, but in 1982 Lizzy decided to do a couple of shows at the Dominion Theatre in London. The band were hoping to film them for future release on VHS. The line up was the same as on the 1981 tour and the set list was classic Lizzy. At the back of my mind, I did wonder why they did not choose to film the gigs at the Hammersmith Odeon. Sadly, the concerts never saw the light of day, and no reason was really given as to why.

Andrew Smyth saw the Dominion show that was filmed for a never realised video release

---

In June 1982, Philip Lynott and the Soul Band toured Ireland, promoting Phil's solo material. Darren Wharton was the only other Lizzy band member involved and Phil played guitar, not bass.

SLANE CASTLE

24 JULY 1982, COUNTY MEATH, IRELAND

I WAS THERE: JUSTIN HEALY

In 1982 the Rolling Stones played Slane. I went to the gig. I was getting into the Stones and I enjoyed the gig but I was saying 'it's not Lizzy, I wish it was Lizzy', the way a kid's brain works. That's how obsessed I was. I walked out at the end to where we were told the bus was going back to Dublin city, on the outskirts of Slane. All the traffic coming out of Slane was moving at a snail's pace because there were thousands and thousands of people on this small country road and it takes forever to get out. There was a tree which had been chopped down beside the bus stop so I was sitting on the side of this tree, waiting for the bus. I turned my head and looked right over and there was Phil, sitting in a long black Merc. I was completely and utterly fucking blown away. I've worked in TV and met all kinds of well-known people like Rod Stewart and other musicians but this was spectacular. I was like 'fucking hell'. I was freaked. I didn't know what to do.

But I managed to get the nerve to walk over to the car and I was real Dublin. I said 'how ya' and he said 'how ya' and he looked at me and smiled. I was wearing a leather jacket with badges on the lapels and he was looking at the badges and going 'they're good… they're good' and then he saw my Lizzy badge and he said 'that's the best one' and smiled. I was completely starstruck. I didn't know what to say to him. He was waiting for me to say something. But he knew I was a snotty-nosed kid. He was drinking a bottle of wine. I said, 'Give us a sup of your wine,' and he started laughing. He said, 'I can't, I can't. It's me missus, she'll kill me you know.' I didn't know what to say so I just grabbed his arm, shook it and walked off.

He was so cool and nice and friendly. A friend of mine met him in Grafton Street and he was just giving out a lot of tickets. He was giving them out to kids and anybody. So many people I know met him or worked with him and I've never heard any bad stories about him.

SNOWY WHITE LEAVES
AUGUST 1982

Snowy White left Lizzy in 1982, telling *Rolling Stone* in 2020 that 'I didn't really fit properly'. Of his lack of stagecraft, he said, 'I'm not the sort that jumps about – I did my best.' Snowy also suggested that there were tensions between Phil's solo career and Lizzy's. 'Scott said to me, 'I'm fed up with this. I don't mind playing on Phil's album, but that's a session. He should pay me for that.' But it all drifted on. It was quite chaotic.'

I think Phil blew it. He got into drugs and he got into a situation where it seemed like he wanted to be a celebrity more than a musician. **Snowy White, as told to *Rolling Stone***

In October 1982, Philip Lynott and the Soul Band went on a Scandinavian and European tour. Again, Darren was the only other Lizzy member involved.

MARKTHALLE

29 OCTOBER 1982, HAMBURG, GERMANY

I WAS THERE: NINO D'ANGELO

This was Phil Lynott's one and only solo concert in Germany. Myself and three friends, all aged between 15 and 17, went along to the venue in the early afternoon, hoping to find out from the roadies which hotel Phil was staying in so that we could go and meet him. They told us he was staying in the Hotel International, just a few metro stops away from Hamburg's main station. We arrived at the hotel and naively asked for 'Mr Phil Lynott' at reception, where they told us we could find him in the hotel bar. We walked through with our bags full of Thin Lizzy records that we were hoping to get signed and - boom! - there he was, sitting at the bar having a drink.

English is not my native tongue but back then I could communicate in what we call in Germany 'school English' and so my friends sent me up to make the first contact. I walked up to this magnificent, charismatic musician and personality and introduced myself. He was really kind, gentle and relaxed. When I asked him if it would be all right for my friends who had hung back to come over and join us, he was like, 'Yeah, sure.' He was wearing a black leather jacket and underneath that a super stylish, elegant jacket made of satin.

As he was doing a solo tour, we asked him if it was true that Thin Lizzy had split up. Phil replied, 'No, no, Thin Lizzy will record with a new guitar player and then also go on tour, shortly after the record release.' Needless to say, we were absolutely thrilled, stunned and happy to hear this amazing news, told to us by the man himself.

We then asked him about the line up in his solo band and he mentioned their names and the only three names, that instantly rang a bell of course, were those of Mark Nauseef, whom we were aware of, through the *G-Force* album of Gary Moore, Darren Wharton, because of Thin Lizzy and Jimmy Bain on keyboards or shall we say on second keyboards of Ritchie Blackmore's Rainbow fame.

Not realising how angry Phil had been at the time about Gary Moore walking out on Lizzy during their US tour supporting Journey, I asked him if he had heard Gary's new album, *Corridors of Power*. Phil, totally laid back and relaxed about everything, asked me if it was any good. Being a die-hard Gary Moore fan, I enthused about it as best I could in my limited English.

Phil agreed to sign our album sleeves but asked us to hand them to him as he had an interview to do. In the meantime, Phil's bass player Jerome Rimson showed up. What a nice, friendly, welcoming and humble guy he was. As we'd given everything to Phil to sign, we gave Jerome some white sheets of paper to sign. Once his interview was over, Phil gave us our record covers back, telling us that he had to leave for the concert and do the sound check.

That evening we saw a great concert, topped off by a great version of 'Dancing in the Moonlight' with a nice bit of audience participation. What a day. Wow, just wow!

The following morning, we returned to the hotel hoping to get some more albums and some music magazine articles signed by him, but Phil wasn't there. We got to meet Darren Wharton and he asked us if we knew where Phil was, as if we were an integral part of the tour management. After signing our records and chatting to us for a bit, he pulled a little book from his bag and started to phone some people, asking them if they knew where Phil was. I guess Phil must just have had a late night!

Philip Lynott and the Soul Band concluded 1982 with an Irish tour in December, in which Brian Downey participated.

THIN LIZZY ANNOUNCE SPLIT
18 JANUARY 1983, LONDON, UK

Phil announced that the upcoming tour in support of the new album, *Thunder and Lightning*, would be their last.

It was really a combination of Scott and Phil who ended the band. Scott was having bad health issues, because of his drug addiction, and wanted to stop so he could work this out. Phil also felt it was time to move on. **Brian Downey, as told to *Classic Rock***

BBC *SIGHT AND SOUND IN CONCERT* REGAL THEATRE
26 JANUARY 1983, HITCHIN, UK

I WAS THERE: KEVIN O'CONNELL

I was invited by the Thin Lizzy Fan Club to attend the BBC *Sight and Sound in Concert* at Hitchin's Regal Theatre. The show was filmed to celebrate the final farewell tour. Once again, the line up had changed, this time to Phil Lynott, Brian Downey, Scott Gorham, John Sykes and Darren Wharton. As I queued to go in, Phil and the band walked past and I was torn as to whether to chase after them and risk losing my place. I regret it now, but I chose to stay put for the opportunity of a better view of the show itself.

Once in, I was placed nicely in front of John Sykes, whilst having a perfect view of Brian Downey and his Tama kit. The show began with a couple of warm up tracks before the filming commenced, which was then followed by Pete Drummond's introduction and the live show as seen on the BBC. After the televised part of the show had concluded, Thin Lizzy performed a number of encores that were really appreciated by the audience, but sadly when Pete Drummond returned to the stage to say that Thin Lizzy had finished performing for the night and that there was no more money available to pay for anymore, the scenes turned ugly and he was soaked in beer and other drinks thrown from the crowd.

I WAS THERE: KEVIN DRISCOLL

I joined the Thin Lizzy Fan Club which meant you had the option of cheaper tickets. I wrote asking if I could take my eight-year-old daughter Julie to a show with me and I got a letter back saying it was okay. She had been playing the cassettes so she knew some of their songs, and she came every time after that gig when they were touring.

Kevin Driscoll's daughter Julie was a big fan of Phil and Phil was a big fan of Julie

We first met Phil at the Regal Theatre in Hitchin which they played for the BBC's *Sight and Sound in Concert* programme. There were only 300 people there. It was a warmup gig for the farewell tour. I'd written to the secretary of the fan club and asked, 'Is there any chance we can meet the band afterwards?' And she wrote back and said, 'Yes, I'll sort that out for you. When you come down, ask for me at the door and we'll take it from there. I took the letter with me. When we got there, I saw the doorman and he said, 'She can't come in because she's underage.' I said, 'I've got a letter here from the secretary of the fan club,' so he went off with the letter and came back and said, 'She's phoned up and said she's not coming because she's ill.' I said, 'What do I do now? We've travelled all the way to Hertfordshire from Nottingham,' and he said, 'I'm sorry, I can't help you.'

Then this other doorman said, 'Tell you what, just go round to the back entrance where the BBC men are and I'll have a word with them and see if they can get you in.' So we went round the back and the doorman was there and the BBC man said, 'Yeah, come on then, we'll take you round.' We got to sit on the steps that went up the top tier.

After the gig had emptied out, we were still stood there. I came through and the bloke I saw said, 'Nobody can see them because they've left to go back to London.' And I thought, 'Oh flipping heck, after all that.' But the doorman who had sent us round to the back door came through the door a minute later and said, 'Haven't you gone up yet?' I said, 'No, that bloke just told us that they've gone,' and he said, 'Come with me.' He took us upstairs to the room where they were. The rest of the lads were sitting at the table talking and Philip was in the corner, talking to two ladies. But as soon as he saw us come in, he said something to the two girls and came straight over to us and started chatting to us.

I said, 'Can I take a picture of you and Julie?' and he said, 'Of course you can.' And he said, 'Lads, come on up here for a photo,' and he got them all lined up with Julie in the middle and I took the photo. He said, 'Right, I want one of these photos. That's the first time I've had a picture taken with the band all together with a fan.' I said, 'Well, we're going to the City Hall in Sheffield when you're up there,' and he said, 'Right, after the gig come round to the back. Come and see me.'

I got the photos developed and we went to Sheffield. Before the gig, I went round the back to see the bouncers and explained that I was going to be coming round afterwards,' and they said, 'No, no, no, nobody can come round here and go backstage.' I said, 'But he told us to meet him,' and the bouncer said, 'No, you can't do that,' and just as he said that Philip came around the corner from out of the changing rooms and saw us. He came straight up to us and said, 'Hi there, are you alright?' I said, 'Well yes, but he's not going to let us in after the gig.' And he said to the security, 'Excuse me, these two will be coming round here after we've done the show and you will bring them to my changing rooms straight away.' And he did.

After the show I showed Phil the photographs. Julie had a silver buckle on her belt and on the photograph, there was a flash reflecting off her belt and Phil said, 'I like that, look at that flash on her belt.'

It was February 14th, which was his wedding anniversary. I was a bit embarrassed because I didn't know this, but my daughter had brought him a present in her bag. It was a platter with a salt and pepper shaker, in the shape of a bull and a cow. She said, 'I've brought you a present,' and he said, 'Oh Julie, that's really good of you.' Caroline came up, looked at the bull and the cow and said, 'I know which one is you.'

Scott Gorham said to Julie, 'Julie, would you like a drink of champagne?' She said, 'No thank you,' and he said, 'I bet you've never had a drink of champagne, have you?' She said, 'Oh yes I have,' and he said, 'Where was that then?' and she said, 'At my mum's wedding.' And Scott looked at me and started laughing. Because her mum had got married again.

Before we left, Julie said, 'We've seen you loads of times and you've never played 'Whiskey in the Jar' but I know you've played it at other venues.' Phil said, 'Right, we're in Nottingham.' 'Yes, we've got tickets for that,' I said and he replied, 'Well, come down in the daytime just after lunch and spend the afternoon with us and we'll do you a personal version of it at the soundcheck.'

THE TUBE, CHANNEL 4

28 JANUARY 1983, NEWCASTLE-UPON-TYNE, UK

I WAS THERE: IAN JOHNSON

On the *Renegade* tour I was lucky enough to see them twice, in December '81 and April '82, both times at Newcastle City Hall, and once again they delivered superb shows. In 1983, John Sykes joined and what a player he was. Then the big news came - the band would be calling it a day after the tour of the new album, *Thunder and Lightning*. I was in the fan club and found out they were going to be on *The Tube*, a music show that was transmitted live with an audience there. Off I went to see them, not knowing you needed a ticket to get in until I was in the queue outside the TV studio. Luckily for me, someone there had a spare ticket and I got in. They only played a few songs but it was brilliant to be there on live TV, and the audience were fantastic.

They came back to Newcastle City Hall in March and I went to one of the two nights they played. I wish I'd gone to both. It was a sad day when it all came to an end, and I always hoped they'd get back together. Then, of course, Phil died – a sad day and definitely no more Lizzy. But their music will live on forever.

SIGHT AND SOUND IN CONCERT
5 FEBRUARY 1983

BBC Two broadcast the Hitchin Regal show that had been recorded on 26 January 1983. The *Radio Times* advised that 'viewers with stereo Radio 1 should turn off TV sound and position their speakers on either side of the screen.'

QUEENS HALL
10 FEBRUARY 1983, LEEDS, UK

I WAS THERE: STEVE FOWKES
I was a massive fan but sadly this was the only time I saw them live. I was at Hull Uni at the time. I can't really remember much about the gig except that I was on the floor, the sound was poor and Lynott seemed off his face. 'Still in Love with You' is my favourite song, but that night it was a mess.

I WAS THERE: MARTYN CROWTHER
I saw Thin Lizzy three times, twice at the Queens Hall in Leeds and once at Milton Keynes Bowl. The first time in Leeds I was only 16. My older brother had got me into Lizzy. He was a bit of a rocker whereas I was into punk but I think Lizzy and punk mixed pretty well. When I first saw them, Snowy White was the guitarist and they started with 'Are You Ready' and Phil Lynott looked very stoned. I also saw them in '83 on the *Thunder and Lightning* tour, with John Sykes. They were wearing matching outfits, like jumpers with a chequered pattern on the chest.

I WAS THERE: ALVIN LEVY
I just remember it being packed. We got searched for drugs before we went in and missed the last bus home so had to walk home from Leeds.

CITY HALL

14 & 15 FEBRUARY 1983, SHEFFIELD, UK

I WAS THERE: ANDY WICKS

I was 16 years old and living with my parents when I went with my friend to see them in Sheffield. They must've already announced that they were splitting up. We were going to miss our last train home to Leeds if we stayed for the encore, but there was some doubt whether the last train would turn up anyway so we decided to stay to the end. Afterwards, we managed to thumb a lift up the M1, getting as far as Barnsley.

We tried sleeping in a stand up telephone box overnight but it was too cold and so we ended up phoning my dad and getting him to come and pick us up for the remainder of the journey. He wasn't too pleased at being called out at two o'clock in the morning. I told him that the last train had been cancelled. I didn't like lying to my parents but that was one time I did.

We also saw the Eric Bell Band play at the Ford Green pub in a rough area of Leeds. As a venue it used to get bands that were on the way up or who were a bit too small to play university refectories. Def Leppard played there on their way up. We went backstage and had a chat with Eric Bell. He seemed like a nice guy. We also went to see Grand Slam a couple of times, which was Phil's band after Thin Lizzy. I remember the early albums were quite difficult to get hold of and my brother ended up paying quite a lot of money to get hold of a copy of *Shades of a Blue Orphanage*. The music changed over the years but they were always a great live band and we never hesitated to buy tickets if they were touring.

We were on the front row at Queens Hall and I accidentally reached out and touched the monitor for one of the lead guitars and got a kick in the face for it. I can't remember if it was Scott Gorham or somebody else. It was a shame that they split up and it was very sad how it all ended. The Seventies was their heyday but they remained a great live band with that fabulous back catalogue.

I WAS THERE: JON NEWMAN

I was in my prime during the classic rock days of the late Seventies and early Eighties. I got into rock on the back of punk and despite worshipping at a broad church when it comes to music, rock has always been my number one genre. What turned me onto rock was travelling in the back of my dad's car when 'Highway to Hell' came on. The funny thing is, I remember everything about that journey.

At school the punks suddenly became the rockers and we used to fight with the Mods who at that time were having a ska revival through the likes of Madness, The Specials and The Beat, etc. We were always outnumbered but everyone made up in time for the local discos, where we went from pogoing to headbanging.

The first concert I ever went to was Rainbow at Leeds Queens Hall, on the *Difficult to Cure* tour. I then saw all the greats - AC/DC, Iron Maiden, Saxon, UFO, Gary Moore, Van Halen, Ozzy, Black Sabbath, Motörhead, Motley Crüe, Van Halen, Purple, Def Leppard, Whitesnake, Guns 'n' Roses, Aerosmith and MSG and, of course, Thin Lizzy. Out of all of those, Thin Lizzy were and remain my second favourite group, just topped by AC/DC. *Live and Dangerous* is still my favourite live album.

DE MONTFORT HALL

17 FEBRUARY 1983, LEICESTER

I WAS THERE: CHRIS NOON

I was introduced to Lizzy by my uncle Colin. *Jailbreak* was my first taste of a band that would mould my style and musical direction for the rest of my life. I became obsessive, collecting Lizzy posters, magazine articles, etc. They were the first band I reached for every time I put on the record player. I was 17 when Thin Lizzy announced they were calling it a day. I saw an interview with Phil on breakfast TV announcing the split and what would in essence be their farewell tour. It was a no brainer that I had to go and say goodbye to the boys. The next challenge was how was I going to pay for it?

Being a full-time student, money was tight so I had the awkward conversation with my parents asking for money. My parents had both grown up as the new breed, all wrapped up in rock 'n' roll - Dad was a Teddy Boy and Mum a Waspy Girl - so they understood how important music was and paid for me to go. To say I was excited is a massive understatement - I was going to see the boys! Days were counted down until finally the day itself came around.

Back then a coach trip would come through towns and village to pick up concert goers so me, Mike Baldwin, Phil Britten and Bob Bonafin waited on a cold late February afternoon for the coach. The coach arrived and the excitement increased, giggling and arsing about all the way to Leicester.

We got into the venue and I headed straight to the merch stand. One t-shirt, scarf, studded wristband and programme later, I made my way to my seat. In no time the support act was announced and Mama's Boys took to the stage, Pat McManus absolutely dominating proceedings and the band was knocking some great music out for over 30 minutes.

They left the stage and it was almost time. My heart was pounding. Finally the lights went down, my giddyometer went up to 12 and in a flash the boys were there, right in front of me - Thin FUCKING Lizzy!

Opening with 'Thunder and Lightning', I was in heaven and jumping up and down like a lunatic. The songs came and went. I can't remember what songs were next but I do remember stopping and taking in the moment. It was magical. The light bouncing off Phil's mirror scratch plate, John Sykes absolutely shredding his Les Paul and flashing his blond mane, the sublime Scott Gorham making it all look too easy, Downey holding them all together and Wharton giving Lizzy the keyboard fill that was so important to the last two albums. It wasn't too loud, it wasn't quiet, it was perfect.

The songs kept coming, classic after classic until the final song, 'Rosalie'. Then it was finished – over. That was it. I'd witnessed one of the greatest bands to ever walk the planet and then came the post-gig blues. We all sat on the coach on the way back in silence. No more Lizzy.

I feel so privileged to have witnessed Phil and the boys. But the story wasn't over for me because 38 years later, going through some boxes brought out from the loft, I came across my concert programme (still with the poster intact) and I grinned like a Cheshire cat. It all came back. Like a warm glow, I remembered Thin Lizzy live. The memory never leaves us. Are you out there?!

I WAS THERE: MARK SMIGGY SMITH

1983 would prove to be the last time I would see Phil in the flesh. I knew it was farewell and the new album didn't come out for another month, so there would be songs that we hadn't heard before, and a new guitarist in John Sykes, of which I had heard nothing before. That February night there were three of us. Angela, myself, and my twelve-year-old nephew, James. This was full circle, because James' dad Rob had introduced me to a lot of music, and now James had picked up the bug. Seeing Lizzy for a sixth time, the excitement was off the scale for me, so I can't imagine what it was like for James seeing his first gig.

It was the first time I sat at a concert. A twelve-year-old in the mosh pit may not have ended well. We were in the balcony, close to the stage. The gig started with 'Thunder and Lightning' which was an unknown quantity to me, and very different to what I'd become accustomed to. The gig was a blinder, and I loved every second. Another degree of brilliance. They gave it to us as a sort of farewell in November as the live album, *Life*, but surely Phil would be back? It was inconceivable that I wouldn't see some sort of reincarnation of Lizzy. I kept hearing and reading stuff but nothing ever seemed to gel.

APOLLO THEATRE

19 FEBRUARY 1983, COVENTRY, UK

I WAS THERE: JOHN ANDERSON

I remember getting on my mate's shoulders and waving at Phil Lynott and him putting his thumb up to me!

ODEON THEATRE

21 & 22 FEBRUARY 1983, BIRMINGHAM, UK

I WAS THERE: JEFF COLLINS

The final time I saw Lizzy was on the *Thunder and Lightning* tour. John Sykes gave them that aggressive sound again. My lasting memory of that night is the opening power chord Lizzy always started with. That night it was one of the loudest things I'd ever heard. Every time I saw Lizzy live, they were awesome.

I WAS THERE: STU HUNTING

I saw Lizzy twice more, both times at the Birmingham Odeon on the *Thunder and Lightning* tour. I was at the front of the stage for the first in February, looking up at the guys, within touching distance. Surrounded by like-minded Lizzy lovers it felt like home, and live shows have been the same since. That sense of belonging.

Stu Hunting met John Earle (on saxophone)

I'm not ashamed to say I had a tear in my eye that last time I saw them, as I stood and watched the band I loved so much say goodbye playing what was basically a greatest hits set. I remember a headline from one of the music papers when they announced they were splitting up, 'The Boys are Backing Down'.

ODEON THEATRE, Birmingham
Adrian Hopkins presents–
Thin Lizzy plus Guests
Monday, 21st February 1983
Evening 7.30
FRONT STALLS
£5.00
11
NO TICKET EXCHANGED NOR MONEY REFUNDED
THIS PORTION TO BE RETAINED (P.T.O.)
A. B. Cooper (Printers) Ltd., Manchester

Birmingham Odeon - Stu Hunting was there

I'm not ashamed to say I had a tear in my eye the last time I saw them

Then came that day in January, I remember it clearly. I went to see my girlfriend at the time and she looked at me and said, 'You don't know, do you?' She told me to sit down and broke the news that Phil was gone.... I was devastated. I've visited Phil's resting place and said my own goodbyes like so many others before and after me. Even so many years on, the love is still so strong for him from so many.

I never had the privilege of meeting Phil but I have been able to spend time with all the other ex-members. Two encounters really stand out, meeting Scott at the London Astoria and spending about 20 minutes sitting on the stairs chatting, and then spending a couple of days in Wolverhampton in August 1994 for the *Are You Ready?* show at the Civic Hall. Talking to Brian, Darren, Eric and all the others that came down for that day, I was in paradise and I got to sit down with Robbo, writing down the lyrics to 'Don't Believe a Word' for Darren. Even John 'Irish' Earle was there, who was a true gentleman.

But that weekend's highlight was without a doubt spending time with Phil's mum, Philomena. She came on the stage towards the end of the show to say a few words and there was such a huge noise from everyone there showing love for her and Phil. It must have gone on for five minutes solid before she could say anything, and when she was able to, it was with tears in her eyes.

After the first time seeing Lizzy, I started collecting albums, singles and memorabilia - anything I could get my hands on. The collection is pretty big now but my most prized items are a mint *New Day* EP, a pair of engraved chopsticks from the *Chinatown* launch party and one of the original 1,000 *Songs for While I'm Away* poetry books. My love of Lizzy has never diminished over all these years. I owe every ounce of pleasure I have ever had from listening to music and seeing live bands over the last 40 plus years to that night in Stafford and I'm forever grateful!

GAUMONT THEATRE

24 FEBRUARY 1983, IPSWICH, UK

I WAS THERE: KEVIN O'CONNELL

I saw Thin Lizzy on their *Thunder and Lightning* tour at Ipswich Gaumont with the same line up I had seen just a month earlier at the Regal in Hitchin. The performance was incredibly special but at times quite emotional. There were almost hidden messages within certain songs, particularly 'Still in Love with You' and the way Phil phrased the lyrics. Deep down I just hoped to see Thin Lizzy reform after the break up, but sadly this was not to be.

BRIGHTON CENTRE

25 FEBRUARY 1983, BRIGHTON, UK

I WAS THERE: GARY WALLIS

I first got into Thin Lizzy in 1982 when I was 15 and new to the rock music scene. I'd heard various songs on the radio over the years but when I purchased *Live and Dangerous,* I was hooked. Such a great album and I played it to death. It was Side 4 that I played the most and still do – 'Suicide', 'Sha-La-La', 'Baby Drives Me Crazy' and 'The Rocker'. No sooner had I discovered Lizzy than they announced they were splitting and that their next studio album would be their last.

I was at the record shop on the day of release to get myself a copy of the limited edition of *Thunder and Lightning* which included a live 12 inch EP. Before that, though, a mate of a mate had told us he was driving over to Brighton to get tickets for the farewell tour. Me and two other mates decided to tag along. These were the days long before internet ticket booking, and the price for a top show in 1983 was just a fiver. This would be my first experience of a live show.

We arrived at the Brighton Centre on the night of the gig and the first thing I remember is having my studded belt confiscated at the entrance, as I suspect did many others. Mama's Boys were the support act and as such the first band I ever saw performing live. They were excellent, but it was Lizzy we were there to really see. As they hit the stage, I got a feeling of euphoria with the opening riffs of 'Thunder and Lightning'. The crowd surged forward and we were off.

Lizzy ripped through their set of new and classic songs. From anthems such as 'Jailbreak' and 'The Boys are Back in Town' to new tunes 'Cold Sweat', 'The Holy War' and my personal favourite from the *Thunder and Lightning* album, 'Baby, 'Please Don't Go'. Towards the end we were treated to a Brian Downey drum solo and a couple more tunes, but all too soon the show was over. I remember having conflicting feelings of happiness, but also sadness as I knew it would be the first and last time I would see Thin Lizzy live. Almost 40 years on, when I listen to the live album that was recorded during the tour, I am taken back to that night.

GUILDHALL

26 FEBRUARY 1983, PORTSMOUTH, UK

I WAS THERE: ELIZABETH MOORE

My friend and colleague at Phonogram married Scott Gorham and they are still together after 40 years. We went backstage after and Phil gave me a kiss. I remember there was a wall of lager cans – I mean, a whole wall - and we never got asked if we wanted a beer! I remember the band coming round Phonogram and giving all the girls a bottle of champagne and a black rose to promote their album, *Black Rose*.

APOLLO THEATRE

27 FEBRUARY 1983, OXFORD, UK

I WAS THERE: ALISON RUSSELL

Phil called me and my friend a 'fanzine'. He was very sweet. We were very young and he treated us so well. On the final tour, he said, 'Spike, come to any gig early and you can have a back stage pass,' so that was it - Southampton, Poole, Portsmouth, Oxford. I remember on the way back from one gig, being at a petrol station in my Mini with Darren Wharton in his Jag and us just chatting.

Phil saw me outside the gig at Oxford and I remember his words so clearly to this day: 'Bejesus, Spike, here you are....' That lovely Irish accent. At Poole Arts Centre, he said before the sound check that he was not sure if they should have stopped Lizzy, but that it was too late now. I said 'noooooo!' - but it was too late.

I also remember being backstage like some starstruck teenager and Scott having a bit of a go at Phil. We were uncomfortable and went to walk out. Phil said, 'Everyone leaves, but not the girls.' Scott was not amused.

I remember Scott having a bit of a go at Phil

COLSTON HALL

3 MARCH 1983, BRISTOL, UK

I WAS THERE: PAUL OWEN

I was in a band called The Bohana Mouse Band and we supported Thin Lizzy! My mate's girlfriend worked at the local radio station and was there when the manager said, 'The support band have rung up to say that their van is broken down and there's no way they can get there tonight. Does anybody know of a local band that could step in at short notice?' My colleague's girlfriend said, 'My boyfriend is in a band.' He said, 'Do you think they can make it to the Colston Hall?' This was five or six o'clock. She phoned her boyfriend, who was the percussionist, and he phoned John, who was the drummer. John then phoned round the rest of the band. I was having tea with my mum when he rang and said, 'We're supporting Thin Lizzy tonight.' I thought he was joking and said, 'I'll see you at rehearsal in a couple of days' time.' He rang back and said, 'It's not a joke, this is for real.' We went down to the venue. They had all their trucks and we just had this little transit van. We set up our kit on the stage in front of the drum kit. The manager came in and said, 'You're on in 20 minutes, and just to let you know there's not an empty seat in the house.'

John rang and said 'we're supporting Thin Lizzy tonight' – I thought he was joking

When we went on stage. 40 per cent of the people went straight to the bar as they always do with support bands. We weren't a rock band. We played funky stuff. We played for about 20 minutes. Then we watched Thin Lizzy's performance from out front. After the gig, we went backstage and met the band and they thanked us for stepping in at short notice. It was pretty surreal. One minute I was having tea with my mum and the next I was playing in front of two and a half thousand people.

I WAS THERE: SHAUN HUTTON, AGE 20

I was fortunate to see Thin Lizzy on the *Thunder and Lightning* farewell tour. Prior to them coming on there was a police presence in the venue.

It seemed like they were looking for someone. There was also an old lady sat several rows from the front who resembled the lady who played with Lizzy on *Jim'll Fix It*. When they first came on, they sounded bloody awful but the mixing desk quickly put things right.

I WAS THERE: MARK WILLIAMS

And so it came to pass that the end was announced. The clan gathered for one last hurrah, and what a send off it was. The album and tour performances were the best they had done for years. How ironic, and amazing when you realise the health of some members at that time. Again, I managed to gain access backstage and got the obligatory programme signed.

I asked a member of the crew where the band was staying, and amazingly he told me. On the way home, I decided to try my luck visiting the hotel bar in case they were having a night cap. In I strolled, not really thinking they would be there, and the first people I saw were Scott Gorham and Darren Wharton, sat chatting to an old lady. She turned out to be May, the lovely lady who appeared on the TV show *Jim'll Fix It* after her granddaughter had written in to Jimmy Savile asking him to 'fix it' for May to play with a rock band. I asked Scott if it was okay to join them and after thinking about it for a bit, he said 'okay'. I was in!

John Sykes turned up and I was chatting away to them all when in walked the Big Man. I was in heaven with my heroes. Phil got the drinks order in and asked me if I wanted a drink. I was all, 'Are you sure? Do you mind?' and Phil said, 'Do you want a fucking drink or what?', a response that makes me smile to this day. There I was, helping John Sykes with the drinks and thinking to myself, 'I don't believe this!'

I stayed in the bar until about 4am, chatting about how they started, their gear and their future plans. Eventually I decided to leave as I had work in the morning. Brian Downey had stayed in his room as he had a bad case of the flu, so he and Gary Moore are the only members of Thin Lizzy I never met.

Of course, we all know how Phil's story ends, a great tragedy. I for one love to know what he would have been doing now if he'd lived, and it still hurts. My wife informed me of his passing in the early hours of the morning when I returned from a night out at a Bristol rock club. I felt like I had lost a close friend, and I'm not ashamed to say that 'I cried, the night the King died…' but, wow, those Thin Lizzy memories….

THUNDER AND LIGHTNING RELEASED
4 MARCH 1983
UK CHART POSITION 4
US CHART POSITION 159

Lizzy's twelfth and final studio album was a heavier sound thanks to the contribution of John Sykes, and for many fans it was a return to form. It spawned three singles – 'Cold Sweat' (number 23 in Ireland, 27 in the UK), 'Thunder and Lightning' (Ireland number 22, UK 39) and 'The Sun Goes Down' (UK 52).

HAMMERSMITH ODEON
9 – 12 MARCH 1983, LONDON, UK

I WAS THERE: PHIL ROSS

I was at Hammersmith Odeon to see Thin Lizzy promoting their final studio album, *Thunder and Lightning*. Yes, the ticket vendor had greeted me with an, 'Oi, Phil mate, what do yer want' as I walked through the door and when I replied 'Thin Lizzy', he shot a sideways glance at his mate next door. 'I knew you would,' he said. 'I saved you a couple seats, middle of the tenth row from the front.' Don't ask me why, but that was always my preferred ticket choice. Close, but not too close if things got a bit lairy, and sometimes they did.

I knew that this was going to be Phil Lynott and Lizzy's last hurrah. His problems with various addictions were well known, and the vehicle that was Thin Lizzy had spent the last few years just trying to keep on the road rather than thundering like a juggernaut through popular culture as they had between '76 and '78.

I was determined to enjoy the Thin Lizzy experience, and I was not in any way disappointed. True, Phil did not look particularly well, and his insightful lyrical edge was not as sharp as it used to be, but the lights, the noise and the consummate stagecraft of all the band members were still there in abundance, and Mr Lynott still held us all in the palm of his hand. He still looked down and grinned at anything that struck him as absurd and he was still committed to giving of his very best. To be on stage was thunder and lightning and God damn, it was so exciting!

If that was to be the end, it was a great way to go out. I could say, hand on heart, I was there. I had witnessed one of the great performers and had savoured the character that he portrayed onstage. Magnetic, engaging, impressive, but also aware that the strutting and posing could verge on self parody. It was just wonderful in so many ways to be a part of that performance, because Phil always made sure that you were part of that performance.

'Are you still out there?'

'Yes!'

'Are you sure you're still out there?'

'YES!'

I WAS THERE: GARY HURST

I was heartbroken when the band decided to call it a day but the resulting tour was terrific, with the newly installed John Sykes giving the band a bit of a kick up the backside after a couple of slightly lesser albums. The four gigs at Hammersmith Odeon were brilliant but very emotional affairs. The last night was made even better by the appearance of three of the four previous guitar players (Bell, Robertson and Moore). Apparently Snowy White wasn't invited. The resulting live album, *Life*, isn't really comparable to *Live and Dangerous*, but served as a fitting ending to a wonderful band.

Being a member of the fan club, you would receive advance information about recordings and tours. There was always excitement over news that the band would be entering the studio soon to start recording a new album, which in those days was one nearly every twelve months, and the knowledge that a new album release meant a new tour. I would be eagerly digesting every piece of news about the band.

I scoured the small ads in the music press to find Lizzy badges that I didn't have. I collected all the tour t-shirts and more. I still have all my 60 or more badges and all the t-shirts.

It took me a while to understand what the ads meant when they advertised 'live tapes'. Eventually I was deep into the world of bootleg tape trading and now have some 150 or more recordings, including one recorded at the St George's Hall in Bradford in November 1976 where the recorder was in a holdall under the stage!

I saw every London gig from July 1976 onwards, and I never came away from a Lizzy gig disappointed. My favourite gigs were July 1976 at Hammersmith Odeon, the 1977 Reading Festival, June 1978 at Wembley Empire Pool and March 1983 at Hammersmith Odeon. My favourite line up was with Robbo and Scott Gorham and my favourite albums are *Jailbreak* and *Live and Dangerous*, although everything from *Nightlife* to *Bad Reputation* was ten out of ten for me.

There were rumours of Lizzy reforming prior to Phil's death. Personally, I don't think that would have been a good idea. I'm not sure if they would have been able to recreate former glories. I am truly grateful for the wonderful recorded legacy the band has left us with and it's great to see the resurgence of interest in the band in the last few years.

I WAS THERE: RICHARD JOHN

My introduction to Lizzy was *Live and Dangerous*. As a kid, I was totally taken in by the intro and 'Jailbreak'. Being half-Irish and a man of colour, I resonated with Phil. My first live gig was at the legendary Hammersmith Odeon on the *Renegade* tour. This was an interesting era for Lizzy with the introduction of keyboards and Darren Wharton. I was critical of this approach at first, but it worked well. The new sound was still dominated by the unique Lizzy sound,

Rich John saw Lizzy twice

but the lyrics moved from lovey-type songs to more meaningful and mature numbers such as 'Angel of Death'.

The second and last time was on the final tour at Hammersmith. Again, it was a new line up and for me it really worked with John Sykes. Hammersmith was alive, with people everywhere. I recall looking down into the stalls and seeing the sea of heads, all moving in time with the bass and beat. I could feel the balcony move with bodies and it was such a loud, strong sound. I also recall the chilling silence of the crowd for the vocal intro to 'Got to Give it Up'. This was the last show for Lizzy; we saw Eric Bell, Gary Moore and Robbo. They all came together at the finale with 'The Rocker'. It was amazing and I don't think anyone really grasped that this was the end. The mood was so high and the sound was one of the best I have ever heard.

If there's one gig that has stayed in my mind for so many years, it's this one.

I WAS THERE: ANDREW SMYTH

Thin Lizzy had decided in 1983 that their new album, *Thunder and Lightning*, with new guitarist John Sykes, would be their swansong as they were splitting up. The new album was jam-packed with riffs and great songs, and my friend Adrian and I decided we would do the last Hammersmith Odeon show. Prior to meeting up with him, I took a wander round to the backstage door to see if any of the band members had arrived.

Andrew Smyth's final Lizzy show was back at Hammersmith

Not long after, a light green Mercedes Benz arrived backstage and out stepped Phil Lynott, looking every inch the rock star. He was beaming, as Manchester United had beaten Everton 1-0 at Old Trafford in the sixth round of the FA Cup. Phil very kindly signed my ticket and then I made my way to the front of the venue. I went inside to look at the notice board to see what future gigs were happening. There was no security around, so I made my way into the stalls area, and managed to hear some of the soundcheck before being asked to leave by security.

The gig itself was a bow out to the fans. The new album was given an airing, but we wanted to hear the old stuff for the final time. Well, we got our wish. Brian Robertson joined the band for 'Emerald', 'Rosalie' and 'Baby Drives Me Crazy'. Next up was Gary Moore for 'Still in Love with You' and 'Black Rose'. And, last but not least, Eric Bell joined the band for 'Whiskey in the Jar'. Then the three guitarists joined the band for a rip-roaring version of 'The Rocker'. What a fitting tribute to this most iconic of bands. We were in dreamland.

They have left a lasting legacy through their live shows, their albums and their singles. And their memory will live on - as long as I'm around!

PLAYHOUSE THEATRE

17 MARCH 1983, EDINBURGH, UK

I WAS THERE: GRAEME THOMSON

I can't remember how I discovered Lizzy. I only had one mate who was into similar music to me and I don't ever remember him mentioning Phil and the lads, so it was probably seeing them in *Kerrang!* or *Sounds*. But the first album of theirs I bought, in 1982, was *Jailbreak* on one of my fortnightly visits to Edinburgh to spend my pocket money and paper round wages in some of the record shops. I grabbed a few more Lizzy albums over the next year or so. The only one I bought soon after release was *Thunder and Lightning*, with that memorable solo on 'Cold Sweat' – wow!

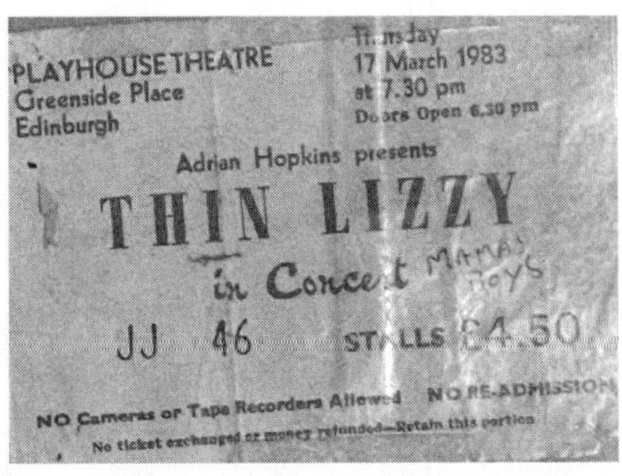
PLAYHOUSE THEATRE
Greenside Place
Edinburgh
Thursday
17 March 1983
at 7.30 pm
Doors Open 6.30 pm
Adrian Hopkins presents
THIN LIZZY
in Concert
JJ 46
STALLS £4.50
NO Cameras or Tape Recorders Allowed NO RE-ADMISSION
No ticket exchanged or money refunded—Retain this portion

Graeme Thomson saw Lizzy at the Playhouse Theatre and the Reading Festival

After getting into them in quite a big way, there was no way I was going to miss the *Thunder and Lightning* tour at my local(ish) venue, the Edinburgh Playhouse. Support was Mama's Boys, who didn't really do anything for me at the time but I hadn't heard any of their music. These days, you can check out a support on the internet first.

Lizzy were amazing! It was a complete show. Phil was one of those frontmen who could control an audience and he had us under his spell the whole night. At the time most bands would play one or two songs for the encore, but Lizzy did four or five songs that night, including a rendition of 'Happy Birthday to You' for Scott, with the crowd singing along. I left the gig with ears buzzing and a huge smile. The only downside was the t-shirt I'd purchased. One wash and it shrank from collar to waist, and yet the width went from a medium to something wide enough for the local scout troop to be able to use at a summer camp. T-shirts have definitely improved over the years!

I WAS THERE: SIXBOLT STEEV, AGE 22

Mama's Boys were in support, who were alright. When the main event started there was plenty of 'wow' factor. With the lights full on from the stage you could see it was a full house. My wife and I were on the balcony, so had a great view of the whole theatre. The Thin Lizzy sign was up at the back of the stage and suddenly the band were on stage.

The first thing I noticed was the blond hair of guitarist John Sykes. I then looked over to see Scott Gorham (with shorter hair), and above and behind him were the keyboards with Darren Wharton, Brian Downey in the rear centre stage on a riser, and of course the legendary Phil Lynott bang in the middle. The band thundered into their set, the frontman dressed in black leather and his by now trademark red Converse basketball boots.

The crowd were loving it. A few audience members were already standing along the front of the stage. John Sykes seemed to be more the focus of the two guitar men, with his hair flowing and his head banging. Gorham seemed happy with more of the rhythm guitar role but during the dual guitar solos they combined in the centre of the stage behind their leader. Rarely do I remember Phil leaving the middle of the stage. With the crowd electrified, Lynott started his between songs patter, asking the girls, 'Do youse have any Irish in ya?' which was answered with screams, and 'Would ya like a little more in ya?' prompting even louder screaming.

Towards the close of the night, Lynott used the house lights with his mirrored guitar scratch plate to pick out various members of the audience, men and women, much to their delight. He had obviously used this trick before as he was very good at it and seemed to enjoy it as much as his audience did.

Throughout the concert, he was the main focus of attention, not only because he was centre stage but because he had an aura about him. He was mesmerising. It all seemed to happen so fast. It was one of the best concerts I have ever attended. It was unforgettable.

I WAS THERE: CRAIG STEWART

Both Phil and Scott looked a little tired but the show was still there. Love or hate John Sykes, he breathed a new life into the music and it's a shame it didn't go further.

I WAS THERE: KEITH MCSHANE

It was Scott Gorham's 32nd birthday. Big flashes of lightning and rumbles of thunder took us into 'Thunder and Lightning'. There was so much power and energy on stage with John Sykes in the band. The atmosphere was wild and terrific. 'Holy War' was brilliant. It was the usual greatest hits territory for that audience. 'Emerald' was very special, with it being St Patrick's Day. I've never ever felt such raw emotion at a gig. They did 'Rosalie', my favourite, going into a medley with 'Dancing in the Moonlight' and then Philip said, 'There is a song I need to do,' and they went into 'Whiskey in the Jar'. I can hardly find words to describe it. It was something more than wonderful.

APOLLO THEATRE

19 MARCH 1983, GLASGOW, UK

I WAS THERE: CAMERON MARTIN, AGE 17

I was there in the second row the night Philip stopped a riot at the Glasgow Apollo. The Apollo had a stage that was 15 feet high, hence the seats were laid out away from the stage, and the crowd usually surged down to the front where there would be a mosh pit. This particular night, when Phil shouted, 'You wanna come a little closer? Then come a little closer,' I jumped over the front row but found that the bouncers were not letting the fans past. I quickly dived back over. The issue escalated until Philip stopped the band playing. At one point, I thought he was going to jump in and start fighting with the bouncers. Needless to say, the bouncers backed off. The rest of the gig was absolute mayhem, with the crowd going even more wild than usual.

I thought Phil was going to jump into the crowd and start fighting with the bouncers

I WAS THERE: FIONA MCCRANOR MURRAY

I was seeing a guy whose birthday was coming up. He was daft about Thin Lizzy. Being a 16-year-old school girl, I was skint but wanted to spoil him so I asked him to pick me up and take me into town, where I treated him to a doner kebab at the newly opened kebab shop next to the Apollo. This was very exotic at the time! We then walked round the corner to the stage door, so he could at least hear the band through the door. We sat on the step but must have bumped against the door. One of the bouncers opened the door and asked us what we were doing. I explained I was treating my boyfriend to dinner and his favourite band. The bouncer told us to go round to the box office, where we could leave our motorbike helmets. He then showed us right down to the front of the Apollo, in the stalls. We probably saw half of the gig!

I WAS THERE: JAMES PETTICREW, AGE 16

Having seen them at the Magnum Leisure Centre in August 1981, Lizzy were back in town, or at least back in Scotland, in December of the same year, this time at the Glasgow Apollo. Boy, did that place rock with Phil on stage. And I was back at the Apollo for the bittersweet experience of the farewell *Thunder and Lightning* tour. The place exploded when they opened with 'Thunder and Lightning'. I much preferred the raw, heavier sound of this album to *Renegade*. I was a Sykes fan, I thought he brought back something of the Robbo to the band. I can't remember who was the guest at the final gig, if it was Robbo or Midge Ure? In retrospect, I think maybe the group had lost some of its edge but as a naïve teenager, I had no idea of the narcotic nightmare Phil had become entangled in. I left the Apollo thinking I would never see anything better than a Phil-fronted Lizzy. I never have....

I WAS THERE: TODD MACLEOD

I had been a massive fan from a young age thanks to my older siblings. For me as a kid, who was getting into heavier stuff and who was blown away with that album, Sykes was a perfect fit. With the keys officially there on stage, the sound was massive. The songs were strong and the delivery awesome. It was the quietest rock gig that I had been to at the Apollo but was crystal clear. The atmosphere was taking the roof off.

Todd MacLeod remembers the return of Robbo

The show kicked off with Mama's Boys, a bit of needle in the groove, and then it was onto Lizzy exploding onto the stage. And - of course - as it was a farewell tour they were bringing back all of the previous guitarists, and as this was Glasgow there was only going to be one! Robbo arrived to a hero's welcome and remained on stage way past the songs he was meant to be on for, with Sykes waving him on and smiling his arse off. Gorham didn't look so pleased but I'm sure he was just trying to make the show go like the way they had rehearsed it. The crowd didn't want Robbo to go but eventually he left the stage. I'm not sure if he came back on. It was a long time ago. I forget my own count ins these days.

I WAS THERE: BILL JONES

I was lucky enough to have my uncle John as a bouncer and so got in to see Lizzy a few times. On the *Thunder and Lightning* tour he got me a triple A pass that guaranteed getting in to see the band. Gig over and on the way up, John Sykes was on the stage with his tech. After a bit of encouragement, I strolled onto the stage to get his autograph. He was talking away to me, asking questions, and all I could do was stare out into the stalls, circle and upper circle thinking, 'Fuck me, I'm on the stage of the Apollo.' I got in to see my hero, big Phil. He had Brian Downey get me a beer and was asking me about how the gig was, how long I'd been a supporter, etc. He was such a great guy. He made sure I was looked after and was genuinely interested in the support. I was speechless. He called Robbo over and got his signature on the programme, and he introduced me to Scott Gorham. I said to Scott, 'Good to hear you've learned the chords to 'Whiskey',' and he said, 'Fuck off.' I handed him the programme and said, 'Well, before I fuck off will you sign this?'

CITY HALL

20 & 21 MARCH 1983, NEWCASTLE, UK

I WAS THERE: PETER SMITH

Snowy White had left Lizzy and his replacement was announced as John Sykes, from local North East band Tygers of Pan Tang. Sykes brought a heavier sound and rock axeman guitar style to Lizzy. Very much a showman, he fitted the Lizzy image and signalled a return to form for the band. The new line up recorded *Thunder and Lightning*, the band's twelfth and final studio album. But this was the beginning of the end for Lizzy and the *Thunder and Lightning* tour was announced as the final farewell tour. Support for the UK tour was Mama's Boys, a hard rock group from County Fermanagh, Northern Ireland who featured three brothers - Pat, John and Tommy McManus. The tour called at Newcastle City Hall for two nights, and I went the first night.

This was very much Lizzy back on form, with Scott Gorham and John Sykes trading and sparking off each other, and Phil and the guys delivering a performance reminiscent of that great rock band of old. This was definitely the best I had seen them for some years. We all knew that this was going to be the last time we saw the band, and we made the most of it, giving them a rousing reception. Thin Lizzy played their hearts out, drawing from throughout their back catalogue. They even played 'Whiskey in the Jar'. It was stunning.

I WAS THERE: PAUL DONNELLY

I was fortunate to see Thin Lizzy at Newcastle City Hall on the *Thunder and Lightning* tour. They had such a huge effect on me that it resulted in me moving to Ulster to research the legends alluded to by Phil on the *Black Rose* album. I was also a huge Rush fan and the concepts being displayed on both *Jailbreak* and *2112* with their narratives of individuals attempting to overcome a dystopian society really resonated with me for some reason. And those themes seem even more pertinent today than the day they were released. Great foresight on the part of all involved!

I grew up in the North East of England and just loved rock music in all its forms. It was just a youth movement that I really got caught up in. It was pre internet and I listened to the radio late at night, notably Tommy Vance's *Friday Rock Show*. I'd record everything on the Toshiba boom box my uncle brought back from Saudi, which had a double tape feature. My father worked in the civil service with a guy called Alan Robson who did a show on Metro Radio in Newcastle called the *Hot 'n' Heavy Express* which I just recorded religiously. That's where I got my first exposure to Lizzy. Prior to this, we were just listening to LP records with friends and family, with my older brother being a fan of The Who, The Beatles and Fleetwood Mac. But they were kind of 'his' bands.

When I had saved up enough pocket money to go and buy my copy of *Jailbreak*, this was something new and - dare I say it – progressive and listening to 'Emerald' in particular was just a paradigm shift for me musically. While I think Lizzy died with Phil, I still turn out to see the various line ups. Just hearing that cymbal intro to 'Emerald' still makes the hairs on the back of my neck stand up.

Hearing that cymbal intro to 'Emerald' still makes the hairs on the back of my neck stand up

---

I WAS THERE: PAUL MIRFIELD

I was in my fourth year at school. My friend had *Live and Dangerous* and he played it to me and I got hooked on 'Southbound'. I bought the album off him for three quid, which in those days was quite a lot of money. I played it so much, it became that scratched and knackered that I had to buy it again. I ended up buying it three times!

I saw them in '81 on the *Renegade* tour. On the *Thunder and Lightning* tour, because I knew it was the last tour, I went to see them three times in five nights, twice at the City Hall in Newcastle on the Sunday and Monday and then on the Wednesday in Carlisle. I'm sure I saw them at the Sands Centre, although the internet says they played the Market Hall. As I recall it was a standing venue. My auntie lived just outside Carlisle so I stayed with her, and my uncle picked me up and I got the train home the next morning.

I was in the sixth form at school. That was a lot of paper round money and money earned washing cars and stuff. It was worth every penny. The biggest thing for me is always thinking what might have been had Phil lived. He was so creative and such a charismatic front man. Limehouse Lizzy are a good tribute band. The guy who sings even looks like Phil. And they play requests. If you shout out a Thin Lizzy song, they'll play it.

NOVOTEL

23 MARCH 1983, BRADFORD, UK

I WAS THERE: JAMES PIERCE

One of the best nights I ever had was as a sales rep staying at the Novotel in Bradford. In the car park at about five o'clock was a rather expensive-looking coach with blacked out windows. To my surprise, Thin Lizzy were going out to do a sound check at the St George's Hall in Bradford. I went out to the car park and got their autographs. Some of the roadies were also leaving and had left a mountain of glasses at the bar. They had been drinking Remy Martin topped up with white wine!

Another rep I knew was also staying at the Novotel and, after having an evening meal, he and I were playing pool when the band returned from the concert, around 11pm. They joined us at the pool table and we started playing doubles, so there I was partnering Scott Gorham in a game of pool. What a fantastic guy. The drink was flowing and at about 2am we decided to play pool lying down on the floor, with plastic glasses on their sides for pockets! I finally turned in about 3am.

Next morning, at Scott's invitation, I joined the band for breakfast. This was the best time I ever had on the road. I never told anyone this story, as most people would think I was making it up.

ST GEORGE'S HALL

23 MARCH 1983, BRADFORD, UK

I WAS THERE: LEE BURKE, AGE 15

Lee Burke was at St George's Hall with a bunch of mates

I was always into rock music and loved going to record fairs and just flicking through albums. I had heard a bit of Tygers of Pan Tang, when John Sykes was in them. I read a lot of music mags as well - *NME*, *Sounds* and *Kerrang!* – so I knew what was going on, and *Live and Dangerous* was shown on the television (on BBC 2, I think) so I had an interest in Lizzy. I was into art as well and did a drawing of the *Chinatown* album cover.

I went to see them with a group of mates. We were up in the wings on Scott Gorham's side. We were mad for the song 'Cold Sweat' and kept yelling it to him. When they were about to play it, he shouted to us and gave us a thumbs up! That's probably my fondest memory – oh, and buying a bottle of Newky Brown with loose change pocket money!

I still listen to Lizzy. Had I have known Phil was only going to live a few more years, I'd have appreciated that gig even more.

I WAS THERE: SARAH ADDERLEY, AGE 16

I had just turned 16. My friend Cheryl and I were in the minority at school in being female rock fans and she asked if I wanted to go and see Thin Lizzy with her. It was so cool to be going to a gig. The ticket was £4 and the coach was a couple of quid more. I had saved some money from a Saturday job I had and my mum gave me the rest of the money for a t-shirt. It was my first ever concert and we were going alone. It was the Eighties and although I did tend to be a bit of a wild child, this was so exciting!

Sarah Adderley's first ever gig was Thin Lizzy

We met the coach headed off to Bradford. When we arrived, we headed into the pub with everyone else. Full of bravado I walked up to the bar and ordered a pint of cider - oh, the good old days of it only being about 70p a pint! After that it was into St George's Hall where we were in the upper circle with a great view of the stage.

I don't recall the support act at all but then… then it happened. There was Phil, all legs and hair and smile. His bass flashed the lights around, the crowd erupted, the music flowed, and we sang, we shouted and we joined in with the banter and the chanting. As we floated back out to the coach, my t-shirt grasped in my sweaty hand, I looked at my friend and said, 'I will never forget that ever.'

It sparked my love of live music and a few months later I went to see Whitesnake on my own. I have seen so many bands since that I've lost count. I'm still going to see bands now. I love live music and feel so privileged to have seen Lizzy and Phil. I didn't know the band would break up soon after that tour and that sadly Phil's demons would take him from us. I recall that concert with such fondness, not just because Lizzy were an amazing band, but because I got to see one of the best front men in rock history.

I WAS THERE: ANTHONY HALEY, AGE 17

Anthony Haley saw Lizzy in '83

Back in the early Eighties I collected a lot of vinyl albums. I bought six Lizzy albums in one go and, of course, when I saw them coming on tour, I had to see them. I went with a school friend. Vic Vergat supported, who was rather good. He stood out because he got a shock off his microphone! Thin Lizzy were just fab and the venue is one of my favourites because the acoustics are great. It was small enough for you to feel as though you were almost up there with them.

I WAS THERE: GLENN DAY

The second time I saw them was at the same venue – Bradford - on the *Thunder and Lightning* tour. While we were queuing to get in, a guy in front of us was saying he had seen them at Leeds a few days earlier and that Phil was out of his head on drugs, which disappointed me. On seeing them it wasn't the same Phil Lynott I had seen before. He was bloated and slurring his words. His singing wasn't slurred but the voice was not quite the same. As we all now know, he passed away a few years later.

I had a friend who was working in Dublin. On his day off he went to find Phil's grave and when he got there, Phil's mother was there. He told her how big a fan I was and she gave him her phone number to give to me. She said that if I ever was in Dublin I should give her a call. I did go to Dublin for a week's holiday and, after a bit of hesitation, I rang her up and said I was going to visit Phil's grave.

She offered to come and pick me and my wife up and take us, but I couldn't let her do that so we got the bus to the cemetery and then walked to her house. We spent a good hour with her and she let us go into a room that held all Thin Lizzy's gold discs, and Phil's private photo albums and personal possessions. It was a dream come true for a Lizzy fan. We had a coffee and chatted with her and then her partner took us to the local train station. What a lovely lady. She thrived off the fans' adulation for her son and rightly so. Sadly, Philomena herself passed away in 2019. She wrote a note in the Thin Lizzy book I had with me, signing it with love to my wife and I. I still listen to Thin Lizzy every week.

ROYAL CENTRE CONCERT HALL
24 MARCH 1983, NOTTINGHAM, UK

I WAS THERE: BEN HAYES, AGE 17

In 1978 I was 13 and really started to get into music. Obsessed with Queen, I began saving up my pocket money to buy the older Queen albums, while my older brother got me into Pink Floyd. I had started playing the guitar and a band played at our school disco. There was an older lad in the band called Andy Lee and all the girls fancied him because he was playing in this band. I thought, 'I could do with a bit of that! That's what I want.' Andy lent me a copy of *Live and Dangerous* and that's what got me into Thin Lizzy. It's still one of my favourite ever albums, with an absolutely iconic cover with Phil with his bullet belt and his leather trousers and the bass between his legs.

Although I was listening to Rainbow, Judas Priest, AC/DC and Whitesnake – all those classic bands of the late Seventies and early Eighties - what I always loved about Thin Lizzy was that there was that crossover appeal, because they were a great pop band. They had quite a few chart hits, so you'd see them on *Top of the Pops* doing their singles. I had a girlfriend that really liked them for that reason. They wrote brilliant songs. They were the chart friendly act.

The concert hall in Nottingham was first opened in 1982 and Thin Lizzy were one of the first raft of bands to ever play in that venue, after Elton John. It was renowned for its acoustics. I got a bus into Nottingham and decided to get something to eat at the chip shop on Parliament Street, round the corner from the venue. I went into the chippy and Phil Lynott was in there with John Sykes. Phil was a massive guy and I remember thinking what a big bloke he was. He'd got his high-heeled platform boots on and the big afro and he was just such a presence. Loads of people in the chip shop were asking him for his autograph and it just made me smile, because he was stood there with a tray of chips and a saveloy about an hour and a half before the gig.

Phil was in the chippy half an hour before the gig with a saveloy and a tray of chips

---

I've been a huge fan of and inspired by two Lizzy guitarists. One was Gary Moore, one of the most underrated guitarists ever, and the other was John Sykes. I was so into guitar and had just started playing in a band, so I was really into 'Thunder and Lightning' and 'Cold Sweat'. I really liked that heavier stuff. I had a girlfriend at the time who loved John Sykes, and I had a massive mane of blond hair like him. I haven't got that mane of blond hair now!

I WAS THERE: KEVIN DRISCOLL

We went down for the soundcheck and sat there while the band were setting up and doing the sound checks. But Philip wasn't there. We were sitting right in the middle, six rows from the front, and we took a few photos and then these two giant legs started climbing over the seats from behind us and it was Philip. He said, 'I'm ever so sorry, we're running late and I've had to go to the local radio station and do an interview with them. I'm not going to have time to play for you now but I'll play 'Whiskey in the Jar' tonight at the end of the gig.'

Next door was the Theatre Royal, where they have plays, and somebody came from the Theatre Royal and said, 'Can you turn the noise down?' Harvey Goldsmith was there and he turned to us and said, 'What do you reckon about this being too loud? It's never too loud when Lizzy play, is it?' and I said, 'No, I don't know what he's talking about.' And the Theatre Royal bloke turned around and toddled off.

In the radio interview, Philip was asked why they never played 'Whiskey in the Jar' and he said, 'We're going to play it tonight. I've got a really good friend called Julie and we're going to do it for her.' They did the gig and they did about three encores. And I thought, 'Oh crikey, I bet he's forgot.' And they went off again after the third encore and about five minutes passed and then came back and Phil said, 'This is for my friend Julie down here. This is a song called 'Whiskey in the Jar',' and the place erupted. We went backstage after and he gave her one of his belts.

ST DAVID'S HALL

27 MARCH 1983, CARDIFF, UK

I WAS THERE: ANDREW KING

I saw them again on the farewell *Thunder and Lightning* tour in March 1983, supported by Mama's Boys. The new choice of venue was because a heavy snowfall in early 1982 had caused the roof of Sophia Gardens to collapse. (The last band to play there was Slade on 14 December 1981). The new venue was seated and the security enthusiastically officious. Their insistence on people staying in their seats resulted in a somewhat stilted show. New boy John Sykes was in for Snowy White, making his presence felt with a change in sound and attack. He wasn't to everyone's taste but it did bring a breath of fresh air to the band on their last tour.

Sadly, Thin Lizzy never played Cardiff with Phil Lynott again.

I WAS THERE: MICHAEL BOWDERY

Michael Bowdery was at Cardiff's St David's Hall

A common thread amongst my mates was Deep Purple, while Rainbow were having chart hits. And it was the beginning of the New Wave of British Heavy Metal. The first gig I went to was Saxon in 1980, on their *Strong Arm of the Law* tour. It was a lot of hard work to convince my parents to let me go to a rock gig as I was only 13 years old. One friend and his brother were massive Thin Lizzy fans and they would sit in the two big armchairs in their lounge extension and listen to Thin Lizzy through headphones on their state-of-the-art stereo. I remember they had a double seven inch single with a live version of 'Bad Reputation' on it.

For a while coach trips to the Colston Hall in Bristol or the Birmingham Odeon were the only gig options if you lived in South Wales. Sophia Gardens in Cardiff had been closed following the collapse of the roof under the weight of heavy snow three days before a Black Sabbath gig, although eventually they opened Saint David's Hall, which is where I saw Thin Lizzy.

Everybody was aware that it was the last tour so the gig was tinged with excitement but also sadness. For those of us who had just got into Lizzy, there was this realisation that this was our one and only chance to see them.

My friend Pete couldn't get a ticket so we smuggled him in. Because it was quite a new venue, they hadn't quite got wise to rock gigs. The venue operated on a series of levels and tiers and they didn't rip the stub off your ticket until you got to the auditorium level, which was where the bar was. If there were three of you with only two tickets, two of you could go in and up the escalator to the lower levels and then one of you would come back out with both tickets and take the third person in. That way, you would gradually work your way up the tiers into the bar. Once the band started and the lights had gone down, and because people moved between the bar and the auditorium, they had no way of checking the tickets once a stub had been torn off, so you could slowly work people into the auditorium. And once the lights were down, it was impossible for them to tell if there were too many people for the seats available.

Lizzy opened with 'Thunder and Lightning' and the sound was awful. This was a surprise because the venue was built as a concert auditorium. They sorted it out after the first track, but I remember Pete saying, 'God, the sound was awful. I almost walked out in protest.' We looked at him in disbelief and said, 'Pete, you didn't even pay!'

Phil Lynott was one of those musicians who formed the bedrock of rock history, who were always there and who you think always will be. Lemmy was another, as was Burke Shelley from Budgie. For me as a rock fan, the whole edifice is built on their achievements. I remember an interview in which Phil talked about Caroline and his Catholicism and how he believed in the institution of marriage and how he wouldn't commit to somebody and have children with them unless he believed he could stay with them. I was brought up in a Catholic household, and to have someone who I admired in the world of rock 'n' roll saying these things really chimed with me at my young age. His death, and the circumstances around it, had a disproportionate impact on my state of mind at the time.

ODEON

28 MARCH 1983, BIRMINGHAM, UK

I WAS THERE: COLIN MASON

By the time I saw them again in 1983 the news had broken that they were splitting up. I was now a 23-year-old married man but when I heard the news, I felt like a little kid who'd just been told his beloved pet had died! I saw them twice more that year, 21st February and 28th March. At the end of that final gig, I cried my eyes out knowing that was the last time I would ever see *my* band. In eight years, I had the privilege of seeing one of the best live bands in the world ever a total of 14 times.

I saw the John Sykes version but I'm afraid Thin Lizzy without Phil Lynott just isn't Thin Lizzy. I'm pleased that the Ricky Warwick version isn't called Thin Lizzy but Black Star Riders, who I've also seen. Don't get me wrong - it's great to hear the music played live again, and to that end I've also seen tribute bands such as Limehouse Lizzy and Dizzy Lizzy. But for me Thin Lizzy were sadly laid to rest on 4th January 1986, along with Phil.

APOLLO THEATRE

29 MARCH 1983, MANCHESTER, UK

I WAS THERE: PAUL DELANEY

Phil was a big Man United fan and at his last Lizzy gig at the Apollo on the *Thunder and Lightning* tour, he dedicated 'Suicide' to all the Man United fans, in reference to Liverpool's dominance of English football at the time. As a Man United season ticket holder, I've always remembered that quote. What a pity he wasn't around to witness United's resurgence in the Nineties and Noughties.

What a pity Phil wasn't around to witness Man United's resurgence in the Nineties

---

CORNWALL COLISEUM

31 MARCH 1983, ST AUSTELL, UK

I WAS THERE: TREVOR RAGGATT

Trevor Raggatt chatted to Phil post-gig

I saw Lizzy twice at the Cornwall Coliseum, with Snowy on the summer pre-*Renegade* tour in 1981 when 'Trouble Boys' was just about scraping into the lower end of the singles charts, and the 1983 *Thunder and Lightning* tour with John. Both were fabulous gigs. The second and final time, we were all aware that this was the final tour and that after this Thin Lizzy were to be no more. School night or not, there was no way I was missing this gig.

Gig savvy by that point, I worked my way down to the front before Mama's Boys came on. Their set left no impression on me. I'm not saying that they were bad, I just have no recollection of them at all. Ensconced slightly stage left, between Phil and Scott's usual positions, I was perfectly set for the main event.

Thunder and Lightning had been out for the best part of a month so the fact that the set relied heavily on that album wasn't a problem. The crowd knew the songs and sang and headbanged at all the right moments. But it was the old crowd pleasers which really lifted the energy levels.

I've personally never been the biggest fan of John Sykes and his recorded output with the band. His style was a touch too NWOBHM for my personal tastes, certainly in the context of a classic hard rock band like Thin Lizzy. On record there's plenty of energy and squealing pinched harmonics, but that's not really classic Lizzy for me. However, watching him live while squashed up against the barrier there were no complaints. Both Scott and John attacked their guitars with gusto, threw the obligatory shapes and… well, John's tousled, flowing locks made up for Scott's shorter haircut! The whole band seemed to be giving it 110% for the final tour, determined to go out on a high. Staring up at Phil, it was clear that a mixture of stage lights, adrenaline and pure commitment were present from the lines of sweat running down his bare arms and dripping off his elbows as he sang and played.

The audience, too, were making the most of this last chance to see the band, singing along with gusto. On the traditional set closer, 'Baby Drives Me Crazy', the whole audience was on point. After an extended echo singalong section, Phil stopped the band to berate us for being far too good at repeating back his increasingly lengthy stuttering '…b-b-b-baby….' Of course, he will have done and said similar things at every show on the tour. However, on that night and for everyone in the audience, this was the show when we all knew that he was talking directly to each one of us and the one time when he really meant it.

When the band returned to the stage for their second encore ('Still in Love with You' and 'Rosalie' had served nicely for the first encore), Phil opened with his usual question, 'Okay, what d'you want to hear?' To be honest, there weren't many favourite songs that hadn't had an airing already so the call went up, "Whiskey in the Jar'!' Phil responded with his usual rebuffs of 'Nah, we don't do that one anymore,' 'Scott's forgotten how to play it,' and 'John's never learned to play it, he doesn't know it….' But a call, now a chant, persisted. 'Whiskey! Whiskey! Whiskey!'

Phil seemed adamant in his denial…. 'Nah, nah, nah… oh, tell you what, we'll do this one instead. You'll know this one….' He nodded to John and Scott, who started up the unmistakable intro guitar line from 'Whiskey in the Jar' and the crowd completely erupted. It might have been a couple of weeks late but the next five or so minutes was a veritable St Paddy's Day party. After a closing rendition of 'Dancing in the Moonlight', the band finally left the stage, waving to the crowd, and a chapter of my personal rock history closed. Except that, about half an hour or so later….

They started up the unmistakable intro to 'Whiskey in the Jar' and the crowd erupted

---

Afterwards, I was hanging around in the empty hall waiting for my dad to pick me up (it was a 25 minute drive from home) and watching the crew breaking down the gear. Phil wandered out on stage, a little wobbly and carrying a huge half-finished vodka bottle. He spotted me standing in the middle of the empty auditorium and shouted over, asking if everything was okay.

I said, 'Sure, just waiting for my dad, and watching the crew break down. It's alright, he'll be here in about a quarter of an hour.' Phil said, 'Well come up here and we'll wait.' I climbed over the barrier and he and a roadie helped me up onto the stage.

We spent the next 15 or 20 minutes sitting on Brian's drum riser, just chatting until my dad turned up. Of course, I asked him if he was really splitting up the band and if he had plans for what he'd do next. The answer to the first was, of course, 'Yes.' And the second just got a wink, a tap of the finger on the side of the nose and, 'I've got a few ideas!' Then we sat there just shooting the breeze, with our legs dangling off the riser. At one point, he accidentally kicked my leg as he was swinging his legs and spent a couple of minutes apologising profusely in the way only happily tipsy people can do.

At one point Scott poked his head out, spotted us and quickly retreated backstage. Eventually Dad showed up at the other end of the hall and I jumped down to get my lift home. Phil and I exchanged a little wave as I went out the rear doors and he wandered back stage. What a lovely guy!

The UK tour was followed by the final Irish tour, with dates in Cork, Galway, Belfast and Dublin.

KING'S HALL

8 APRIL 1983, BELFAST, UK

I WAS THERE: ROBERT BURNS, AGE 16

It was their last show in Belfast, with Mama's Boys supporting. I still have the ticket stub and programme. When my older brother and cousin both said they were happy to hear everything from the back of the King's Hall I said, 'Yeah right, see you here at the end of the concert,' and left to work my way towards the front and join a huge line of head bangers. The reflecting bass of Phil Lynott often shone into my face. I loved it.

ROYAL DUBLIN SOCIETY

9 & 10 APRIL 1983, DUBLIN, IRELAND

I WAS THERE: SHAY CAHILL, AGE 18

My first Lizzy memory is of listening to my sister's *Live and Dangerous* LP. I remember thinking, 'Wow, that sound was amazing,' and then I remember seeing them on *Top of the Pops* with Phil catching the lights with his bass, playing 'Waiting for an Alibi'.

When I was 16, I worked in a pub in Clontarf in Dublin as a lounge boy. I came in for the evening shift and heard Phil had been there about an hour before so I just missed him! I was 18 when I saw them at the RDS in Dublin. They were playing two shows on successive nights and I had bought a Sunday night ticket. My mates had Saturday night tickets, so I just went on the Saturday night, handed my ticket to the guy and made a run for the door!

I WAS THERE: JUSTIN HEALY

When the news came that they were breaking up it was heartbreak. I was so, so disappointed. I went to the RDS. I had a ticket for the first night. The second night I didn't have a ticket but I went back and chanced my arm. In those days you could talk your way in, and I talked to a bouncer who very kindly let me into the second gig for nothing. Phil was in better form for the first gig.

At the end of one of the gigs, Brian Downey walked up to the front of the stage and threw out a drumstick. I was five foot nothing and all these huge hairy guys around me were six footers. It was like Brian threw the stick in slow motion, and I don't know how the hell I did it, but I jumped up so high and got the stick in my hand. I went down to the floor and I huddled and was jumped upon by three or four people who were trying to get the stick off me. But I held onto it for life and ran home out of the arena clutching hold of it. My friend Ian reminded me a couple of years ago that I took the drumstick to school the very next day to show it off to everybody. I'd forgotten that.

I WAS THERE: JOHNNY CAHILL

I was living in a flat in Ranelagh, Dublin, just a shortish walk from the gig at the RDS. The first night we had a decent spot in the centre, about a third of the way back, and had a mind blowing time. I remember Phil talking to us, saying that there were so many who missed that night that another gig was being organised for the following night. Phil said it was going to be memorable and that possibly we would see him cry. Myself and my flatmate Pat begged, stole and borrowed a few shekels from the girls who lived upstairs from us and then hunted down two tickets.

For the second gig we were up front in the mosh pit, slightly to the right and only three or four back. As it was all standing, I was at times almost within touching distance of the man himself. My take away memory is Phil's lovely way of bouncing the spotlight off his pick guard and into my face. It was a magical experience. I still get goosebumps today thinking about those gigs, and the fact that my head is there somewhere on the last filmed gig is priceless!

Lizzy's short final European tour included shows in Denmark and Sweden. Planned German dates were cancelled.

VEJLBY-RISSKOV HALLEN

27 APRIL 1983, AARHUS, DENMARK

I WAS THERE: JAN HVEDHAVEN

The next concert was with John Sykes on guitar. This time I went as a reporter for a small music magazine. Phil was playing a Roland custom made synth bass. They had pulled out all the synth stuff and turned it into a normal bass. After the concert we went to their hotel and I spoke to Phil about his choice of equipment. We had a few drinks. Sykes was there as well. It was one of the greatest moments of my life. Phil was such a nice person to talk to, with a great sense of humour, and we had a good time.

I WAS THERE: JØRN SØRENSEN

I lived in a small town just outside Aarhus in Denmark and discovering Thin Lizzy helped prepare me and my mates to go out into a bigger, better and more rocking world than the boring middle class one we knew. It all started with a copied cassette of *Live and Dangerous* which split 'Still in Love with You' into two parts. Even now, when I hear that song, I remember the point at which I had to turn the tape over!

I only saw Thin Lizzy once, in Aarhus, Denmark. I was 15 or 16 and Lizzy blew the roof of my head off. I also saw Phil solo in Aarhus at the smaller university concert hall the previous year. I still have all of Lizzy's studio albums in my living room and enjoy listening to the intelligent energy and magic of this band - loud!

SCANDINAVIUM

29 APRIL 1983, GOTHENBURG, SWEDEN

I WAS THERE: STEVAN TOMULEVSKI

An audience member threw a condom up onto the stage. Phil picked it up and said 'too small!'. The day after the concert, all the members of Lizzy were down at the front desk on Hotel Park Avenue except for Phil. Through the speakers at the hotel, you could hear Phil Lynott taking a phone call. Scott asked the lady at the front desk who was looking for Phil? The receptionist said, 'Phil's wife.' As she said that, Phil stepped out of the elevator with a blonde beauty.

JOHANNESHOVS ISSTADION

30 APRIL 1983, STOCKHOLM, SWEDEN

I WAS THERE: DAN WESTMAN

I grew up in the north of Sweden, in a small village with just 350 people, and in the mid-Seventies there were quite a lot of kids in my own age or a few years older. In the summertime, we played football and spent most of the time outdoors, but winters were always cold and snowy. There was no café or other places to meet. Fortunately, there was a small library, which was open a few evenings a week.

In the library, there was a sofa and some armchairs, with headphones close by, and a selection of records to choose from. You gave your choice to the librarian who handled the record player and then the kids would

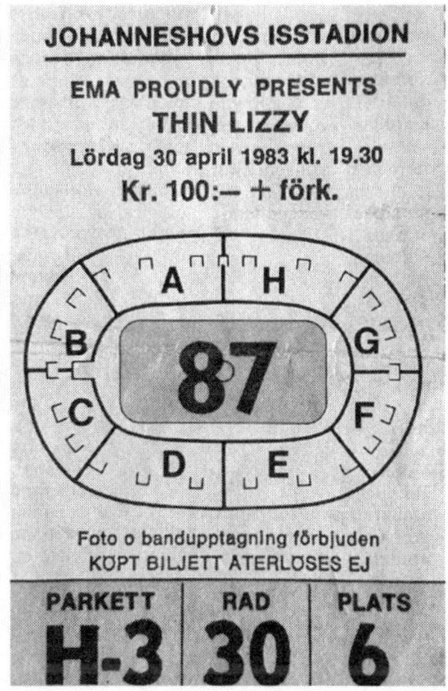

Dan Westman was at the last Stockholm show

all listen to the same record through their headphones. The librarian was a kind, elderly woman who let the older boys choose from a record catalogue and order the items they wanted. They were mostly rock albums by artists such as Led Zeppelin, Black Sabbath, Deep Purple, Queen and, of course, Thin Lizzy.

You could also take records home, and since my big brother just had bought his first stereo I started doing that. I was thrilled by all the great rock music released in that era. I was browsing through the records at the library when one album stood out. I took *Johnny the Fox* home with me and from the first listening I realised that this was an extraordinary album. I played 'Don't Believe a Word' over and over again. But I did the opposite. I believed everything Phil Lynott was telling me.

I started dreaming of seeing Lizzy live in concert. To begin with I was too young, but when the farewell tour was announced in 1983, I knew it was now or never. Most of the guys I grew up with still lived in the village and were still great fans of Thin Lizzy, so I wasn't on my own. Stockholm was a day long 600 kilometre bus ride away, so we occupied the back seats of the bus and spent the day playing Thin Lizzy songs on a portable stereo and singing along.

Johanneshovs Isstadion was a classic rock venue in Stockholm in the Seventies and Eighties. Our tickets were near the back of the stadium but as soon as we got in, I sneaked past the guards, worked my way forward and finally ended up where I wanted to be - just in front of the stage a few metres from the band.

The crowd went crazy when the band entered the stage, and everything exploded with 'Thunder and Lightning'. Positioned just in front of a wall of speakers, it was extremely loud, so loud that my ears couldn't handle it and I couldn't hear a single note of the first three songs. But I was so close that by reading Phil's lips and watching what the band played, I could work out which song it was. With the fourth song, 'Baby Please Don't Go', the sound was adjusted and was great for the rest of the concert.

The band really gave their best and we got to hear most of the classics. It was a wonderful night and every song was performed excellently. After a superb ending with 'Rosalie' the band left the stage, the lights went on and I was standing there, blown away, on top of a chair, exhausted but with a happy smile on my face. Was this for real? After 90 minutes of the best music there was, I felt like I had been run over by something.

I have been to many concerts in the 40 years since, and seen many great artists and bands, but this remains the greatest musical experience of my life. Nothing compares to that night when the boys were back in town.

Nothing compares to that night when the boys were back in town

---

FALKONECENTERET

28 APRIL 1983, COPENHAGEN, DENMARK

I WAS THERE: ROGER JÖNSSON, AGE 15

I saw Lizzy play in Copenhagen in 1983 on their farewell tour. It was my first real concert experience. I had discovered the band through the radio broadcast of the 1981 Hammersmith show on the *Renegade* tour and I became an instant fan. Together with a friend, I made the long trip from the east coast of southern Sweden to Denmark. It was quite an adventure at my young age.

We arrived early and waited outside the venue, the Falconer Theatre. Suddenly we heard the sound of glass breaking. Some Danish Hell's Angels members had arrived and they were wreaking havoc outside the venue. They stole the posters from inside the display monitors they had smashed. Me and my friend had bought similar posters, at great expense, from the peddlers of bootleg merchandise. We walked to the other side of the building in order to avoid trouble....

Roger Jönsson remembers some trouble caused by Danish Hell's Angels

When we got to the other side, a large white limousine drove up next to the stage entrance and a large man stepped out. When we saw a few autograph hunters approaching the man in front of us, and noticed the large man's big afro hair, we realised that we had actually stumbled upon our hero, Phil Lynott. He was dressed in a big fur coat. It was an unforgettable moment but it was over in a flash because Phil got inside the building as soon as he had signed the autographs for the small group of fans outside. I managed to get his autograph on a small piece of paper and we also exchanged a few words.

Our excitement before the show couldn't have been higher. When we got inside, we rushed to the stage and stood in the first row. There was a distinct smell of marijuana smoke in the room. The show began. It was very loud and the vocals were hard to hear on the first few tracks but after a while the sound got better. When they played 'The Boys are Back in Town', the pressure from behind became enormous and I could lift both legs from the floor and just hang in the air, pressed toward the security railing in front of the stage. 'Angel of Death' and 'Suicide' were two of the highlights in the setlist for me but I treasured every second of the show. It was truly mesmerising.

At one point we could hear sirens outside between two of the songs - actual sirens and not sound effects. When the concert was over and we came to the exit, we saw an ambulance outside and we were met by a long double row of policemen with helmets, shields and batons at the ready.

They were prepared for - and expecting - trouble! It was very tense and almost surreal. My friend and I escaped unharmed and arrived home safe, but the next day we read about post show riots in Copenhagen.

Thin Lizzy played a rescheduled UK show in Gloucester that was originally planned for two months before.

LEISURE CENTRE

4 MAY 1983, GLOUCESTER, UK

I WAS THERE: DANIEL HALPIN, AGE 21

Gloucester Leisure Centre is not the most famous of musical venues, but it was a day to remember. Now I had seen Lizzy throughout the years at various venues such as London, Reading, Milton Keynes, Birmingham, Bristol and Cardiff – just to name a few - but this one stands out. Myself and my friend Philip Coopey headed for the local ticket agent, Roxcene Records in Newport, South Wales, to book our tickets for the up-and-coming Lizzy tour. The usual tickets were bought – Bristol, Cardiff and Birmingham were all relatively easy to get to. And they had Gloucester on the list. Why Gloucester? We checked the transport. The Newport to Gloucester train was okay but there was nothing back home after 11pm. 'What the hell. It's Lizzy - let's book it!' And, boy, am I glad we did.

Up early (well, middayish) I headed into town to meet up with Coopey and a few others that were travelling up with us. We had a few jars in the local and then went onto the train to Gloucester with cans in hand. We arrived at Gloucester station and walked to the venue just to suss it out. It was still early and there was nobody about. We went around the back and could see the big trucks had already arrived and that the last of the kit was being loaded in through the stage door. We had a sneaky look in. The stage was up, the lights were going in and the Lizzy sign was being raised. There was no sign of the band, but the excitement was starting to rise.

More beer was needed to refuel so off we went to find a shop. Most of our gang went into a local where many fans were starting to congregate but myself and Coopey decided to grab some cans from a shop and head back down to the venue.

As we walked around the corner a black Merc pulled up to the doors and out stepped John Skyes - and then Philip Lynott! Philip looked sheepishly around and then got ushered in through the doors and they slammed shut. Damn, we missed them – we were gutted! We hung around, sat next to that door, hoping to catch Downey, Gorham or Wharton but nothing. We could hear the soundchecks were going on but it sounded like it was the crew playing, not Lizzy.

Then – bang – the doors were flung open and Phil stepped out shouting, 'I need some fresh air!'

I was dumbstruck, awestruck. Here was my idol stood in front of me and I didn't know what to say. He seemed a bit aggravated. John stepped out and said, 'C'mon Phil, let's just do it.' Phil lit up a cigarette and decided to stay outside. 'Guys, where you from?' He started pounding me with questions. 'Have you seen the tour? Have you got the album? What's your favourite track? What do you think of our new guitarist?' He went on to say how good Sykes was and how he hoped that we would really enjoy the gig.

We finished our little chit chat and he turned to go back in. Then – bang - the door would not open. He pushed and pushed again. It wouldn't budge. He banged his fist on the door shouting, 'Open the fookin' door, will ya?' We could faintly hear some laughter behind the door. Oh my god, he was going mad, now kicking the door shouting all sorts of obscenities.

We offered to help and kicked the door with him but it was solid. Not surprisingly, it was quiet on the other side of the door. There were no laughter sounds any more. Then Philip asked if we could go to the front and ask someone to open the stage door for him. We ran around and told the man in the office that Phil Lynott was locked out and could he open the door – now! We ran back around, the doors opened and Lynott stomped in raging, cursing and shouting. He was not a happy chappy at all. The guy then shut the door and that was that.

As to the gig, we got there early to get our place at the front.

'Thunder and Lightning' opened the set and then into 'Waiting for an Alibi'. Then we went through all the emotional up and downs of a Lizzy gig, into a crescendo for 'Emerald' and back down to earth with 'Still in Love with You'. Then it finally ended with 'Baby Drives Me Crazy.' We were thoroughly exhausted by the end and turfed out into the cold Gloucester air with no means of getting home back to Wales.

But who cared? I'd just had the experience of a lifetime!

SAXON AND GUESTS QUEENS HALL

28 MAY 1983, LEEDS, UK

I WAS THERE: RICHARD HUDSON

I did see Lizzy again, but they never quite matched that first time in 1978. As a fan, it was painful to see the effect that drug and alcohol abuse had on Phil. Some of the new songs no longer told those stories, and sometimes even sounded like other bands, almost as if he was searching for new direction or inspiration in his writing.

I wasn't surprised when they bowed out in 1983. I caught them in Nottingham, and whilst still head and shoulders above most of the competition, the glory days had gone and it was definitely time for a rest. But our paths did cross again a couple of months later....

A few of us travelled to the Queens Hall in Leeds for an indoor festival headlined by Saxon. The venue was a real dump, someone had turned a fire hose on and flooded part of the venue, and there were rumours of skinheads waiting for us outside. The whole place stank of piss and chips. Early in Saxon's set, a few men pushed their way through the crowd. One was Phil, and he accidentally stood on my foot! I excitedly told my mate next to me, who said I was mistaken and that he'd not seen him. Later in Saxon's set, Phil joined them on stage. I kept those shoes for years and never cleaned them!

In May 1983, Thin Lizzy toured Japan for the last time, playing five shows. After this, the Philip Lynott Band - comprising Phil, Brian Downey, John Sykes, Mark Stanway and Doish Nagle – undertook *The Three Musketeers* tour and performed 14 Swedish shows in late July and early August.

GRÖNA LUND

8 AUGUST 1983, STOCKHOLM, SWEDEN

I WAS THERE: OLLE ÖSTERGÅRD

Poster Magazine was a Swedish magazine full of beautiful music posters which you could put on your wall. It was in this magazine that I first saw Thin Lizzy. But I didn't listen to them until a friend played me the *Jailbreak* and *Bad Reputation* albums. I thought *Jailbreak*'s beautifully drawn cover was very, very cool-looking.

Olle Östergård got Phil's autograph

The first time I saw Lizzy was May 1979 on the *Black Rose* tour, and seeing Gary Moore and Scott Gorham together live is just one of my best ever gigs. I saw Lizzy again in 1980 on what was billed as the *Solo in Soho* tour, I guess because Lizzy didn't have an album to promote that year and I got a photo of Phil backstage with the promoter Thomas Johansson. Then I saw them on the *Chinatown* tour and Snowy White was good, but completely different from Gary Moore. Finally, I saw Lizzy on the *Thunder and Lightning* tour with John Sykes in 1983. They were more heavy metal by then.

Phil came back to Sweden later in 1983 when the promoter EMA Telstar asked him to play some Swedish festival dates originally booked for Dave Edmunds. He put a band together called the Three Musketeers with John Sykes, Brian Downey and a couple of others. I don't think Scott Gorham was involved. They played the Gröna Lund, an amusement park where Bob Marley had previously played to 40,000 people. Earlier that day Phil did a signing session at a record store in Stockholm and I went along. I had him autograph the backstage photograph of him and Thomas Johansson and Phil drew a moustache and an earring on Thomas!

Thin Lizzy fronted by Phil were only to play four more shows - a handful of European festival dates, which included their last ever UK show.

23RD NATIONAL JAZZ BLUES AND ROCK FESTIVAL

28 AUGUST 1983, READING, UK

I WAS THERE: STUART FAVILL

Phil was born in West Bromwich, not that far from me. Phil's mother came over to England to have him because to have an illegitimate child in Catholic Ireland was anathema, and to have a black illegitimate child must've been absolutely horrendous for her. Phil always saw himself as a black Irishman from Dublin. He had to find an identity and that's where he identified. One of my heroes was Hendrix, so when Thin Lizzy did 'Whiskey in the Jar' I thought, 'He looks a bit like Hendrix'. The first album I bought was *Vagabonds of the Western World*, because I used to go to a disco at the Leicester University Rock Society and they would play 'The Rocker' constantly.

The first time I saw them live was in 1976 at the Hammersmith Odeon, and that show was recorded for part of the *Live and Dangerous* album. My jaw hit the floor and I don't think I picked it up until a couple of weeks later. They were phenomenal.

After Hammersmith I then saw them on the last ever English show at Reading. I'd been married about 18 months and my son was five months old, so my mother looked after our son so that my wife and I could go to Reading. When Lizzy played 'Still in Love with You' on that Sunday night, you could have heard a pin drop. I think every single person across the whole of the festival site had a tear in their eye.

When they played 'Still in Love with You', every single person at the festival had a tear in their eye

I WAS THERE: STEVE WILLIAMS

I saw them a number of times, from the *Black Rose* tour to their last appearance at Reading in 1983. I used to go to two gigs on each tour - Portsmouth and Hammersmith. The highlight for me was watching Gary Moore playing with them - he was absolutely sensational – and, at the same gig at Pompey, I was picked out by Phil when he did the spotlight on the mirror scratchplate thing. The band were always great, but you could tell that Lynott and Gorham weren't at their best on the *Thunder and Lightning* tour.

I WAS THERE: GRAEME THOMSON

So on to the final gig. My main motivation to travel 500 miles was to see Sabbath but as a 15-year-old who had recently left school with only O grades in arithmetic and woodwork, I probably had no idea where Reading actually was. Maybe I should have taken geography too. Thankfully, the City Link bus driver knew how to get from Edinburgh to London Victoria and we grabbed a train from there, camped up next to the Thames (not a good idea, it's bloody cold at night next to a river of that size even in August) met up with mates and checked out the arena.

Friday wasn't the strongest day but Hanoi Rocks and Big Country were awesome. Saturday had Stevie Ray Vaughan on the bill, I'd never heard of the guy before but I certainly checked him out after, he was phenomenal. Sadly, my reason for being there wasn't as much fun. I fought for hours to get down the front of the stage for Sabbath but as soon as Gillan opened his mouth, I knew this wasn't for me. Ian's a brilliant singer but it just didn't work. He was constantly forgetting the lyrics and playing 'Smoke on the Water' contributed to one of the worst gigs I've been to.

But on Sunday Lizzy saved the day. They'd extended the stage over the front of the crowd so Phil, Scott and John could use one of the three platforms to get closer to the fans. As the scaffolding holding them up was where the audience was, it would have been easy to climb up and join the band on stage. However, sitting on the platforms were a couple of Hells Angels from the Windsor Chapter to deter any would be stage invader.

The March show had been brilliant but this one was even better. Maybe it was due to it being my first festival (how the hell did I convince my parents to let me go to a festival at the age of 15?). Maybe it was because it was the last gig. Maybe it was because Phil was in tears during 'Still in Love with You' and perhaps his passion transferred over to the crowd to make it even more special. Whatever the reason, this was a phenomenal show and in 40 years of gigs and festival attendance this is still up there with the best for me.

Phil was in tears during 'Still in Love with You'

Maybe it wasn't Thin Lizzy at their peak but it was still a great line up and, being a drummer myself, it was great to see Brian Downey in action, who is a very underrated musician in my opinion.

As for the newer versions of the band? I saw them with Sykes and Warwick singing, and yeah, they were a good tribute and both good at what they did. But as Queen without Freddie will never be Queen, Lizzy without Phil wasn't real Lizzy.

I still regularly listen to the real Lizzy on this new format they call vinyl. I'm sure it'll catch on.

I WAS THERE: SIMON BURTON

Even after all these years I remember that they were awesome, extremely tight. John Sykes had joined by then. I also remember big scary-looking biker types passing me as they walked away from the stage as the band played 'Still in Love with You'. It was a great performance.

I WAS THERE: SIMON GILBEY

Fast forward to '83 and back to Reading Rock for the heartbreaking farewell show. We sat in the sun, drank beer, listened to bands and passed out. My girlfriend started nudging me, 'Wake up, Lizzy are coming on!' It was dark and my head was pounding from sun and cider. I sat up and looked toward the stage. Red and blue police lights each side of the stage, a ton of dry ice and a curtain. It dropped and – bang! – 'Jailbreak'. 'Jesus, that's loud!' We made our way to the stage. It was jammed, but we rocked.

Let's skip Phil's death and move on and remember the good times. Eight years ago, I discovered bass and now I own five of them. I play Lizzy just about every weekend on them and *Live and Dangerous* lives in my car and on my phone, along with the other albums. My two girls know all the tracks and my eldest plays bass (better than me, but don't tell her I said that). She's 18 this year and off to Reading Rock in her dad's footsteps. My baby girl, my Sarah.

RIP Phil Lynott, thank you for the music and memories.

I WAS THERE: MICHAEL GREANEY

As each album was released and tour announced, tickets were bought. *Bad Reputation* followed and although Robertson played on several tracks, he was replaced on the tour by Gary Moore. *Live and Dangerous* followed that and then the music world heard Thin Lizzy live on vinyl and realised just how awesome they were. Each subsequent tour seemed to feature a different guitarist lining up alongside Gorham and I never saw the same line up twice. I saw Gary Moore on two separate tours, and sadly only ever saw Brian Robertson on the '78 tour. I did however see him in Wild Horses supporting Rush, with whom Lizzy became friends (Rush are mentioned in the credits on *Bad Reputation* and Lizzy on a Rush album).

Michael Greaney met Scott Gorham in 2019

The only member I hadn't seen was Eric Bell and that was rectified in 1983 when Thin Lizzy headlined Reading on the Sunday night. All the previous members including Eric were on stage for 'Still in Love with You' and they then played through a set of Lizzy classics in which each was involved individually. It was the last concert they ever played in England.

I have seen the reformed Lizzy with Sykes and Gorham. Whilst in Dublin with my wife one night to watch the band, I was on the way to the Olympia Theatre and saw Phil's mum having her picture taken under a giant mural of Phil, just off Temple Bar. We had our photo taken with Philomena but unfortunately the picture never got sent to me. She said to call in and see her before we headed home but time didn't allow it. I viewed the recently erected statue of Phil on Grafton Street and felt obliged to have a pint (or two) of Guinness in Bruxelles Irish bar. Several years later, we returned to Dublin and this time visited Phil's grave.

Of all the times I saw Lizzy, the greatest line up was Lynott, Robertson, Gorham and Downey. Although I admired Moore as a guitarist, I never felt he had the same connection with Scott Gorham as Brian Robertson did. Lizzy lost their way a little with all the personnel changes and Phil's heavy drug abuse. At a concert in Manchester, Phil was clearly under the influence and I remember him asking if any United fans were in (I'm a lifelong City fan). After the cheers, he said he had been to Old Trafford and spoken to 'the Doc'. But Tommy Docherty had been sacked several years before. I noticed that the energy levels of 1978 had dropped and that was sad. *Thunder and Lightning* was the best album after *Black Rose* and although quite heavy and less melodic it was somewhat of a return to form.

My parents were both Irish (one from the north, one from the south). I saw at first hand how ultra conservative the south of Ireland was in the Seventies. As an 18-year- old visiting Cork with long hair and denims, I looked like a fish out of water. It must have been incredibly difficult for Phil to be growing up in Dublin as a black man who wanted to take the musical direction he chose.

I WAS THERE: ROGER KNIGHT, AGE 18

I saw Lizzy headline on the Sunday. I was blown away! I had been a fan for a few years but sadly this was the only time I got to see them. They were so tight and the sound was exceptional. John Sykes was mind blowing and Phil had us in the palm of his hand. Over the years I've heard the stories of *Live and Dangerous* being heavily overdubbed but in 1983 no fillers were required - they were outstanding. The only downside was some bloke a few rows back kept shouting for 'Whiskey' at every single break. They didn't play it!

I WAS THERE: JONI FRIEND

I'd already been to my first gig at 15 - Black Sabbath with Ozzy - and I had loads of grief from my mum about going to a festival. It was amazing. I can remember the long hair and the patchouli oil and the smell of dope. Coming from a small village it was quite something to see so many people. My brother and his friends were all bikers and used to play Lizzy in the pub on the jukebox. The man who changed the records used to let me have them for 10p each.

I WAS THERE: CRAIG STEWART

My last Lizzy gig with Phil was the 1983 Reading Festival. It was an occasion of huge emotion. You could feel the - for want of a better word - sadness in the air. The performance was still there though, as were the interactions with the crowd and there were even some surprises. It was well worth the trek all the way from Edinburgh!

I WAS THERE: ALISON RUSSELL

The last time I saw them was their last gig at Reading. I always felt that on the last tour they seemed like they were rushing through the songs. The Grand Slam days were very odd. 'The Sun Goes Down' still makes me cry, because it's a song about how sad Phil was. He had many demons as well as being a big romantic and a softie. I remember hugging him and saying goodbye on the final tour. That is the way I will remember him. What a lovely man he was. He had such a huge impact on my life, and made me who I am.

There will never ever be another Phil Lynott.

MONSTERS OF ROCK 83 VFR FUSSBALLSTADION

3 SEPTEMBER 1983, KAISERSLAUTERN, GERMANY

I WAS THERE: ALEXANDER BEH ROCKSTATION KIEL, AGE 19

I saw Lizzy's last but one ever show. I already knew some of their songs but got into them through *Thunder and Lightning*. I had been listening to hard rock and heavy metal since the summer of 1979. Now I regret not discovering Lizzy earlier.

I WAS THERE: GREG NUSZ, AGE 15

I went with my junior high school friend. I'd heard of them before and it was just cool seeing them perform. They performed their more popular songs. I don't remember if they played any songs off the *Thunder and Lightning* album, but I do remember that it was a great show!

MONSTERS OF ROCK FESTIVAL

4 SEPTEMBER 1983, NUREMBERG, GERMANY

The Nuremberg show was Thin Lizzy's last ever gig, in front of a crowd of 35,000 people.

I WAS THERE: NORBERT GÖSS

I was a DJ for 20 years at the one and only rock disco in Nürnberg during the Seventies and into the late Eighties and met many musicians when they came into my discotheque after their gigs, as my best friend worked for the local concert agency and he would bring the guys in. I met Wishbone Ash, Lynyrd Skynyrd, Frank Zappa, UFO, Mink de Ville and Thin Lizzy, who I met three times. The first time he came, Phil Lynott asked me to play 'something by Thin Lizzy'.

I WAS THERE: STUART FAVILL

After Reading, they played a few gigs in Ireland and a few gigs on the Continent. And Scott says they then said 'goodbye' to each other at the airport and that was it. No more Lizzy.

After the final show, we just shook hands and said goodbye. Simple as that. **Brian Downey, as told to *Classic Rock***

Phil performed one more solo show in 1983.

SAVOY ENTERTAINMENT CENTRE

23 DECEMBER 1983, WATERFORD, IRELAND

I WAS THERE: RODDIE CLEERE

I've been following the band since I was about 12. The only music we had in Ireland at the time was the showbands. They would cover all the hits of the day. It was a uniquely Irish thing. They were good but they were just not my kind of music. Even today talking about showbands makes me gag a little bit.

How I got into Lizzy in the first place was that my brother was doing a cull of his record collection and he gave me their very first album. 'You might like these,' he said. 'They're Irish.' Now I hadn't a clue at that stage who Thin Lizzy were. To find out they were Irish was quite amazing given that my entire musical education up to that point was the showbands. But to then find out that the lead singer was not only from Dublin but he was also black? A black man in Ireland was a huge rarity, and to see a black man speaking with this really thick Dublin accent just blew our heads off.

I saw Lizzy over 20 times over the years from the incarnation with Eric Bell right up to the end. I'd go and see them every time they came home to Ireland. To say I'm obsessed with them is probably putting it too mildly. The only line up I didn't see was with Midge Ure, who was in the band for six months in America.

I first saw them in 1972. I was 12 at the time. I remember reading that they were coming to play a little ballroom in my home town of Kilkenny. I asked my mother could I go and of course she said no and that I was too young. And like any rebellious 12-year-old I decided to pretend I was going to bed, slipped out the back window and went off to see them. I cycled into the venue. It must have been an early gig at around eight o'clock because I don't recall it being very late and I certainly wouldn't have gone in the depth of the night.

I remember getting to the gig. I couldn't get in because I was too young but I found the toilet window was open and I climbed in there. Subsequently, I slipped and got my foot into the bowl of the toilet. A doorman came out and was ready to chuck me out but I pleaded with him and begged him to let me stay, and for some reason he allowed me to. My only memory is a sea of heads and a purple haze and that famous silhouette of Philip standing on stage.

'The Hero and the Madman' is my ultimate favourite Thin Lizzy song, and I think it's because that's the song they were singing when I saw them onstage and it's stayed with me all these years. I don't remember how they did the Kid Jensen part on stage but funnily enough, I did the Kid Jensen part myself at the Vibe for Philo a few years ago. And ironically of course Kid was a radio DJ and that's what I am now.

Then 'Whiskey in the Jar' came out. That was also a bit of a revelation for me. At the time we only had the one radio station, Radio Eireann, and they pretty much played all the crooners and the easy listening music. Not that there was anything wrong with that but it wasn't the kind of music I wanted to be listening to.

I was alone in the kitchen at home listening to the radio and cooking dinner or something and I remember the radio presenter coming on and saying, 'After the break we have 'Whiskey in the Jar',' which of course is a very well-known Irish folk song. I threw my eyes up to heaven and can remember thinking, 'Oh god, 'Whiskey in the bloody Jar'.' But it wasn't a case of me rushing up and switching the channel or walking away and the opening line came in and I thought, 'Bloody hell, what is this?' and then I realised it was Thin Lizzy. I already liked the band at that point but the single coming out copper fastened my love for them.

Then I started watching for anything in the music press or on the television or wherever. We had a magazine called *Spotlight* which was a sort of cross between the *NME* and *Smash Hits* and it had all the Irish stuff which was going on which would be about all the showbands, but occasionally you'd get something about Rory Gallagher or Van Morrison and of course Thin Lizzy. So any time any of that stuff came out I'd cut it out and put it in my scrap album.

It took a long time between 'Whiskey in the Jar' and 'The Boys are Back', so I thought maybe they were just a one hit wonder band and they were going to fade away and that would be the end of it. Eric had left and I went through all of those emotions: 'Oh god, my favourite band are going to break up.' Then I read somewhere that they had recruited two new members and that piqued my interest again. And suddenly there was an awful lot more about them in the press. And then 'The Boys are Back in Town' hit and the rest, as they say, is history.

However hooked I was up to that point, I was now even more hooked. Suddenly I was listening to a band that was melodic. I always knew that a band was good if my mother liked them, even though she wasn't shy when it came to her music. You wouldn't expect your mother to like the band that you were into, and particularly a hard rock band like Thin Lizzy were. But even years and years later she would say to me that she always liked the melody of the band.

People would often say to me, 'How can they be an Irish band when you've got a Scotsman and an American in the line up?' But two of the members – the mainstays - were Irish. They were always an Irish band and were never going to be otherwise with me.

I soaked up anything and everything about Thin Lizzy like a sponge. Even today, if something's on the television I get a dozen texts telling me.

I was working a full time job at Waterford Crystal as a cutter but in the late Seventies pirate radio kicked off in Ireland and I was interested in that. There were two pirate stations in Waterford at that time. I said 'any chance of a programme?' and I eventually got a programme. But then the station I was on closed down and another one, run by a bunch of English guys, called ABC Radio started up and I got an invitation to join them.

1981 was the first time I met Philip. Somebody else was doing the interview. I just tagged along and was the open-mouthed fan, gaping at this man. The other chap did most of the talking. Then in 1983, Thin Lizzy were past their peak but still a powerful force when Philip was on a solo tour of the country. It was coming up to Christmas 1983 and I got word that he was playing in my hometown. There were two radio stations in the town at that time and I heard that the other radio station was doing a live interview with him. I wanted something for posterity anyway so I said I'd go along and record an interview with him. I got in touch with the guy that owned the venue and asked him to set it up for me.

You know how they say you should never meet your heroes? It was a mixture of excitement and sheer terror on my part at the fact of meeting Philip Lynott. I was waiting in this little side room and I could hear him talking to somebody as he approached the room that we were doing the interview in. I recognised his accent straight away. He came in and I was shaking like a leaf.

The one thing that stays in my mind to this day is that when I shook hands with him, his hands were really rough like a builder's hands, I presume from playing bass. He had a vice-like grip. It wasn't threatening. It was very solid. My mother always said that when you shake hands with someone you know the character of the person from their handshake. It was one of the first things that impressed me about him.

In that moment I found him to be very personable and I think he sussed that I had only been on the radio a couple of years. My interview techniques would have been pretty woeful. I'd have a lot more confidence today. Back then it was, 'Bloody hell, it's Philip Lynott. What am I going to ask him?' I spent days and days writing down questions making sure I got all the right ones. I didn't want to delay the man.

He was wearing this brown leather jacket and he had a rimmed hat on. He sat down. I had one of those old Marantz tape recorders and I had another chap with me who looked after me to make sure everything went okay. This was all on cassette as well, so you got one chance to do the recording and you had to make sure your batteries were up, etc., which all worked out fine.

I think the first question I asked him was what brought him back to Ireland so soon after Thin Lizzy had been back in the country and he said, 'I just needed some money for Christmas.' I asked him if getting married and having kids was an influence on his life. I had read somewhere that when he did interviews, he didn't talk about his private life. He half answered me and then nicely sidestepped the question and I remember thinking back and realising I shouldn't have asked that question. To his eternal credit he didn't say, 'I'm not talking about that, how dare you?' There was none of that at all.

We spent about 20 minutes talking and at the end of the interview he said to me, 'Thank you.' I said, 'Thank you.' He said, 'Are you happy with that?' I said, 'Yeah, yeah, sure. No problem. Thanks very much.' 'I'm not too sure about that last question,' he said. 'Ask me that again and I'll give you a better answer. Do you know how to edit?'

Now I didn't know how to edit at that time but I said, 'Oh yeah, of course I can,' knowing that there were people back at the station who could help me with that if needs be. So I re-asked the question and he gave me another answer. We finished and he shook hands with me, gave me a couple of tickets for the gig that night and a couple of t-shirts.

But then the other side of him kicked in, inasmuch as we walked out of the room and were saying our goodbyes and you could hear on the stage somebody had knocked over his bass guitar. There was this kind of bang and he said, 'I've gotta go.' The mood changed and he was visibly annoyed that someone had knocked over the bass so he went storming off saying, 'What the fuck are you doing with my equipment?' And that was the last I saw of him.

But I went away a happy bunny and couldn't wait to get back to the studio and relisten to the interview again and again and again. I didn't edit out the last question at the end of it all. I left it all in because I thought the answer was perfectly fine.

Whatever my feelings were before I met him, they were again copper fastened after I met him. He was perfectly professional. If he sensed me being a rawhide newbie he didn't let on. He answered the questions as best he possibly could, and I found out years later from talking to his mum that he was always like that. He was one of these men who would go to the after show parties and he'd look particularly for the fans who were there, who he knew were out of place and shouldn't be there inasmuch as they didn't know anybody else in the room. He would make it his business to go over and talk to them and put them at ease. He'd make a beeline for them rather than the journalists or the people who were hanging off his coat tails.

1984 saw Philip launch his new band, Grand Slam, with an Irish tour in April 1984. The line up consisted of Phil, Laurence Archer, Robbie Brennan, Doishe Nagle and Mark Stanway. Brian Downey quit the band three days before the first gig.

I'd get there for 2pm (for rehearsals) but nobody else turned up until six… Phil turned up at all hours, because he'd go out every night, get drunk and not make it home to 6am.

Brian Downey, as told to *Classic Rock*

The Irish dates were followed by a series of UK shows from May 1984 onwards. The bookings for Grand Slam were at smaller venues than Lizzy were used to playing, and not always to packed houses.

TOWN HALL

11 JULY 1984, MIDDLESBROUGH, UK

I WAS THERE: PETER SMITH

This gig, unfortunately, was not well attended. Grand Slam came along after Thin Lizzy disbanded and, although still possessing some of the qualities that made Lizzy great, were in many ways also a shadow of Thin Lizzy. The band played a few Thin Lizzy songs - 'Whiskey in the Jar', 'Sarah' and 'Cold Sweat' – and Phil's great solo track, 'Yellow Pearl', which he'd written with Midge Ure and which was

Peter Smith saw Grand Slam at Middlesbrough Town Hall

adopted as the theme to *Top of the Pops* in the early Eighties, as well as 'Parisienne Walkways', which he co-wrote with Gary Moore.

Grand Slam's line up was Lynott (bass, vocals), Laurence Archer (lead guitar; ex-Stampede, Wild Horses, Lautrec), Donal 'Doish' Nagle (guitar; ex-The Bogey Boys), Robbie Brennan (drums), and Mark Stanway (keyboards; ex-Magnum). They were all excellent players and, had this band come about under different circumstances, I could really have seen them doing well. Sadly, Phil Lynott didn't look well. His face was bloated and his performance lack lustre. Whilst some of the old energy shone through at times, he seemed too unwell to give us the level of performance from his Lizzy days. As a result, the concert was a disappointing, sad affair, particularly in comparison to the power and glory days of Lizzy.

I prefer to remember Phil as the wild rover, the cowboy, the vagabond, the Rocker, 'one of the boys' that he wrote and sung about, and to think about the many magnificent Thin Lizzy performances I saw in the north east and at the Reading festival. RIP Phil. You were, and remain, my hero - a rocker, a cowboy and a legend, the like of which we will never see again.

NOSTELL PRIORY MUSIC FESTIVAL

27 AUGUST 1984, WAKEFIELD, UK

I WAS THERE: ROB SHARMAN

Phil Lynott was on the bill. Neal and I had gone to see Marillion, so anyone else was a bonus. We parked up and walked towards the event. Walking through the grounds the first thing we saw was a white canvas tent with an advert for every drug you wanted on a blackboard. We carried on walking towards the event. The next sight we saw was a totally naked woman dancing with only a belt on with a knife fitted to it. I don't recall Phil's set!

MR KIESA'S

16 OCTOBER 1984, LEICESTER, UK

I WAS THERE: STUART FAVILL

In 1983, Phil had put Grand Slam together and they were due to play a tiny little club in Leicester. My wife was pregnant and she said, 'We can go, but on one condition. I've got to wear a dress so you've got to wear a suit.' And so there we were, on the front row in this tiny little club, with her in a dress and me in the three-piece suit I got married in, watching one of my all-time heroes. Phil would burst into peals of laughter every time he looked at us.

We hung around afterwards and got invited backstage. And he said, 'Man, I thought you were a lawyer. I can't remember the last time somebody came to see me in a suit.' We just laughed so much. We probably spent an hour talking to him about our kids and his kids. We had a copy of his limited edition poetry book which he signed for us that night. Phil was a rock star, but he was also a gentleman. If he'd run away with my wife that night, I probably would've forgiven him. What a wonderful human being he was. He was a bit overweight but he was very cognitive. He wasn't slurred in his speech or anything like that.

And that was the last time we saw him, because just over a year later he'd gone. We couldn't believe it when we heard the news. We were just sat on the sofa, crying like babies. We found out years later that he would disappear off after shows and shoot up in his feet. And he kept that away from everybody.

A year later, we went to see Magnum. Mark Stanway had gone back to Magnum from Grand Slam and he saw my wife and went up to her and said, 'Hello, I remember you. What did you have? A little boy or a little girl?'

Phil burst into peals of laughter when he saw us

UNIVERSITY OF HULL

24 OCTOBER 1984, KINGSTON-UPON-HULL, UK

I WAS THERE: STUART ASHLEY

My introduction to Lizzy was an epiphany. It was very tribal in '77 and '78. You had the Northern Soul crowd, the Mods, the punks and the grebos, so all types of music were played at our local youth club disco. I was mainly into ABBA and pop. But I was stood near the speakers at the disco when the *Live and Dangerous* version of 'Rosalie' came on. I thought, 'What is this?' Some mates were into rock so I asked them. Within a few weeks I'd saved money from my paper round and bought *Live and Dangerous*. I've been into Lizzy ever since. I got to high five Phil when he played Hull Uni with Grand Slam.

AYR PAVILION

26 OCTOBER 1984, AYR, UK

I WAS THERE: STUART CUNNINGHAME

I had the pleasure of meeting Phil when he was with Grand Slam. We were in the venue before the band took to the stage and he was at the bar on his own, drinking a pint of Guinness. We chatted away for five or ten minutes and he was as nice as you'd expect him to be. I said, 'Any chance of Thin Lizzy reforming?' and he said, 'No, I don't think so.'

He seemed fine when I met him. He seemed to be getting himself back in order. He was rake thin. He looked very bloated on videos of the last Lizzy tour, but I think he'd tried to 'give it up', as the song goes. My memory is that he was looking quite healthy.

What pissed him off that night was that the crowd were all shouting for Lizzy songs and they didn't do any at all. He said, 'No, no, I know what you want to hear but this is my new band with new members and we're playing new songs.' He got quite annoyed at one point because somebody was shouting out for 'Cowboy Song' and 'Jailbreak'. I wasn't overly impressed by the Grand Slam thing. I thought the magic of Lizzy had gone.

CLOUDS NIGHTCLUB

1 OCTOBER 1984, PRESTON, UK

I WAS THERE: STEVE HARRISON, AGE 18

Growing up in Liverpool, I moved to Preston in September 1984, studying at Lancashire Polytechnic. Being a massive Lizzy fan, I noticed a Grand Slam poster at the front of Clouds Nightclub, which had rock nights every Thursday. Briefly mentioning this in passing conversation, my mate said he worked for Clouds as an in-house roadie. He said, 'Why don't you come down late afternoon on Thursday? I'll let you in round the back and you may get to see some of the band.' I wasn't sure whether this was too good to be true and what the chances would be of this actually happening. But I went down to the venue at about 3.30pm with a couple of albums, a couple of singles and my ticket for the night.

Steve Harrison got Phil's autograph on his Grand Slam ticket

It was a gloomy day and the back entrance of Clouds was deserted. I was so disappointed, believing I would just have to return home and wait for the gig that evening. However, I then noticed flight cases and boxes marked 'Thin Lizzy' which felt so exciting. It reminded me of the beginning of the *Live and Dangerous* video and I began thinking about where these boxes had previously been over the years. I felt like I was seeing a piece of Lizzy's history.

The back door was open! Apprehensively I entered, but still there was silence and no one was around. I realised I was at the side of the stage, which had been completely set up and obviously finished sometime earlier. I wasn't sure whether to stay, and risk a member of staff walking in and throwing me out, or leave on the basis that maybe the band had already completed the sound check and gone. I decided to risk it and stay. It was quite surreal sitting in a nightclub in the middle of the day in almost total darkness.

Within minutes, some doors opened, some house lights were switched on and people started entering the room. I was still waiting to be asked to leave, but nobody said anything. The crew started turning on the mixing desk and stage lights and one or two of the band climbed on stage. Then Phil came in, bounced down the steps, afro bouncing backwards. It's a moment I will never forget. Still no one said anything about me being there. After a few minutes tuning up, they started rehearsing 'Yellow Pearl'.

For some reason I decided to move from one side of the room to the other to get a better view. This would be the test of my invisibility! Whilst playing, I slowly walked behind the mixing desk and to one of the nightclub-style seating booths. I had a great view of Laurence Archer, who was only about 20 feet in front of me. My stealth move had worked once again, as it had not caused anyone to ask who I was and what I was doing there? This was becoming more than I could have expected. I was watching Phil and Grand Slam gig - on my own!

I thought that sound checks might only last two or three songs but I watched as Laurence positioned himself and a chalk 'X' was marked on the floor, to hold the long note in 'Parisienne Walkways', and the songs kept coming.

Then, during one of the songs, there was some feedback and buzzing coming through the PA speakers. Phil was trying to arrange the echo effect with the sound engineer but during the next song, the onstage buzzing got worse. Phil was getting frustrated and announced, 'There's two things on this stage going fuckin' mental, sort it out!'

He jumped off stage, came and sat in the opposite booth across from me. A tray of Holsten Pils arrived. Phil took one, sat back and took a swig. I decided this was my one chance, even though he looked a bit annoyed. I walked over and said, 'Not sure if this is a good time but could you sign these for me?' He smiled, took a bottle off the tray and put it in front of me. Once Phil and I started talking, slowly the rest of the band came over, took a bottle and I think the tension was lifted.

As I continued chatting to Phil whilst he was signing my records, he realised I was a genuine fan, particularly when I talked about all the Lizzy records I had and those I hadn't managed to buy. I mentioned the single 'Philomena' (about Phil's mum) that I didn't have and he quipped, 'I think only me mother bought that one.'

I specifically wanted to ask him about a song I hadn't heard before, that was on the recording of the last UK gig at the 1983 Reading Festival, called 'A Night in the Life of a Blues Singer'. I didn't know that he had continued to play this song a few further times with John Sykes, Brian Downey and Mark Stanway as the Three Musketeers after Lizzy had split up. Phil seemed pleasantly surprised that I'd picked upon this track, as it had not been played during the *Thunder and Lightning* main tour.

He said, 'I kept playing the bass intro when we were warming up all the time and eventually the guys asked what it was.' Phil explained to me that he had recorded the track in 1979 with Gary Moore and there were strings on it. He slightly drifted as he thought back and explained the history of the track. I said that I loved the fact that there were amazing guitar solos and was so impressed with the track.

We chatted a little more and he asked if I was coming to the gig that night. I promptly produced my ticket, which Phil signed, which made me feel a little better for sneaking in that afternoon. Overall, we chatted for about 15 to 20 minutes before the sound check recommenced.

It was my own personal Grand Slam performance. I began to relax as the songs kept coming. I seem to remember them playing 'Military Man' twice, which eventually featured on the 'Out in the Fields' single and Gary Moore's *Run for Cover* album. I was also surprised and delighted to hear 'Sarah', which sounded chunkier live. My final recollection from that afternoon was 'Whiter Shade of Rolling Stone', which took me a few minutes to grasp.

Overall, I was in the venue for about two hours and got to speak to Phil on a one-to-one basis which obviously meant so much to me, particularly after Phil's passing. I will never forget that day. They say 'never meet your heroes' but I'm glad I did. I've heard many stories about how important the fans were to Phil and even after Lizzy had split, on a dull Thursday afternoon in Preston, he still had plenty of time for one of them.

Returning for the gig in the evening I had to explain to the doorman that he couldn't take my ticket, or rip it in half, because Phil had signed it! Strangely, I can't remember much about the gig, except it was heaving and the crowd were very close to the stage. Phil asked them to move back due to the pyrotechnics.

Eventually Grand Slam ran out of money and folded without getting a record deal. There are other theories why Grand Slam didn't happen, but Phil seemed to get his own deal straightaway. However, how surprised was I when on the B-side of the 12 inch of Phil's first single, 'Nineteen', was the original version of 'A Night in the Life of a Blues Singer', recorded with Gary Moore in Thin Lizzy. I like to think….

I WAS THERE: ROGER DYSON

I've been a massive Thin Lizzy fan since the late Seventies and was lucky enough to see them on a number of occasions at the Guild Hall in Preston on the *Black Rose*, *Chinatown* and *Renegade* tours. On two of the three gigs I was lucky enough to get back stage where I met all of the various members, including Gary Moore, Snowy White, Darren Wharton and – of course - Phil, Scott and Brian.

Roger Dyson saw Lizzy and Grand Slam

My last meeting with Phil was after Thin Lizzy had called it a day and Phil went on to form Grand Slam with Laurence Archer. I was heartbroken when Lizzy split but was very keen to see Phil's new venture and went along to see Grand Slam at Clouds Night Club in Preston in 1984. I remember being so excited about seeing Phil live on stage again. The gig was great and the club was packed. After the show finished the 500 to 750 people in the audience were filing out of the place, but I decided that I wanted to try and meet Phil again so I hung around.

The security guys were trying to usher me out but I said to one of them, 'Please, can I go back stage as I want to meet Phil.' After a lot of badgering on from me the security guys said, 'Go on then, but be quick.' I didn't need telling twice. I managed to get back stage, knocked on the dressing room door and got a 'yeah' reply. I knew it was Phil.

I went in and there he was, sat on a chair in all his stage gear, sweating like mad as he always used to on stage. I asked him if he would sign my Grand Slam postcard that had been handed out at the gig as promo stuff. We exchanged a few more words and, after getting my postcard signed by the rest of the band, I went back to Phil who was still sat there on this chair and said, 'Phil, can I ask you a big favour?'

He said, 'What's that, then?' He had two gloves on - one leather and one fingerless glove made of silk. I said, 'Phil, please could I have one of your gloves?' He said, 'Sure, which one would you like?' I said, 'Could I have the black leather one please?' He replied, 'No, but you can have this one,' and gave me his silk black and pink fingerless glove. I still have it today, kept in a plastic wallet to protect it, as I do my autographed Lizzy concert programmes.

Some years after Phil's passing, I got very friendly with Philomena, Phil's mother, and felt very honoured to be able to play in front of her on several occasions with my own Thin Lizzy tribute band, which had been going for 21 years.

ROCK HOUSE

6 DECEMBER 1984, DERBY, UK

I WAS THERE: KEVIN DRISCOLL

I saw Phil a few times again with Grand Slam. I went to Rock City in Nottingham but I didn't take Julie with me. The show had finished and I just stood there on the dance floor as it was emptying out and Lizzy's manager, John Salter, who I knew shouted out to me, 'Hello, Kev, nice to see you. Would you like to see Philip?' and he took me down into the changing room and three or four minutes later Philip came in. He saw me, looked around and said, 'Where is she then?' I said, 'I didn't bring her because, due to her age, I don't think I'll be able to get her in.' And he said, 'No, wherever I'm playing she can come in. If she can't come in, I won't play.'

I said, 'Okay then, I'm very sorry about that. Where are you playing locally around here then?' Phil said, 'In two weeks' time we're over at the Derby Rock House.' I phoned the venue up on the day of the gig, told them I was coming and bringing my daughter and they said, 'No, you can't bring her in here. She's too young, she's not old enough to get in.' I said, 'I'm coming over,' and he said, 'If you're bringing your daughter, it's a waste of time.' I said, 'Okay then mate, I'll leave it at that.'

We went over to the gig. I got to reception and this guy says, 'Did you phone up today?' I said, 'Yes, we've come to see Philip,' and he said, 'No, no, you can't come in here. She's too young.' As he was saying that, John Salter walked past and said, 'Hey up Kev, how are you going on?' and I said, 'We've got a bit of a problem. This guy is not going to let her in.' John Salter said to the guy on reception, 'I'm sorry to inform you that if she can't get in, you haven't got a band on.' I said to the guy, 'I'm sorry mate. I'm not trying to cause trouble. I'm just telling you what the situation is.' And he let us in.

Phil saw us from the stage and waved. We waited about after and he came and started speaking to us. Julie had bought him a Christmas present. It was a bottle of brandy all wrapped up in paper and tinsel. And he said, 'Julie, you've made me blush now.' He said, 'I can guess what this is. Can I open it now?' and she said, 'Oh, go on then.' He opened it and took a few swigs and then he said, 'Wait there.' He went off and came back a few minutes later with a book of all his songs and poems. He was the perfect gentleman.

We went over to Dublin on the 10th anniversary of the *Vibe for Philo*. I met Philomena, who seemed a bit overwhelmed by it all. Julie and her mates were there with me, and Julie said, 'We have been talking to Philomena and she's invited us up to her house tomorrow.' The next day we went to Philomena's house and chatted with her and I took loads of photos, including in Philip's room, which she said we could just go into and browse around.

I said to Philomena, 'Philip had great charisma and was a great guy and I can see where he got it all from now,' and Philomena turned to Julie and said, 'You'll have to go on your own. I'm keeping your dad.' And she said to Julie, 'I can see why Philip took a shine to you. You are the spitting image of the girl he used to go out with at school.'

Julie passed away just after her 48th birthday.

I WAS THERE: MARK STANWAY, MAGNUM

I really miss Phil, rest his soul, and am so proud to have been such close friends with him and indeed to have worked with him performing the likes of 'Parisienne Walkways', 'Whiskey in the Jar' and 'The Boys are Back in Town' etc. along with the many Grand Slam songs I co-wrote with him. Phil Lynott: a true talent, a real gentleman, a genuinely funny man and the epitome of a rock star.

1985 saw Phil play fewer gigs during the year than at any point in his career.

CUBA, DISCOTECA MARBELLA
6 AUGUST 1985, MARBELLA, SPAIN

I WAS THERE: NICK HARNEY

The summer of 1985 was pretty amazing. I was 20 years of age and was given the opportunity to stay in a luxury beachfront apartment in Marbella, Spain with my best buddy, Simon. By then, the new wave era was in full swing and, although I had adopted a John Taylor-style mullet, my heavy rock roots were still as strong as ever.

Nick Harney with the main man

Our days were spent sunbathing on the beach until around 4pm, returning to the apartment for a nap until 9pm, getting showered and ready for the pubs and clubs and out by 10pm, and then returning to the apartment at 4am. Get up at 10am and rinse and repeat! Girls in those days were also plentiful and I met a like-minded rock chick from Milngavie, Glasgow called Tracy who was affectionately nicknamed T-Babes by Simon.

The three of us were walking along the promenade when Simon pointed out a flyer. 'Don't you follow this lot?' he questioned. The flyer was advertising Phil Lynott solo playing at a well-known club called Cuba, where T-Babes just happened to be working as a promoter. I was then singularly focused on obtaining tickets for the gig and promptly sent T-Babes off to secure them. Simon was more of a Durannie and not interested in the gig, so on August 6th 1985 I donned my leather pants and machine gun belt and set off with T-Babes to see the Rock God himself at work.

Phil was as talented as ever but the musicians supporting him were embarrassing to say the least, certainly in comparison to Brian, Scott, Darren and the previous Lizzy guitarists through the years – Robbo, Gary, Snowy and John. Phil was clearly frustrated with his band mates but despite that, his voice, his talent on the bass and his presence were unmistakable Phil, always at his best. I didn't realise as I was stood a few feet away from him that this would be the last time I would ever be able to hear or see him live in action.

Through the Eighties and Nineties, I continued to build my Thin Lizzy vinyl collection and still have some rarities. I became friends with a music promoter and agent called Will Robinson as a result of us both having premature babies in neonatal care. Will was to invite us to a small charity event at his house near Congleton in Cheshire. We arrived, grabbed a drink and casually glanced around at the other guests. I nearly dropped my drink when I saw that one of them was Darren Wharton! I raced over to him but my brain froze and rather than me ask all the questions that I subsequently remembered, we just made small talk.

I consider myself incredibly lucky to have enjoyed such memorable times. I often think of Scott when I pass through his home town of Glendale in California (my son is at university in California) and am lucky to be connected to Darren on social media. Scott has recently announced his retirement from Black Star Riders to 'focus on Thin Lizzy'. Although Darren is currently busy with Dare and Brian Downey occupied with his band, Alive and Dangerous, maybe I'll get a chance to see the legendary rock trio in action again?

ROYAL DUBLIN SHOWGROUND

18 AUGUST 1985, DUBLIN, IRELAND

I WAS THERE: ALAN GRAHAM

We were at a ZZ Top concert in Dublin. They had just headlined Donington. We were standing in the audience and Phil was standing beside me so I was talking to him. After the concert we went outside and got photos and he signed a bit of paper for me, 'To Alan & Rosie, from Phil.' We stood talking to him and then went on our way.

Alan Graham got Phil's autograph

APOLLO THEATRE

23 SEPTEMBER 1985, MANCHESTER, UK

I WAS THERE: NIGEL EUBANK

I was lucky enough to see Phil Lynott on one other occasion. Gary Moore had played a gig at Manchester Apollo, which almost became a second home to me, backed up by a group of well-established musicians. The theatre was only half full and had not sold well and John Sloman was not the vocalist to match the music. But this was my favourite Gary Moore era - *Corridors of Power*, *Victims of Fury*. While I enjoyed it, I would have liked to see more of Gary on vocals.

Gary returned to the Apollo the year after, taking the lead vocals himself. At the time he had released 'Out in the Fields' with Phil Lynott, which is still a stomping track. For the latter half of the gig, Moore said, 'This next song I can't do on my own,' and Phil Lynott walked on. It still lifts the hairs on my arms and the back of my neck to think about it. The place went totally bonkers and they couldn't start the song for the noise, but 'Out in the Field' was amazing, with the place barely intact after that. Phil knew how to handle us - when he asked for quiet, he got it. The first three bars of 'Parisienne Walkways' echoed around the Apollo, and I suspect very few people were ever treated to the original singer and bass player on stage playing this rock classic together. It was magical.

Soon after Phil passed away. It was possibly the last time he played on stage - my mate saw Moore at another venue on the same tour and Phil wasn't there. He was sick, of course, and when he died it was the first time I had experienced one of my heroes leaving us.

I WAS THERE: KEV HUMPHREY

I'd seen Gary Moore before, but a chance to see him in '85 after his collaboration with Lynott was too good to miss. Their single releases, 'Out in the Fields' and 'Military Man', were wicked. '85 had Moore still shredding and being a speed merchant, so the gig was everything I expected. Material from his solo albums *Corridors of Power*, *Run for Cover* and *Victims of the Future* were hammered out. Everyone expected 'Parisienne Walkways' as an encore, but I never even thought about Phil being there to help out with that, and with 'Out in the Fields'. I can still see him walking on stage from the left, in a floor-length leather trench coat, bass strung up high and a pearly grin. What a finish to an already bostin' gig.

Kev Humphrey caught one of Phil's last live appearances

I consider myself so fortunate to have seen Phil Lynott live just months before his untimely passing. I've dined out on this tale a number of times, and recalling it still makes me grin!

HAMMERSMITH ODEON

27 & 28 SEPTEMBER 1985, LONDON, UK

I WAS THERE: PHIL ROSS

September 1985 and 'Oi Phil Mate' had been to the Hammersmith Odeon box office again, this time coming away with a pair of tickets (in the middle of the tenth row from the front - saved for me as usual!) to see Gary Moore in concert.

The first song of the encore was 'Back on the Streets', and at the close of that number, one Phil Lynott stumbled onto the stage. To say he was a little the worse for wear would be understating it. However, a miraculous transformation was about to occur. Already the crowd were yelling so Gary Moore simply said that he had a very special guest to join him on stage that night, and without further ado they launched into 'Out in the Fields'. The sudden transformation in Phil as the performer took over was incredible. The wandering eyes and the stagger had been replaced by the sharp-eyed front man thundering out the bass notes. The lyrics were delivered with clarity and conviction, and not with the sozzled giggle he had made upon his entrance. Phil the electrifying performer was back, bestriding the stage like a colossus, and once more, albeit briefly, I got to relieve the magic of those Thin Lizzy concerts I had seen. The closing number for the night was 'Parisienne Walkways', and the closing notes were greeted by a tumultuous roar from the crowd.

I saw three different nights in the life of one of the truly great rock performers. Sadly, he was also a troubled individual with many personal demons, but for all his faults, of which he was only too aware, there was something energising, enigmatic and life affirming about the man.

Over 40 years later, and with many hundreds of concerts and thousands of CD purchases under my belt, I still count myself very blessed that my oh so very special first live concert was on the promotional tour for *Live and Dangerous*, and that I got to see one of the truly great bands and performers at their peak.

If someone were to play me Phil Lynott's voice asking, 'Are you still out there?', I would respond loudly and proudly with my fist in the air – 'yes!' - because I am still out there, itching to get a couple of tickets in the middle, ten rows from the front.

I WAS THERE: PETER PHILIP SNEESBY

I only got to see Phil Lynott once, with Gary Moore during his *Run for Cover* tour, when Phil came out for the encore as Gary's special guest and played 'Out in the Fields' and 'Parisienne Walkways'. It was amazing.

PINK ELEPHANT

NOVEMBER 1985, DUBLIN, IRELAND

I WAS THERE: DAVID SWEENEY

I subsequently saw Lizzy at parties and stuff for their tours in London and we would always be invited along. Phil was extremely nice and supportive the last time I met him. I'd gone back to college and I met Phil in this nightclub. We had a chat. It was just great to be with him. He was a bit down in the mouth. He told me his marriage had broken up but I had no idea how bad his health was or that he was drinking a lot. He just seemed the same Phil. This was maybe six weeks before he died. I'd got qualified and stuff and he was really congratulatory. When I said the same thing to Bob Geldof, he said to me, 'That sounds fucking boring!'

PHIL'S HOUSE

DECEMBER 1985, KEW, LONDON

I WAS THERE: ROBIN GEORGE

I used to go to a club in Wolverhampton called the Lafayette which was a great rock club. I ended up playing a residency there every Friday night, which was brilliant. Sometimes we'd open for bands but mostly we'd headline, and one night a band called Thin Lizzy happened to be playing. And I watched them and thought, 'Wow, I like this band.' I was having a drink at the bar after the gig and Phil was standing next to me and he just started chatting to me. We had a really good conversation and I thought, 'He's a nice fellah.'

Many moons later, they were auditioning for a guitar player when Gary left halfway through a tour. I got the call the night before to come down for the audition. I wasn't that familiar with their stuff so I managed to get hold of a copy of *Live and Dangerous* and spent all night learning most of it and had literally no sleep. I raced down to Shepperton Studios where the auditions were and I'd learnt all the wrong bloody tracks! Snowy White got the gig in the end. Phil later told me, when we finally met properly, that he wanted me for the gig but was overruled – 'politics' - which I was pleased to know. Mark Stanway, the keyboard player from

Magnum who played keyboards with Phil in Grand Slam, invited Phil to a session that I was doing for my *Dangerous Music* album. I was working on a track called 'Showdown' and Phil said, 'I've got my bass in the car - do you want me to go and get it? I'll play bass on this. I really like it.' So I said, 'Brilliant - yes please!' and he sat there and played on the tape and it was so relaxed and casual and fabulous.

Then I read an interview with him in *Kerrang!* in which he mentioned my single 'Go Down Fighting' and how much he liked what I was doing and my album. Then I got a call out of the blue asking me if I'd play on Phil's 'Nineteen' single, so of course I said yes. I went to the session and we had a few rehearsals, most of which were just set up for the Musicians Union, who used to come and check loads of bands in those days. We all hung around the studio for a few hours waiting for them and Phil and I were just jamming, playing guitars together, and then we did the single.

He invited me to his house to start writing with him and to travel with him and Brian Downey to Newcastle to do 'Nineteen' on *Razzamatazz* and *The Tube*. We got on amazingly well. Flying back afterwards, Phil said, 'I've come to a decision. I want you guys to reform Lizzy with me.' When we were filming the 'Nineteen' video he kept complaining about a back ache. 'Oh, my back's killing me today.' I didn't know that he was seriously ill.

I went to Phil's house again and we were just sitting around, mostly in his bedroom, cross-legged on the floor writing. It was going really well. He had a studio in his garden and the same tape machine as me. We did some demos. The songs were really good, really vibey. He asked his driver to take me to Euston because I was going back to Wolverhampton for the Christmas period and he said, 'I'll come with you' and we had a chat on the way. He was playing the songs on a cassette in this old Volvo estate, and when I was getting out of the car, I said, 'Can I have the tape to listen to and work on over Christmas?' and he said, 'Tell you what, give me the tape and I'll give it you back when we get together in the New Year.' Of course, unfortunately that was not destined to happen.

PHIL LYNOTT DIES

4 JANUARY 1986, SALISBURY, UK

Phil collapsed on Christmas Day following a heroin overdose. He was found by Philomena, his mother, who called his estranged wife, Caroline, who took him to a drug clinic. It was decided to refer him to Salisbury Infirmary. Diagnosed with septicaemia and kidney and liver damage, his condition worsened and he died a few days later from heart failure and pneumonia. He was 36 years old.

I HEARD THE NEWS: DAVID SWEENEY

I remember the date well. It was really shocking. I'd heard a few days beforehand that Phil had taken badly ill in London. He had this big house in Kew. I'd visited there a few times. He was locked away and I think his mother called and was shocked by the state of him. He got really bad and then they called Caroline, his wife, and I believe she drove him to Salisbury. By coincidence the same doctor that attended Phil had attended my uncle when he died at Salisbury hospital the year before. I later went to see this doctor, who was a friend of my family, and talked to him about my uncle. And then I said, 'What about Phil Lynott? You looked after him too.' He said that when Phil got to the hospital, there was nothing they could do for him.

I HEARD THE NEWS: ROBIN GEORGE

I got the terrible news when a radio DJ rang me live on air and said, 'Can you comment on Phil's death?' I put the phone down with a few choice words. I was in shock.

I WAS THERE: JUSTIN HEALY

I really did think they were going to come back. Brian Downey turned down gigs with Paul McCartney and AC/DC because he was holding out for Thin Lizzy to get back together. I heard it on the news that Phil had been admitted to hospital the day before. I was thinking 'he'll pull through' and then I didn't hear very much. I was listening out and I was asking friends what they knew but nobody heard anything. I think I heard reports saying that he was doing good. The day that he died was just a complete fucking shock. I'd lost my mother five years before that. My dad actually got up to switch the channel off when the news came on and I grabbed his arm and said, 'Listen, I'm watching that.' Fuck off, basically. I was that serious about it. My family knew that I was such a huge fan. I was gutted. I was shocked. It was horrible.

I HEARD THE NEWS: RICHARD HUDSON

Heading home in a taxi after a party sometime between Christmas 1985 and New Year it came over the radio that Phil had been taken to hospital. He sounded in a bad way, and I wasn't surprised when he passed away a few days later. Of course, I was sad, but I was also angry. How could it have come to this?

I HEARD THE NEWS: MARK SMIGGY SMITH

I really don't remember a lot about the January day he died. I blocked it out. All I know is that I couldn't bring myself to listen to any of the music for something like ten years. When anything came on the radio, I had to switch it off. It was all too emotional, a weird feeling. My heart was broken for a very long time. Time has a way of healing, but it still leaves the scars.

When my sister's husband passed away, I escorted her and his ashes to Belfast so that he could rest in peace at his birthplace. After the solemnity of the occasion, we drove through the Mountains of Mourne and down to Dublin. I'd read that Philomena was welcoming to fans and I had come across an email address so got in touch and was given a contact number for when we got there. In the two or three days we were in Dublin, we spent our pilgrimage visiting Philip's grave at Howth and his statue, as well as having a cheeky Guinness or five in the Bruxelles bar and spending an evening in Temple Bar. On the morning of our last day in Dublin, I called the number I had been given and spoke to Philomena. She was poorly and her doctor had told her to rest so, sadly, I would not be able to visit her home and see her memories of Philip. But it felt such an honour just to be able to talk to her.

Ever since that autumn night in '76, the affinity initially created by Phil, Brian, Scott and Brian has grown into an unshakeable bond. Maybe I have become a music snob, but I find nothing exciting about the chart music I sometimes find myself listening to in the car of the hotel I now work for, as I transport staff to and from work. The motivation I once felt back in the day slips away by degrees. But I listen to even more of Thin Lizzy and their ilk, and am grateful that I lived through a golden age of rock music. And I'm most grateful that I'm still led by Phil Lynott and Thin Lizzy.

I WASN'T THERE: JOHN SMALLSHAW

My Thin Lizzy story began at a record store called Peaches, in Milwaukee, Wisconsin. It was part of a national chain. It was a supermarket for records. We always spent time in the bargain bins looking for something special and my friend found *Fighting* as what was then called a cut-out (a hole was punched in the jacket so it could be discounted.).

We were totally blown away, those twin guitars and some absolutely great songs. This was followed by *Jailbreak* and I got into the nasty habit of putting 'The Boys are Back in Town' on heavy rotation in the jukeboxes at our favourite bars. I also loved *Chinatown*,

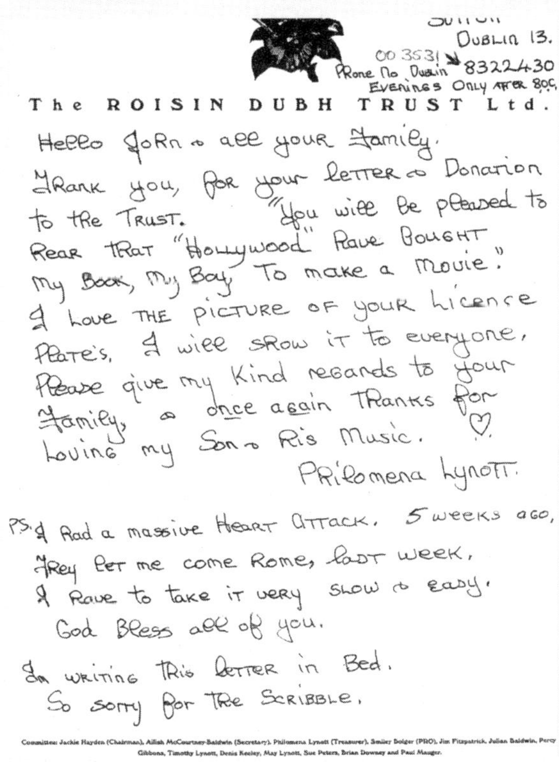

Dublin 13.
00 3531
Phone No Dublin 8322430
Evenings Only after 8 o'c.

The ROISIN DUBH TRUST Ltd.

Hello John & all your Family.
Thank you, for your letter & Donation to the Trust. You will be pleased to hear that "Hollywood" have bought my Book, "My Boy, To make a Movie."
I love the picture of your licence plate's, I will show it to everyone, Please give my kind regards to your Family, & once again Thanks for loving my Son & his Music.
Philomena Lynott.

P.S. I had a massive Heart Attack, 5 weeks ago, they let me come home, last week, I have to take it very slow & easy.
God Bless all of you.
I'm writing this letter in Bed.
So sorry for the Scribble.

Committee: Jackie Hayden (Chairman), Ailish McCourtney-Baldwin (Secretary), Philomena Lynott (Treasurer), Smiley Bolger (PRO), Jim Fitzpatrick, Julian Baldwin, Percy Gibbons, Timothy Lynott, Denis Keeley, May Lynott, Sue Peters, Brian Downey and Paul Mauger.

John Smallshaw never saw Lizzy with Phil but remains a devoted fan even though it didn't get the best reviews. I was living out in West Texas at the time and had some very long drives between sales calls. Every time I started getting tired, I would play 'We Will Be Strong' and snap out of it!

But I really fell in love with Lizzy when I was posted to the UK from 1986 to 1988. They became 'my band' and I bought every release that I could. My favourite latter day release was *Thunder and Lightning* with the incredible guitar work of John Sykes. I spent a great deal of time looking for anything from Grand Slam, but there wasn't much out there.

In the early 2000s, my work took me over to Asia and I found quite a few Thin Lizzy bootlegs in Japan, Hong Kong and Singapore. I now have about 40 in my collection - live recordings, outtakes, B-sides and the like. When I returned to the States, I got a 'THN LIZY' vanity plate in Texas and when I moved to Illinois, I got another. I sent my Texas plate to Philomena and received a very nice letter attached. I still have my Illinois plate.

I saw Lizzy four times in concert, three with John Sykes and once with Ricky Warwick. I also found a number of concert DVDs here in the US from various sources. If I were stuck on a desert island with only one band, it would be Lizzy. They have been truly my most favourite band since I first heard them in 1975.

Thin Lizzy have continued to perform intermittently in the years since Phil's death. For fans born too late to see Lizzy in their heyday, seeing members of the original line up play even without Phil remains an opportunity not to be missed.

ACADEMY

7 FEBRUARY 2004, BRISTOL, UK

I WAS THERE: LAUREN O'HAGAN, AGE 13

I had just turned 13 and went with my dad to see the latest incarnation of Lizzy in concert - John Sykes on vocals along with Scott Gorham, Marco Mendoza and Tommy Aldridge. I hadn't long before discovered Lizzy and I was totally obsessed with Scott. Lizzy did an incredible two hour set and we were right at the front the whole time. It saddened me not to see Phil but I was overjoyed to be up close to Scott and John. The atmosphere when the police siren went off on 'Jailbreak' was electric, and the sound of hundreds of us doing the coyote call together on 'Cowboy Song' was spine tingling.

Lauren O'Hagan waited backstage to meet her hero Scott

As we filed out of the club, I asked my dad if we could head round to the backstage door and wait. He was totally up for it, so we went round there with a small group of others and waited for a good hour or so with nervous anticipation. Suddenly, the back door swung open and Scott was standing there in a leather jacket, blue shirt, black jeans and black boots. 'Hey, I hope you haven't been waiting too long,' he said, with a smile and in that cool Californian accent. I nearly passed out on the spot. My actual response was to blush and babble, by which time he said, 'How was the sound for you? Cos we can't hear much when we're up there.' Cue more babbling from me until I finally managed to say, 'Yeah, it was good.' Thankfully my dad was there to keep the conversation going and we talked for 15 minutes.

Scott turned to me, pointed at my camera and said, 'I'm guessing you want a photo.' I couldn't believe I was standing so close to this guy I admired so much and who I was totally besotted with. He took my ticket and pulled out a pen to sign it, then gave me one of his plectrums from his pocket. As I took it, he noticed the turquoise stone ring on my finger (I'd bought a replica of his!) and said, 'Hey, cool ring. I used to have one just like that!'

I went to sleep that night with the plectrum clutched tightly in my fist. The next day at school, I was out of control telling my friends what had happened. Nobody else was a Lizzy fan so they couldn't really get my joy, but I didn't care. It was the greatest night of my life and one that I will never forget.

STATUE OF PHILIP LYNOTT UNVEILED

19 AUGUST 2005, DUBLIN, IRELAND

A statue of Philip Lynott was unveiled on Harry Street in Dublin, the result of campaigning by his mother Philomena and the Roisin Dubh Trust, which was set up to protect his legacy.

Photo Kate Sullivan

The author pictured with the statue of Philip Lynott

REGENT THEATRE

24 NOVEMBER 2007, IPSWICH, UK

I WAS THERE: KEVIN O'CONNELL

The line up was John Sykes, Scott Gorham, Francesco DiCosmo and Tommy Aldridge. I was hesitant about going but curiosity got the better of me. My lasting memory of that night was John Sykes saying to me 'thank you' at the end, as I sat in my wheelchair (as a result of having contracted meningitis). Sadly, the show itself did little for me. The sound balance was not good and within it there was no Brian and no Phil.

CITY HALL

8 JANUARY 2011, NEWCASTLE-UPON-TYNE, UK

I WAS THERE: PETER SMITH

For 20 odd years I didn't have much Thin Lizzy in my life. I thought of them sometimes and would visit the statue of Phil off Grafton Street when I went to Dublin which, because of work, is quite often. In 2007, a group of us went to see Deep Purple, Thin Lizzy and Styx at Newcastle Arena. I was intrigued by the inclusion of Thin Lizzy on the bill. How could there be a Thin Lizzy without Phil? But they seemed pretty good (as good as any support act can be in a big arena) and performed credible versions of all the well known songs.

In 2011, I found myself at the back of a packed City Hall waiting for Thin Lizzy to take the stage and wondering what this incarnation of the band would be like. Would it work? Could it work? How could the new Thin Lizzy, who might be considered a tribute band by some, sell out the City Hall? I prepared myself by playing the *Live and Dangerous* double album. My favourites were always 'Emerald' and 'Cowboy Song'. I'd forgotten how good they were.

The 2011 line up was Scott Gorham on guitar, Brian Downey on drums, Darren Wharton on keyboards, Def Leppard guitarist Vivian Campbell, former Whitesnake bassist Marco Mendoza and singer Ricky Warwick from The Almighty. Thin Lizzy exploded onto the stage with 'Are You Ready'. They were loud and sounded pretty true to the original.

Ricky Warwick hails from Northern Ireland and his voice sounded very much like Phil's.

The twin guitar sound was as great as it ever was, and Scott Gorham looked good, the only visible difference being the lack of that great long mane of hair that I was always so jealous of. The crowd jumped to their feet, where they stayed throughout the entire performance. Everyone was singing along. I got to hear my favourites, 'Emerald' and the 'Cowboy Song', and also a great version of 'Whiskey in the Jar', with Viv Campbell squeezing wonderful licks from his guitar. It was great to hear it included in the set again. Now and then, the screens at the back of the stage showed images of the old band and of Phil.

Did this come back of one of the greatest rock bands of all time work? Definitely. The band consisted of the right blend of previous members, excellent musicianship and Irish heritage to do justice to the material and to pay tribute to Phil in a fitting way.

UNIVERSITY OF EAST ANGLIA
23 MAY 2012, NORWICH, UK

I WAS THERE: KEVIN O'CONNELL

This was a new Thin Lizzy line up of Ricky Warwick, Brian Downey, Scott Gorham, Damon Johnson, Marco Mendoza and Darren Wharton. It was at this intimate venue that I sat next to Brian Downey's auntie. We chatted for ages and, after the show, waited behind with her to meet the band and ultimately my childhood hero, Brian Downey. Brian did not disappoint and neither did Ricky, Scott, Damon, Marco and Darren. We chatted for some time and Brian said to me that if I ever go to see him again, to let backstage know and to ask to be let in. The bass drum and snare sound that night was incredible and the band performed superbly with a balanced sound that dispelled my concerns about ever seeing Thin Lizzy again.

To this day, I still have all of my programmes, scarves, t-shirts and sweatshirts and my *Thunder and Lightning* embroidered jacket. I would never part with them as they hold so many wonderful memories.

GENERAL POST OFFICE, O'CONNELL STREET

3 OCTOBER 2019, DUBLIN, IRELAND

I WASN'T THERE: STUART CUNNINGHAME

The Irish Post Office issued Thin Lizzy stamps and held a launch event at O'Connell Street general post office. My mate Mark Graham was the HR director for the Irish Post Office and he helped set up a gig inside the post office, where Brian Downey and his band came along and did some covers of Lizzy songs. Phil's widow and his daughters were in attendance. The post office produced large artwork copies of the stamps, which Jim Fitzpatrick designed, and thanks to Mark I've got one of only five in the world. I've got the *Black Rose* album cover stamp.

Stuart Cunninghame has one of the reproduction stamps issued by the Irish Post Office

HMV CARDIFF

24 OCTOBER 2019, CARDIFF, UK

I WAS THERE: LAUREN O'HAGAN, AGE 13

Over the next decade or so, I went on to see Scott perform live at least a dozen times, whether with Lizzy or Black Star Riders, including a very special night at the unveiling of Phil's statue in Dublin, but I never had the pleasure of meeting him again. That was until autumn 2019, when I heard through the grapevine that Black Star Riders were doing a secret acoustic set and meet and greet at my local HMV in Cardiff. I was due to be in work but, luckily, I had a really cool line manager who knew I was obsessed with Thin Lizzy. I just told her straight that I needed to leave work for a few hours to meet Scott Gorham (as you do) and she let me go.

I walked down to the city centre feeling like I was that nervous 13-year-old again, but this time, I didn't have my dad with me to do the talking! I joined a 50 strong queue of predominantly men in their fifties and sixties. There was no fighting for a good spot and I was able to get to where I knew Scott would be. The band walked out and played four acoustic numbers. Hearing Scott play is always amazing, but it felt especially magical in this intimate setting. They then took seats at a long table and we lined up ready to talk to them. I was first in the queue.

Just like all those years ago, Scott smiled and said, 'Hey, how's it going?' This time, I actually managed to reply. I told him what a huge impact Lizzy had had on my life and how much their music meant to me. Then I said, 'By the way, I actually met you about 15 years ago and you gave me your plectrum.' I told him I had been just 13 and he said how great it was that I had got into Lizzy so young and was still a fan now. He signed my copies of *Black Rose* and *Another State of Grace* and I asked if it would be okay to have a photo and give him a hug. 13-year-old me would have probably had a heart attack then and there, but older me managed to somehow keep myself in check even though my hands were starting to shake like mad. I mean, this was Scott-freaking-Gorham, one of my heroes and an absolute guitar legend.

'See you at the gig tonight. Come down the front and I'll give you another plectrum,' he said. I pretty much floated down the line past the other members of BSR and didn't utter a single word to any of them. I stayed there soaking up the atmosphere until the only people left were the band, the HMV staff and me. I cheekily gatecrashed the promo photos for the event and helped pack up their stuff just so I could stay even longer and talk to Scott. Then I somehow made my way back to work on jelly legs, once again feeling like I did when I was 13 years old.

ENCORES

A book about Thin Lizzy and Phil Lynott told in chronological sequence doesn't have a happy ending, because Phil's story doesn't have a happy ending. But just when you think the band have left the stage for the last time, they come back out…

COLSTON HALL

5 DECEMBER 1972, BRISTOL, UK

I WAS THERE: DAVID SMALE

I saw Lizzy a number of times during the Seventies, right up to 1983 on their final tour at Bristol Colston Hall. The first time I saw them was in late 1972, when they were support to Slade and Suzi Quatro. To be fair, the crowd were mainly there for Slade, but it was still a memorable show and you felt that Lizzy could become something. They were only a three piece then, as it was 'Whiskey in the Jar'-era Lizzy.

Post-Phil, I've seen Lizzy at the Colston Hall in 2011 and 2012 and at the *Giants of Rock* festival at Minehead. I've seen Black Star Riders (who did ten Lizzy songs when I saw them – 'Are You Ready', 'Bad Reputation', 'Jailbreak', 'Suicide', 'Dancing in the Moonlight', 'Emerald', 'Cowboy Song', 'The Boys are Back in Town', 'Whisky in the Jar' and 'Rosalie', the Eric Bell Band and Brian Downey's Live and Dangerous.

Lizzy's music is still out there, even today.

WINTER GARDENS

18 JANUARY 1975, MALVERN, UK

I WAS THERE: LOUISE NEEL, AGE 15

The concert was at my local concert hall, Malvern Winter Gardens. I had no idea what to expect and thought I was going to see the three piece made famous by the hit 'Whiskey in the Jar'. My expectations weren't high and I certainly wasn't expecting the tour de force that came on stage that night. Goodness me, they were bloody fantastic!

Louise Neel (right) with her friend Bev

This line up of Lizzy were special… EXTRA special; a charismatic, ultra-confident front man, two duelling guitars and a solid, steady drummer. They weren't bad to look at either - very important to a teenage girl of 15 who was still at school. They belted through a repertoire of songs that would become live favourites in the coming years including 'The Rocker', 'Little Darling', 'Rosalie' and 'Still in Love with You' which, even then, was obviously a future classic. New guitarists Brian Robertson and Scott Gorham melded beautifully, while the rhythm section of Phil and Brian Downey, founding members of the band, held everything together. Already Phil was the band's focus and a fully formed rock star, relishing in the adoration of the hundreds of people in the crowd that night.

In the hall there was a feeling of excitement. Very little happened for rock music fans in the area and the Winter Gardens was the only place that held regular concerts. Young people, including me and my friends, would go to every gig regardless of what we knew about the band - it was a meeting place for young people from the area, which largely consisted of rural areas and small towns. On this particular night, there was definitely a feeling amongst the crowd that we were witnessing something very special. And indeed we were: the beginning of the phenomenon that was Thin Lizzy, one of the best live acts ever.

After the show, I couldn't wait to get backstage. Access was so easy in those days - no special passes or security necessary. All that was needed was will - the will to get into the inner sanctum, the dressing room. To see a band live on stage was never enough for me - I wanted to meet and hang out with them. There they all were - towelling themselves down after the show. Brian R was moody, Scott friendly and very American, Brian D quiet and Phil slightly scary - right from the start I was intimidated by his hypnotic presence and overwhelmingly masculine charisma. There was a friendly atmosphere in the dressing room, and I fell in love with all of them that night. There was no lewd behaviour and I felt attached to them very quickly. In fact, I didn't want them to leave Malvern that night so me and my friend stayed until the bitter end, finally waving them off as they started the long drive back home to London around 1am.

That night Thin Lizzy became MY band, and I was devoted enough to hitchhike all over the country to see them a further 25 or so times over the next two years, including twice more at Malvern. I would try to get to see them before and after each gig, attending sound checks and going to hotels… watching as they grew bigger crowds, became more famous and, sadly, attracted more hangers on. Despite spending so much time with Thin Lizzy and their roadies and lighting technicians for those couple of years - especially Robin, Pete and Charlie - I was always a fan and remained a fan. Despite how friendly we became, I never crossed the line and got too close… my relationship with them was strictly platonic… strictly no shenanigans.

By 1977 the band were really breaking into the big time and it became harder to get close to them. Much as I loved them, I felt the time had come to end my treks across the country to see them. It broke my heart but I could see the changes happening right before my eyes so I stopped going to see them. Punk rock was happening so I moved on to musical pastures new, getting into a new scene and grabbing that by the balls, as I had with Thin Lizzy.

I never saw them live again, although a few years later, after moving to London, I did bump into Phil a few times in nightclubs and we would exchange a knowing smile and a few words. I never really knew what to say to him in those moments; it was obvious that he was changing and there were negative junkie rumours surrounding him. The rest, as they say, is history… as are my memories, of which there are many.

I truly loved Thin Lizzy and they were a massive influence on me in my formative teenage years. Once seen never forgotten. Marvellous.

TOP RANK

24 MARCH 1976, CARDIFF, UK

I WAS THERE: AL RAYNER

The *Jailbreak* tour was the one that hit me hard in the eyes. I had seen them at Cardiff before, but that *Jailbreak* album and tour is what relaunched Lizzy. My late friend John 'Irish' Earle was the sax player on the *Live and Dangerous* album. Irish was originally the sax player in Graham Parker's Rumour brass section that later went on to be the brass in Shakin' Stevens band, which is where I met him. Irish was a right character. That whole Rumour brass section was amazing.

CITY HALLS

29 MARCH 1976, GLASGOW, UK

I WAS THERE: ALAN BAXTER

I first saw Thin Lizzy after the official release of *Jailbreak*. Phil announced, 'This is our new single, 'The Boys are Back in Town',' and I was hooked. He introduced the 'baby' of the band - Brian Robertson - who had just turned 20 years old. Les Paul in hand, he was my guitar 'god' and I bought my first black Les Paul copy because of Robbo. Outside after the gig, I briefly met Phil and got a signed photo of the band that I still have on my living room wall today.

Alan Baxter saw Lizzy several times starting in 1976

I went on to see Lizzy with Phil eight times and saw him with Grand Slam a couple of times, but nothing beats that era between '76 and '78 and the releases of *Jailbreak*, *Johnny the Fox*, *Live and Dangerous* and *Bad Reputation*. That was the ultimate line up for me and everything afterwards pales into insignificance. I last saw them on the *Thunder and Lightning* tour in Edinburgh and Glasgow. Phil looked drained. You could see he was not well. The sun was indeed going down…

I went to the *Vibe* in Dublin for 10 years in a row after the 10th anniversary of Phil's passing. Great stories, great memories, great friends all brought together by Smiley and Philomena's love for her son, Philip. I visited her once at her home, White Horses in Howth, and she was always very warm and hospitable and loved telling the stories about 'her boy'.

All the Lizzy reunion bands that have come and gone without Phil were in my eyes tribute bands and not Thin Lizzy. There will never be another Lizzy without Phil, but he left a great musical legacy which many bands acknowledge and are influenced by to this day. Thin Lizzy were a moment in time of rock music history, and I'm so glad I was around to be part of it. 'Til the next time….!

APOLLO THEATRE

17 JUNE 1978, GLASGOW, UK

I WAS THERE: STEVIE REID, AGE 14

I saw them as a 14-year-old, in 1978 on the *Live and Dangerous* tour at the Glasgow Apollo. It was my first concert ever and it all went by in a blur of excitement. I saw them again at the Apollo on the *Black Rose* tour, and I was only six rows from the front. Although I'm a Robbo fan, Moore was fantastic and I was blown away by his skill, energy and stage presence. In the late Nineties, my mate worked for an antiques company in Glasgow and visiting one older lady's house, he saw an electric guitar and said, 'My mate plays too.' She said, 'Yes, my son plays in bands. Brian Robertson was with Thin Lizzy…'.

MCELROY AUDITORIUM

21 MARCH 1979, WATERLOO, IOWA

I WAS THERE: DANIEL BOSS

Thin Lizzy opened for Nazareth in support of the upcoming *Black Rose* album. Waiting outside for the doors to open, a limo passed by the faithful out front. It slowed to a crawl in front of us, and waving through the back window was Phil Lynott. He had a big grin on his face and was checking out the long-haired crowd waiting to get a good standing position in front of the stage. Back then, the earlier you got there the closer you could get to the stage.

When the doors finally opened, I made a mad dash to front, securing a spot on the second row of bodies. I was able to sneak my parents' cheap 126 format camera into the concert by sticking it down the front of my pants. The real trick was also bringing along the flash cubes needed to get a photo. Those took up both my front pockets so I was running funny to get to the front!

Photos Daniel Boss

Daniel Boss saw Lizzy in Waterloo, Iowa

When Thin Lizzy started, the volume level was crushing. Not many people wore earplugs so we just accepted the fact that our ears would be ringing the next day. And Lizzy was a very satisfying loud! I don't remember all of the setlist, but they played all the fan favourites like 'The Boys are Back in Town', 'Cowboy Song', 'Emerald', 'Don't Believe a Word' and 'Whiskey in the Jar'. They also played a previously unheard song called 'Black Rose'. That song really took off with Gary and Scott ripping it up. Even though no one was familiar with it, the song was a highlight of the whole show.

After an encore by Lizzy, Nazareth played their set. They seemed tame compared to what Lizzy had just put us through. Safely to say that Thin Lizzy smoked the headlining band and put on a show for the ages. I never got to see Phil Lynott again, but I will always remember the concert that I saw as one of the best opening bands ever. Too bad they didn't headline - that would have been something!

ODEON THEATRE

16 APRIL 1979, EDINBURGH, UK

I WAS THERE: GORDON THOMSON

They were amazing live and Phil was a great front man. I saw them with Robbo and the year after, when Robbo had a problem and the late, great Gary Moore was on guitar with Scott Gorham. Both times they were brilliant.

CITY HALL

18 APRIL 1979, SHEFFIELD, UK

I WAS THERE: CAROLINE DEWAR

I first started following Thin Lizzy around 1977. I listened to my older brother's copy of *Johnny the Fox* (still one of my favourites) and in '78, after hearing various tracks on the John Peel and Alan Freeman radio shows, decided to buy *Jailbreak*. About this time, my friend and I started seeing Lizzy whenever they played Sheffield City Hall, which was included in all their UK dates. I remember seeing them with Brian Robertson and then Gary Moore.

The first album tour I remember well is *Black Rose*. 'Waiting for an Alibi' was in the charts, and I had seen Lizzy live at least three times before and was so looking forward to seeing Scott Gorham on stage again. I always thought he was absolutely lovely and had such amazing hair, especially when it was really long. He was such a beautiful guy and such a good poser! So I could not believe it when I had to go into hospital the day before the concert for a small but urgent operation. I begged the surgeon to be allowed out of hospital to be at the concert. He agreed to see if I had recovered sufficiently from the anaesthetic following the operation that I might be strapped up and discharged, provided I avoided being knocked or jostled, went in a taxi and stayed at the back of the hall. Needless to say, I made sure I was absolutely fine, watched from the back of the stalls as instructed and made it through the concert. It took me a week to recover afterwards, but it was worth it.

Lizzy concerts at the City Hall were truly memorable. Phil Lynott was a master of controlling and playing to the audience. *Live and Dangerous* might have been slightly less 'live' than originally recorded, but the experience of actually being at those concerts is captured on that album. Phil would catch the spotlight with his bass guitar and reflect the light across the audience. A glitter ball would announce the 'starry night' for the 'Cowboy Song' and 'Rosalie', while the audience would howl like coyotes at the right moment – if they didn't, Phil would make them do it again! The medley of 'Baby, baby, b-b-b-baby' could go on and on, until the audience lost track and Phil won. And of course, all the audience seemed to know the words of all the songs, particularly those classics always played at every concert – 'Emerald', 'The Rocker', 'Suicide' and 'Dancing in the Moonlight'.

Despite line up changes, Lizzy were always superb live, partly because of the continuity provided by Downey/Gorham/Lynott. Whether it was Robinson, Moore or White, there was a consistency in the twin guitars and the showmanship from the whole band that was gripping and highly entertaining. I have been to many concerts of many bands; live on stage were the best I have seen!

From then on, I bought every album and went to every concert in Sheffield, even when they played two nights running. The *Thunder and Lightning* tour was truly great, although the second night was better as the first suffered from technical problems.

Hopes of Lizzy getting back together ended with Phil's death in 1986 and I cried for the loss of such a great talent. Now that I have children of my own who have discovered Thin Lizzy's music, it's interesting to hear their opinions on the albums from a new generation. They agree that *Johnny the Fox* is a favourite and underrated, while one of the best tracks is 'Black Rose'. Perhaps tastes are genetic.

CITY HALL

13 APRIL 1980, CORK, IRELAND

I WAS THERE: TREVOR THOMPSON, AGE 15

I have been a Thin Lizzy fan since I was eight years old. My older brother George introduced me to the band and their amazing music, and Philip Lynott and his music have inspired me through the years as they continue to inspire younger people today. I have seen Thin Lizzy at least twelve times in concert and Grand Slam four times and they delivered every time. There was no such thing as a bad show.

It was Christmas 1979 when my mother Kitty bought me a concert ticket to see Lizzy at Cork City Hall the following April 1980. This was my first time seeing my heroes live and they rocked it to its foundations on the *Chinatown* tour. The excitement and the atmosphere were just electric for this 15-year-old young fella. They did all the favourites as well as the *Chinatown* LP, including 'Killer on the Loose', 'Chinatown' and 'Hey You'. A few weeks later, the band released 'Chinatown' as a single, the B-side of which was called 'Sugar Blues' and which was recorded live at the City Hall that night I saw them. For months after the concert, I was on a high. I had seen the greatest rock band in the world live and now I had a single recorded at the same gig!

I've seen some of the greatest bands live through the years but nothing ever beat Philip Lynott and his super group, Thin Lizzy. My dear friends William Magnier, Denis Ryan and Mark McGoey are all lifelong Lizzy supporters and together we followed Thin Lizzy all over Ireland on their tours. That Christmas morning in 1979, in addition to the ticket for Cork City Hall, my mother presented me with a Lizzy tour scarf and belt buckle. They accompanied me to all of the Lizzy concerts I went to and I still have them to this day, along with the memories.

CITY HALL

1 MAY 1980, NEWCASTLE-UPON-TYNE, UK

I WAS THERE: DOUGIE WALSH

I saw them on the *Chinatown* and *Thunder and Lightning* tours. The *Chinatown* tour had Snowy White filling in the other guitar spot. It was a great gig, Phil was up front as usual and they sounded great. Robbo joined them for 'Emerald' and 'Rosalie'. For the final tour, I remember being down at the bar at the City Hall. It was rammed, and the band were electric.

FESTIVAL HALL

13 OCTOBER 1980, BRISBANE, AUSTRALIA

I WAS THERE: TRACEY HIGGINS

A group of us loved Thin Lizzy. I was particularly impressed by Phil Lynott's musical part in Jeff Wayne's *War of the Worlds* and I'd mimic it with my electric guitar when I used to play. We went to see them at the Festival Hall in Brisbane and they were loud and proud. Unfortunately, we were quite a way back but I remember Phil's brilliant black and silver stage clothes and the vibrant atmosphere. It was a magical time and youth was on my side. My ears were buzzing for days after. It was a great experience for a 17-year-old.

LOGAN CAMPBELL CENTRE

25 OCTOBER 1980, AUCKLAND, NEW ZEALAND

I WAS THERE: TONY GEORGE, AGE 16

My friend and I were a couple of 16-year-olds who were mesmerised by the two lead guitarists laying the lead and rhythm down for Phil. They were as good as anyone I've seen. There were two little platforms in semi-circles connected to the stage, and it was like a duel between them playing lead and rhythm. They worked it.

The concert ended and us young lads went around the back, walked up the stairs to the back stage and knocked on the door. 'Let us in!' No answer. We knocked again. Still no answer. On our next knocking attempt, we were greeted by an Irishman with an afro hairstyle. Hallelujah! We have achieved our goal. We got invited into Phil's dressing room. My punk mate had Stiff Little Fingers written in felt pen on his Sex Pistols jeans and Phil saw that and said, 'I love those guys.'

Phil asked us teenagers who had gatecrashed his after gig function if any of us were from Ireland. I raised my hand like a boy in school and Phil gave me a can of Lion red beer. It's a night to remember for a very young shaver.

COLSTON HALL

12 NOVEMBER 1981, BRISTOL, UK

I WAS THERE: KEVIN OAKMAN

My first ever gig was at the Colston Hall on the *Renegade* tour. My mate, Nige, asked if I wanted to go. Knowing them only from their singles,

I jumped at the chance. The ticket was five quid which I felt was good value. I asked Nige what to wear as I didn't have a suit and he laughed like a drain and said, 'Jeans and t-shirt and leather jacket!' He lent me a tape of *Live and Dangerous* so I could hear more of their stuff before I saw them.

We caught the train to Bristol Temple Meads and walked to the Colston Hall. The atmosphere inside was electric. We were in the stalls and when Lizzy came on stage the place erupted. It was absolutely mental. We had to stand on the seats to see them, which is not great when you're headbanging!

Phil Lynott was in his usual customary tight trousers but he didn't strut much. I guess it's pretty hard to do when you're playing a bass guitar and singing, and he never really needed to strut on stage. He just had a presence. He drew the eye. Scott Gorham had the longest, sleekest hair I had ever seen on a man. They all moved about but it was never frenzied or over the top. There was an overall sense that they just loved being up there and playing their stuff.

My mum and dad provided the transport home, which was fantastic of them as we lived over an hour away from Bristol by road. There was no security out front so they came into the hall and saw the last half hour of the show. It turned my mum onto gigging. She loved the atmosphere, the noise and the showmanship. And Phil Lynott had that in spades.

The next gig was the *Thunder and Lightning* tour at the Colston Hall in March 1983. By then we had transport and there was a group of us. A couple of my friends had never been to a gig before and they asked what to wear, as I had eighteen months previously. The show was pretty much the same as before, with a slightly different set list to reflect the new album. They played the old favourites and again the last encore, of the two or three they played, was 'The Rocker'. This time they had big American police car-style light bars on either side of the stage which were turned on during 'Jailbreak'. After the gig, one of our party bemoaned the fact that they hadn't used the police lights - he'd been so caught up in the performance he'd just not noticed.

DOMINION THEATRE
30 APRIL 1982, LONDON, UK

I WAS THERE: MATT PETERS

In autumn 1981 I was attending a little private school in Surrey when a new arrival called Graham was sat down next to me at a vacant desk. My form teacher Mr Wales told me to look after him and help him to settle in. At some point Mr Wales - a rather unorthodox teacher to say the least - mentioned to me about Graham's dad being a drummer in some rock band. He lifted his jumper up to reveal a black band t-shirt underneath. I had no idea what it said on it and was too awkward to ask.

I was only 11 and, having much older brothers and a sister, I had access to their huge collective vinyl treasures. I would access it whenever they went out and listened to anything I could get my hands on: Black Sabbath, Iron Maiden, Aerosmith, Kiss and Led Zeppelin. But I couldn't see anything that looked like the mysterious logo that my teacher had shown me. At home that night and around the dinner table I excitedly gabbled my story in front of my siblings - probably desperate to garner their approval. They asked me the name of the band and I said I didn't know. They rolled their eyes at the pointlessness of my story.

A few evenings later around the dinner table my new classmate cropped up again. I mentioned that he was from Ireland. 'What's his surname?' my brother asked. 'Downey,' I said. 'Thin Lizzy!' said my brother. 'His dad is the drummer in Thin Lizzy.' 'Yes,' I said. I now realised that's what was printed on Mr Wales' t-shirt. My sister Sarah said, 'They play my song!' I didn't have a clue what she meant.

The next day I was packed off to school with a well-worn vinyl copy of *Johnny the Fox* to be signed as a test to the veracity of my story. It came back a few days later duly autographed by the band, who were recording the *Renegade* LP at the time. Somewhat unbelievably, it was agreed that I could go and see the band when they next played live and my form teacher Mr Wales took us on the Underground up to London.

We arrived at the backstage door of London's Dominion Theatre around the back of Tottenham Court Road and somebody asked the security for Brian Downey. He came to the door through a massive throng of people and we were ushered in. Other fans in the queue started shouting out his name and were also waved through.

I first went into the gent's toilet next to the dressing rooms and there was the sound of frantic banging on the outside of this little frosted window. Some guy opened the little catch and suddenly fans started scrambling through this tiny window, coming through head first and landing in a heap on the toilet floor. It was complete chaos until the security guards twigged what was happening and closed the window.

We got shown into a packed cream-coloured dressing room and introduced to various people. I remember saying hello to Scott Gorham who smiled his big Californian smile. Phil Lynott shook my hand and said, 'Howyah, Matt - can I get you anything?' He fetched me a can of Coke from the table at the opposite end of the room and cracked it open for me. I always thought it was very nice that he had time for a daft little kid. I remember Lynott being very tall and wearing a tight red top. Midge Ure was also there and Lenny Henry pulled this crazy face at me as I walked past him.

We then got taken out onto the side of the stage. There were cables snaking everywhere across the floor and technicians were running around making last minute touches. We stood behind huge stacks of black amps, looking out across the audience as the whistling and cheering got louder in anticipation.

The auditorium lights went out as sirens started up and these two red and gold Renegade flags at the back of the stage started to blow in wind generated by the biggest electric fan I'd ever seen. A strobe light flickered as the keyboard intro to 'Angel of Death' began. A couple of flash pots went off and scared the life out of me. Once the drums and bass kicked in, the volume became unbelievable - the loudest thing I'd ever heard and my ears were ringing for days afterwards.

I didn't understand the rush I'd just 'felt' but I was bitten and from that moment knew that I had to be involved in music somehow. Back at school I came down to earth with a bump. My music teacher told me I didn't have a musical bone in my body. Any career in music was certainly not going to involve me playing an instrument.

Aged 14, I was being driven to the cinema to see *Who Framed Roger Rabbit?* as my birthday treat and I heard on the car radio that Phil Lynott had died. I felt sick and honestly watched that film in complete shock.

I never wanted to go to university. I just wanted to be involved in live music and thought my best route into a career in music was by just getting a foot in the door and making connections. Aged 16, I started helping out at a little indie record label (Food Records) listening to demo tapes, doing post and making studio bookings.

There was a constant name on the sleeve notes of most Thin Lizzy LPs: Adrian Hopkins. He was both concert promoter and the band's merchandiser. I called them up on the off chance of a job but there was nothing going. He did however give me some other companies to contact and within a few weeks I had landed a job developing merchandise ranges for various bands.

I later went on to work with The Prodigy for a few years and toured around Europe with Lou Reed as he performed his *Berlin* album and had the best time with his crew. So, a chance meeting with an Irish kid took me on a 25 plus year career of working with some of the world's biggest acts, witnessing amazing gigs and events in Europe, the US and Japan. If I had followed a different path, could I still have travelled to such places? Possibly.

Would I have had as much fun? No way.

Graham's family moved back to Ireland after the band split and I lost touch with him. He went on to play bass for The Frames for a few years. I still listen to Lizzy most days. Still my favourite band.

GUILDHALL

26 FEBRUARY 1983, PORTSMOUTH, UK

I WAS THERE: KAREN WOODS

I first heard Thin Lizzy on *Top of the Pops*. I looked forward to watching it every week. Me and my older brother, who was buying records by Judas Priest and ELO, would get the tape recorder ready and record our favourite songs, and we would do the same with the radio. We lived in London at the time and would listen to Capital Radio 194 - I still remember the jingle. I was born in 1966 so I expect this would have been in the mid-Seventies. I am sure Thin Lizzy's records were making their way into my psyche as I listened to the radio as often as I could, buying myself a little transistor radio to keep with me.

When I was old enough to start going to pubs and gigs, Thin Lizzy were on my agenda. They had such a recognisable sound and Phil was just so cool in his leather trousers, studded belts, wild afro and laidback understated ego, like a modern day cowboy-biker. He was a mesmerising frontman without the glam-fanfare that was all the rage in the Eighties. I was often able to get to the front of gigs as I'm so small. I could duck under people's armpits and elbows and wangle my way to the front and get pinned to the stage for the rest of the gig.

I saw Thin Lizzy at the Portsmouth Guildhall in 1983 and then Grand Slam at Portsmouth Polytechnic, as well as appearances at all-dayers like Crystal Palace. At one of these gigs, I had the absolute pleasure of meeting Phil Lynott in person. My boyfriend at that time was Paul Miller who was writing for his own fanzine, *Forearm Smash*, and later wrote for *Kerrang!* magazine. He interviewed Phil for an article and brought me along to sit in. Phil came across as such a gentleman, so respectful and generous. He posed for a photo with me afterwards. He towered over me and stooped down to my level and gave me a respectful hug around the shoulders and smiled for the photo. Oh, I wish I still had that photo!

The gig that night was phenomenal. There was something about Thin Lizzy that brought the rawness of heavy rock with the slick professionalism of an experienced and passionate bunch of artists, totally committed to their craft and entertaining their fans. I remember in art class, I drew from the point of view of looking from behind, through the legs of a frontman like Phil Lynott out to an audience of adoring fans, arms in the air, mouths wide, hair flailing - the epitome of people in their element, in rhapsody. Every Thin Lizzy fan will know exactly what I was trying to capture in that moment. They'd all been there. Of that there is no doubt.

FULHAM GREYHOUND

30 AUGUST 1983, LONDON, UK

I WAS THERE: LARS FORSETH

I got to meet Scott at a Loudness gig in Fulham around the time Lizzy played their last UK gig at Reading.

Lars Forseth (left) with Scott Gorham

LEIGHLIN ROAD, CRUMLIN
1958/59, DUBLIN, IRELAND

MY DAD WAS THERE: COLIN DEAN

When Philomena (Phil's mum) moved Phil to live with his grandmother at 85 Leighlin Road in Crumlin, my dad (John Dean) and his brothers lived at number 81. People on the road protected Phil as he grew up... My dad passed away in 2019 at the age of 90. He was a great photographer down the years and, after he passed away, I went through his picture collection and came across some he had taken of Phil, his uncles and friends in around 1958 or '59 on Leighlin Road. This is my favourite.

Phil Lynott (left) playing on Leighlin Road in the late 1950s

POSTSCRIPT

It's been almost 40 years since Thin Lizzy headed by Phil Lynott last graced the stage. That they are still fondly remembered is evident from reading these memories, as is the continued sense of loss at Phil's untimely death. For many fans, the memories of Phil doing what he did best – reflecting the spotlight off his mirror scratchplate, smiling as he pumps his fist and encouraging the crowd to get involved – 'we need your helping hands' – are indelible.

Are you out there?

Did you see Thin Lizzy live? If you have any memories of classic rock gigs, please send your story to: iwasatthatgig@gmail.com.

WARRIORS

Thank you to the following Warriors for their support:

Robert Acquaviva, Claude Airoldi, Stephen Ambrose, Steev Amos, Stavros Apostolidis-Parisi, Allan Atkins, Helen Bakaszynsky, Mike Barber, David Barry, Elizabeth Baverstock, Melanie Benerth, Kevin Bergin, Phil Birch, Daniel Bjerknes, Antony Booth, John Bradbury, Murtagh Brennan, Tania Briddon, Andrew Brookes, Steen Bugtrup, Lee Burke, Noel Byrne, Jim Cameron, Graham Clark, John Cockerham, Jeff Collins, Richard Collins, Nigel Cottrell, John Cowpar, John Craig, Peter Crammer, Adrian Curran, Nino Gabriele D'Angelo, Anthony Darcy, David Davies, Martin Davis, Scott Davis, Glenn Day, Ian Dennis, Adriano Di Ruscio, Linda Dobson, Damien Doherty, Colin Dotchin, Steve Driscoll, Cheryl Duncan, Roger Dyson, David Edwards, John Fitzgerald, Michael Flanigan, Ingrid Foan, Nigel Forde, Steve Fowkes, Christopher Francis, Glenn Gallocker, George Galloway, Mike Galway, Leslie Gilbert, Simon Gilbey, Scott Gill, David Godsey, Dave Goodhand, Michael Greaney, John Grogan, QE Grul, Chuck Guzik, Erin Guzik, Anthony Haley, John Hall, Carl Hamilton, Nicholas Harney, Steve Harrison, Marcel Hartenberg, Hume Hawkins, Peter Heijting, John Heseltine, Garry Hindley, David Hinds, Pat Hogan, David Hood, Gavin Hogg, Ian Horsfield, John Howell, Rebecca Hudson, Michael Hulbert, Kev Humphrey, Stu Hunting, Gary Hurst, Morten W Jørgensen, Roger Jönsson, Andy Jackson, Claire-Willow Jackson, Richard John, Ian Johnson, Hugh Jones, Bill Jones, Patrick Kelly, Michael Kempster, Zenobia Khan, Andrew King, Andy King, Kelby Lane, Jo Leighton, Ian Lidbetter, Alan Liddle, Paul Litchfield, Frank Loughrey, Keith Luckey, Gary Malorey-Vibert, David Manwering, Marie Marie, Sergio Martos, Colin Mason, George Matakonis, Cora McCrystal, James McCafferty, Michael McDonald, Alistair McLauchlan, Graeme McNaughton, Keith McShane, James Mohr, Eric Mongan, Stephen Morris, Sally Morrison-Griffiths, Chris Noon, Geoffrey North, Anthony O'Shea, Ultan O'Sullivan, Kevin O'Connell, Enda O'Donnell, Dave O'Donovan, Lauren O'Hagan, Stephen Page, Kerry Palmer, Rob Parkin, Harald Pfeiffer, Chris Puttock, Thomas Pytel, Trevor Raggatt, Justin Ramadan, Martin Redford, John Regan, Peter Reynolds, Tim Roberts, Phil Ross, Magnus Rouden, Paul Ryan, Jarl Sävqvist, Vijay Seedarsan, Graeme Selkirk, Robert Sharman, John Smallshaw, Rhonda Smith, Duncan Smith, Peter Smith, Mark Smith, Michael Somers, Frank Sørensen, Janne Stark, Craig Stewart, Andrew Sutherland, David Sweeney, Keith Thompson, Peter Thomson, Stevan Tomulevski, Rob Trewhella, John Truman, Trevor Tucker, Roger Tully, John Vasey, Gary Wallis, Kevin Warren, Dan Westman, Paul Whiston, Andy White, Alan White, Paul Whitehouse, Ian Williams, Mark Williams, Harry Wolf, Julia Young, Jackie Yuill, Nanki Sato, Brian Bannister, Stuart Langsbury, Clark Craig, Tony Ratton, Paul Cumberlidge, Dan Halpin, Stuart Cunninghame, Michael O'Brien, Richard Rhodes, Cris Martin, Michael Morgan, Fiona Murray, Chris Gaywood, Keith Parker, Lee Jones, Lauren Stiles, Toni Kass Trevizo, Gary Powell, Rob Paric, Alan Baxter, Gordon Thomson, Toby Medhurst, Gerard Butterfield, Margaret Dean, Janice Marshall, Andy Francis-Mackie, Karen Woods, Norman Thomson, Richard Hein, George Frith, Danielle Keogh, Michael Bickley, Paddy Lennon, Peter Boyle, Ralph Kynoch, Alison Smith.